Mobile App Development for iOS and Android

Edition 2.0

Jakob Iversen
University of Wisconsin Oshkosh

Michael Eierman
University of Wisconsin Oshkosh

Prospect
Press

Founded in 2014, Prospect Press serves the academic discipline of Information Systems by publishing innovative textbooks across the curriculum including introductory, emerging, and upper level courses. Prospect Press offers reasonable prices by selling directly to students. Prospect Press provides tight relationships between authors, publisher, and adopters that many larger publishers are unable to offer in today's publishing environment. Based in Burlington, Vermont, Prospect Press distributes titles worldwide. We welcome new authors to send proposals or inquiries to Beth.Golub@ProspectPressVT.com.

Editor: Beth Lang Golub
Production Management: Kathy Bond Borie
Cover Design: Annie Clark

eTextbook
  • Edition 2.0
  • ISBN: 978-1-943153-27-5
  • Available from Redshelf.com and VitalSource.com

Printed Paperback
  • Edition 2.0
  • ISBN: 978-1-943153-28-2
  • Available from Redshelf.com and CreateSpace.com

For more information, visit
http://prospectpressvt.com/titles/iversen-mobile-app-development/

Contents

Preface

Welcome to mobile application development!

Developing apps can be fun and is potentially lucrative, but is also quickly becoming a core skill in the information technology field. Businesses are increasingly looking to mobile apps to enhance their relationships with their customers and improve their internal processes. They need individuals skilled in developing the mobile apps that support these initiatives.

This book is intended to be an introduction to mobile app development. After you successfully complete the book, you will have the basic skills to develop both Android and iPhone/iPad apps. The book walks you from the creation of an app through the publication of the app to its intended audience on both platforms. We (the authors) have been teaching technology for many years at the collegiate level and directly to professionals, and we strongly believe that the only way to learn a technology is to actually use it. That is why the book is structured as a series of tutorials that focus on actually building a complete app on both platforms.

While the book is an introduction, it does cover many of the unique features of the mobile platforms that make apps a technology that offers new capabilities that businesses may use to enrich or augment their operations. The features covered in the book include using the device's ability to determine its location, using hardware sensors and device components in apps, and mapping. The book covers both Android and iOS because we designed it for our curriculum, where it is used in a senior-level course where we teach both platforms. Our goal in doing so was to provide experienced programmers with the knowledge to continue development for either platform. With the background in many aspects of mobile development, they have a solid base they can build on. That said, the book could also be an option for a two-course sequence covering both platforms. Being tutorial-based, it is also a good basis for a self-paced course for either platform.

If you have suggestions, bug fixes, corrections, or anything else you'd like to contribute to a future edition, please contact us at jhiversen@gmail.com or michael.eierman@gmail.com. We appreciate any and all feedback that helps make this a better book.

—Jakob Iversen & Michael Eierman, July 2017

What's New in the Second Edition

Since writing the first edition of this book in 2013, the world of mobile development has changed drastically. Google released Android Studio in December 2014 to replace Eclipse as the primary development environment for Android apps. Meanwhile, Apple released Swift in June 2014 as the primary programming language for iOS development. In this edition of the book, we have completely rewritten all the development chapters to cover these changes.

The second edition is completely revised and updated to cover Android Studio and Swift. In addition, we also introduce AutoLayout for managing layout of iOS apps.

The general chapters (1, 2, 15, and 16) have been edited and updated with additional examples and reflecting changes to the mobile development landscape over the last three years.

Appendix A has been rewritten to cover how to fix a number of common code problems in Android and Android Studio.

Appendix B has been rewritten to explain how to use ConstraintLayout in Android. This is an emerging approach to controlling placement of user interface elements in Android. However, as it is still in beta, and not very stable, it is not integrated into the main tutorials.

Appendix C has been updated to cover Swift instead of Objective-C.

What You'll Need

You can begin learning mobile application development with very little investment. However, you will need a few things. The following list covers the basics of what you need for Android programming:

- **Android Studio**—You can download Android Studio from Google (https://developer.android.com/studio). It is available for Windows, Mac, and Linux platforms. The book was written based on version 2.2 of Android Studio.

- **An Android device**—This is not necessary for purely learning, but if you plan on releasing your apps to the public, you really should test them on at least one device. The more different types of devices, the better, because Android on different manufacturer's devices can sometimes behave in different manners. Certain features covered in Chapter 7 and 8 can only be fully tested in a physical device.

- **Familiarity with Java**—Android apps are programmed using the Java programming language. You should be able to program in Java. At a minimum, you should have experience programming in some object-based programming language such as C# or C++ so that you can more easily pick up Java.

The following list covers the basics of what you need for iPhone/iPad programming:

- **A Mac running macOS Sierra 10.12 or OS X El Capitan 10.11.5 or later**—iPhone/iPad programming can only be done on a Mac. That Mac should have a fair amount of disk space available and a significant amount of RAM so you don't have to spend as much time waiting for things to compile and execute.

- **Xcode**—Xcode is an IDE provided by Apple available from Apple's iOS Dev Center (http://developer. apple.com/ios). Xcode is free but limits how many physical devices you can test your apps on. If you want to distribute your apps, you must sign up as a registered developer ($99/year for individuals, $299/year for enterprise developers). The book was written based on Xcode 8 (iOS 10).

- **An iOS device**—As with Android, this is not necessary for learning how to program an iOS app but is important for testing apps that you wish to release to the public. Additionally, some features of iOS programming cannot be tested on the simulator. Chapter 9, "Using Xcode for iOS Development," has more details on what is needed to be able to test your apps on a physical iOS device.

- **Knowledge of Swift**—Two programming languages can be used to develop iOS apps: Swift and Objective-C. Since 2014, Swift has become Apple's recommended programming language. It is a modern and powerful object-oriented language with a simple syntax. Appendix C contains an introduction to Swift and Objective-C that will help you learn what is needed to be successful with iOS development.

Your Roadmap to Android/iOS Development

This book is intended as an introduction to mobile development for both Android and iOS. While the book provides everything you need to know to begin creating apps on both platforms, it is not intended to be a comprehensive work on the subject. The book assumes programming knowledge. At a minimum, you should have taken at least one college-level programming class in an object-oriented programming language such as Java, C#, or Python. Mobile development introduces issues and concerns not associated with traditional development, but at its core requires the ability to program. Experience with an Integrated Development Environment (IDE) is a plus. This book will help you learn the Android Studio and Xcode IDEs, but if you have some understanding and experience prior to working through this book, it will ease your learning curve.

As a beginner's book, that should be enough to successfully work through the tutorials. However, to truly master Android and iOS development, there is no substitute for designing and implementing your own app. For this, you will likely need some reference books. Of course, if all else fails—Google It! And then you'll likely end up with the good folks at StackOverflow.com, which has quickly become a trusted source for answers to programming questions.

How This Book Is Organized

This book guides you through the development of mobile applications on both Android and iOS. It focuses on building a single, complete app on both platforms from beginning to publication. The book is meant for the beginner but goes in enough depth that you could move into developing your own apps upon completion of the book. The philosophy embedded in the book's approach is that the best way to learn to develop is to develop! While the book begins with Android development, the reader could choose to begin with iOS without any problem or setback in understanding. However, we do suggest that you read Chapter 2, "App Design Issues and Considerations," before beginning either platform. After that, you can choose either Chapters 3–8 on Android or Chapters 9–14 on iOS. You could even switch back and forth between the platforms, first reading the introduction to Android in Chapter 3, then the introduction to iOS in Chapter 9, and then continuing to switch back and forth between the platforms.

Here's brief look at the book's contents:

Part I, "Overview of Mobile App Development"

- **Chapter 1, "Why Mobile Apps?"**—Mobile apps are a potentially disruptive technology—technology that changes the way business works. This chapter explores the potential impact of mobile technology and discusses how apps can and do change the way organizations do business.

- **Chapter 2, "App Design Issues and Considerations"**—Mobile technology has different capabilities and limitations than more traditional computing platforms. This chapter discusses many of the design issues associated with app development.

Part II, "Developing the Android App"

- **Chapter 3, "Using Android Studio for Android Development"**—Eclipse is an open source development environment commonly used for Android development. Chapter 3 shows how to use Eclipse to build a simple "Hello World" app. The chapter is your first hands-on look at app development.

- **Chapter 4, "Android Navigation and Interface Design"**—The limited amount of "real estate" on a mobile device typically requires multiple screens to build a complete app. This chapter introduces how you program movement between screens in Android. The chapter goes in depth on how a user interface is coded in Android, where the number of screen sizes that your app has to accommodate is relatively large.

- **Chapter 5, "Persistent Data in Android"**—Business runs on data. An app has to be able to make sure important data is preserved. This chapter explores two types of data persistence methods in Android: the persistence of large and complex data in a relational database using SQLite and simple data persistence through the `SharedPreferences` object.

- **Chapter 6, "Lists in Android: Navigation and Information Display"**—Chapter 6 introduces a structure ubiquitous in mobile computing—the list. Lists display data in a scrollable table format and can be used to "drill down" for more information or to open new screens. This chapter explains how to implement a list in an Android app.

- **Chapter 7, "Maps and Location in Android"**—Displaying information on a map can be a very effective way to communicate information to an app user. This chapter examines implementing Google Maps in an app and also demonstrates how to capture the device's current location.

- **Chapter 8, "Access to Hardware and Sensors in Android"**—Mobile devices come equipped with a number of hardware features that can enhance an app's functionality. The code required to access and use these features is discussed in this chapter.

Part III, "Developing the iOS App"

- **Chapter 9, "Using Xcode for iOS Development"**—Chapter 9 begins the book's discussion of iOS with an introduction to Xcode, which is the development environment used to develop iPhone and iPad apps. Xcode and iOS development is introduced by guiding you through the implementation of a simple "Hello World" app. This chapter also covers how to register and use physical devices for testing.

- **Chapter 10, "iOS Navigation and Interface Design"**—Just as in Android, interface design and navigation between screens are important concepts to master in mobile development. This chapter guides you through the development of a Storyboard for app navigation and demonstrates how to use Xcode's Interface Builder to implement a user interface, as well as how to use AutoLayout to control the placement of user interface elements on the screen.

- **Chapter 11, "Persistent Data in iOS"**—Many of the same data persistence features available in Android are also present in iOS. One primary difference is that the database feature of iOS is implemented through a wrapper kit called Core Data. Core data enables the updating and querying of an underlying SQLite database.

- **Chapter 12, "Tables in iOS: Navigation and Information Display"**—Tables in iOS provide the same type of information presentation format as Lists in Android. Tables display data in a scrollable table format and can be used to "drill down" for more information or to open new screens. In this chapter, you will learn how to implement this very important mobile computing concept in an iOS app.

- **Chapter 13, "Maps and Location in iOS"**—Chapter 13 covers the implementation of maps and capturing device location information on an iOS device. It is analogous to the Android chapter on maps and location.

- **Chapter 14, "Access to Hardware and Sensors in iOS"**—This chapter demonstrates the techniques used to access hardware features of the device. It covers many of the same sensors and hardware features covered in the Android chapters on the topic.

Part IV, "Business Issues"

- **Chapter 15, "Monetizing Apps"**—One of the reasons many people consider getting into mobile application development is to make money. Both Android and Apple provide a marketplace for apps that has a wide reach. This chapter discusses various approaches to making money from your apps and briefly discusses the organization of your app development business.

- **Chapter 16, "Publishing Apps"**—Once you have developed an app, you'll likely want to make that app available to its intended audience. This chapter discusses publishing apps on Google Play and the App Store, as well as distribution of corporate apps that are not intended for the public at large.

Appendices

- **Appendix A, "Fixing Code Issues Using Android Studio"**—This appendix shows you how to use Android Studio to fix a number of common code issues.

- **Appendix B, "ConstraintLayouts in Android"**—This appendix contains a brief tutorial on how to use the new ConstraintLayout in Android to place user elements on the screen. This material is kept as an appendix, as the ConstraintLayout is not yet ready for prime time.

- **Appendix C, "Introduction to Swift"**—This appendix provides a brief introduction and tutorial on the Swift language.

About the Sample Code

The sample code for this book is organized by chapter. Chapters 3 and 9 contain a single "Hello World" app in Android and iOS, respectively. Chapters 4 through 8 build a complete Android contact list app, and Chapters 10 through 14 build the same contact list app in iOS. Each chapter folder contains the code for the completed app up to that point. For example, at the end of Chapter 7, the code will include that developed for Chapters 4, 5, 6, and 7. The exception to this single completed app per folder model is in Chapters 7 and 13. These chapters demonstrate several different approaches to getting location information on the mobile device. Each technique has a folder with the complete app that demonstrates the technique. If a book chapter requires any image resources, you will find those images in the respective chapter.

Getting the Sample Code

You'll find the source code for this book at https://github.com/LearningMobile/BookApps2.0, on the open-source GitHub hosting site. There, you will find a chapter-by-chapter collection of source code that provides working examples of the material covered in this book.

You can download this book's source code using the git version control system. The Github site includes Git clients for both Mac and Windows. Xcode and Android Studio also include built-in Git support.

Typographical Conventions

In order to make it easier to read and follow the instructions in the book, we have followed specific typographical conventions while writing this book:

- **Code**—When referring to specific code constructs, such as variable names or methods to call, we have used a fixed-width font. Example: Change the code in the `initSettingsButton()` method so that the button is disabled.

- **Descriptions of classes and code concepts**—When introducing new code concepts and classes, we have generally used bold typeface on first usage of a particular construct. Example: The **Activity** class is designed to handle a single task that the user can perform.

- **New Concepts**—We have used italics to highlight important concepts when they are first introduced. Example: You also learn how to use *AutoLayout* to control placement of controls.

- **Actions to take in IDE**—You will often be directed to take some action in the IDE as you are developing. These actions are highlighted with bold typeface. Examples: Drag a **View Controller** into the Storyboard. Select **Cocoa Touch Class** and click **Next**.

- **Values to enter in the IDE**—As you are asked to enter values or change settings in the IDE, these values are also highlighted in bold typeface. Example: Select the **Contact:** label and change its **Horizontal Content Hugging Priority** in the **Size Inspector** to **251**.

Both Android Studio and Xcode are complex software applications, and many of the procedures required to create apps involve a number of steps that have to be carried out carefully. We are very confident that the instructions in the tutorials in the book are correct, but there are times when you have to carefully read the instructions to do them correctly. As you go through the book, take your time and study the screenshots carefully to make sure you carry out the steps as we have intended them to be done.

Instructor Resources

A test bank, instructor's manual, and a set of basic lecture slides are available at the publisher's website at http://prospectpressvt.com/titles/iversen-mobile-app-development/. The test bank includes true/false, multiple choice, and matching questions for each chapter in the book. The instructor's manual includes overview, teaching objectives, suggested teaching approaches, answers to end of chapter questions, suggestions for alternative exercises, and answers for those exercises for each chapter in the book.

Acknowledgments

We would like to thank the reviewers for this edition: Elizabeth D. Diaz, University of Texas at Arlington; J. Bryan Osborne, Oral Roberts University; and Mark Sherriff, University of Virginia. Their effort created a much better final product. We also would like to thank Beth Golub and Rachel Paul at Prospect Press for the support and help they provided in completing the book. Our families also must be acknowledged for putting up with the time we spent away from them in the rewriting of this edition.

About the Authors

Jakob Iversen, PhD, is Professor of Information Systems and Interim Associate Dean at the University of Wisconsin Oshkosh College of Business. His current research interests include software process improvement, agile software development, e-collaboration, and mobile development. Dr. Iversen teaches and consults on web development, mobile development, technology innovation, information systems management, strategy, and software development processes.

Michael Eierman, PhD, is a Professor of Information Systems and Chair of the Information Systems Department at the University of Wisconsin Oshkosh College of Business. Dr. Eierman has worked in the information systems field for nearly thirty years as a programmer, analyst, consultant, but primarily as a teacher. From the very first class he took in college at the suggestion of an advisor, information systems have been his passion. His research has taken many directions over his years as a professor but is currently focused on the impact of collaborative and mobile technology. Dr. Eierman is also co-owner and manager of Ei-Sor Development LLC, a provider of Android and iOS apps designed for the outdoorsman.

PART I

OVERVIEW OF MOBILE APP DEVELOPMENT

CHAPTER 1

Why Mobile Apps?

Mobile, mobile, mobile! Mobile technology is certainly receiving a lot of attention in the IT world as well as the general business world right now. It seems everyone is executing a mobile strategy, designing a mobile app, or worrying about managing mobile devices. But why all the buzz? What makes mobile so special that it garners this much attention? In this chapter, you explore some of the key reasons behind the hype. It really is *not* "much ado about nothing!"

Transformative Devices

For all the hype, there must be something that makes these devices important. There is! Mobile devices add a host of new possibilities for business and personal software because they are truly the first mobile computing platforms. Although laptops and netbooks are moveable, their size significantly impacts how easily they are transported. Very few people carry a laptop during their every waking hour to every location they visit. However, if this were their only advantage, mobile devices would not be causing such a stir. There are many technical and nontechnical reasons behind mobile's surging popularity.

One key feature of mobile devices is the capability to be made aware of their current environment through built-in sensors. Mobile devices have sensors designed to capture where they are, where they're going, and the environment around them. Sensors can identify their present location to within a few meters and capture their current heading, orientation, and acceleration. Additionally, they can recognize how close they are to another object through a proximity sensor. These devices also have the capability to capture information about the ambient environment, including light levels, temperature, pressure, and magnetic field.

Another important feature of mobile devices is the capability to communicate with other computing devices through a variety of mechanisms. A laptop typically can communicate using Wi-Fi and Bluetooth. However, mobile devices can also communicate via cellular signals and near-field communication (NFC). Each communication standard has different characteristics with regard to communication range, bandwidth, and power usage, making each standard suitable for different usage scenarios. Whereas Wi-Fi has a lot of bandwidth and reasonable range, it is often not available. Its range is measured in yards, whereas cellular's range is measured in miles. Bluetooth offers communication with low power usage, but is relatively short range, measured in feet, whereas the range of NFC is measured in inches. If a device wants to communicate with another device based on its proximity, broadcasting in inches may be preferable to broadcasting and listening in feet.

In addition to these capabilities not present in other computing platforms, mobile devices have most of the same features, such as being able to display and manipulate data. Some of these features have enhanced usability because they are on a device that is easily moved. One example of this is the camera. Although many laptops and desktops have cameras built in, their usefulness is limited because they cannot easily be moved and easily pointed in specific directions, making mobile device cameras useful for both taking pictures as well as scanning bar codes and QR codes. While data input may at first seem limited due to the diminutive size of the keyboard, a mobile device offers software keyboards that can easily be switched to offer different character sets, which can be useful for international applications as well as for inputting business-specific symbols. The availability of high-quality microphones allows a user to use speech to enter data or instruct the device to perform some operation. Again, these features may be more useful because data can be entered at its source when it is produced, rather than after the fact when human memory errors can impact the integrity of the data. Another similarity is that mobile devices also have the capability to store data in a number of formats, including in relational databases. Finally, mobile devices are also computers.

When equipped with enabling applications, mobile devices, with their built-in screen readers, cameras, and internet connectivity, comprise a technology bundle that affords blind people new and powerful ways to interact with visual aspects of their environment. For example, the K-NFB Reader app, developed collaboratively by Ray Kurzweil and the National Federation of the Blind, allows blind users to snap pictures of printed text on any nearby surface and hear that text read aloud. Leveraging pattern recognition software and the image-processing technology built in the device, blind users can read menus, browse classroom handouts, read instructions, watch PowerPoint presentations, and perform other tasks that could be daunting or impossible absent the technology. AppleVis.com, a community-powered weblog dedicated to blind and low-vision users of Apple products, has catalogued more than 130 commercially available apps developed specifically for blind people or people with low vision. The purpose of these apps is to assist people with disabilities doing everyday tasks and increase their independence in their daily life.

Research by one of our colleagues at UW Oshkosh, Don Heath, has shown that the use of mobile applications makes blind people better able to perform in the workplace, and allows them to perform tasks that were previously impossible to do and perform other tasks more efficiently. The research also shows that when managers become aware of the capabilities that mobile apps have in terms of allowing blind people to interact with their environment, they are more likely to hire blind people and more likely to give them far more responsible tasks to perform.

Taken together, the added capabilities of mobile devices compared with traditional computing platforms means that the smartphone and tablet are the most dramatic changes in technological capability since the introduction of the personal computer. Dramatic change in technological capability enables the reexamination of the assumptions that business processes and products are based on. Organizations base the design of what they do and how they do it on available technology. If technology changes, the assumptions about what can be done are no longer valid. This invalidation of previous assumptions is disruptive, and if existing organizations don't reexamine their products and processes, it is likely that their competitors and start-ups will.

Reaching Customers

Smartphone users almost always have their device within reach. Organizations want to be ready when a potential customer is interested in a product or service. If customers have to wait until they get home to their computers, or worse yet, go to an actual store to get information about or purchase their product, it may be too late. Individuals may forget about what they wanted, or a competitor's product may be available and then the sale is permanently lost. In addition, the smartphone adoption rate and sales have greatly outpaced PC sales in recent years. In many homes, smartphones may be the only way to access the Internet. Many consumers are choosing tablets instead of a PC, rather than in addition to a PC. In fact, tablet sales surpassed PC sales in 2016. Companies that provide their service over the Internet may be left behind in these situations if they do not have a mobile strategy.

In many cases, a website designed to be mobile friendly may be enough to hold or attract the customer. However, to truly tie your organization to the customer, an app is required. Many organizations are pursuing both approaches. Apps can provide a stronger link to your organization because static data and the basic interface is always available on the device, reducing the amount of data that needs to be transferred and providing quicker access than having to always download this information. An app also can provide some functionality, even when the device cannot connect to the Internet. In these situations, customers could make a purchase when they get the urge, and the transaction could be uploaded when the device gets a data connection. Having the app always available on the device may also lead to your organization being one of the first choices when the consumer is in the buying mood. Additionally, the app's consistent interface may help the individual learn it so that working with your organization becomes quicker and easier than working with others.

Having a mobile app can also support brand loyalty and awareness. Some organizations have developed apps that allow customers to interact with their brands in positive ways. For example, Starbucks lets customers define their favorite drinks and collect rewards within their app. AXE has developed several games where the player has to collect AXE cans to earn points. Nestlé has an app that promotes fitness, and Zyrtec gives asthma patients tools to keep track of symptoms and current pollen levels. Finally, Kimberly-Clark helps parents with potty training their toddlers in the Pull-Ups Big Kid App. Although these apps could also be available on a traditional computing platform, having them on a mobile app allows the customer to access them quickly when they happen to think of it, even if they are standing in line or sitting on a bus. This allows companies to have positive interactions with the customer in more situations than only when the customer is sitting at a computer.

The Good Old Days

Ever hear the phrase "Banker's Hours"? Many years ago, banks had very limited customer service times, and getting to the bank to perform your business required going at hours not particularly friendly to many people's schedules. The technology of that time required that the bank have time to complete transactions after the customer left. To have enough time in the day to complete the work, they had to limit the amount of time they were available to the customer. This phrase became pejorative because people thought that the customer service hours were the only time that bankers worked and because the limited access frustrated customers.

However, with the advent of better technology, banks were able to expand their customer services hours, and the Internet made interacting with your bank something you could do anytime, anywhere. These days, a bank would not have much of a customer base if it did not provide online access. Mobile devices expand this problem. With many customers using a smartphone as their only Internet access, banks that don't provide mobile-friendly access will begin to lose customers to those that do—or never have a chance to gain new customers.

One area where mobile devices enable a strong potential for disruption of the assumptions made about a business process is the payment industry, where a lot of companies are innovating to provide consumers and businesses the capability to make and receive payments. For instance, Square provides small retailers a simple solution to accept credit cards via a mobile device and even use an iPad as a cash register, complete with inventory and listing of all products in the store. Although customers may not be able to easily get a printed receipt, the capability to easily e-mail receipts may be even better. PayPal also allows for sending money easily to individuals. Although PayPal has this capability on a traditional computing platform, the capability to do it on a mobile device enables the customer to get money quickly to someone, wherever they may be.

The final, and potentially most important, advantage of an app is that it can take full advantage of the device's hardware and software capabilities to provide the customer with capabilities that make your products an easy option for them. The device's location could be used to guide potential customers to a nearby store or even find a product within a store. The device camera could be used to present your products that are similar to a product image capture. Captured UPC codes could be used to provide product information and prices. NFC or Bluetooth could be used to alert customers that they are near your product in the store. The potential is there. An app provides the capability to realize that potential. For example, Amazon has an app that the consumer can use to scan UPC codes to compare a competitor's product to theirs.

Changing Business Process

One of the most exciting possibilities associated with mobile technology is the potential it has to impact business processes. Processes are designed within the parameters of the available technology. When technology drastically changes, new forms are enabled. When that technology is cheap, change is enabled in areas that may have previously seen limited impact of the technology. Businesses are paying significant attention to mobile because these qualities suggest that the technology may have implications for strategic and tactical advantage, or as demonstrated with the banking app, become competitive necessities.

Several years ago, business process reengineering (BPR) received significant attention in the business and academic worlds. The idea of reengineering was important because of what was termed the "productivity paradox." For years, organizations were investing a significant amount of money in information technology without realizing corresponding significant increases in productivity. Investigation found that a major contributor to this problem was that organizations were using the new technology to simply automate existing processes. Information technology was applied to portions of the existing process to make it faster or increase accuracy. This approach produced improvements, but they were incremental rather than revolutionary. As businesses became more adept with the technology and the technology became more capable, it was recognized that the full potential of the technology was not being realized, and companies began rethinking entire processes to take advantage of the technology. Noteworthy improvements in process measures were realized, and BPR was born.

Mobile technology is likely to follow a similar path in application to business processes. However, that path could be traversed much more quickly because of the past experience of applying technology to business processes. The excitement over mobile technology is evidence that a more aggressive approach to reengineering processes may be truer than a simple automation approach.

Still, there is room for automation, especially in smaller businesses that may have found that the cost, complexity, and nonmobile nature of traditional computing platforms made technological solutions to their business process infeasible. Bossy (Figure 1.1) is an example of this. The app is designed for the dairy farmer. As the farmer attends his cows, with Bossy, he has at his fingertips a complete display of the actions that need to be taken on different animals in his herd. This automates the process of tracking the animals on paper or on a desktop computer with written notes used while attending the herd.

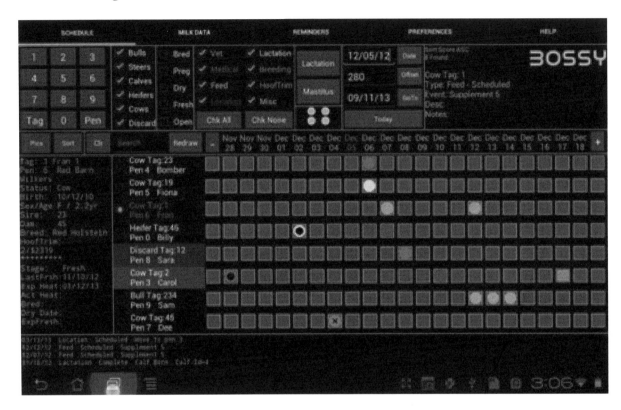

Figure 1.1 Bossy—an app for the dairy farmer.

Fence Builder Pro (Figure 1.2) is an app designed to support the fence-building indust. Although some big fence-building organizations exist, the majority of fence-building companies are much smaller, family-owned businesses in which technology plays a very limited role. Fence Builder Pro is designed to manage job scheduling and communication. Jobs performed by these smaller organizations typically last on the order of hours, rather than days or weeks, precluding the need for more traditional project management software. Additionally, a need exists to quickly rearrange the schedule because of outside influences such as the weather, material delivery errors, and interaction with external agencies. Because these externalities can change quickly, and because of the short nature of jobs, there is a need to quickly communicate the new schedule to the field crew. Fence Builder Pro is innovative for the industry because the schedule is also loaded on the crew foreman's device. When the company's owner changes the schedule, it is automatically communicated to the foreman.

Figure 1.2   Fence Builder Pro—an app for the small job shop.

These two apps represent innovation in business process that could not have been done without a mobile device. In contrast to consumer apps, these apps sell for much more money. They represent a significant investment by the developer in analysis and design, and are focused on a much smaller market.

Large organizations can also benefit from process redesign based on mobile technology, and many are creating mobile development teams to explore, design, and implement process solutions. The focus for these companies is on internal processes, and they are large enough to absorb the cost of creating apps to support their processes, so these are generally not available to other companies via an app market, although some apps available to consumers hint at the internal process changes. One such example is the insurance company apps that allow customers to submit insurance claims.

Although this provides an added convenience to the consumer, the benefit is much larger to the insurance company, because claims are reported electronically and with no people at the insurance company involved in receiving and recording the claim. These claims can also potentially contain much more accurate, richer, and timelier information. For example, State Farm's Pocket Agent app allows their customers to report an auto incident; they can include pictures taken with the device camera, tag the report with GPS coordinates, and draw a sketch of the scene. It's not hard to imagine that State Farm also has mobile apps for insurance agents and claims adjusters that use the data entered into Pocket Agent, so the entire process can be changed to take the mobile devices into account.

Making Money

A final reason that mobile is all the rage is that many enterprising individuals see the potential to start businesses and make money. The Google Play Store and the Apple App Store provide the app developer access to the market of app purchasers. The developer does not have to worry about product distribution, returns, or payment collection. The store does all this and conveniently deposits the proceeds into the developer's bank account. In addition, smartphone users automatically go to these stores to get new apps or browse for apps that might interest them. One final and very big reason for the strong focus on app development is that Google and Apple either support or provide the development environments needed to create apps for their stores. Taken together, this creates significant potential for individuals or small businesses to make money in the app market.

Apps make money for their producer through several approaches. Apps can be sold for a one-time fee, like other products. Consumers buy the app through the appropriate store, and it is theirs for use whenever they like. The more apps the developers sell, the more money they make. Ad-supported apps make money by including an advertisement on a small portion of the screen. Anytime a user clicks an ad, the developer makes money. Both Google and Apple provide developers access to the code to display ads and a service to provide the ads and track the clicks. In contrast to a paid app, the only time the developer gets paid is if an ad is clicked (Apple's ad service also pays per view of the ad, but the amount is significantly less than a click). The amount of money generated by a single click is very small, so to make significant money, it is important to get a lot of users of the app. A third approach to making money is to provide for in-app purchases. With this model, the user gets the app for free but needs to make a purchase to get additional features. For example, a developer might provide a game for free but require a purchase for more advanced levels of the game. Another approach is subscription based. The app provides functionality that requires access to the developer's data or other services. To use the service, users buy a monthly or annual subscription.

The combination of device capabilities, an accessible market, and a diverse and large number of developers makes the app market exciting and innovative. Because the market for consumer apps puts a significant focus on free or low-cost apps, the challenge for a developer is to create a product that appeals to a lot of people. Fortunately, the capabilities of the mobile computing platform enable the implementation of apps that can do things in a variety of domains that could never be done before. Chapter 15, "Monetizing Apps," provides a more in-depth discussion of how to make money from the apps you have created.

Figure 1.3   An app that innovates based on device capabilities.

Innovation Using Device Capabilities

Figure 1.3 shows an app that takes advantage of device capabilities to provide a product not previously available. This is a paid app called GoFishing! It uses the device's capability to capture its location, connect to the Internet, and store data to allow fishermen to record their fish the moment they catch them, including where they were, what the weather conditions were like, and how the fish was caught. The app provides search and mapping capability so that the fisherman can locate previously successful locations, methods, and conditions to use in future efforts. This functionality is not possible without the mobile device's sensors and Internet access.

Summary

Mobile technology is receiving significant attention in the business and IT worlds. The technology represents a dramatic change in technological capacity that has enabled potential economic advantages for those able to capitalize on it. Mobile technology is the basis of innovations in reaching customers, and in redesigning business processes and software products that lead to the creation of many new small businesses.

Exercises

1. Find an app that uses device capabilities to provide a product that previously couldn't exist. Explain what makes this app important or innovative.
2. Find an app designed to support a business process. What is the business process? How does the app propose to improve it?
3. Identify and explain a specific business process. How might this process be automated with mobile technology? How might it be completely redesigned?

CHAPTER 2

App Design Issues and Considerations

App development for mobile devices is, in many ways, similar to development for other platforms. However, development requires attention to items that are not even present in traditional development. Mobile devices have operating systems that run apps differently than traditional programs, have access to environmental sensors that are not available in laptop and desktop computers, have a limited power supply, and have a much smaller screen. This chapter provides an overview of the design issues associated with these differences. The chapter also discusses differences between iOS and Android devices that impact design. The chapter concludes with an introduction to the app that will be developed to illustrate design and development for both platforms.

App Design

Designing for the specific device your app will run on is extremely important! Applications that work well on a traditional computer may be complete disasters if ported to a mobile platform without redesigning the logic to fit the device's capabilities. Additionally, the capabilities of the device enable you to design an application that can do different things than an application on a traditional computer. Apps are cheap and easy to obtain. If yours doesn't work well, there is likely to be an acceptable alternative. A well-designed app can be a delight to use. A poorly designed app will not be used for long, if at all. The operating system, device size, and mobility all impact design and must be accounted for.

Operating System Design Issues

The primary technical difference between mobile device operating systems and operating systems used on laptop and desktop computers is that the mobile operating system is not a true multitasking system. On mobile devices, only one app can be active at a time. When another app is started, or the app is interrupted by another app (e.g., a phone call), the app that was running gets put in the background. It remains in the background until the user specifically accesses it again. If it remains in the background too long, or if available memory gets too low, the operating system may kill it. This back-and-forth between different states is called the app's *life cycle*. Both Android and iOS apps have a life cycle. The life cycle is based on the user's interaction with the app and the operating system's need for memory and processing resources. As users interact with the device, they may switch between apps or different views within a single app. When this happens, the app goes through different states, requiring the developer to handle this switch so that users don't lose data or aren't unnecessarily interrupted in the task they were performing. This makes understanding, and designing for, the app life cycle extremely important to the successful app developer.

Android Life Cycle

To understand the Android life cycle, it is useful to first understand the states that an Android app user experiences. When users touch an app's icon, the app is started and becomes visible to the users. While the app is visible, the users can interact with it. This is considered the *Resumed* or running state. As the users interact with the app, they may be interrupted with a pop-up window, or they may be distracted and not touch the screen for a period of time. If the users stop interacting for a period of time, the app will fade but still be partially visible. In either of these two cases, the app enters the *Paused* state. If the users close the pop-up or touch the screen, the app becomes fully visible again, and the app again enters the *Resumed* state. If users don't touch the screen for a longer period of time and the screen goes black, or the user starts another app so that the original app is no longer visible, the app enters the *Stopped* state. If users turn on the screen or use the Back button to get back to the app, the app again enters the *Resumed* state. An app can remain in the *Stopped* state for quite some time. However, if the device is rebooted or a user runs a number of other apps before coming back to the original app, that app can be *Destroyed* by the operating system to free up resources for other apps that the user is actually interacting with. To design an app that functions well, given this pattern of use, developers must understand what happens as the app enters and leaves these states, as well as what they should design the app to do in those instances. This requires understanding the Android life cycle.

The Android life cycle (see Figure 2.1) begins when a user touches an app's icon. This action causes the `onCreate` method in the app's initial activity to execute. This method includes code to load the screen (called a *layout*) associated with the initial activity to load. The developer needs to place code in this method that initializes variables and layout objects to the settings required for the user to begin interacting with the app. After the activity has been created, the `onStart` method is executed. This method does not have to be implemented but is useful if the app requires certain settings to be the same for every time the app starts, whether it is an initial start after the activity is created or restarted after the activity is brought back from a stopped (but not destroyed) state. After the activity has started, the `onResume` method is executed. This method also does not have to be implemented but is very useful to return the app to the running state that the app was in before it paused. This includes turning on system services used by the app (e.g., the GPS or the camera), restarting animations, and any other settings needed to allow users to pick up where they left off.

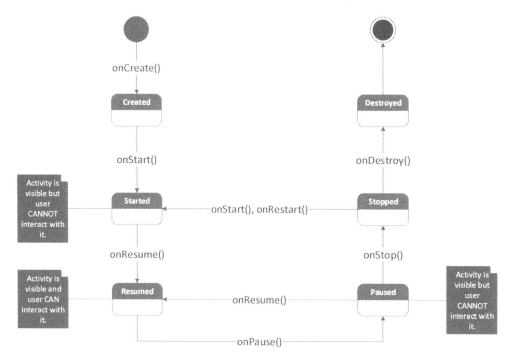

Figure 2.1 Android life cycle.

When a user stops directly interacting with the app, the path to destruction begins. None of the methods executed on the path to destruction have to be implemented. However, they often serve a useful purpose and should be considered. The first method executed is `onPause`. This method should be used to stop services that the app is using, to stop animations, or to store important state information so that users can start using the app exactly as they left it. If the app is about to become invisible, the `onStop` method will be executed. This method should make sure important data is permanently stored so that as system resources are consumed by other apps, they are not lost. Finally, if not restarted, the `onDestroy` method will be executed just before the operating system takes away all the app's resources. This is your last chance to capture important data before all is lost.

iOS Life Cycle

The life cycle for iOS is similar to Android's. However, iOS uses both an app life cycle and a screen (called *view*) life cycle to accomplish essentially the same things. As with Android, the life cycle (see Figure 2.2) begins when the user taps an app's icon. The didFinishLaunchingWithOptions method is similar to an Activity's onCreate method. However, in iOS this method is used to set up the operating environment for the complete app, not just a single activity.

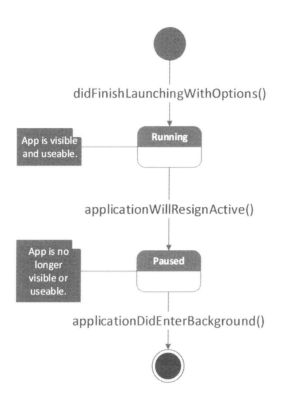

Figure 2.2 iOS App life cycle.

The applicationWillResignActive method is executed when the app is interrupted, similar to when the onPause method is executed in Android. Finally, when the app is no longer visible, the applicationDidEnter-Background method is executed. As with Android, code in these methods should be used to turn off services and save important data for the user before it's potentially lost.

Unlike Android, iOS has a separate life cycle for displayed screens (called ViewControllers). The view life cycle (see Figure 2.3) begins after the application has finished loading or the user goes to a different page in the app. After the view is loaded into memory, the viewDidLoad method executes. This method is executed only once if the view stays in memory. You should write code in this method to set the initial state of the view. After the view has loaded into memory, just before the view is visible to the user, the viewWillAppear method is executed. Code in this method should be used to load any data into the views that will be visible to the user and turn on services that the user needs to interact with the app. This method executes every time the view reappears on the device.

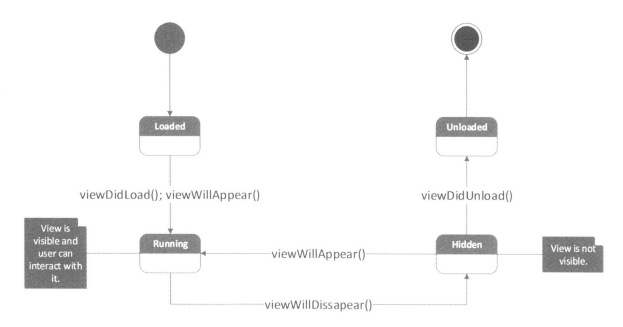

Figure 2.3 iOS view life cycle.

Just like in Android, if an app is interrupted, or the user doesn't interact with the device for a period of time, or the user moves to another view in the app, the view is pushed into the background. Just before this happens, the `viewWillDisappear` method is executed. Code in this method should turn off services and take steps to save the user's data. If the user doesn't interact with the view for a period of time while it is in the background, iOS may reclaim its resources. Just before the view is released from memory, the `viewDidUnload` method is executed. This is the developer's last chance to preserve important data used in the view.

Understanding and properly coding the app to take advantage of the methods associated with the life cycle are important to ensuring a good user experience with your app. Take the time to understand these life cycles, and your app development experience will be significantly less frustrating!

Screen Size and Orientation Issues

The most obvious difference between mobile and traditional application design is the amount of real estate you have to work with. The mobile device has significantly less area to design the interaction that your users can experience with your app. Poor interface design is the easiest way to get bad reviews for your app. Mobile devices are also used in different situations than traditional computing devices. App users are often multitasking (walk, talking with friends, and so on). The app design must allow users to switch to your app and do what they want to do right away, before they are distracted again. If users can't easily figure out how to use the app, no amount of help will satisfy them. This is no different from traditional development. However, the very limited screen real estate makes it a significant challenge. In addition, the focus among app developers has been on very good user interface design, so the competition is fierce for apps that work really well.

In response to the limited screen size, both iOS and Android have the capability to scroll to interface elements not on the screen. Scrolling can be both horizontal and vertical. However, both scrolling capabilities should be used judiciously, especially horizontal scrolling. Scrolling down a list has become a natural action on both traditional computers and mobile devices. However, horizontal scrolling has not. Horizontal scrolling should be reserved for use for elements that start on the main screen and extend off the screen. Users won't naturally think to horizontally scroll to look for items they can't find on the main screen. Even vertical scrolling should be limited. Lists are obvious choices for vertical scrolling, but other types of interface elements should be limited. In addition, when scrolling, you must also fix certain elements so that the user can perform needed operations without scrolling back through the entire contents of the screen.

The obvious answer to the limited screen size is to carefully plan the user's interaction with your app. Screens should focus on one, or a very limited and coherent, set of tasks that the user can or would want to do. Navigation should be planned and designed so that it is obvious to the user how to proceed to the next task. If a task requires multiple steps, those steps should be designed as distinct screens, and the user should be guided through the screens needed to complete the whole task.

Although screen size is a nontrivial design issue, the fact that by default a screen's orientation can change as the user turns the device also presents design issues. When the user turns the device from vertical to horizontal orientation, the layout or view reorganizes to that orientation. This significantly changes the amount of vertical and horizontal real estate for your interface. Interface elements that were obvious to the user in the vertical orientation may become inaccessible in the horizontal orientation. Again, this can be a very frustrating experience for your user, unless you carefully plan for the layout in both orientations, and thoroughly test it as well. Scrolling can be implemented to alleviate some of the problems associated with orientation change. However, simply adding scrolling may not solve the user experience issues. If you cannot make it work in an alternative orientation, as a last resort you can code the app to work in only one orientation.

The solutions to these screen size and orientation issues are planning and design. What does the user want to do with your app? What can your user do with your app? What are the logical steps needed to accomplish those tasks, given the device limitations? These are the types of questions you must answer to design a successful app.

Connectivity Issues

One of the most important aspects of mobile devices is that they are able to communicate with other devices and the Internet. This enables the capability to create very powerful and useful apps. However, this also poses design problems. The device's capability to connect can be lost, or the connection speed may be very slow. Additionally, these problems can arise if the device moves even a few feet. Compounding the problem is that users may not recognize or even understand that there is a connectivity problem while they are using your app. Apple requires that all apps submitted to the app store include a user warning when the network connection is lost, but this doesn't address slow speeds, and is not required by Android at all.

Again, design and planning are your solutions.

The primary issue that the app developer has to be concerned with is blocking the user from working with your app. When the app receives or sends data, it can take a significant amount of time. Users are unlikely to be happy waiting for this action to complete before doing other tasks. This means you have to plan for uploading and downloading data asynchronously, which means you have to make it run outside the main thread of the app. It also means that the rest of the app should be designed to provide other things users can do, unless the data is absolutely necessary for the task. If a user tries to do something that requires the data, provide a warning. The warning should provide enough information to help users decide what they should do next. If there is no connection or if there is a weak signal, tell them and give them options.

Users Can't Wait!

In my first app, I (Michael) made this mistake. The app retrieved weather information as part of its functionality. I included it on the main thread of the application. Everything worked fine in testing because I was in an area with good connectivity. But the first time I used it in the field where there were connectivity problems, I couldn't use the app at all! I could see the screen, but nothing worked because it was waiting for the weather. The screen eventually timed out, and I retried starting the cycle again. This was very frustrating. If I had purchased the app, I would have immediately demanded a refund.

Uploading important data is also a concern. As with a download, uploads should be performed asynchronously. You need to check that the upload was completed fully so that if a connection is lost during the upload, the user's data is not corrupted. This means that the data should be cached locally until it is successfully uploaded. Finally, you may need to provide functionality to upload the data when a good connection becomes available.

Communication problems external to the app can impact your app's performance. You must plan for this possibility to provide the best user experience possible.

Battery Issues

Mobile devices are just that—mobile. This means that they are not always connected to a power source. They rely on batteries for their power, and batteries can be drained. Your job as a developer is to not drain those batteries unnecessarily. This is not just a courtesy issue. If every time your app is used the user's device quickly becomes a brick, it will be noticed. An app that quickly drains power will not get used, will get bad reviews, and eventually will not get downloaded at all.

The primary power draw for devices is the display. You cannot do much about that except make sure that your code is efficient and doesn't take an unnecessary amount of time to complete the work that the user wants to do. Also, you should make sure that users can pick up where they left off if the app is interrupted, so the screen doesn't need to be on so long.

After the screen, the primary power drains are the sensors. The global positioning system (GPS), camera, communication, and other sensors are all big power draws. Fortunately, it is within your power to control these things. You control access to device hardware within your app and should turn on these capabilities only just before the user needs them. You should also turn them off as soon as the user completes the task that requires these items.

The app's life cycle plays an important role here. If the app is interrupted, all device access or use should be suspended immediately. When the app is about to become active, turn on as late as possible only those device capabilities needed. For example, in the previously mentioned app that uses weather data, the weather retrieval is started as one app activity becomes active. If the weather data is successfully retrieved, it is time stamped. The next time the activity becomes active, the weather data will be retrieved only if it is outdated, thus saving battery power.

Some battery issues are beyond your control. You cannot make an app that extends battery power. However, you can definitely make an app that significantly reduces battery life. Be sure to account for battery use when designing your app.

Hardware Issues

A very cool aspect of mobile computing is the set of hardware components available on the device. Many devices have the capability to locate the device within a few meters using the GPS, have sensors that can capture device orientation, have lights that can be turned on and off, have cameras, and have other hardware components that allow the device to interact with the environment. Access to these components can make for fun and useful apps. However, employing them within your app is not without potential problems. The battery issue was discussed in the previous section, and this is always a concern when using hardware devices. However, each component has its own set of issues that, when used poorly, can make an app less desirable.

The first issue to be aware of is the availability of the component. Different manufacturers make Android devices, and some include devices that others do not. iOS devices are generally more homogeneous, but differences still exist. Because of this, it is very important to consider how important the component is to the primary functionality of your app. If it is only tangential, you may want to consider not using it, because its use will often prevent the app from be loaded onto the device. At best, the absence of the hardware component on the user's phone or tablet will cause frustration with your app. Another concern is situational availability. For example, for a device to get a GPS signal, the device has to have the capability to get the satellite signal required for operation. If the user is indoors, the GPS may not work.

It's My Fault!

Early on in my app development efforts, I (Michael) created an app that used GPS data to map certain points. This app was made available in the Android Play Store, but to try to expand the availability of the app, I submitted it to the Amazon App Store. Unlike Android, Amazon reviews the apps submitted to them before they make them available. They rejected it because it didn't work! I couldn't believe it. It always worked for me. However, they were testing it indoors where it never got a GPS reading, and therefore nothing worked. My design didn't account for this possibility, and the entire functionality was dependent on getting a GPS reading. Realizing that much of the app's functionality did not require the GPS, I redesigned it to handle the situation, and Amazon eventually accepted it. However, if this happened to a user, you might not get a second chance—or worse, the user might write a scathing review of your app.

A second issue to be aware of is time delays. To access a hardware component, you must use the component's application program interface (API). The component may take some time to turn on and respond with the information you need. If this delay is significant, it may impact the user experience in such a way that your app is viewed negatively. For example, the GPS system takes time to acquire enough satellite signals to accurately locate your device. This could take more than a minute. Stopping app function until this happens should be avoided, if possible. If the user is left waiting for the device to respond, the screen may time out. This issue may be encountered even if you did everything properly and turned off the services when the app is about to be sent to the background, and then turned them on again when the user reopens the app. However, if the activation of the device takes time, your app will end up hanging every time it returns from the background. This vicious circle will not please the user. The proper solution to this particular problem is to use a separate execution thread to do the initialization, thus allowing the user to interact with other parts of your app while the services are being activated.

A final important issue with the use of hardware devices is accuracy. There are several aspects of this issue. First, the accuracy of the component can differ among manufacturers. Consider the minimal level of accuracy needed for effective use of your app, and design for that. Be sure to give the user options if the required level of accuracy is not available. Second, accuracy often takes time. For example, finding the location of the device within a few hundred meters is often very quick. However, accuracy of a few feet often takes much more time. What is the required level of accuracy for your app's functionality? What can the user do if the device cannot achieve this? How quick does the acquisition of location need to be? All are important considerations when you are designing the app. A very good design strategy when you need better accuracy is to keep the user informed of progress. The Google Maps app provides an example of this. When finding your location on the map, the app first shows a big blue circle that gets progressively smaller as the accuracy improves. Finally, how the device returns data to the app may impact the level of accuracy your app can access. Again, using GPS as an example, the number of digits reported for the latitude and longitude coordinates dictate the level of accuracy of those coordinates. In some cases, the number of digits reported can differ. This is primarily an issue for the Android platform because it can differ among versions of the Android OS.

Device Differences

Android devices (phones and tablets) and iOS phones and tablets each have a unique set of hardware and software capabilities that make the way the user interacts with the device different for each. Again, to fully capture the device's capabilities and not degrade the user experience, you must design for those unique characteristics. Remember, users can and will do things you are not expecting. Even if it makes no sense to you, they will do it! If the app crashes or loses important data because of something they did, it does not matter—*it is your fault*. Plan accordingly.

It's Your Fault!

I (Michael) have an app that uses GPS data to map certain points. Against my better judgment, I was asked to allow the manual entry of GPS coordinates for the app. One user contacted me about why his app was always crashing when he tried to display the map. We went back and forth on potential fixes. (He really liked the app and wanted to use it. Most users would just delete your app.) I could not figure it out, so I finally asked him to send me his data. It turns out that he wasn't entering GPS coordinates; he just entered information about the location. I assumed that my users would know to enter the exact GPS coordinates, not just the location name without exact coordinates. I had to add an error message to the manual location entry to handle the situation. You never know what a user is going to do!

Android

Android devices originally used four hardware buttons (see Figure 2.4) to support the user's use of the device. These buttons were the Home button, the Menu button, the Search button, and the Back button. The user could press any of these buttons at any time during use of your app, which would impact the functioning of your app. The Home and Back buttons worked independently of your code, whereas the Menu and Search buttons provided functionality only if your app was specifically coded to use these buttons.

Figure 2.4 Android hardware buttons.

However, more recent Android devices (running Android 3.0, API 11, and greater) have replaced these buttons with virtual buttons at the bottom of the screen and an action bar at the top of the screen (Figures 2.5 and 2.6, respectively). It should be noted that the exact shape of these icons is dependent on the manufacturer of the device. In some devices, the Home button is an actual hardware button. The Back and Home virtual buttons remain the same in both form and function. However, the Menu and Search buttons were eliminated, and a Recents virtual button was added. The Recents button shows the user's recently used apps. The action bar displays the app's icon and title and the menu. Menu items will be displayed with an icon (if defined). If there are too many menu items to be displayed with an icon, the extra menu items are accessible through the three vertical dots on the right side of the menu bar. If an app is targeting older versions of Android as well as newer, the action bar presents only the three dots at the far right. When pressed, these dots perform the same function as the Menu button.

Figure 2.5 Android virtual buttons.

Figure 2.6 Android action bar.

The Home button immediately moves your app to the Stopped state. This causes the onPause and onStop methods to execute. It will not destroy the app unless it needs the system resources. This means you must pay attention to these events, even though you may not be anticipating this behavior when your app is in use.

The Back button immediately goes back one action or activity. This can have several implications for your code. For example, if the user is looking at an activity and presses the Back button, the visible activity will be immediately moved to the Stopped state (causing the onPause and onStop methods to execute). It will move the previous activity into the Running state. This will cause the onStart and onResume methods to execute for that activity. If your activity has displayed a pop-up, the activity is currently in the Paused state (because it is partially visible). Pressing the Back button will hide the pop-up and cause the onResume method to execute, and your activity will be placed in the running state. If the soft keyboard is displayed, your app is also in the Paused state. Pressing the Back button will hide the keyboard and again put your activity in the Running state.

If the user presses the Menu button, your app will not do anything unless you have specifically programmed it to have a menu. Menus can be useful ways to provide the user with access to functionality that is not used as the normal course of events in using your app; thus you don't want to waste valuable screen real estate to provide access to that functionality.

Finally, the Search button also does nothing unless you code it. You can use this button to allow the user to search for information within your app.

The hardware/virtual buttons provided by Android devices either have an impact on your app or can be used to extend the functionality of your app. In either case, it is important to plan for the impact of these buttons when designing your app.

iOS

The primary hardware button of concern on iOS devices is the Home button. This button immediately moves any app presently running to the background. The viewWillDisappear(), applicationWillResignActive(), and applicationDidEnterBackground() methods will all be called. Plan your app so that this action will not cause problems.

Both Android and iOS have a button that puts the device to sleep or reboots it. This action also must be handled. Fortunately, the same methods that put the app in the background for other actions are executed, so typically no additional programming is required to prepare for this.

Introducing Your First App

To learn both Android and iOS design and development, you will build the same app on each platform. Building the same app on both platforms is useful for understanding differences and similarities between the platforms. The app you will build is called *MyContactList*. For two reasons, building a contact list app is a good way to learn mobile development. First, its purpose and function are generally understood, so a significant part of any application development effort (understanding the functional requirements) does not need to be explained. Second, a contact list app requires utilizing many basic and advanced features of mobile development; therefore it is very useful in providing a context for learning these concepts.

The MyContactList app consists of four different screens. Each screen is used to illustrate basic app development concepts you will use in almost any subsequent app you develop. In addition, you'll learn how to navigate between screens in an app.

Contact Screen

The contact screen shown in Figure 2.7 is used to enter, edit, and save information about people in your contact list. While developing this screen, you learn some of the fundamental concepts of mobile user interface design and data entry. Later on, you use this screen as a way to learn how to create and store data in a database on a mobile platform. Finally, the contact screen shows you how to integrate hardware capabilities into an application by using the device's camera to capture a contact's picture and to make a phone call by tapping the contact's phone number.

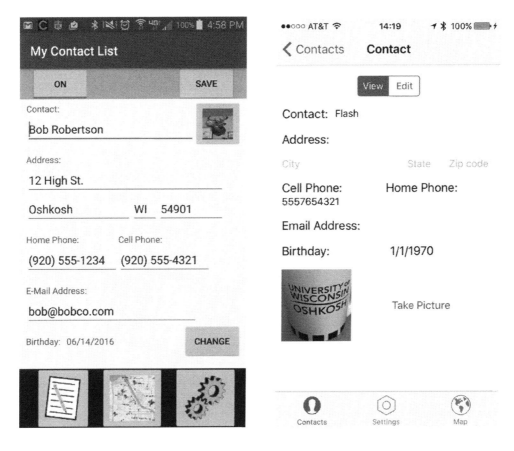

Figure 2.7 The contact screen.

Contact List Screen

The contact list (see Figure 2.8) is used to search for basic contact information and allow selection of a contact for further action (e.g., editing and deleting). Lists are very important components of many apps on both Android and iOS. Developing this screen teaches you how to integrate them into any future app. This screen also demonstrates how to access information provided by hardware components of the device.

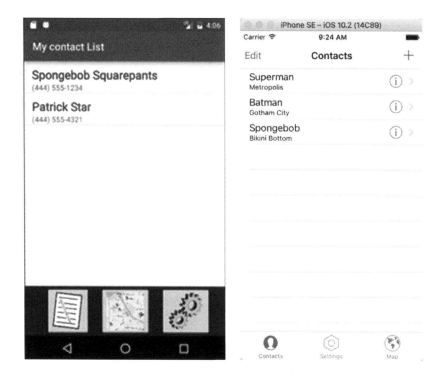

Figure 2.8 The contact list screen.

Map Screen

The map screen (see Figure 2.9) is used to display the recorded location of a single contact or all your contacts on a map with a pin. The screen also demonstrates how to display the device's present location on the map and how to switch between different map views. The usefulness and importance of maps on mobile devices needs no further explanation. Through the development of this screen, you learn how to integrate mapping into your apps. In addition, the screen will be used to demonstrate another approach to accessing sensor information.

Figure 2.9 The map screen.

Settings Screen

The settings screen (see Figure 2.10) is used to set the sort order for the contacts in the contact list. In developing this screen, you learn to use a method of data persistence designed for capturing and storing individual pieces of data. This type of data persistence is often used to capture user preferences for an app. You also learn to use a different type of display widget (view).

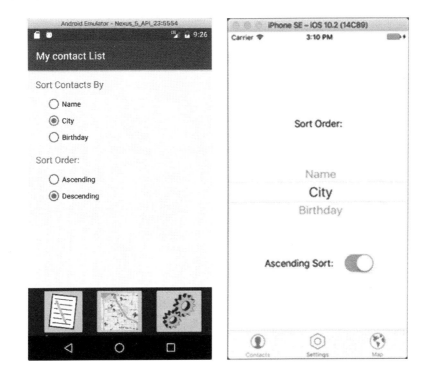

Figure 2.10 The settings screen.

Summary

App development is different from traditional software development. You must design to take advantage of, and be aware of, the impact of the mobile operating system and the hardware that the app is running on. If you do not design your app to account for these differences in the device, you will ensure that your app doesn't get much use. Android and iOS devices have many similarities and differences that require planning when you are developing an app that will run on both device families. To learn both platforms and learn the differences between them, you will learn to develop the same app for both platforms in the next two sections.

Exercises

1. Find an app that runs on both platforms. Download and run it. Identify the similarities and differences between the platforms.

2. Find out what uses the most battery power on the mobile device. On Android, find the battery usage information. This can be in different places on different Android devices but is typically in the Settings app. Scroll through the list of power draws. What requires the most? What requires the least? Note: This feature is not available on iOS.

3. Open an app that uses the GPS (e.g., Google Maps). Look at the status bar at the top of the device. What icons are there? What are they doing? Watch until the device goes to black and then turn it on again. What changes occurred in the status icons? Now switch to the home screen. What happened to the status icons?

PART II

DEVELOPING THE ANDROID APP

CHAPTER 3

Using Android Studio for Android Development

This chapter is an introduction to building a complete Android app and includes creating a new app project, exploring the components of an Android app, setting up the emulator to run and test apps, and building a variation of the traditional Hello World app. This and the following chapters in Part 1 assume that you have access to Android Studio and that it is set up for Android development. If this is not the case, visit https://developer.android.com/studio and follow the instructions to download and install Android Studio on your computer.

Starting a New App

Android Studio is an integrated development environment (IDE) provided by Google as their official tool for developing Android phone and tablet applications. This tool is continually being refined and has become quite powerful and reliable with recent versions. Especially useful is the enhanced ability to identify deprecated code, inefficient code, and code that doesn't conform to Android design guidelines.

Android is a mobile operating system designed for smartphones and tablets. The operating system is very powerful, enabling access to a diverse set of hardware resources on a smartphone or tablet. Android is provided by Google and is continually updated, improved, and extended. This makes the development of apps for Android smartphones and tablets both exciting and challenging. The many features of the Android environment are best explained through the act of developing an app.

Starting a New Project

Android Studio organizes apps into projects that are stored in a folder designated by the developer. The folder contains the application's code and resources, code libraries used by the application (or references to them), and metadata that is used to keep track of environment information for the workspace.

To begin, run Android Studio. Android Studio will open the project you were working on when you last closed the IDE. If no project was open, the IDE displays the Welcome window, which lists a number of quick start options, including starting a new project, opening an existing project, importing a project from another IDE (e.g., Eclipse), and other update and configuration options. Most IDEs are designed with the idea that developers are going to be working on the same machine each time they work on a project. This can cause problems in the education environment, where students do not have the ability to work on the same machine and/or store their work on the machine they are currently working on. However, moving projects in Android Studio is really just moving the project folder and opening it on the new machine.

Creating the Project

The traditional beginning tutorial for many different languages and development platforms is "Hello World." Your first Android app will be a slightly modified "Hello World" app. In Android Studio, all Android apps are created within a project. To create your first app, you will have to create your first project. Creating a new project requires stepping through a series of windows and making choices to configure your app. To get started, from Android Studio's Welcome window, choose **Start a new Android Studio project**. You should see the **New Project** dialog window, as shown in Figure 3.1.

Figure 3.1 New Android Studio project.

Fill out the screen as shown in Figure 3.1, except project location, which will be unique to your computer. Click the ⬚ button and choose a location that fits your needs. If this is your own computer where you will be doing most of your work, you can keep the default location. If not, you may want to change the location to a USB drive. The application name is displayed on the phone's screen as the name of the app. You can use spaces if you want. As you type the name, the project location and package name will be completed. There are no spaces allowed in these items. The wizard will remove them as you type. Don't put them back in either of those fields. The package name is important. For this initial project, you don't need to change the default. However, if you are building an app for sale, in place of "example" you should put your company name. This identifier will be used in the Play Store to link your apps to the services they use and connect all your apps.

Once you have selected your location, click **Next**. The **Target Android Devices** window should be displayed (Figure 3.2).

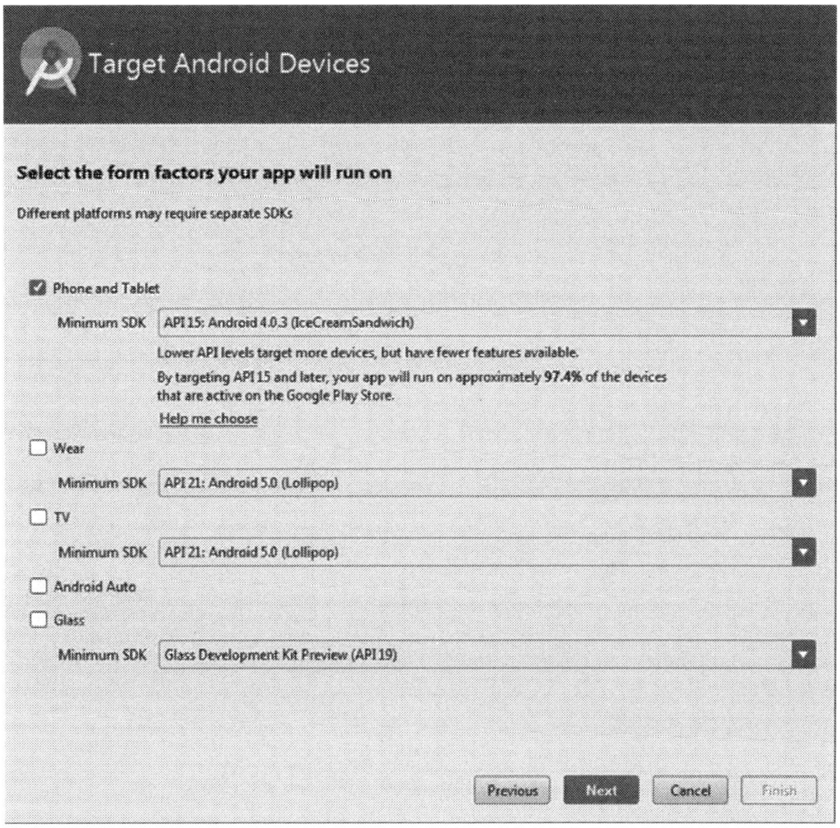

Figure 3.2 Target Android Devices window with default selections.

This window allows you to select the oldest version of Android that your app will be able to run on. A suggested minimum Android SDK is displayed. SDK stands for Software Development Kit, and it is a set of tools and code libraries used to write software for a specific platform. Each release of the Android OS is associated with an SDK so that programmers can write code for that platform. An application programming interface (API) is a set of routines that allow a program (app) to access the resources of the operating system to provide functionality to the user. The minimum required SDK determines what phones and other Android devices will be able to install your app. (Phones and tablets using Android operating systems earlier than this selection will not even see your app in the Play Store.) This selection will also determine the features you can program into your app. The recommended minimum is the default: *IceCreamSandwich API 15*. An app that has this minimum will be accessible to more than 95% of the devices "in the wild." This means devices running the minimum up to the current version. If you are building apps for devices other than phones or tablets, you can target them in this window. For this book, we are only targeting phones and tablets so leave the default selection.

Click **Next** and the **Add an Activity to Mobile** screen will be displayed. An activity is a core component of any Android application. Activities are typically associated with a visible screen. Most of the core functionality of an app is provided by an activity and its associated screen (called a *layout*). The choices of activity are limited by your choice of minimum and target SDK. If you had selected an SDK less than fifteen, a number of layouts would not be available. Select **Empty Activity** and click **Next**. We are doing a very basic application and want to demonstrate some basic concepts without Android Studio doing some of the work for us.

The **Customize the Activity** window is displayed. In this window, you will name the activity and choose if a layout should be associated with the activity. In the Activity Name text box, delete **MainActivity** and type **HelloWorldActivity**. Notice below Activity Name is Layout Name. As you typed in the activity name, the text in this box changed to reflect the text you entered. A layout is an XML file that specifies the user interface for the activity. Layouts are discussed in detail later. For now, just remember that every activity has an associated layout file if it is to have a visible interface. Verify that the **Generate Layout File** checkbox is checked (default) and verify that the **Backwards**

Compatibility (AppCompat) checkbox is checked. Click **Finish**. Android Studio will create the project (which may take some time). A layout file will be created for the activity. This is essentially the interface for the activity. Checking backwards compatibility includes files to make your app run with older versions of the Android operating system. When finished, you should see something like Figure 3.3. You may have to click on the **Project** tab on the left side of Android Studio, drill down into the **app** folder, and double click on the **HelloWorldActivity**.

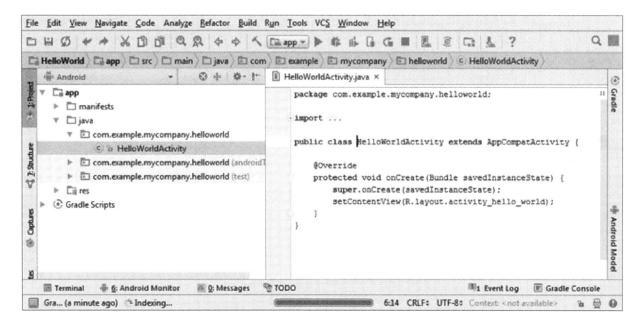

Figure 3.3 Android Studio with the newly created Hello World project.

Components of the IDE

Many of the items in the IDE will be explained as needed. For now, let's examine just a few. The right section is the *Editor*. Much of the development work is done here, including the UI design and writing code. It should currently be displaying the code file for the HelloWorldActivity. It will also display a tab for the layout file associated with the HelloWorld Activity. Click on the **activity_hello_world.xml** tab. This will display the XML that creates the activity's interface. You can switch between graphical layout and the XML code that generates the layout with the tabs below the layout. One tab, labeled **Design**, shows the interface as the user would see it (on the left) and the blueprint view of the layout (on the right). The blueprint view shows the relative position and sizes of the items in the display. This view is new in Android Studio 2.2. The other tab, labeled **Text**, shows the XML that generates the visual interface. Click on the **Design** tab to see the display. It should look like Figure 3.4. Note that if the properties window on the right-hand side is not displayed, click on **Hello World!** in the design view or blueprint view.

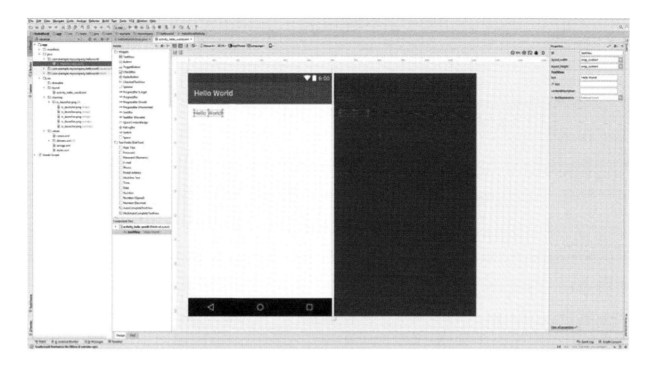

Figure 3.4 Layout file in design view (Design/Text tabs).

The left side of the IDE shows the Project window. The Project window displays the structure of the Android app and is used to move between different components of the app. Many of these items will be generated for you, and you will work with many others as you create your app. The java folder will contain all the Java code files for the app. Each file typically represents one class. Click the **disclosure button** to the left of the java folder and its subfolders until you see HelloWorldActivity.java (which may already be displayed). This is where the code to create the activity's functionality is written. Double-click the **HelloWorld.java** file. The file contents are displayed in the editor with some Java code listed (again, this may already be displayed). This code is explained later.

Next, look for the **res** folder in the Project window. This folder contains a number of subfolders that all contain a different kind of resource file needed for your Android app. Remember one very important note about resource files—there are no capital letters allowed in the file names! The **drawable** folders are for images. There can be multiple subfolders in drawable. Each is associated with images of a different size to match the size recommendations for different screen resolutions. Android uses portable network graphics (PNG) files for its images. While drawable is empty at this point, you can see the multiple subfolders in the **mipmap** folder. When your app is installed on a device, Android automatically uses the image appropriate for the device it is installed on by selecting it from the correct folder.

Next is the **layout** folder. This folder holds all the layouts for the user interface of your app. The **menu** folder holds the menu items to be displayed in your app when a user clicks the device's menu button. Menu functionality is not required for an app, and this book will not work with them.

The **mipmap** folder holds your app's launch and screen icon. This is the image for the icon the user taps on to start your app. Click the **disclosure button**. You should see five png files with the same name. These are the different sized icons for different screen sizes. The icon in this folder is currently the default app icon. You may change this by deleting the existing png files and adding your own.

The final set of folders is that of the **values** folders. Click the **disclosure button** to the left of the **values** folder. Four XML files will be displayed: **colors.xml, dimens.xml, strings.xml, and styles.xml**. The values files hold configuration data for an Android app. Android uses this information to limit the hard-coding of potentially changeable data. For example, the dimens.xml file could hold a value for screen title size that could be reused on each layout in the app. If you later decide that you want the screen title size to be different (e.g., `<dimen name="screen_title_size">24sp</dimen>`), you only have to change the value in the dimens.xml file and it automatically applies the new size to all titles that use that dimension. The values folders with a dash and number or other information are for values to be used for specific versions of the Android operating system (note that these may not be in new apps). This enables the developer to take advantage of different OS capabilities within the same app. Some common values files are described as follows:

- **dimens.xml**—Values for the display size of items in a layout.
- **color.xml**—Values for the displayed color of item in a layout.
- **strings.xml**—Values for text.
- **array.xml**—Defines string arrays and the values in those arrays.
- **ids.xml**—IDs that cannot be reused by items in layouts.
- **styles.xml**—Defines a look and format for layouts or app as a whole.

The Android Manifest

The final and very important item in the Project window that we will examine is the **AndroidManifest.xml** file. The manifest file is in the **manifests** folder. Double-click this file. The **manifest** will be displayed in the editor. The manifest is used to configure the whole app and tell the device it is installed on what it can and should be able to do. You can open it by double-clicking the file name in the left sidebar.

Interpreting the XML

Although the tabs in the **manifest** editor can be used to create a basic configuration of the manifest, the ability to read and manipulate XML is a critical skill for the Android app developer. Modifying a manifest to allow your app to do more advanced behaviors is common, and most online help documentation on doing so, either from the Android Developer site or developer forums, is provided in XML. To get started, take a look at the manifest components in the **AndroidManifest.xml** file (Listing 3.1).

Listing 3.1 Manifest XML

```
1    <?xml version="1.0" encoding="utf-8"?>
2
3    <manifest xmlns:android="http://schemas.android.com/apk/res/android"
4        package="com.example.mycompany.helloworld" >
5
6        <application
7            android:allowBackup="true"
8            android:icon="@mipmap/ic_launcher"
9            android:label="HelloWorld"
10           android:supportsRtl="true"
11           android:theme="@style/AppTheme" >
12
13           <activity android:name=".HelloWorldActivity" >
14               <intent-filter>
15                   <action android:name="android.intent.action.MAIN" />
16                   <category android:name="android.intent.category.LAUNCHER" />
17               </intent-filter>
18           </activity>
19       </application>
20
21   </manifest>
```

The manifest contains a number of XML elements. Those elements and their attributes define basic operational aspects of your app. Refer to the numbers in Listing 3.1 to see the complete code associated with each element explanation as follows.

- **Lines 3–4**—The `<manifest>` component is the root element. The attributes associated with this element define the application package and potentially other attributes of the application such as the version name or installation location preference.

- **Lines 6–11**—The `<application>` element has both attributes and child elements that configure ho
app works. Application attributes in this manifest define the app icon, theme, and name. Note that the a
bute android:label displays HelloWorld with a greenish tint (note that the tint may differ depending on your
device parameters). Hover your cursor over it, and the string resource file entry that has the value "HelloWorld"
will be displayed.

- **Line 13**—Each activity in an app must have an entry in the `<application>` element. In our manifest, there
is one activity: the one created when we created the project. Its attributes identify the Java class file for the
activity and the display name of the activity. Currently, that name is the same as the app's name. The `<activity>`
element tells the operating system that an activity has permission to run in your application. All activities used
in an app must be defined in the manifest. If they are not, the app will crash when the user navigates to that
activity. In this element, the Java source file for the activity and the activity's title are identified.

- **Line 14**—A child element of the `<activity>` element, the `<intent-filter>` element, defines what the
Android OS should do with this activity. Not all activities will have an intent-filter. Specifically, activities that
you want users to launch when they are using the app do not need intent-filters. However, for this app, you
want this activity to be displayed when the user runs it.

- **Line 15**—Therefore the `<action>` tag identifies the activity as the main or first activity to run.

- **Line 16**—The `<category>` tag tells the OS to use the app launcher to start this activity.

Gradle Scripts

Now turn your attention back to the Project window. Below the app portion is a section labeled **Gradle Scripts**.
Click the **disclosure button** to display the files (if not already displaying). *Gradle* is the build system Android Studio
uses to compile and package apps. The items listed here include files that have settings for the app and files that have
instructions for building the app. For now, we will just examine one of these. Double-click on **build.gradle (Mod-
ule:app)**. The script file will be displayed in the editor, and you should see something like Listing 3.2. If the version
numbers in your app are lower than those in Listing 3.2, you either do not have the latest version of Android Studio
or the latest SDKs for Android. To update the SDKs, select **Tool > Android > SDK Manager**. Make sure the **SDK
Platforms** tab is selected. A list of SDKs will be displayed. Select the newest (top of the list) at a minimum and click
OK. Click the defaults as they come up to download and install the SDKs. This will take a while. When complete,
change your version in the **Gradle** script to the highest one you downloaded. To update Android Studio and other
associated tools, click **Help > Check for Updates**. Click **Update** if any are found.

Listing 3.2 Gradle Build Script

```
1    apply plugin: 'com.android.application'
2
3    android {
4      compileSdkVersion 25
5      buildToolsVersion "25.0.0"
6
7      defaultConfig {
8        applicationId "com.example.mycompany.helloworld"
9        minSdkVersion 15
10       targetSdkVersion 25
11       versionCode 1
12       versionName "1.0"
13           testInstrumentationRunner "android.support.test.runner.AndroidJUnitRunner"
14     }
15     buildTypes {
16       release {
17         minifyEnabled false
18         proguardFiles getDefaultProguardFile('proguard-android.txt'), 'proguard-rules.pro'
19       }
20     }
21   }
22
```

(continued)

Listing 3.2   Gradle Build Script (*continued*)

```
23          dependencies {
24              compile fileTree(dir: 'libs', include: ['*.jar'])
25              androidTestCompile('com.android.support.test.espresso:espresso-core:2.2.2', {
26                  exclude group: 'com.android.support', module: 'support-annotations'
27              })
28              testCompile 'junit:junit:4.12'
29              compile 'com.android.support:appcompat-v7:25.0.0'
30          }
```

The Gradle build file contains a number of important elements:

- **Lines 4–5**—The `compileSdkVersion` and `buildToolsVersion` tell the Gradle system what version of Android should be used to compile the code into an app. By default, the latest version of the Android SDK installed on your development machine should be identified here.

- **Lines 7–14**—The `defaultConfig` element has both attributes provide information about the specific version of the app that is being compiled. All of these except `applicationId` can, and should, change in newer versions of your app. Both the minimum and target SDKs will change as new versions of Android are released. After the initial project creation, you will have to change these manually by opening the build script in the editor as you need to release new versions to your users.

  Note the `versionCode` and `versionName` elements. Version code is an integer value. It is used to indicate that there is a new version of the app available. Increasing the value enables the Play Store to notify users of the app that a new version is available. It also controls the install of the upgrade so that no user data is lost during an upgrade. The Version Name is the displayed version of your app. Beyond that, it is nonfunctioning. However, it is good practice to have a consistent approach to changing this so that you know what version of the app is at issue when communicating with users about their problems with the app. The `testInstrumen-tationRunner is used in testing code that needs to access the Android API. The default configuration for these tests is AndroidJUnitRunner.`

- **Lines 15–20**—The `buildTypes` element is used to configure different "flavors" of the same app. Here we have only one flavor, the release version. Proguard is enabled by default, but is also recommended. Proguard is a tool that shrinks and optimizes your compiled code. It also obfuscates your code by renaming classes, fields, and methods so your app is more difficult to reverse engineer.

- **Lines 23–30**—The `dependencies` element identifies packages external to the app that are required to ensure proper operation. The items noted previously are included by default, but you may add others to enhance your app. For example, if you wanted to have your app interact with Facebook, you would include a dependency to the Facebook SDK here (e.g., `compile 'com.facebook.android:facebook-android-sdk:4.1.0'`).

Configuring the Emulator

Now that you have some understanding of the development environment, you are almost ready to start creating the app. Don't worry—future projects will take less time to set up. You could start coding at this point, but until you tell Android Studio how to execute the app, you will not be able to see your results. Therefore the next step will be to set up the test environment.

> **Note**
>
> If you are running Android Studio on a virtual machine (such as VMWare Fusion), you will not be able to use a virtual device. This is essentially running a virtual machine on a virtual machine, and it won't work. If that is the case, you will have to test on a real device by attaching the device to a USB connection on your computer.

Android apps may be tested on either the emulator provided by the Android Studio IDE or on an Android device. The emulator is a program that simulates an Android device. If you choose to test on the emulator, you should also test on several varieties of real devices before you publish your app. Real devices often perform differently than the emulator. If you do not test on a real device, you will likely have many unhappy users.

To set up the emulator, we first must set up an **Android Virtual Device** (AVD). An AVD is a software replication of one or more types of Android devices. Multiple AVDs with different characteristics may be set up for testing. To set up an AVD, we use the AVD Manager. From the main menu, select **Tools** > **Android** > **AVD Manager** to display the **Your Virtual Devices** window. Click the **Create Virtual Device** button, and the **Select Hardware** window will be displayed (Figure 3.5).

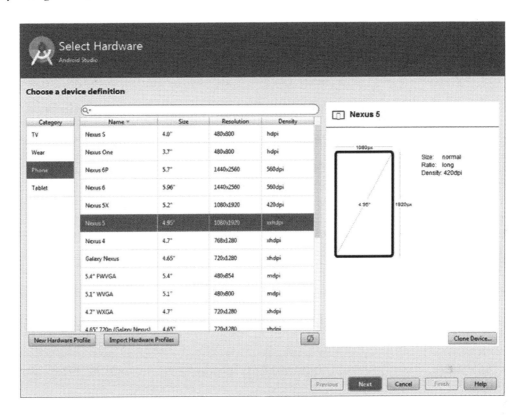

Figure 3.5 AVD initial window.

Select whatever phone or tablet type you would like to test your app on and click **Next**. Depending on what SDKs you have installed, you will see one or more SDKs listed. You can also download more SDKs from this window. Click the SDK that you want your virtual device to emulate running. Click **Next**, and on the next window enter a name for the device (or keep the default). Leave all the other defaults. Click **Finish**. The AVD will be created (which may take some time), and the **Your Virtual Devices** window will open, displaying your newly created AVD. Close the window.

> **Note**
> We like to start our development with one of the smaller devices because we find it easier to scale up when developing the user interface than to scale down. Also, we like to pick a lower API for the device for similar reasons. Later, you can create different AVDs to test different device configurations.

Setting Up Run Configurations

The final step in setting up the test environment is to confirm the run configuration for your app.

1. From the main menu, select **Run > Edit Configurations**. The **Run Configurations** window is displayed.
2. Click the **disclosure button** to the left of Android Application on the left side of the screen. Then click **app**.
3. Find **Deployment Target Options** on the right side of the screen and verify that **Open Select Deployment Target Dialog** is selected (if not, use the dropdown arrow to select it).
4. Click **OK**. Now when you run or debug your app, a device chooser will display all your AVDs and real devices connected to the computer. You can then choose which one you want to test on.

Coding the Interface

As mentioned earlier, the user interface for any Android app is created through the use of a layout file. A layout file is an XML file that contains the XML used to create the objects and controls that the user can interact with. The first step in coding the HelloWorld app is to modify the layout so that it has some controls that the user can interact with. Your modifications will be simple. You will make the app take a name entered by the user and display "Hello" followed by the entered name after a button click (e.g., Hello Jane).

Double-click the **activity_hello_world.xml** file in the layout folder of the Project window to begin work coding the interface. If it is already open in the editor, click the **activity_hello_world.xml tab** at the top of the editor. If the Design view is displayed, click the **Text** tab at the bottom of the editor. The XML code that creates the user interface is displayed with two *elements* in it. The root element is a **RelativeLayout**. A RelativeLayout allows the user interface to be designed by placing controls by specifying their position relative to other controls or the parent screen. Because Android devices have so many screen sizes and resolutions, it is often best to design the UI components as relative to one another, rather than designing them as a fixed position. Because the RelativeLayout is the root, it encompasses the whole screen. You must have only one layout root in an Android layout file. All other items are children of this root element.

Examine the attributes of the RelativeLayout element (Listing 3.3). A closer look at the attributes reveals a certain structure. Attributes have the format *library:attribute name = "attribute value"*. First, all the attributes in the listing start with `android:`. This indicates that the attribute is associated with the Android SDK library, and that is where the compiler should look for information on what to do. Other libraries are available from third parties. Adding other libraries will be covered in Chapter 7, "Maps and Location in Android." The attribute name and values differ based on the element to which they are applied.

Listing 3.3 Layout XML

```
1    <RelativeLayout xmlns:android="http://schemas.android.com/apk/res/android"
2        xmlns:tools="http://schemas.android.com/tools"
3
4        android:id="@+id/activity_hello_world"
5        android:layout_width="match_parent"
6        android:layout_height="match_parent"
7
8        android:paddingBottom="@dimen/activity_vertical_margin"
9        android:paddingLeft="@dimen/activity_horizontal_margin"
10       android:paddingRight="@dimen/activity_horizontal_margin"
11       android:paddingTop="@dimen/activity_vertical_margin"
12       tools:context="com.example.mycompany.helloworld.HelloWorldActivity" >
13
14       <TextView
15           android:layout_width="wrap_content"
16           android:layout_height="wrap_content"
17           android:text="Hello World!"
18           android:id="@+id/textView"
19           android:layout_alignParentTop="true"
20           android:layout_alignParentLeft="true"
21           android:layout_alignParentStart="true" />
22
23   </RelativeLayout>
```

- **Lines 1–6**—The first attribute of interest in the RelativeLayout is `android:id="@+id/activity_hello_world"`. This is the id of the root layout in the layout file. It is used in the code to access the root layout. The next two attributes are `android:layout_width="match_parent"` and `android:layout_height="match_parent"`. These attributes define the size of the element. In this case, the value `"match_parent"` indicates that the layout should be the height and width of the device screen. If a child element of RelativeLayout has this value for either `layout_height` or `layout_width`, it will fill up as much of the RelativeLayout as it can.

- **Lines 8–11**—The next few attributes, `paddingRight`, `paddingLeft`, `paddingBottom`, and `padding-Top`, all tell Android that it should not fill the entire screen with the RelativeLayout. Instead, there should be blank space between the edge of the screen and the edge of the layout. The amount of space is dictated by the value. The values in these attributes are your first introduction to the use of the XML files in the values folder. To refer to values from these XML files, Android also has a specific structure. That structure is `"@xml_file_name/value_name"`. All values are enclosed in quotation marks. The value for the attribute `android:paddingBottom` is `"@dimen/activity_vertical_margin"`. This tells Android it should use the value named `activity_vertical_margin` from the dimens.xml file. Double-click the dimens.xml file in the values folder in the Package Explorer. This displays the XML used to define the dimensions. The `<dimen>` tag is used to define each dimension. Each dimension has a name attribute, a value, and then a closing tag that looks like this: `</dimen>`. The value between the beginning tag and the closing tag is the value that Android uses as the size of the padding. You may have a disclosure button next to dimens.xml. In this case you have two dimens files. One is for wide displays (w820dp). Android will automatically select the correct file at runtime.

  Valid dimensions for Android include `px` (pixels), `in` (inches), `mm` (millimeters), `pt` (points), `dp/dip` (density-independent pixels), and `sp` (scale-independent pixels). It is generally recommended that `dp` be used for most dimensions and `sp` be used for specifying font sizes. These two units of measure are relative to screen density. They help keep your UI consistent among different devices. The reason that the `sp` unit is recommended for fonts is because it also scales to the user's preference in font size.

- **Line 12**—The `tools:context` identifies that activity that is associated with layout. This is used at design time support development but has no impact once the app is compiled.

- **Lines 14–21**—Switch back to activity_hello_world.xml. The only child element of the RelativeLayout, and thus the only item on the screen, is a TextView. TextView is Android's version of a label. It is primarily used to display text. This element currently has several attributes. The two size attributes differ from the RelativeLayout in that they have the value `"wrap_content"`. This tells Android to adjust the TextView to the size of the text displayed in it. The third attribute tells Android what text to display. In this case, its value is "Hello World!". The fourth attribute assigns an id to the TextView. Again, the id is to access the element in the code. The final three attributes describe the position of the TextView in the RelativeLayout. In this case, the TextView is aligned with the top of the RelativeLayout (its parent) and to the left. AlignParentLeft and AlignParentStart do the same thing. AlignParentStart is required to support languages that read right to left.

Switch back to the **Graphical Layout (Design** tab) view of the activity_hello_world.xml file (click the **Design** tab below the code window). At the left of the layout is a panel titled **Palette**. Palette contains a set of folders with different components (called widgets) that can be used to design a user interface. If it is not open, click on the **Widgets** folder in the Palette. The Widgets folder contains a set of widgets for designing the user interaction with your app. Notice that some controls have multiple versions that enable you to pick the size that you want for your interface.

A TextView that displays "Hello World" is already on the layout. This is used to display your app's message. However, the size of the text needs to be bigger. Below the Palette should be a panel with the label **Component Tree** (Figure 3.5). If this is not present, click **View > Tool Windows > Designer** to display it. The top of the tab should show the structure of the layout. It should have the **activity_hello_world (RelativeLayout)** as its root; the **TextView** should be indented below the RelativeLayout. The TextView should be displaying "Hello World" after it. As widgets are added to the layout, they are displayed in the structure. This is very useful because sometimes controls are added to the layout that get lost (not visible) in the Design Layout. However, if they are in the layout, they will be displayed in the structure. Alternatively, they will also be visible in the blueprint view.

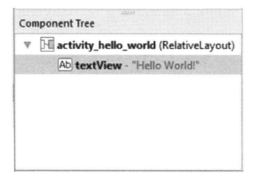

Figure 3.6 Layout outline.

To the right of the Design and Blueprint views is the **Properties** panel (Figure 3.6). If you haven't clicked anything in the Design view, Blueprint view, or Component Tree, that panel will be empty. Click the **Hello World TextView** in the Design view. The Properties window should populate with the basic attributes that can be set for a TextView widget. Click the **All Properties** button at the bottom of the Properties panel. All properties for the the TextView are displayed. Locate the **textSize** attribute (you may have to scroll down). It should have `@dimen/text_size_small_machine` as a value. Hover over the value and click on the **wrench** icon that appears. A new row will appear below with an empty box and a ▢ button next to it. Click on the button. The **Resources** window is displayed. All the resources created when the project was created are listed. Click the **Add new resource dropdown** on the upper right of the window and select New Dimension Value… (which may be the only choice). In the window that opens, enter **message_text_size** as the Resource name and **24sp** as the Resource value. Click OK until you have closed these two windows. The size of Hello World! should be increased. Open the **dimen.xml** file and switch to the XML view to see the dimension you created. Close this file and click back to the **activity_hello_world.xml** tab. Switch from **Design** view to the **Text** view and examine the XML changes to the TextView element.

Figure 3.7 Basic and All Properties views.

Note

The values files are used to hold values that are going to be reused in your app. Unfortunately, the only way to know what values are available is to open the file and inspect its contents for the value you'd like to use. We recommend that when you add values, you name them very clearly and limit the number of values you use to keep it somewhat manageable. Naming clearly is very important because Android Studio's code completion capability will list the value names but not their actual value.

Switch back to the **Design** view, and locate the TextView widget in the Widgets folder in the Palette. Click and drag it to the layout, position it as in Figure 3.7, and drop it. Notice the green arrows pointing to the left side of the layout and to the Hello World! TextView. These arrows show what object the widget is relative to for positioning purposes. Click the **Text** view (Listing 3.4). A number of changes have been made to the XML (some of your dimensions may be different).

Listing 3.4   Layout XML with TextView Added

```
1    <RelativeLayout xmlns:android="http://schemas.android.com/apk/res/android"
2        xmlns:tools="http://schemas.android.com/tools"
3        android:layout_width="match_parent"
4        android:layout_height="match_parent"
5        android:paddingBottom="@dimen/activity_vertical_margin"
6        android:paddingLeft="@dimen/activity_horizontal_margin"
7        android:paddingRight="@dimen/activity_horizontal_margin"
8        android:paddingTop="@dimen/activity_vertical_margin"
9        tools:context=".HelloWorldActivity" >
10
11       <TextView
12           android:layout_width="wrap_content"
13           android:layout_height="wrap_content"
14           android:text="Hello World!"
15           android:id="@+id/textView"
16           android:layout_alignParentTop="true"
17           android:layout_alignParentLeft="true"
18           android:layout_alignParentStart="true" />
19           tools:textSize="@dimen/message_text_size" />
20
21       <TextView
22           android:text="TextView"
23           android:layout_width="wrap_content"
24           android:layout_height="wrap_content"
25           android:layout_below="@+id/textView"
26           android:layout_alignParentLeft="true"
27           android:layout_alignParentStart="true"
28           android:layout_marginLeft="41dp"
29           android:layout_marginStart="41dp"
30           android:layout_marginTop="36dp"
31           android:id="@+id/textView2" />
32
33   </RelativeLayout>
```

- **Line 22**—The `android:text` attribute indicates what text should be displayed. Delete `"TextView"` and replace it with `"Name:"`. This line may now be highlighted in gold. This warning indicates that you are not following Android coding standards. Hover over the highlighted line and the warning is displayed, saying that the value `"Name:"` is a hard-coded value. Android wants all values to be referenced from a value's XML file. This is for ease of maintenance. You can change a string value used multiple times just once in the strings.xml file, and the changes will be made throughout your app. Also, by substituting a different string's.xml file, you can adapt your app to different languages more easily. To simplify this example, leave the string hard-coded for now.

- **Lines 25–27**—As the arrows on the Design view showed, this widget is positioned relative to the Hello World! TextView. The layout attributes are the XML used to do the relative positioning. `alignParentLeft` and `alignParentStart` tell Android to align this widget's left edge with the referenced widget's left edge. `alignBelow` tells Android to position the widget below the referenced widget. In this case, the referenced widget is the Hello World! TextView that has the id `textView`.

- **Lines 28–30**—The margin attributes `layout_marginLeft`, `layout_marginStart`, and `layout_marginTop` tell Android how much space to put between the widget and the referenced locations. Change the left margin to 20dp and the top margin to 55dp. You will often have to tweak these values to get the layout to look exactly the way you want it. Switch back to the **Design** view. The TextView you added should now be displaying `Name:`.

- **Line 31**—The new TextView also has a `+id`. However, it is different from the first one. `+id`s may be reused in different layouts but cannot be reused within the same layout!

- **Line 15**—We want to use the TextView that current displays Hello World! to display Hello and the name entered (how to enter a name will come next) when a button is clicked. Since we will use this TextView in the code, we should change its id to something that has some meaning. In the first TextView, change `android:id="@+id/textView"` to `android:id="@+id/textViewDisplay"`. Once you do this, the `layout_below="@+id/textView"` line in the second TextView will be underlined in red. This is because that id no longer exists in the layout. Change it to `@+id/textViewDisplay` and the underline will go away.

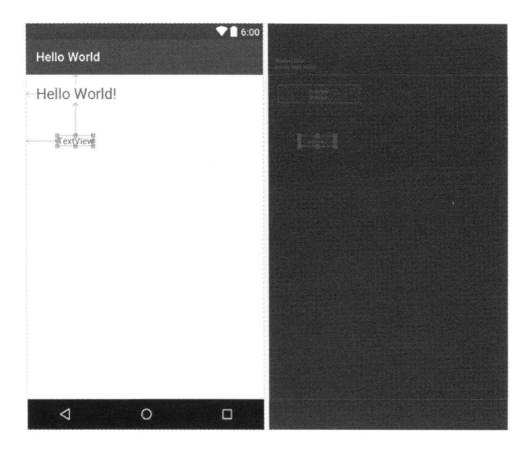

Figure 3.8   A TextView positioned properly on Design view.

UI Design—Android Versus iOS

UI design in Android is done through relative positioning of the controls that make up the interface. However, in iPhone and iPad, absolute positioning is used. Absolute position holds the control to a fixed position on the screen. The use of absolute position makes the design of the UI easier. Unlike in Android, when you move a control, it has no effect on other controls in the UI. Often in Android, moving one control changes the whole design. This can be frustrating! When moving or deleting a control in an Android layout, especially if you do this in the XML, be sure to check the impact of the change in the Design view.

Interface design is not without its challenges in iOS. Devices that run iOS have a fixed screen size, which is controlled by Apple. This enables the use of absolute positioning because all device screen sizes are known by the developer. However, this means that the UI has to be created multiple times for each device that you want your app to run on. These different screens all run on the same code, so during design, the developer must be sure to be perfectly consistent among the different screens needed.

In more recent versions of Xcode, Apple has introduced a more relative layout type approach called AutoLayout. Android Studio also has a similar approach with ConstraintLayout, which is discussed in Appendix B, "ConstraintLayouts in Android."

Locate the **Text Fields** folder in the Palette (you may have to switch to design view). A number of widgets for entering information are displayed. The widget for entering data in Android is called an **EditText**. Each of the Edit-Text widgets listed is configured for the entry of a different type of data. The different configurations dictate what soft keyboard is displayed when the widget is clicked and, in some cases, how the text is formatted as it is entered. For example, the EditText named Number will display a keyboard with only numbers on it, whereas the EditText named Plain Text will display a full keyboard. Drag the **Plain Text EditText** to the right of the **Name: TextView**. As you are dragging it, pay attention to the arrows. You want this relative to the **Name: TextView**, so there should be only one arrow, and it should point at the TextView. A dotted line should go from the bottom of the TextView through the EditText. This aligns the EditText with the bottom of the TextView.

Go back to the **Widgets** folder and drag a **Button** to the layout, centering it below the EditText. In this case, you want the arrow pointing to the EditText and the dotted line going through the middle of the bottom from the top of the screen to the bottom to center it horizontally in the **RelativeLayout**.

Note

Although Android Studio is a very powerful and useful tool in Android development, the need to make all items in the UI relative makes designing a layout difficult. We recommend that you use the Design view to get the UI approximately correct and then fine-tune in the XML.

Switch to the **Text** view for the layout. Locate the `EditText` element. Change the default `id` to `"@+id/editTextName"` so that we have some understanding about what data that widget is handling. Change the `layout_marginLeft` and `layout_marginStart` attributes to `"5dp"`. There are four new attributes. The first new attribute is `android:inputType`. This attribute tells Android how you want text handled as it's entered and the type of keyboard to display when the user is entering data. It is currently set to `textPersonName`, which will capitalize the first letter of each word entered into the EditText. The second is `android:ems`. This attribute sets the displayed size of the layout to 10 ems. Ems is a size measurement equal to the number of capital Ms that would fit into the control. Note that all these attributes can be changed in the Properties section of the Editor on the right-hand side, but it is important to develop an understanding of the xml, so we have you do it in the code. The final two new attributes are `layout_toRightOf` and `layout_toEndOf`. These attributes tell the EditText to align relative to the right of the name: TextView.

Switch to **Design** view. Note that the button is out of place. Since you changed the name of the EditText, the `layout_below` attribute of the button no longer knows its relative position. Switch back to **Text** view, locate the `Button` xml, and change the `layout_below` attribute value to `@+id/editTextName`. Next, change the id to `"@+id/buttonDisplay"`. There is also a new attribute in this element: `layout_centerHorizontal`. This attribute is set to true to tell Android to center the widget in the parent. Finally, change the text attribute to `"Display"`. Switch to the **Design** view to see the changes.

Run the app in the emulator using **Run > Run App** (or click the green triangle on the toolbar). Choose your **AVD** from the chooser window to see the layout as it would appear running (Figure 3.8). The first time you run the emulator, you may have to slide the lock to unlock the device (like a real phone). Note that the emulator might be behind Android Studio, so you will have to minimize windows or in some other way bring it to the foreground. The button clicks but does not do anything. For this to work, you need to write code. Your display may be different based on the selections you made for hardware during AVD creation.

Figure 3.9   Initial run of Hello World!

> **Note**
>
> Either close the activity_hello_world.xml file or switch to the Text view after you are done editing it. The reason is that if you close Android Studio with the layout file open in Design view, Android Studio will take a long time opening the project the next time you want to work on it.

Coding App Behavior

Code to give behavior to the layout is written and stored in the Java class file associated with the layout. Open the **HelloWorldActivity.java** file by double-clicking it. If it is already open, click its tab in the editor. You should see the basic code structure (Listing 3.5). Note that you may have to expand the import section by clicking the + button to the left of the keyword `import`.

Listing 3.5 Initial Activity Code

```
1      package com.example.mycompany.helloworld;
2
3      import android.os.Bundle;
4      import android.support.v7.app.AppCompatActivity;
5
6      public class HelloWorldActivity extends AppCompatActivity {
7
8          @Override
9          protected void onCreate(Bundle savedInstanceState) {
10             super.onCreate(savedInstanceState);
11             setContentView(R.layout.activity_hello_world);
12         }
13     }
```

This code was generated when you created the activity at the start of the HelloWorld project. It is important to understand what this code does to properly code an activity.

- **Line 1**—At the top of the file is the keyword "package" followed by com.example.helloworld. This identifies this class as belonging to the Hello World package. All source Java files (in src folder) will have this entry as the first code in the file.

- **Lines 3–4**—After the package line and before any other code are the imports. Click the plus (+) sign in front of the import... line of code. You should now see two import lines. This code is used to get the source code needed for your activity. The AppCompatActivity class provides the functionality required by any class that uses or interacts with other Activities used in this class. The Bundle import requires a bit more explanation.

    In Line 3, a Bundle is an object for passing data between activities. In this way, we can have an application that can perform some activity based on what another activity has done or the data it has used. You will use this functionality later in the book. However, Bundle also performs another very important function. It passes data back to the activity itself. When the user rotates the device, the displayed activity is destroyed and re-created in the new orientation. So that the user doesn't have to start over if this happens, the activity stores its current state in a bundle just before it is destroyed and passes that data to itself when it re-creates the activity in the new orientation.

- **Lines 6–13**—The public class line of code begins the Activity class and declares that this class is referred to as HelloWorldActivity and that it is a subclass of the SDK-provided AppCompatActivity class. Within the class is one method, onCreate. Before the method declaration is @Overide. This annotation tells the compiler that the method immediately following the annotation is to be used in place of the super class's method of the same name.

- **Lines 9–11**—The onCreate method is the first method executed by the Activity when it is started. The method has a parameter that is of type Bundle named savedInstanceState. This is the object that contains information on the state of the Activity if it was destroyed in an orientation change, as explained earlier. The next line super.onCreate calls the super class's onCreate method. Because your onCreate method is overriding the Activity class's inherited onCreate method and thus all the work it does to create the activity, you must call the super class method explicitly to use that functionality to create the Activity. It is passed the savedInstanceState bundle. The final line of code is setContentView(R.layout.activity_hello_world). This code tells the activity to use the activity_hello_world.xml file as the layout to be displayed when the activity is running. It is very important to understand the parameter R.layout.activity_hello_world. The R parameter tells the compiler that we want to use a resource from the layout folder named activity_hello_world. Whenever we want to access or manipulate a resource, it has to be referred to in this manner. However, this does not refer directly to the res folders; instead, it refers to a file generated by the compiler that is named R.java. To see this file, double-click into the gen folder in the Package Explorer until you see it. You should not edit this file because it is automatically generated by the compiler. The onCreate method will be modified with our code to add further functionality to the activity.

Adding Code

Our app has only one function—to display the name entered into the EditText when the Display button is pressed. Enter the code in Listing 3.6 before the last curly bracket in the activity Java file.

Listing 3.6   Display Button Code

```
1     private void initDisplayButton() {
2         Button displayButton = (Button) findViewById(R.id.buttonDisplay);
3         displayButton.setOnClickListener(new OnClickListener () {
4
5           @Override
6           public void onClick(View arg0) {
7             EditText editName = (EditText) findViewById(R.id.editTextName);
8             TextView textDisplay = (TextView) findViewById(R.id.textViewDisplay);
9             String nameToDisplay = editName.getText().toString();
10            textDisplay.setText("Hello " + nameToDisplay);
11          }
12        });
13    }
```

This code does the work and illustrates a number of important concepts in Android development.

- **Line 1**—This line declares a new method in the HelloWorldActivity class. The method is only useable by this class (`private`) and does not return any value (`void`). The method signature is `initDisplayButton()`. The signature, or name, of the method is completely up to you. However, you should name it to give some idea what it does.

- **Line 2**—Associate the code with the button on the layout. This line of code declares a variable of type `Button` that can hold a reference to a button and then gets the button reference using the command `findViewById`. All widgets on a layout are subclasses of the `View` class. The method `findViewById` gets a reference to a widget on a layout so it can be used by the code. The method can return any `View` object, so you have to use `(Button)` before it to cast the returned `View` to a `Button` type before it can be used as a `Button` by the code. `Button` is underlined in red after you type it in. This is because the code for the button class is not automatically available in the class. You have to import it. Fortunately, this is easy. Click on and then hover your cursor over the underlined word, and a message will display asking if you want to import. Once you get the message, press Alt + Enter to import. Do this for any other items underlined in red. You will get two options for onClickListener. Choose the `View.OnClickListener` option.

- **Line 3**—Set the button's listener. There are a number of different listeners for widgets, which gives great flexibility when coding app behavior. For this button, we use an `onClickListener`. The code creates a new instance of the listener and then adds a method (`public void onClick(View arg0)`) to be executed when the button is clicked.

- **Lines 4–5**—The code for when the button is clicked gets references to the `EditText` where the name was entered and the `TextView` where the message will be displayed.

- **Line 6**—The name entered by the user is retrieved from the `EditText` and stored in a `String` variable named `nameToDisplay`.

- **Line 7**—The `text` attribute of the `TextView` is changed to the value of the `String` variable. This will be highlighted in yellow. Android does not like concatenating strings while setting the text. It will work, but the preferred method is to use a string value with a placeholder in it. To fix this, open the strings.xml file in the values section of the Project Explorer. Enter the following as a new string resource: `<string name="welcome_message">Hello, %1$s!</string>`.

  The `%1$s` is the placeholder for the text you want to put in the string; `%1` indicates it's the first placeholder value (you can more than one). The `$s` indicates it's a string value. Next switch back to the activity code. Before the setText line of code, add the following lines:

```
Resources res = getResources(); //Asks the system for access to the values files
String displayString = res.getString(R.string.welcome_message, nameToDisplay); //creates the string
                                                            with message and name
```

Finally, change the setText line to `textDisplay.setText(displayString);` and the yellow should go away.

Notice that `initDisplayButton()` is light gray in color. This is because the method is never called by the code. To call it and get the behavior associated with the ▶ button to execute, you have to call the method in the `onCreate` method. After the `setContentView` line of code, enter

```
initDisplayButton();
```

The name gets normal code color and your code is done! Run the app in the emulator using **Run > Run App**. You could also run your app using the button in the top toolbar.

Connecting Code to UI—Android Versus iOS

In both Android and iOS (iPhone and iPad), the user interface (UI) and the code that makes the UI work are stored in different files. This means that both types of app coding require that the code has to be linked to the UI in some way. The chapters in this book that cover iOS explain the process of "wiring up" an interface using the features of the Xcode IDE. However, in Android, connecting the UI to the code is done entirely in the code itself.

Whenever some code needs to use a widget on a layout, it has to get a reference to it using the `findViewById` command. This requires extra coding but provides great flexibility. Forgetting to connect the code to the UI widget needed in both operating systems will result in a runtime error.

Summary

Congratulations! You have built your first app. You created an Android project, designed and coded a user interface, and finally, made the app do something. Along the way you learned the process of Android App development, the Android Studio development environment, and the components of an Android app.

Exercises

1. Change the Hello World app to allow the entering of a first and a last name and display "Hello *firstname lastname*!" when the button is clicked. Be sure to label the `EditText`s to reflect the new data that is to be input.

2. Add a Clear button. The Clear button should remove any data in the `EditText`(s) and change the display back to "Hello world!"

3. Create a new Android Virtual Device that uses a bigger device to test your app on a different screen size. Run the app using the new AVD.

CHAPTER 4

Android Navigation and Interface Design

App development for mobile devices is, as discussed in Chapter 2, "App Design Issues and Considerations," both similar to and different from development for other platforms. Navigation within an app has these similarities and differences. Different functionality is provided on different screens (windows in a traditional environment), and the app designer has to both provide the capacity to switch between those screens and make it easy and relatively obvious for users to do so when they want or need to access the functionality provided by those screens. Likewise, screen design is both similar to and different from the traditional user interface design. In a traditional environment, a window design is made up of a set of visible objects that give the user the ability to accomplish some component of the overall task. This is the same in the mobile environment. However, the objects available for design differ in both form and function, the amount of screen real estate available is much more limited, and often the amount of real estate available changes among devices that can use your app. This chapter introduces you to many of the principles and components of interface design and navigation in the Android platform. To learn these things, the chapter guides you through the development of MyContactList navigation and the development of the Contact interface.

Activities, Layouts, and Intents

The primary structural components for an Android app are Activities and Layouts. These components work together to present a display that the user can interact with. Intents are objects that are used to switch between activities in an app. All three objects are used as the basis for the structure of your app. Understanding the role and responsibilities of these objects is very important to effective development of an Android app.

The Activity Class

The **Activity** class is designed to handle a single task that the user can perform. Activities almost always have a visible component that allows the user to interact with the activity to perform the task. The activity class is not directly instantiated in an Android app. Rather, it is subclassed for every activity that the user needs to perform in the app. These subclasses are stored as .java files in the app project's java folder. This allows developers to inherit all the functionality of the Activity class and add their own unique functionality through Java code. One of the most important inherited functions of the Activity class is the capability to respond to life cycle events such as onCreate and onPause (refer to Chapter 2, "App Design Issues and Considerations," for a discussion of the Android life cycle).

The Activity class has a number of important subclasses. Only two of these subclasses are used in this book. The first of these is **AppCompatActivity**. This activity is a subclass of **FragmentActivity**, which is a subclass of Activity. Fragments allow the developer to include multiple tasks or panes within a single activity. The AppCompatActivity allows implementation of fragments and makes this functionality and others compatible with earlier versions of the Android operating system. Since we are making our app available on Android version 15 and later, we will need to use this as the super class of all our activities.

Layout

A **layout** is the visual component of a user interface in Android. The layout is not a class but rather an XML file that is used to tell the operating system what visual objects are to be displayed, how those objects are configured, and where those objects should be displayed on the screen. The XML in the file does use objects. The objects that make up an

Android interface are referred to as *widgets*. Widgets are subclasses of the View class. Android widgets include widgets to define where other widgets are displayed (e.g., RelativeLayout), to directly interact with the user (e.g., RadioButton), and to provide some type of navigation within the interfaces (e.g., ScrollView). Developing an understanding of how to describe the layout in the XML is a critically important task for the new Android developer.

Layouts can also be defined at runtime by instantiating the widgets that make up an interface and configuring them as needed. This can be very useful in some cases. However, designing the interface is more difficult because you cannot see the layout until you run the app. You will be designing your interface with XML in this book rather than at runtime.

Intents

An **Intent** is an object that is used to describe an operation to be performed. Intents are the primary way in which the developer starts new activities within the app. This is how you will use them in the app you develop for this book. However, Intents can also be used to communicate between activities. An Intent is essentially a message that defines an action to be taken and the data that the action is to be performed on. Intents can be used to start activities or broadcast both within and outside the app to provide instructions and data to other activities.

Activities, layouts, and intents are important components of an Android app. You will use all of them in almost every app you develop. Figure 4.1 provides a graphical relationship between these objects.

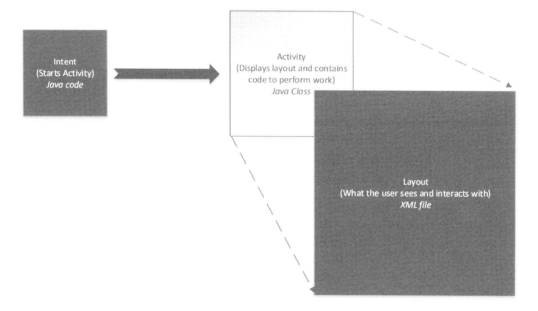

Figure 4.1   The relationship between Intents, Activities, and Layouts.

Creating the Interface

The MyContactList app requires four activities and four layouts to provide the functionality described in Chapter 2, "App Design Issues and Considerations." The app will use Intents to switch between activities and pass data between these activities. Your first task in creating the MyContactsList app is to make sure you have access to the image resources provided with this book. You will need four image files. One image is the app icon (appicon.png) and the other three are used in the app for navigation (contactlisticon.png, settingsicon.png, mapicon.png). Every app needs a project, and MyContactList is no different. Your second task is to create a new project.

Importing a Project

The completed project for each chapter is available in the online resources for this book. You can import the project by following these steps:

1. Unzip the chapter code.
2. Close any open projects in Android Studio to get to the Android Studio Welcome screen. Select **Open an existing Android Studio Project**.
3. Navigate to the unzipped code folder. Select **MyContactList** and click **OK**. The project will be imported and opened in Android Studio.

If you don't want to import the whole project, you can inspect the different files by navigating through the MyContactList folder.

Create the Project

Create a new Android project by selecting **File > New > New Project** from the menu if you have a project open. If you don't have a project open, you can select **Start a New Android Studio Project** from the Quick Start menu.

1. Use the following values for the first window presented by the project creation wizard:

   Application Name: **My Contact List**

   Company Domain: **example.com**

   Project location: Choose a location appropriate for your environment.

2. Click **Next**. Accept the defaults on this screen by clicking **Next** again.
3. In the **Add an Activity to Mobile** window, select the **Empty Activity**. Click **Next**.
4. In the **Customize the Activity** window, change the **Activity Name** to **ContactActivity**, and click **Finish**.

   To code the navigation, you need more than one activity. Create three more empty activities using the following process. Expand the **app** folder in the Project window and then expand the **java** folder. Right-click on **com.example.mycontactlist** and select **New > Activity > Empty Activity** (Figure 4.2).

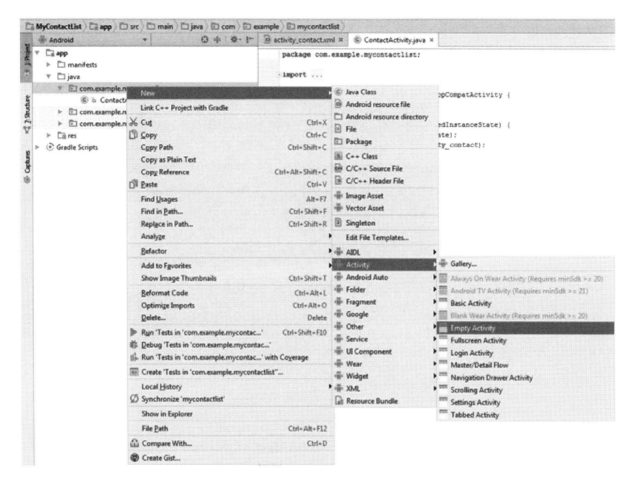

Figure 4.2 Adding a new activity.

In the **Customize the Activity** window, change the **Activity Name** to **ContactListActivity**. Accept the defaults (check **Generate Layout file** and **Backwards Compatible**; uncheck **Launcher Activity**). Click **Finish**. Repeat this process to add another two activities to your project. Give the activities the names **ContactMapActivity** and **ContactSettingsActivity**. Find the **res** folder in the Project Explorer and expand the **layout** folder. You should now have four layout XML files, one for each activity.

Set the Launch Icon

The launch icon is the picture displayed above the app's name in the device's Apps screen. An icon should give the user some idea about the function of the app. Launch icons are stored in the **mipmap** folder of the **res** folder in the Project window. You should have a number of app icons of different sizes named exactly the same name. To set the launch icon, you will copy the launch images provided to the **mipmap** folder in your Android project. There are four versions of the launch image provided. Each is in a different folder. Each will have to be individually copied to your project. Follow this procedure:

1. Expand the **res** folder, which is in the **app** folder, until you see the **mipmap** folder.
2. Open Windows Explorer and navigate to the folder where you placed the **Images** folder, and open one of the HDPI, MDPI, XHDPI, XXHDPI, or XXXHDPI folders. Right-click on the **contactlist_launch_icon** and choose **Copy**.
3. Go back to Android Studio and right-click on the **mipmap** folder. Choose **Paste**. On the window that opens, select the folder that has a name that ends with characters matching the folder you copied the image from. Click **OK**. Repeat for all five images in individual folders.

4. Open the **AndroidManifest.xml** file and find `android:icon=` attribute. Replace `@mipmap/ic_launcher` with `@mipmap/contactlist_launch_icon`.

Your app will now display the image as the app's launch icon rather than the default launch icon.

Create the Navigation Bar

The navigation bar for the MyContactList app sits at the bottom of the screen and allows the user to quickly move between different activities in the app by tapping one of the images on the bar (Figure 4.3). The navigation bar is made up of three `ImageButtons` contained within a RelativeLayout. The `RelativeLayout` is set to be just big enough to hold the three buttons and placed within the root `RelativeLayout` that was placed in the layout file by the wizard when you created the activity. The navigation layout is anchored to the bottom of that layout so that it always appears at the bottom of the screen.

    `ImageButtons` can only use image files that are within the project. To add the images to the project,

1. Expand the **res** folder, which is in the **app** folder, until you see the **drawable** folder.
2. Open Windows Explorer and navigate to the folder where you placed the **contactlisticon.png, settingsicon.png**, and **mapicon.png** files. Select all three files, right-click, and choose **Copy**.
3. Go back to Android Studio and right-click on the **drawable** folder. Choose **Paste**. Click **OK** on the window that opens.

Figure 4.3 Complete navigation bar layout.

4. Open the **activity_contact.xml** file if it is not already open by double-clicking it in the Project window. Make sure that it is open in the **Design** view in the Editor window.
5. Click the **Hello World! TextView** and delete it.
6. Scroll to the **Layouts** folder in the **Palette** to the left of the Design view. Locate the **RelativeLayout** and drag it onto the MyContactList layout. Position the layout anywhere on the screen. You will set the exact location and size in the XML later in this chapter. You should see a RelativeLayout in a RelativeLayout in the Component Tree, and the new RelativeLayout should be outlined in light blue in the Design view and the Blueprint view.
7. Click and drag an **ImageButton** from the **Images & Media** folder in the Palette, and place it inside the **RelativeLayout** you just put on the screen. Again, exact position does not matter at this point.
8. The **Resources** window will open with a set of images listed. The images you put into the project should be listed at the top of the window. Double-click on **contactlisticon**. The image will be displayed in Design view in the ImageButton.

    Now that the RelativeLayout has some content, it is easier to work with.
1. Drag another **ImageButton** to the right of the first one and set its image to the mapicon image using the same procedure used with the first button. Use the **Blueprint** view to make sure the new button is to the right of the first button and aligned with it.
2. Repeat step 1 for the last button. Use the **settingsicon** image and make sure it is positioned to the right of the **mapicon** button.

3. Click on the **RelativeLayout** you added to layout in either the **Blueprint** view or the **Component Tree**. The **Properties** panel on the right should display the basic properties of the layout (id, layout_width, layout_height). Change the `layout_height` value from `match_parent` to `wrap_content` using the dropdown.

    The layout may look a little strange, but that's OK for now; final configuration will be done with XML. However, before you do that, you have to create a color resource to give the layout the proper background color.

To create a color resource, navigate to the **values** folder in the **res** folder and double-click the **colors.xml** file. Add the following line before the `</resources>` closing tag:

```
<color name="navbar_background">#1a1a48</color>
```

This line creates a new color resource. The #1a1a48 is a hexadecimal value that the Android OS will use to display the color we want wherever we want to use that color. Your XML should look like Listing 4.1.

Listing 4.1   Resource XML

```
1    <?xml version="1.0" encoding="utf-8"?>
2    <resources>
3        <color name="colorPrimary">#3F51B5</color>
4        <color name="colorPrimaryDark">#1303F9F</color>
5        <color name="colorAccent">#FF4081</color>
6        <color name="navbar_background">#1a1a48</color>
7    </resources>
```

Close the color resource file by clicking the **x** to the right of the **colors.xml** name tab at the top of the editor. Android Studio saves changes as they are made, so there is no need to explicitly save the file. Switch to **activity_contact.xml**. The rest of the navigation bar will be configured in XML, so be sure to choose the **Text** view (click on the **Text** tab) at the bottom of the editor window.

Several changes need to be made to the XML to give the navigation bar the correct look. First, you will change the default layout of the whole screen. Second, the navigation bar **RelativeLayout** is modified to position it at the bottom of the screen and have the blue background color. Finally, the layout of the **ImageButtons** are modified to center the middle button and position the other two buttons around it. Refer to Listing 4.2 and the explanations that follow to complete the navigation bar.

Listing 4.2   Contact_Activity.xml

```
1    <RelativeLayout xmlns:android="http://schemas.android.com/apk/res/android"
2        xmlns:app="http://schemas.android.com/apk/res-auto"
3        xmlns:tools="http://schemas.android.com/tools"
4        android:id="@+id/activity_contact"
5        android:layout_width="match_parent"
6        android:layout_height="match_parent"
7        tools:context="com.example.mycontactlist.ContactActivity" >
8
9    <RelativeLayout
10           android:layout_width="match_parent"
11           android:layout_height="wrap_content"
12           android:id="@+id/navbar"
13           android:background="@color/navbar_background"
14           android:layout_alignParentBottom="true" >
15
16           <ImageButton
17               android:layout_width="wrap_content"
18               android:layout_height="wrap_content"
19               app:srcCompat=="@drawable/contactlisticon"
20               android:layout_centerVertical="true"
21               android:layout_toLeftOf="@+id/imageButtonMap"
22               android:layout_toStartOf="@+id/imageButtonMap"
23               android:layout_marginRight="20dp"
24               android:layout_marginEnd="20dp"
25               android:id="@+id/imageButtonList" />
26
```

(continued)

Listing 4.2   Contact_Activity.xml (*continued*)

```
27              <ImageButton
28                  android:layout_width="wrap_content"
29                  android:layout_height="wrap_content"
30                  app:srcCompat=="@drawable/mapicon"
31                  android:id="@+id/imageButtonMap"
32                  android:layout_centerVertical="true"
33                  android:layout_centerHorizontal="true"/>
34
35              <ImageButton
36                  android:layout_width="wrap_content"
37                  android:layout_height="wrap_content"
38                  android:id="@+id/imageButtonSettings"
39                  app:srcCompat=="@drawable/settingsicon"
40                  android:layout_marginLeft="20dp"
41                  android:layout_marginStart="20dp"
42                  android:layout_toRightOf="@+id/imageButtonMap"
43                  android:layout_toEndOf="@+id/imageButtonMap" />
44          </RelativeLayout>
        </ RelativeLayout >
```

Very specific changes need to be made to the XML to get the desired look. The following explains the changes to each widget in the activity_contact.xml.

- **Lines 1–7**—The first change is to change the default layout attributes of the whole screen. By default, the Blank Activity Wizard puts padding around the layout. To use the whole screen, these attributes need to be removed. Locate the paddingBottom, paddingTop, paddingLeft, and paddingRight attributes in the root RelativeLayout and delete them. This attributes have been removed in Listing 4.2 but will show up in this section in your code.

- **Lines 9–14**—The RelativeLayout that contains the ImageButton is changed to a position at the bottom of the layout and is given a dark blue background and a meaningful ID:
   o Add an id attribute with the value @+id/navbar.
   o Add the background attribute and set its value to "@color/navbar_background". This refers to the color resource file previously created.
   o Add the layout_alignParentBottom attribute and set its value to "true". This tells Android to always position the layout at the bottom of the screen regardless of any other widgets in the layout.
   o Finally, remove all other attributes not shown in the listing. These are left over from the random positioning of the layout when it was first dragged to the layout. Be careful not to delete the closing angle bracket.

- **Lines 15–24**—The two image buttons on either end of the navigation bar are positioned relative to the middle button, which is centered in the layout. All buttons are given meaningful IDs:
   o Change the id of the first button to "@+id/imageButtonList".
   o Add the attributes layout_toLeftOf and layout_toStartOf and set their values to "@+id/imageButtonMap".
   o Add the attributes layout_marginRight and layout_marginEnd and set their values to "20dp" to position it to the right of the centered Map button.
   o Add the attribute layout_centerVertical and set its value to "true".
   o Remove all other attributes not shown in the listing. Note the src attribute and its value. This is where the image file is associated with the ImageButton. The image can be changed by changing its value.

- **Lines 26–42**—Modify the remaining buttons in a similar way to match the XML in the listing. Delete any attributes not included in the previous listing.

> **Note**
>
> You may get two warnings after you have completed the preceding changes. The first warns that the `RelativeLayout` may be useless. This is because you have a `RelativeLayout` within a `RelativeLayout` that has no other objects in it. After you add other objects later in this chapter, this warning will go away. The second warning is "Missing contentDescription attribute on image." The `contentDescription` value is used by alternative access modes, such as a screen reader that describes what is on the screen. You can safely ignore this warning. If you want your app to be accessible in a nonvisual manner, include the following in your `ImageButton` XML: `android:contentDescription="your description of the image"`.

Switch to the **Design** view. The navigation bar should be dark blue, positioned at the bottom of the screen, and the map button should be positioned in the center. If this is not the case, review the XML to make sure it matches Listing 4.2.

When the navigation bar is properly configured, you can copy it into each of the other three layouts. Note that it is possible to set up the navigation bar as its own layout that can be included rather than copied. This is a way to reuse code and make the app more maintainable. However, since this is more advanced than this book, we will not do it here. Refer to https://developer.android.com/training/improving-layouts/reusing-layouts.html if you'd like to learn how to do this.

1. Switch to **activity_contact.xml**, and then highlight and copy all the XML that defines the navigation bar. Be sure to include the start `<RelativeLayout` and end `</RelativeLayout>` tags.
2. Open the **activity_contact_list.xml** file in the layouts folder by double-clicking it. Switch to the **Text** tab and paste the copied code just before the last `</RelativeLayout>` tag in the file.
3. Delete the **padding attributes** in the root **RelativeLayout**.
4. Add the following attribute to the root **RelativeLayout** in each XML file: `xmlns:app="http://schemas .android.com/apk/res-auto"`. This line was generated for us in the first layout when we manually added ImageButtons with images we provided. This ensures that the images we added are properly displayed during layout design.
5. Repeat for the other two layouts.

Switch to **Design** view to verify that the navigation bar is properly displayed. Close the file and repeat the process to add the navigation bar to activity_contact_map.xml and activity_contact_settings.xml. Verify that all were properly copied by switching Design view for each file to check that each layout looks like the first layout, that a dark blue navigation bar is at the bottom, and that three image buttons are included in it. Note that you may get a rendering error. Close the error window with the **x** on the top right. Oftentimes, when making whole-scale changes with cut and paste, this error occurs. If the layout is correct, there is no need to worry about it.

Create the Contact Layout

The contact activity provides functionality associated with adding and modifying information about individual contacts. Although it is the most complicated layout in the MyContactsList app, it also demonstrates the use and configuration of a significant number of interface elements available in the Android platform. The relative nature of Android layouts makes development challenging; however, the concepts discussed in this chapter should help make the creation of a layout routine.

Figure 4.4 Complete layout.

There are three major sections in this layout (Figure 4.4). The navigation bar completed in the previous section is one of these. The second is another **RelativeLayout** at the top of the screen to display the buttons that allow the user to access overall functionality for the screen—in other words, a layout that will function as a toolbar. The third is a **ScrollView** that holds all the widgets that allow the user to enter information about a contact. A ScrollView is used to ensure that users can access all the data entry widgets regardless of the size of their device.

Create the Toolbar

The toolbar consists of a **RelativeLayout** positioned at the top of the root layout, a **ToggleButton** to switch between editing and viewing modes, and a **Button** to allow the user to save changes to the contact's information.

1. Open **activity_contact.xml** if it is not already open. Switch to **Design** view and drag a **RelativeLayout** to the screen. Don't worry about its position, but do not put it on the navigation bar.

2. Drag a **ToggleButton** from the Widgets folder on the Palette to the new RelativeLayout in the **Blueprint** view.

3. Click on the new **RelativeLayout** in the Blueprint or Component Tree views and change the `layout_height` attribute's value to `wrap_content` in the Properties panel.

4. Drag a **Button** from the Palette to the right of the **ToggleButton**.

5. Create another color resource for the toolbar's background. Double-click the **color.xml** file. Add the color resource with the name **toolbar_background** and value **#bebebe**. Close the color resource file.

6. Switch to **Text** view and refer to Listing 4.3 to modify the XML so that the toolbar appears at the top of the screen with the proper size and widget spacing. Note that Android Studio will position XML associated with the new items added to the Design view at the bottom of the XML file. You can verify or modify these via the **Properties** pane as well. Click on each widget and click **View all properties** to see full set of attributes.

Listing 4.3 Toolbar XML

```
1        <RelativeLayout
2            android:id="@+id/toolbar"
3            android:layout_width="match_parent"
4            android:layout_height="wrap_content"
5            android:background="@color/toolbar_background"
6            android:layout_alignParentTop="true"
7            android:layout_alignParentLeft="true"
8            android:layout_alignParentStart="true" >
9
10           <ToggleButton
11               android:layout_width="wrap_content"
12               android:layout_height="wrap_content"
13               android:text="ToggleButton"
14               android:id="@+id/toggleButtonEdit"
15               android:layout_marginLeft="20dp"
16               android:layout_marginStart="20dp"
17               android:layout_centerVertical="true"
18               android:layout_alignParentLeft="true"
19               android:layout_alignParentStart="true" />
20
21           <Button
22               android:layout_width="wrap_content"
23               android:layout_height="wrap_content"
24               android:text="Save"
25               android:id="@+id/buttonSave"
26               android:layout_centerVertical="true"
27               android:layout_alignParentRight="true"
28               android:layout_alignParentEnd="true"
29               android:layout_marginRight="20dp"
30               android:layout_marginEnd="20dp" />
31
32       </RelativeLayout>
```

There are only a limited number of new attributes to discuss in the XML. Make sure your toolbar XML matches the listing.

- **Lines 1–8**—The `layout_alignParentTop` attribute locks the relative layout to always appear at the top of the device's screen. The `layout_alignParentLeft` and `layout_alignParentStart` attributes lock the `RelativeLayout` left edge to the left edge of the screen. Technically, the `alignParent` attributes do not lock to the screen but refer to the containing layout. Since the root `RelativeLayout` is the containing layout, it has the effect of locking to the screen edges.

- **Lines 10–30**—The `layout_alignParentLeft`, `layout_alignParentStart`, `layout_alignParentRight`, and `layout_alignParentEnd` attributes used in the `ToggleButton` and the `Button` refer to the toolbar `RelativeLayout` as the parent. With these attributes set to `true`, it does not matter where the layout is placed. They will always remain fixed to those positions within the layout.

Switch to **Design** view. The toolbar should appear at the top of the screen with a gray background (see Figure 4.5). Note that you may get a Rendering problem (Path.isConvex is not supported) now when you switch to Design view. This is caused by the **ToggleButton**. At runtime it will have rounded corners, but that is not supported in Design view. Click **Ignore for this session** if it occurs.

Figure 4.5 Complete toolbar layout.

Create the Data Entry Form

The data entry portion of the ContactActivity allows users to enter information on their contacts. The data entry form primarily relies on the **EditText** and **TextView** widgets that were introduced in the Hello World! app. New concepts introduced include configuring the **EditTexts** to limit and format the input, movement (tabbing) through the data entry widgets, using a custom pop-up window to enter the birthday with a **DatePicker** widget, and using a **ScrollView** to expand the "screen real estate" available. The Birthday button and its functionality shown on the screen in Chapter 2, "App Design Issues and Considerations," are added in Chapter 8, "Access to Hardware and Sensors in Android."

Open the **activity_contact.xml** file (if it is not already open) and switch to **Design** view. Scroll to the **Containers** folder in the Palette. Drag a **ScrollView** to anywhere between the toolbar and the navigation bar, or to the **Component Tree** (Figure 4.6). Switch to the **Text** view to edit the XML so that it is usable. Refer to Listing 4.4 to properly configure the **ScrollView**.

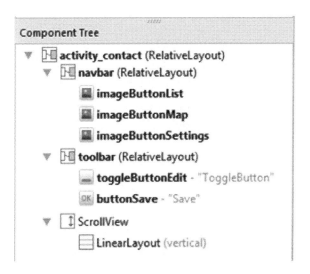

Figure 4.6 Component Tree with ScrollView added.

Listing 4.4 ScrollView XML

```
1    <ScrollView
2        android:id="@+id/scrollView"
3        android:layout_width="match_parent"
4        android:layout_height="wrap_content"
5        android:layout_alignParentLeft="true"
6        android:layout_alignParentStart="true"
7        android:layout_below="@+id/toolbar"
8        android:layout_above="@+id/navbar"  >
9
10       <RelativeLayout
11           android:layout_width="match_parent"
12           android:layout_height="wrap_content" >
13
14       </RelativeLayout>
15   </ScrollView>
```

Examine the XML on your screen. Notice that it is somewhat different from Listing 4.4. These differences are explained as follows. Change your XML to match Listing 4.4.

- **Lines 1–8**—The `layout_width` attribute is changed to `match_parent` to use the full screen. The height is left as `wrap_content` to allow the ScrollView to expand or contract based on its contents and the device size. The margin attributes are eliminated to allow the use of the full screen. Finally, the `layout_above` attribute is added to prevent the ScrollView from overwriting the navigation bar.

- **Lines 10–14**—By default, the ScrollView has no contents. ScrollViews can have only one widget as their content. However, if that widget is some type of layout, more widgets can be added as long as they are within that layout. Change the XML in the listing from `LinearLayout` to `RelativeLayout` in the ScrollView. Delete the `orientation` attribute. A LinearLayout only allows widgets to be placed one after the other either vertically or horizontally. We want more control over the positioning of widgets in the layout, so we change it to `RelativeLayout`.

After making the changes to the XML, switch back to **Design** view. The basic structure of the data input screen is complete. The next step is to add the widgets that the user can interact with to save contact information.

Drag a **TextView** onto the **ScrollView**. You might have trouble with this. The ScrollView is set to be the area between the toolbar and the navigation bar. However, you cannot place a widget in the ScrollView because it already has its one widget, the RelativeLayout. Although the RelativeLayout is set to match the parent ScrollView's height and width, the lack of content is making it wrap its content to a very small area. If you are having problems, drag the **TextView** to the **RelativeLayout** in the ScrollView in the Component Tree area instead. Then switch to **Text** view and modify the **TextView's** attributes so that its ID is **textContact** and is aligned to the **top** and **left** of its parent, and it has left and start margins of **10dp**, a top margin of **5dp**, and displays **Contact:** as its text.

Add an EditText for the user to enter the contact name. Scroll to the **TextFields** folder in the Palette and drag a **plain EditText** to underneath the **TextView** in the RelativeLayout in the Component Tree. Switch to the XML and refer to Listing 4.5 to configure the **EditText**.

Listing 4.5 Contact Name EditText XML

```
1        <EditText
2            android:id="@+id/editName"
3            android:layout_width="wrap_content"
4            android:layout_height="wrap_content"
5            android:layout_alignParentLeft="true"
6            android:layout_alignParentStart="true"
7            android:layout_marginLeft="10dp"
8            android:layout_marginStart="10dp"
9            android:layout_below="@+id/textContact"
10       android:ems="14"
11       android:imeOptions="actionNext"
12       android:inputType="textCapWords" >
13
14       <requestFocus />
15   </EditText>
```

Modify the XML as shown. You have worked with many of the attributes already. However, a few require additional explanation:

- **Line 10**—The `ems` attribute tells Android how big the `EditText` should be. The unit `ems` is the number of capital Ms that could fit into the widget. It often takes some experimentation with the number to get the widget to size the way you'd like it.

- **Line 11**—The `imeOptions="actionNext"` attribute/value pair tells Android to show a Next button on the soft keyboard. When the user presses that button, focus will move to the next `EditText`. This is how tabbing is implemented in Android apps.
- **Line 12**—The `inputType` attribute tells Android what type of keyboard to display and how to format the data as it's entered. The value `textCapWords` tells Android to display an alpha keyboard and to capitalize each word as it's entered.
- **Line 14**—The final item in the XML `<requestFocus />` is not an attribute. It is a tag to tell Android to put the cursor in this widget when the layout is displayed. You should have only one of these in a single layout file.

Switch back to **Design** view to review the impact of the changes. You'll need to look at the **Blueprint** view to see the position of the EditText, since there is no text currently in it. Switch back to the XML. The next widget will be added completely through XML. Locate the **TextView** XML and copy all of it from the `<TextView` initial tag, including the `/>` closing tag. Paste it after the **EditText** XML. Modify the XML to match Listing 4.6.

Listing 4.6 Address TextView XML

```
1      <TextView
2          android:id="@+id/textAddress"
3          android:layout_width="wrap_content"
4          android:layout_height="wrap_content"
5          android:layout_alignParentLeft="true"
6          android:layout_alignParentStart="true"
7          android:layout_below="@+id/editName"
8          android:layout_marginLeft="10dp"
9          android:layout_marginStart="10dp"
10         android:layout_marginTop="15dp"
11         android:text="Address:" />
```

Next, copy all the **EditText** XML and paste it after the **TextView** XML. Be sure to include the `</EditText>` closing tag. Delete the `<requestFocus />` tag. Refer to Listing 4.7 to configure the XML.

Listing 4.7 Address EditText XML

```
1      <EditText
2          android:id="@+id/editAddress"
3          android:layout_width="wrap_content"
4          android:layout_height="wrap_content"
5          android:layout_alignParentLeft="true"
6          android:layout_alignParentStart="true"
7          android:layout_marginLeft="10dp"
8          android:layout_marginStart="10dp"
9          android:layout_below="@+id/textAddress"
10         android:ems="15"
11         android:imeOptions="actionNext"
12         android:inputType="textCapWords" >
13     </EditText>
```

Switch to **Design** view. Your layout should like Figure 4.7. If it doesn't, return to the XML and verify your settings.

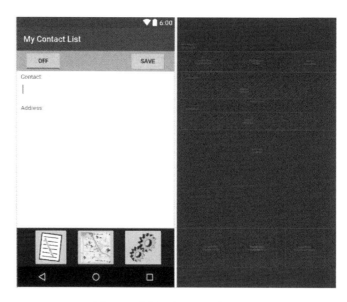

Figure 4.7 Contact layout.

The next step is to add the three **EditTexts** required to enter the city, state, and zip code of the contact. Drag and drop or copy XML to add these widgets to your layout. Refer to Table 4.1 for parameter values for each **EditText**. Attributes that have a value --- in the table should not be included for that particular widget. The table introduces three new attributes. The `layout_toRightOf` attribute is used in place of the `layout_below` attribute to position a widget next to another widget. The `layout_alignBottom` attribute tells Android to lay out the widgets so that their bottom edges match, regardless of the height or width of the widget. Some input has a limited number of characters that should be entered. The `maxLength` attribute is how the developer limits the number of characters that can be entered into an **EditText**. Finally, the `nextFocusDown` attribute is used when it is difficult for Android to figure out which of the **EditTexts** should get focus next. This attribute is used to specifically identify which widget should get focus after the current one.

Table 4.1 Attribute Values of City, State, and Zip Code EditTexts

Widget	City	State	Zip Code
Attribute			
+id	editCity	editState	editZipcode
layout_width	wrap_content	wrap_content	wrap_content
layout_height	wrap_content	wrap_content	wrap_content
layout_alignParentLeft/Start	true	---	---
layout_marginLeft/Start	10dp	---	---
layout_below	@+id/editAddress	---	---
layout_toRightOf/EndOf	---	@+id/editCity	@+id/editState
layout_alignBottom	---	@+id/editCity	@+id/editState
ems	8	2	5
maxLength	---	2	5
imeOptions	actionNext	actionNext	actionNext
nextFocusDown	@+id/editState	@+id/editZipcode	@+id/editHome
inputType	textCapWords	textCapCharacters	numberSigned

Verify with **Design** view that the interface looks like Figure 4.8. If everything looks correct, the next step is to add the phone number fields. You will need to add two **TextViews** and two **EditTexts** to the layout for the phone information. Configure the widgets using the information in Table 4.2

Table 4.2 Attribute Values of Phone Widgets

Widget	Home Text	Home Edit	Cell Text	Cell Edit
Attribute				
+id	textHome	editHome	textCell	editCell
text	Home Phone:	---	Cell Phone:	---
layout_width	wrap_content	wrap_content	wrap_content	wrap_content
layout_height	wrap_content	wrap_content	wrap_content	wrap_content
layout_alignParentLeft/Start	true	true	---	---
layout_marginLeft/Start	10dp	10dp	---	---
layout_marginTop	15dp	---	---	---
layout_below	@+id/editCity	@+id/textHome	---	---
layout_toRightOf/EndOf	---	---	---	@+id/editHome
layout_alignBottom	---	---	@+id/textHome	@+id/editHome
layout_alignLeft/Start	---	---	@+id/editCell	---
ems	---	7	---	7
maxLength	---	14	---	14
imeOptions	---	actionNext	---	actionNext
nextFocusDown	---	@+id/editCell	---	@+id/editEMail
inputType	---	phone	---	phone

The phone number labels (TextViews) are above the EditTexts used for input of those phone numbers. This layout poses challenges because the size of the EditText inputs can and will change based on the device the user runs the app on. Given that, you cannot set the labels at a fixed position, because the inputs below them will change and no longer align with their labels. This makes the interface look sloppy.

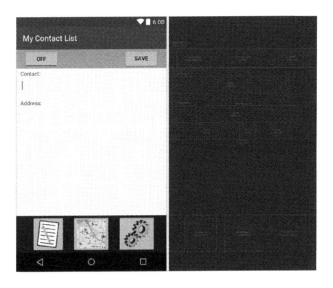

Figure 4.8 Contact layout with address fields.

The solution implemented in XML provided earlier is to align the cell phone label with the bottom of the home phone label, but rather than position it to the right of the home phone label, you align it with the left edge of the cell phone input. That way, as the `EditTexts` change size, the cell phone label will always be directly above the cell phone input. A new attribute value/pair, `layout_alignLeft="@+id/editCell"` and `layout_align-Start="@+id/editCell"`, is used to implement this solution. One other item of note in these widgets is the `maxLength` attribute of the `EditTexts`. Note that they are set at 14 rather than 10, which is the number of digits in a US phone number. The `maxLength` of input is the total length, including formatting and spaces. When formatting is added to the phone number, the input length becomes greater than 10. For example, a phone number formatted as (111) 222-4444 would be 14 characters long. When completed, your layout should look like Figure 4.9.

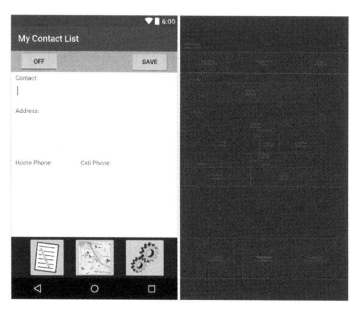

Figure 4.9 Contact layout with phone fields.

The final elements of the contact activity layout are the e-mail and birthdate inputs. You need a **TextView** and an **EditText** for the e-mail input, and two **TextViews** and a **Button** for the birthday input. One of the birthday `Text-Views` will be used to display the birth date, and the `Button` will be used to open a pop-up window. Configure these widgets as identified in Tables 4.3 and 4.4.

Table 4.3 Attribute Values of E-mail Widgets

Widget	E-mail Text	E-mail Edit
Attribute		
+id	textEMail	editEMail
Text	E-Mail Address:	---
layout_width	wrap_content	wrap_content
layout_height	wrap_content	wrap_content
layout_alignParentLeft/Start	true	true
layout_marginLeft/Start	10dp	10dp
layout_marginTop	15dp	---
layout_below	@+id/editHome	@+id/textEMail
ems	---	13
inputType	---	textEmailAddress

The **Change Birthday** button uses several new attributes. The button should be anchored to the right side of the screen so that its position doesn't change as the birthday value changes. To do this, you use the `layout_align-ParentRight="true"` and `layout_alignParentEnd="true"` attribute/value pairs, and to make it have a margin from the screen, you use the `layout_marginRight="10dp"` and `layout_marginRight="10dp"` attribute/value pairs. The birthday widgets are all on one line. To make this work, the `layout_toRightOf`, `layout_toEndOf`, and `layout_alignBottom` attributes are used with the birthday date display `TextView`. However, the button is aligned to the right of the screen with the attribute previously discussed. To make it line up with other widgets, a new attribute, `layout_alignBaseline`, is used. This aligns the center of the button with the bottom of the widget it refers to. Because a button is bigger than the other widgets, aligning it bottom to bottom would make it tall enough on the screen to cover a portion of the e-mail `EditText`.

Test this yourself by executing the app on the emulator before you add the padding attribute. You can select the same device as you did in the previous chapter. When the layout is displayed on the emulator, click and hold on any whitespace in the layout and drag to the top of the emulator screen. Try it again after you add the padding.

Table 4.4 Attribute Values of Birthday Widgets

Widget	Birthday Text	Date Text	Button
Attribute			
+id	textBday	textBirthday	btnBirthday
text	Birthday:	01/01/1970	Change
layout_width	wrap_content	wrap_content	wrap_content
layout_height	wrap_content	wrap_content	wrap_content
layout_alignParentLeft/Start	true	---	---
layout_alignParentRight/End	---	---	true
layout_marginLeft/Start	10dp	10dp	---
layout_marginRight/End	---	---	10dp
layout_marginTop	15dp	---	---
layout_below	@+id/editEMail	---	---
layout_toRightOf/EndOf	---	@+id/textBday	---
layout_alignBottom	---	@+id/textBday	---
layout_alignBaseline	---	---	@+id/textBirthday

When the layout is complete, verify that it looks like Figure 4.10. Examine the bottom of the figure closely. The `ScrollView` was selected (surrounded by a thin blue line) before the screenshot was taken. Notice that the bottom blue line runs through the navigation bar. This is where the bottom of the Change button would be if the `padding-Bottom` attribute had not been added. In other words, it would have been partially obscured by the navigation bar.

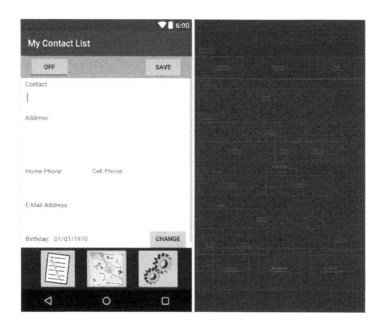

Figure 4.10 Completed contact layout.

Congratulations! You have completed your first real layout in Android. However, there is one more layout task to complete before you write the code to make the layout do something: creating a layout for the birthday selection dialog box.

Create the Dialog Layout

Although Android provides a `DatePickerDialog` class that provides the functionality needed, you are going to create the dialog from scratch to learn how to create and use custom dialogs in an app. The birthday selection date dialog is relatively simple. It displays a `DatePicker` widget, which allows the user to select a specific date, and Cancel and OK buttons. Refer to Figure 4.11 to see the final layout.

Begin by adding a new XML layout file to the project.

1. Right-click the **Layout** folder in the Project window and select **New > Layout resource file** from the pop-up menu.

2. Enter **select_date** as the file name of this new layout and change the **Root element** to **RelativeLayout**. Leave all other defaults.

3. Click **OK**, and the new layout will open in the editor and select_date.xml will be displayed in the layout folder of the Project window.

Switch the layout to **Design** view (if not already there). Locate the **Date & Time** folder in the Palette and drag a **DatePicker** to the screen. Switch to **Text** view and edit the XML such that the DatePicker The XML should look like Listing 4.8.

Listing 4.8 Birthday DatePicker XML

```
1      <DatePicker
2          android:layout_width="wrap_content"
3          android:layout_height="wrap_content"
4          android:id="@+id/birthdayPicker"
5          android:layout_alignParentTop="true"
6          android:layout_marginTop="5dp"
7        android:layout_centerHorizontal="true" />
```

Note

Adding the DatePicker to the layout may cause an error screen to show up at the bottom of the editor. You can ignore this. Although it says it can't find the DatePicker class, it will at runtime.

Next drag a **LinearLayout (horizontal)** to the screen and place it below the **DatePicker**. Now drag **two buttons** from the Palette and place them in the **LinearLayout**. This may not look exactly like Figure 4.11. It is difficult to place widgets exactly where you want them. We'll correct that next. Select the **LinearLayout** in the Component Tree and change the `layout_height` attribute to `wrap_content` in the **Properties Panel**. The buttons should appear side-by-side, with the text **BUTTON** below the DatePicker. The rest of the configuration will be done with XML. However, before editing the layout, we need a new color, so open the **colors.xml** file and add the following line:

```
<color name="dialog_button_color">#26C6DA</color>
```

Switch back to **select_date.xml** and switch to **Text** view to edit the XML. Modify the **LinearLayout** and **Button** code to match Listing 4.9.

Listing 4.9 Birthday Dialog LinearLayout

```
1    <LinearLayout
2        android:id="@+id/buttonLayout"
3        android:orientation="horizontal"
4        android:layout_width="match_parent"
5        android:layout_height="wrap_content"
6        android:layout_alignParentBottom="true"
7        android:gravity="end"
8        style="?android:attr/borderlessButtonStyle" >
9
10       <Button
11           android:layout_width="wrap_content"
12           android:layout_height="wrap_content"
13           android:text="Cancel"
14           android:textColor="@color/dialog_button_color"
15           android:id="@+id/buttonCancel"
16           style="?android:attr/borderlessButtonStyle" />
17
18       <Button
19           android:layout_width="wrap_content"
20           android:layout_height="wrap_content"
21           android:text="Select"
22           android:textColor="@color/dialog_button_color"
23           android:id="@+id/buttonSelect"
24           style="?android:attr/borderlessButtonStyle" />
25
26   </LinearLayout>
```

This XML introduces some new items. The addition of these items ensures that the layout conforms to design guidelines for dialogs specified by Android. These items are explained as follows:

- **Lines 1–8**—The `orientation="horizontal"` attribute tells Android to layout widgets side-by-side rather than stacked on top of one another within this LinearLayout. The `gravity="end"` attribute tells Android to position the widgets within the LinearLayout horizontally rather than starting at the right side of the screen. This is the Android recommended position for buttons on a dialog. The `style="?android:attr/ borderlessButtonStyle"` removes borders from the widget.

- **Lines 10–24**—Android design guidelines specify that the affirmative button, or the button that continues the task, should be the rightmost, so it is last in the LinearLayout XML. The discontinue or cancel button should be immediately to the left of the continue button, so its XML comes before the continue button code. The `textColor` attribute sets the text color of the button to the color you created in the colors.xml file.

Once you have completed these changes, switch to **Design** view. Your display should look like Figure 4.11.

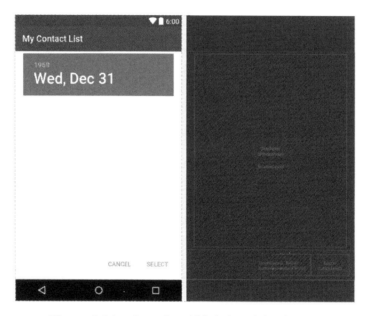

Figure 4.11   Completed birthday picker layout.

The contents of the DatePicker widget will display only at runtime. However, you won't write the code to open the dialog until later in this chapter, so you will have to wait to test it.

Activating the Interface

The primary function of the Contact activity is to save information about the user's contacts. The saving of data is beyond the scope of this chapter but is addressed in Chapter 5, "Persistent Data in Android." However, other functions can be implemented at this time. This section demonstrates the coding of the navigation bar, coding the toggle button to switch between editing and viewing modes, coding the Change Birthday button to display the dialog window, and coding the dialog.

Code the Navigation Bar

Movement and data transfer between activities is done with `Intents`, as discussed earlier in this chapter. The use of `Intents` makes coding navigation relatively simple. The `Intent` does most of the work. Open the **ContactActivity.java** file in the **src** folder by double-clicking it. Begin by coding the **List ImageButton**, which will switch to the list of all contacts. Enter the code in Listing 4.10 before the last } in the **ContactActivity.java** file. Pay attention as you enter the code, as the editor may complete several parts of it for you.

Listing 4.10   List Button Code

```
1     private void initListButton() {
2       ImageButton ibList = (ImageButton) findViewById(R.id.imageButtonList);
3       ibList.setOnClickListener(new View.OnClickListener() {
4         public void onClick(View v) {
5           Intent intent = new Intent(ContactActivity.this, ContactListActivity.class);
6           intent.setFlags(Intent.FLAG_ACTIVITY_CLEAR_TOP);
7           startActivity(intent);
8         }
9       });
10    }
```

After you have entered the code, some of the objects may be underlined in red. This indicates that the compiler doesn't know what that object is. To fix this, click on the underlined object and then hover the mouse button over it until the message `?nameOfObject ? Alt + Enter` message is displayed. Press the **Alt + Enter** keys simultaneously to import the object. If there is no import option, it is likely that you misspelled the object name.

This code is used to associate the ImageButton named imageButtonList on the activity_contact layout with the code that is executed when it is pressed.

- **Line 2**—A variable to hold an `ImageButton` is declared, and `findViewById` gets the widget named `image-ButtonList`. `FindViewById` returns the widget as a generic object, so it must be cast (`ImageButton`) to an `ImageButton` before it can be assigned to the variable.
- **Line 3**—A listener is added to the `ImageButton`. A listener makes a widget able to respond to different events. In this case, the listener makes the `ImageButton` able to respond to the user pressing it.
- **Line 5**—An `Intent` variable is declared and a new `Intent` is created and assigned to it. The intent constructor requires a reference to its current activity (`ContactActivity.this`) and to know what activity it should start (`ContactListActivity.class`).
- **Line 6**—An intent flag is set to tell the operating system to not make multiple copies of the same activity.

The completed method name `initListButton()` is grayed out. This indicates that the method is never used. To use it, enter `initListButton();` after the `setContentView(R.layout.activity_contact)` line of code in the `onCreate` method at the beginning of the file. This code calls the button initiation code at creation of the activity, so that it is ready for use when the user sees the layout. The method name should turn black. Complete the navigation bar code by copying the preceding code for each of the two remaining ImageButtons, and make the following changes for the first new method:

> `initListButton()` to `initMapButton()`
>
> `R.id.imageButtonList` to `R.id.imageButtonMap`
>
> `ContactListActivity.class` to `ContactMapActivity.class`

Similar changes should be made to the second new method:

> `initListButton()` to `initSettingsButton()`
>
> `R.id.imageButtonList` to `R.id.imageButtonSettings`
>
> `ContactListActivity.class` to `ContactSettingsActivity.class`

Be sure to call the new methods in the `onCreate` method. The navigation bar is now ready for testing. Run the app on the emulator and test that each button opens the correct activity. Because the navigation bar is not currently coded for these activities, you will have to use the Back button to return to the ContactActivity. However, you can add the three methods to each of those activities at this time if you wish. Just copy the code for the buttons from **ContactActivity.java** to the other Activities. When you do, you will get error messages that **ContactActivity** is not an enclosing class. Replace **ContactActivity** with the **name** of the **class you are working in**. We do not include a button in the navigation bar for ContactActivity. Accessing that activity will be done through the working of the app. This is implemented in later chapters.

Code the Toggle Button

Coding the ToggleButton is relatively easy, if not somewhat tedious. It is easy because you need only to enable or disable the interface. It is tedious because each widget that the user could interact with must be enabled or disabled separately. The ToggleButton's functionality requires the creation of three methods. One method will initialize the button to respond to the user. A second method will enable all the data entry widgets, and the third will disable all the widgets. First enter the code in Listing 4.11 in **ContactActivity.java** after the navigation bar button code to initialize the ToggleButton. Remember to import any items underlined in red.

Listing 4.11   ToggleButton Initialization Method

```
1    private void initToggleButton() {
2        final ToggleButton editToggle = (ToggleButton)findViewById(R.id.toggleButtonEdit);
3        editToggle.setOnClickListener(new OnClickListener() {
4
5          @Override
6          public void onClick(View arg0) {
7              setForEditing(editToggle.isChecked());
8          }
9        });
10   }
```

The code is very similar to the navigation button initialization methods. A reference to the widget is grabbed, and an onClickListener is added to the button. There are a few differences that require some explanation.

- **Line 2**—The final keyword is added to the statement that gets the reference to the ToggleButton to prevent the variable assignment from changing. This is required because it is being used in the button click code. It ensures that the widget referred to cannot change, so the code is always working on the same thing.

- **Line 7**—The onClick method calls the setForEditing method, passing it true if the button is toggled for editing and false if it is not.

The next step is to code the methods to do the enabling and disabling of the form. Enter the code in Listing 4.12 to create the setForEditing() method.

Listing 4.12   Code to Enable the Data Entry Form

```
1    private void setForEditing(boolean enabled) {
2        EditText editName = (EditText) findViewById(R.id.editName);
3        EditText editAddress = (EditText) findViewById(R.id.editAddress);
4        EditText editCity = (EditText) findViewById(R.id.editCity);
5        EditText editState = (EditText) findViewById(R.id.editState);
6        EditText editZipCode = (EditText) findViewById(R.id.editZipcode);
7        EditText editPhone = (EditText) findViewById(R.id.editHome);
8        EditText editCell = (EditText) findViewById(R.id.editCell);
9        EditText editEmail = (EditText) findViewById(R.id.editEMail);
10       Button buttonChange = (Button) findViewById(R.id.btnBirthday);
11       Button buttonSave = (Button) findViewById(R.id.buttonSave);
12
13       editName.setEnabled(enabled);
14       editAddress.setEnabled(enabled);
15       editCity.setEnabled(enabled);
16       editState.setEnabled(enabled);
17       editZipCode.setEnabled(enabled);
18       editPhone.setEnabled(enabled);
19       editCell.setEnabled(enabled);
20       editEmail.setEnabled(enabled);
21       buttonChange.setEnabled(enabled);
22       buttonSave.setEnabled(enabled);
```

(continued)

Listing 4.12 Code to Enable the Data Entry Form (*continued*)

```
23
24     if (enabled) {
25         editName.requestFocus();
26     }
27  }
```

Add the following two lines of code to the **onCreate** method to initialize the ToggleButton, and set the screen so that it is not in editing mode when it opens:

```
initToggleButton();
setForEditing(false);
```

Run the app to test the button. You may find one "error." The Contact name field looks disabled when the app opens, but it has focus and will allow data to be entered. Earlier versions of the Android OS always want to put focus on an EditText and will do so on the first EditText they find in a layout. This is a relatively well-known bug/feature. There are a number of hacks to get around it. For demonstration purposes, one such hack is included in the sidebar. However, not every approach works or is reasonable for all circumstances. If you want to stop the autofocus from occurring, you should do it on a case-by-case basis.

Hacking Autofocus of EditText

One approach to stopping the autofocus places a dummy layout in the root layout to grab the focus. It is set to be focusable but has no size, so it is not visible. This approach also clears the focus from all widgets in the `setForEditing()` method, allowing the `LinearLayout` to grab the focus. Enter the following XML as the first element in the root `RelativeLayout` in the activity_contact.xml file.

```
<LinearLayout
    android:focusable="true"
    android:focusableInTouchMode="true"
    android:layout_width="0px"
    android:layout_height="0px" />
```

Next, modify the if statement at the end of the `setForEditing()` method in the ContactActivity.java file so that it looks like the following:

```
if (enabled) {
    editName.requestFocus();
}
else {
    ScrollView s = (ScrollView) findViewById(R.id.scrollView);
    s.clearFocus();
}
```

After you disable all the widgets, this code clears the focus from all of them so that the dummy LinearLayout can grab it. If you enter this code, your app will now properly switch between editing and viewing modes.

Code the DatePicker Dialog

The DatePicker dialog is a window that opens when the user presses the Change button. A custom dialog requires both a layout, which you have already created, and a class that contains the code that gives the dialog its behavior.

Using a custom dialog in an activity also requires changes to the activity code. The following describes how to code the **DatePickerDialog** class and make changes to the ContactActivity to display and use the dialog.

The first task is to create a new class to hold the custom dialog code. Right-click **com.example.mycontactlist** in the java folder and select **New > Java Class** from the pop-up menu. Enter **DatePickerDialog** for the **Name** and click **OK**. The new class opens with a limited amount of code. Replace all that code except the first line (package com.example.mycontactlist) with the code in Listing 4.13.

Listing 4.13 DatePickerDialog.java

```
1    import android.os.Bundle;
2    import android.support.v4.app.DialogFragment;
3    import java.util.Calendar;
4    import android.view.LayoutInflater;
5    import android.view.View;
6    import android.view.ViewGroup;
7    import android.view.View.OnClickListener;
8    import android.widget.Button;
9    import android.widget.DatePicker;
10
11   public class DatePickerDialog extends DialogFragment {
12
13       public interface SaveDateListener {
14           void didFinishDatePickerDialog(Calendar selectedTime);
15       }
16
17       public DatePickerDialog() {
18       // Empty constructor required for DialogFragment
19       }
20
21       @Override
22       public View onCreateView(LayoutInflater inflater, ViewGroup container,
23                       ⮱Bundle savedInstanceState) {
24           final View view = inflater.inflate(R.layout.select_date, container);
25
26           getDialog().setTitle("Select Date");
27
28           final DatePicker dp = (DatePicker)view.findViewById(R.id.birthdayPicker);
29
30           Button saveButton = (Button) view.findViewById(R.id.buttonSelect);
31           saveButton.setOnClickListener(new OnClickListener() {
32               @Override
33               public void onClick(View arg0) {
34                   Calendar selectedTime = Calendar.getInstance();
35                   selectedTime.set(dp.getYear(), dp.getMonth(),dp.getDayOfMonth());
36                   saveItem(selectedTime);
37               }
38           });
39           Button cancelButton = (Button) view.findViewById(R.id.buttonCancel);
40           cancelButton.setOnClickListener(new OnClickListener() {
41               @Override
42               public void onClick(View v) {
43                   getDialog().dismiss();
44               }
45           });
46           return view;
47       }
48
49       private void saveItem(Calendar selectedTime) {
50           SaveDateListener activity = (SaveDateListener) getActivity();
```

(continued)

Listing 4.13 DatePickerDialog.java (*continued*)

```
51              activity.didFinishDatePickerDialog(selectedTime);
52              getDialog().dismiss();
53         }
54    }
```

A significant number of important concepts for Android app development are introduced in this code. Fortunately, dialog coding follows the same pattern, so after you understand the components, you can apply them whenever you need your app to show a dialog window.

- **Line 11**—The declaration of the class includes the keywords `extends DialogFragment`. This makes the `DatePickerDialog` class a subclass of the `DialogFragment`, which in turn is a subclass of the `Fragment` class discussed earlier in this chapter. All custom dialogs in an Android app should be created in this way.
- **Lines 13–15**—A listener must be created with the `DialogFragment`. This is how the dialog communicates the user's actions on the dialog back to the activity that displayed the dialog. The listener must have a method to report the results of the dialog. The activity will have to implement the listener to handle the user actions.
- **Lines 17–19**—A constructor for the class is required. It almost always is empty.
- **Lines 22–24**—The `OnCreateView` method is the workhorse of the class. It creates the `View` from the resources in the layout file associated with it by the line `inflater.inflate(...)`. The method also gets references to the widgets on the layout and sets up listeners for the widgets in the layout so that they can respond to user action.
- **Lines 34–36**—`Calendar` objects are used to hold dates and times. This object stores a time/date as a number of milliseconds (millis) from January 1, 1970. A new time object is created, and when the user clicks the OK button, it grabs the user selections on the `DatePicker` and sets the time object to that time. Finally, it calls the `saveItem` method to report the selection to the main activity.
- **Lines 49–54**—The `saveItem` method gets a reference to the listener and calls its method to report the results of the dialog.

This pattern is always used with custom dialogs. Each dialog needs a listener interface and associated method, a constructor, an `onCreateView` method, and a call to the listener method. The call to the listener method does not necessarily have to be in its own method, as it is here. Finally, the dialog must be dismissed at the end of every code path in the `DialogFragment`.

Before the dialog can be tested, the code to present it and use its results must be implemented in the activity that uses it. In this case, it is the ContactActivity. Switch to or open the **ContactActivity.java** class. The following steps must be done in the exact order listed here, or potential problems may occur.

1. Locate the class declaration and verify that it extends **AppCompatActivity**: `public class Contact-Activity extends AppCompatActivity`. If it does not, change it to do so.
2. If the `AppCompatActivity` is red and a whole bunch of other errors show up in the code, place your cursor in `AppCompatActivity` and press **Alt + Enter**; then select **Import Class**. This will import the AppCompatActivity class from the android.support.v4.app library, which is a set of code that provides objects to make some features in newer Android operating systems work in older versions.
3. Add the words `implements SaveDateListener` after `AppCompatActivity`, so that the class declaration is `public class ContactActivity extends AppCompatActivity implements SaveDateListener {`. After making the change, `SaveDateListener` may be highlighted in red. If so, hover over it to get the pop-up menu and press **Alt + Enter**.
4. The whole line will be highlighted in red. Click anywhere on the line and press **Alt + Enter**. In the menu, select **Implement methods**. Click **OK** on the dialog window that opens up. When an activity implements a listener, it must implement the methods associated with the listener so that the results may be used in the activity.
5. Scroll down to the bottom of the **ContactActivity.java** file. You should find the following code. If not, delete your changes and repeat the previous steps.

```
@Override
public void didFinishDatePickerDialog(Calendar selectedTime) {
}
```

The `didFinishDatePickerDialog` method is the code that will handle the date that the user selected. Enter the following two lines of code in the method:

```
TextView birthDay = (TextView) findViewById(R.id.textBirthday);
birthDay.setText(DateFormat.format("MM/dd/yyyy",
↪selectedTime.getTimeInMillis()).toString());
```

Some of the code may be highlighted in red, indicating that it needs to be imported. In the case of `DateFormat`, you may see two import options. Choose **android.text.format**. This code gets a reference to the TextView that will display the date and set its text attribute to a string produced by the `DateFormat.format` method.

The last thing to do for the dialog is to code the Change button to make it display the dialog. Add the code in Listing 4.14 to the ContactActivity.

Listing 4.14   Change Birthday Button

```
1     private void initChangeDateButton() {
2         Button changeDate = (Button) findViewById(R.id.btnBirthday);
3         changeDate.setOnClickListener(new View.OnClickListener() {
4
5             @Override
6             public void onClick(View v) {
7                 FragmentManager fm = getSupportFragmentManager();
8                 DatePickerDialog datePickerDialog = new DatePickerDialog();
9                 datePickerDialog.show(fm, "DatePick");
10            }
11        });
12    }
```

Most of the code is standard initialization of a button to respond to the user pressing the button. The code to be executed when the click occurs displays the dialog.

- **Line 7**—A `FragmentManager` is a required object to manage any and all fragments displayed in an activity. It needs to be imported.
- **Line 8**—A new instance of the `DatePickerDialog` class is created.
- **Line 9**—The `DatePickerDialog`'s show method (inherited from `DialogFragment`) displays the dialog. The method requires an instance of a `FragmentManager` and a name, which the `FragmentManager` uses to keep track of the dialog.

Be sure to call the `initChangeDateButton()` method in the `onCreate` method of ContactActivity. The app interface is ready to be tested! Run it to be sure that the dialog is displayed and the correct date is placed in the TextView.

Summary

Creating layouts is a lot of work! In this chapter, you learned how to use Android Studio to create an Android layout file that is the user interface for an app activity. Development of a layout requires the use of both the graphical editor and modification of the associated XML to get the exact design you want. Experimentation is often the key to getting the layout to look the way you want it to.

Intents are used to switch between Activities and sometimes pass data to those Activities. You learned how to use Intents to implement a navigation bar that allows the user to move between different Activities in your app.

Finally, you learned how to use Fragments to implement a custom dialog window. You also learned how to display the custom dialog and to communicate the results of the user interaction with the dialog back to activity so that it could act on those actions.

Exercises

1. Create a new color resource to be used as the background for the data entry part of the ContactActivity. Search on the web for the color and associated Android color code (color codes always start with a # symbol), and add it to the color.xml file. Set the background of the data entry part of the layout to that color resource.

2. Make the navigation work for all activities in the app. Copy the navigation bar XML code to the layout associated with each activity. Copy the Java code that makes the buttons work to the Java file associated with each activity. You will have to modify that code to reference the activity it is in, rather than ContactActivity. Add code to disable the `ImageButton` associated with the activity that is displayed.

3. Modify the DatePickerDialog layout so that the Cancel/OK buttons are centered. Hint: You'll have to use the gravity attribute in the LinearLayout.

4. Add the hack to your code to stop the autofocus of the EditTexts.

CHAPTER 5

Persistent Data in Android

The capability to have data that the app uses or relies on to continue to be available regardless of changes to the app's state as it moves through the app life cycle is vital to the user experience with the app—and for the app itself to be a useful tool. For this to occur, the data needs to persist through these life cycle changes. Android provides several ways in which the developer can make data persist. This chapter introduces you to three of these data persistence approaches. A significant amount of time will be spent on understanding and using the SQLite database system incorporated with Android, but the chapter also discusses storing data in files and demonstrates how to store individual pieces of data in an object that persists across an app's life cycle.

Preferences, Files, and Database

The three approaches to data persistence discussed in this chapter are SharedPreferences, standard flat file input/output, and the SQLite database system. Each of these approaches provides capabilities that are relevant for different tasks in an app. SharedPreferences are often used for a limited set of data that represents user choices about the way they want the app configured. They may also be used for other data that needs to persist across life cycle changes. Flat files are useful for backing up data and transmitting to other users. Finally, databases are the workhorses for data manipulation, storage, and retrieval. Developing an understanding of where, when, and how to use these data persistence approaches is very important for effective development of an Android app.

Preferences

Preferences are implemented through use of the **SharedPreferences** class. A SharedPreferences object can be used to store primitive data (e.g., integers and strings) in a key/value pair. Each value has its own key for storage and retrieval of that data. SharedPreferences are stored in memory private to the app and will persist as long as the app remains installed on the device. App upgrades will not impact the values stored with SharedPreferences. Data such as login information, app layout settings, or data settings are good candidates for storage in this object.

Files

Files are written and read as a stream of bytes. This means that to the Android system, a file is a single thing. It does not have parts, such as different objects, within it. The advantage to this is that the system stores the data efficiently and does not have to worry about what the data is—that is stored within the stream. Thus many kinds of data can be stored in a file. The disadvantage is that it is up to the developer to code the reading and writing of the file so that the data can be used appropriately when needed. For example, the developer can embed XML, JSON, or commas in the stream to identify the different pieces of data. However, in either case, the user of that file must know its structure to use it correctly.

Files can be written to either internal or external storage. Those written to internal storage are private to the app. They will persist as long as the app is installed on the device. Files written to external storage (such as an SD card) are not private to the app. Other apps can access them, and if the device is connected to a computer, they are accessible (including modify and delete) to the user of the computer. Data from the app that needs to be moved between devices (export and import) or for backup is a good candidate for this type of storage.

Databases

Android supports the use of SQLite databases. SQLite is a fully functional relational database management system (RDBMS) that can integrate into any host application. It does not have to run in an independent server process. A relational database system allows the developer to give meaning to the data stored within it by separating the data into tables (e.g., a customer table and an order table. Each table will hold data pertinent for each instance of whatever is stored in the table (e.g., data for each customer). SQLite also provides capabilities for retrieval and manipulation of the stored data through the use of queries written in Structured Query Language (SQL). Almost any type of data can be stored and manipulated using a SQLite database, although some data types have more limited support than other RDBMSs.

Data stored in a SQLite database is private to the app and will persist as long as the app is installed on the device. An app may create and use multiple databases, and each database can have many tables, making data storage via SQLite both extensive and flexible. Databases are the workhorse data storage of many apps, and many types of data are stored in databases.

Android Versus iOS: Data Persistence

Android and iOS offer essentially the same three types of data persistence mechanisms discussed in this chapter. The functionality provided by **SharedPreferences** in Android is provided by the **UserDefaults** object in iOS. File input and output is also provided in iOS. Finally, iOS also implements SQLite databases in a very similar manner to Android. However, most iOS apps will instead use a storage solution called Core Data that offers an object-oriented approach to storing data, implemented on top of a SQLite database. Although in all cases the code has different commands because the programming languages are different, the functionality is the same. So while porting data persistence between platforms requires work, the concepts are easily replicated.

Using Preferences

SharedPreferences are an easy way to store bits of information that need to persist over the life cycle of an app. There are two main modes for accessing SharedPreferences: `getSharedPreferences("String preference name", integer mode)` and `getPreferences(integer mode)`. The `getSharedPreferences` mode is used when you want to have more than one set of preferences for an app, or you want the preferences available to any Activity in the app. Each set is given a name that is used as the key to access that particular set of preferences. If you need a set of preferences only for a single Activity, then you can use the `getPreferences` method. With each of these methods, you need to set an access mode. Using 0 (zero) makes the preferences private to the app. Preferences may also be given a mode that makes them readable or writeable from outside the app. However, this is discouraged because it opens potential security holes. Data is stored by using a method appropriate to the value being saved (e.g., `putBoolean` or `putInt`) and supplying a string that will be the key for future access to that value. Likewise, data is retrieved from the object using the string key with the appropriate get method (e.g., `getBoolean` or `getInt`).

In the MyContactList app, some settings are set in the ContactSettingsActivity and stored using SharedPreferences. This activity is developed so that you can learn how to use SharedPreferences. To do so, the layout is first coded, and then the Java file is edited.

Create the Settings Layout

Open the **activity_contact_settings.xml** file. If you have not already done so, add the navigation buttons to the layout (note that this is already done in the project that you can download from the book's website). Do this by opening the activity_contact.xml file and copying the **RelativeLayout** xml with the `+id` set to `navbar` to the **activity_contact_settings xml**. Be sure to include the end `</RelativeLayout>` tag. While in the XML view, delete any the XML not associated with the root RelativeLayout and the navbar, and delete the padding attributes in the root `RelativeLayout`. Switch to **Design** view to verify that the navigation bar is visible and in the correct position. There should be no whitespace around the navigation bar and no other widgets on the screen.

In Design view, drag a **TextView** from the **Widgets** folder to the layout and position it near the top. Next, drag a **RadioGroup** from the **Containers** folder and position it below the TextView. Now drag three **RadioButtons** from the Widgets folder and place them in the **RadioGroup**. Position them one above the other. You may have to do this in the Component Tree because the RadioGroup is too small on the Design view to accurately place the buttons inside it. However, once you have one button in the group, it gets easier to use the Design view for this. Repeat this procedure to add another set of widgets below the first set. Positioning of these widgets should be similar to Figure 5.1. Don't worry if it is not exact. We will fix the positioning in the XML.

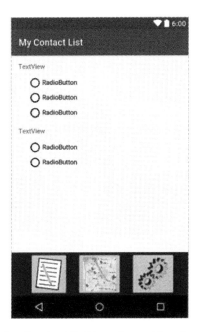

Figure 5.1   ContactSettings layout loading widgets.

Switch to **Text** view and modify the XML to match Listing 5.1. Only attributes that need to be added or modified are shown for each widget in the listing. Do not change or modify any other attributes.

Listing 5.1   RadioButton and TextView XML

```
1    <TextView
2        android:layout_width="wrap_content"
3        android:layout_height="wrap_content"
4        android:textAppearance="?android:attr/textAppearanceMedium"
5        android:text="Sort Contacts By:"
6        android:id="@+id/textContactSort"
7        android:layout_alignParentTop="true"
8        android:layout_alignParentLeft="true"
9        android:layout_alignParentStart="true"
10       android:layout_marginLeft="15dp"
11       android:layout_marginStart="15dp"
12       android:layout_marginTop="15dp" />
13
14   <RadioGroup
15       android:layout_width="match_parent"
16       android:layout_height="wrap_content"
17       android:layout_below="@+id/textContactSort"
18       android:layout_alignParentLeft="true"
19       android:layout_alignParentStart="true"
20       android:layout_marginLeft="35dp"
21       android:layout_marginStart="35dp"
22       android:layout_marginTop="10dp"
23       android:id="@+id/radioGroupSortBy">
```

(continued)

Listing 5.1   RadioButton and TextView XML (*continued*)

```
24
25        <RadioButton
26            android:layout_width="wrap_content"
27            android:layout_height="wrap_content"
28            android:text="Name"
29            android:id="@+id/radioName"
30            android:layout_weight="1" />
31
32        <RadioButton
33            android:layout_width="wrap_content"
34            android:layout_height="wrap_content"
35            android:text="City"
36            android:id="@+id/radioCity"
37            android:layout_weight="1" />
38
39        <RadioButton
40            android:layout_width="wrap_content"
41            android:layout_height="wrap_content"
42            android:text="Birthday"
43            android:id="@+id/radioBirthday"
44            android:layout_weight="1" />
45    </RadioGroup>
46
47    <TextView
48        android:layout_width="wrap_content"
49        android:layout_height="wrap_content"
50        android:textAppearance="?android:attr/textAppearanceMedium"
51        android:text="Sort Order:"
52        android:id="@+id/textViewSortOrder"
53        android:layout_below="@+id/radioGroupSortBy"
54        android:layout_alignParentLeft="true"
55        android:layout_alignParentStart="true"
56        android:layout_marginLeft="15dp"
57        android:layout_marginStart="15dp"
58        android:layout_marginTop="15dp" />
59
60    <RadioGroup
61        android:layout_width="match_parent"
62        android:layout_height="wrap_content"
63        android:layout_below="@+id/textViewSortOrder"
64        android:layout_alignParentLeft="true"
65        android:layout_alignParentStart="true"
66        android:layout_marginLeft="35dp"
67        android:layout_marginStart="35dp"
68        android:layout_marginTop="10dp"
69        android:id="@+id/radioGroupSortOrder">
70
71        <RadioButton
72            android:layout_width="wrap_content"
73            android:layout_height="wrap_content"
74            android:text="Ascending"
75
```

(continued)

Listing 5.1 RadioButton and TextView XML (*continued*)

```
76              android:id="@+id/radioAscending"
77              android:layout_weight="1" />
78
79      <RadioButton
80              android:layout_width="wrap_content"
81              android:layout_height="wrap_content"
82              android:text="Descending"
83              android:id="@+id/radioDescending"
84              android:layout_weight="1" />
85      </RadioGroup>
```

After making the modifications, switch to **Design** view and verify that the layout looks like Figure 5.2.

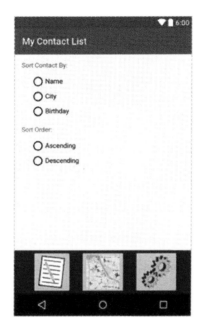

Figure 5.2 Completed ContactSettings layout.

Code the Page's Behavior

The settings activity's function is straightforward. When a user presses one of the choices, that value is stored as a key/value pair in SharedPreferences. When the page is accessed, the activity reads the stored preferences and sets the RadioButtons to the stored value. The value stored in a SharedPreferences will be used in ContactListActivity to sort the list of saved contacts.

Open the **ContactSettingsActivity.java** file, and if you didn't implement the navigation bar previously, complete the following steps:

1. Copy the **ImageButton initialization methods** from the ContactActivity.java to the ContactSettingsActivity.java file so that the navigation bar will work. These methods are `initMapButton()`, `initListButton()`, and `initSettingsButton()`. Paste this code before the last } in the `ContactSettingsActivity`.java file. A pop-up will ask if you want to import required code. Click **OK**.

2. When the code is pasted into the ContactSettingActivity class, it will produce errors. That is because the current activity in the Intent code is referencing the ContactActivity. Change this for each to be the **ContactSettingActivity**.

3. Change the code in the `initSettingsButton()` method so that the button is disabled. Use the following code:

```
private void initSettingsButton() {
    ImageButton ibSettings = (ImageButton)findViewById(R.id.imageButtonSettings);
    ibSettings.setEnabled(false);
}
```

4. Call the three methods in the `onCreate` method.

After you have completed coding the navigation bar, you have to code the activity so that it displays the current preference. Create a method called `initSettings` and refer to the code in Listing 5.2 to get it to properly configure the activity at startup. Be sure to call `initSettings();` in `onCreate`.

Listing 5.2   Code to Initialize the Activity

```
1    private void initSettings() {
2        String sortBy = getSharedPreferences("MyContactListPreferences",
3            ↪Context.MODE_PRIVATE).getString("sortfield","contactname");
4        String sortOrder = getSharedPreferences("MyContactListPreferences",
5            ↪Context.MODE_PRIVATE).getString("sortorder","ASC");
6
7        RadioButton rbName = (RadioButton) findViewById(R.id.radioName);
8        RadioButton rbCity = (RadioButton) findViewById(R.id.radioCity);
9        RadioButton rbBirthDay = (RadioButton) findViewById(R.id.radioBirthday);
10       if (sortBy.equalsIgnoreCase("contactname")) {
11           rbName.setChecked(true);
12       }
13       else if (sortBy.equalsIgnoreCase("city")) {
14           rbCity.setChecked(true);
15       }
16       else {
17           rbBirthDay.setChecked(true);
18       }
19
20       RadioButton rbAscending = (RadioButton) findViewById(R.id.radioAscending);
21       RadioButton rbDescending = (RadioButton) findViewById(R.id.radioDescending);
22       if (sortOrder.equalsIgnoreCase("ASC")) {
23           rbAscending.setChecked(true);
24       }
25       else {
26           rbDescending.setChecked(true);
27       }
28   }
```

The `initSettings` method gets the values stored in SharedPreferences to set the RadioButtons to the value that the user checks.

- **Lines 2–5**—A string variable is declared, and the value for the field to sort contacts by is retrieved from `SharedPreferences`. The `getSharedPreferences` method is used to get the `SharedPreferences` object because there is no need to have multiple `SharedPreferences` objects in this app. The `Shared-Preference` file is opened as a private object. The `getString` method is called on the `SharedPrefer-ence` object to retrieve the string value associated with the sortfield key. If there is no value stored for that key, the default value of `contactname` is assigned to the variable. The next line does the same thing for the preferred sort order.
- **Lines 7–9**—A reference to each radio button in the sort field `RadioGroup` is assigned to a variable.
- **Lines 10–18**—The value retrieved for the preferred sort field is evaluated to determine which `RadioButton` should be set as checked.
- **Lines 20–27**—The same operations are performed to set the sort order to the order preferred by the user.

The next step is to create a method to store the selected user preference for each option. Two methods are required—one for each RadioGroup. When the user presses a RadioButton in one of the groups, the method determines which RadioButton was pressed and then the value associated with that RadioButton is saved in SharedPreferences. Refer to Listing 5.3 for the code for these methods.

Listing 5.3 RadioButton Click Code

```
1    private void initSortByClick() {
2        RadioGroup rgSortBy = (RadioGroup) findViewById(R.id.radioGroupSortBy);
3        rgSortBy.setOnCheckedChangeListener(new RadioGroup.OnCheckedChangeListener() {
4
5            @Override
6            public void onCheckedChanged(RadioGroup arg0, int arg1) {
7                RadioButton rbName = (RadioButton) findViewById(R.id.radioName);
8                RadioButton rbCity = (RadioButton) findViewById(R.id.radioCity);
9                if (rbName.isChecked()) {
10                   getSharedPreferences("MyContactListPreferences",
11                       ➥ Context.MODE_PRIVATE).edit()
12                       ➥.putString("sortfield", "contactname").commit();
13               }
14               else if (rbCity.isChecked()) {
15                   getSharedPreferences("MyContactListPreferences",
16                       ➥ Context.MODE_PRIVATE).edit()
17                       ➥.putString("sortfield", "city").commit();
18               }
19               else {
20                   getSharedPreferences("MyContactListPreferences",
21                       ➥ Context.MODE_PRIVATE).edit()
22                       ➥.putString("sortfield", "birthday").commit();
23               }
24           }
25       });
26   }
27
28   private void initSortOrderClick() {
29       RadioGroup rgSortOrder = (RadioGroup) findViewById(R.id.radioGroupSortOrder);
30       rgSortOrder.setOnCheckedChangeListener(new RadioGroup.OnCheckedChangeListener() {
31
32           @Override
33           public void onCheckedChanged(RadioGroup arg0, int arg1) {
34               RadioButton rbAscending = (RadioButton) findViewById(R.id.radioAscending);
35               if (rbAscending.isChecked()) {
36                   getSharedPreferences("MyContactListPreferences",
37                       ➥ Context.MODE_PRIVATE).edit()
38                       ➥.putString("sortorder", "ASC").commit();
39               }
40               else {
41                   getSharedPreferences("MyContactListPreferences",
42                       ➥ Context.MODE_PRIVATE).edit()
43                       ➥.putString("sortorder", "DESC").commit();
44               }
45           }
46       });
47   }
```

Much of the code in these two methods has already been discussed. The only new code is the code used to save the selected preference. Examine the listing to find the getSharedPreferences method. This method gets a reference to the SharedPreferences object using private mode. It then sends the message edit() to the SharedPreferences object to open it for editing. Next, the message putString is sent to the editable SharedPreferences object to save the value. The first parameter in the `putString` method is the key and the second is the value to be saved. Finally, the message `commit()` is sent to the changed `SharedPreferences` object to make the changes persist.

Add calls to these methods in the `onCreate` method and then run and test the Settings activity. You should select a sort field value and a sort order value. Navigate to another activity and then navigate back to the Settings activity. If the values remain as you selected them, the activity is completed. These values stored in the `SharedPreferences` object are used in Chapter 6, "Lists in Android: Navigation and Information Display," to present a sorted list of contacts to the user.

Using Files

The MyContactList does not really have a need to store data in a file. Accessing and storing contacts in a database is a better solution than in a file. One possible use for a file in the app could be to export the contacts in the database for export to another app or for backup. This is beyond the scope of the book at this point. However, we will discuss some of the options.

First, an app can store data in the standard file storage on the device. This is considered external storage, and data stored here is accessible to other apps. The other option is internal, which stores the data in the app's private storage area. Files stored here are only accessible by the app and will be deleted if the app is ever uninstalled. Whichever storage location is selected, Android encourages developers to use standard folders such as Documents or Pictures provided by the operating system, so that the OS knows how to treat those files.

The process of storing data in a file starts with converting the data to text (if it is not already). The next step is to get a reference to the storage location. For example,

```
File filePath = new File(Environment.getExternalStoragePublicDirectory(Environment.DIRECTORY_
↪DOCUMENTS), "contacts");
```

This path is a document folder external to the app with the name **contacts**. The next step is to create a folder using this path and then create a new file in that folder. The final step is to use `FileOutputStream` and `OutputStreamWriter` to write the text to the file. Reading the file is essentially the same process, except the data would be read in from an existing file using `FileInputStream` and `InputStreamReader`.

For more details on file storage, you can reference the Android developer's site, which provides plenty of information on how to do this.

Creating the Database

The MyContactList app uses a simple database with a single table to provide the data storage and manipulation functionality described in Chapter 2, "App Design Issues and Considerations." You will create two new classes to provide the database functionality. One class is a database helper class used to create, modify, and delete the tables included in the database. The other class is used for data access. It provides methods to open and close the database and the queries used to store, access, and manipulate the data in the tables. The focus in this chapter is to enable the ContactActivity to store a contact's data. Retrieval and manipulation of that data is introduced in later chapters.

Create the Database Helper Class

The recommended approach to using SQLite in an Android app is to create a Database Helper class whose only function is to provide for the creation, modification, and deletion of tables in the database. The new class is defined as a subclass of the `SQLiteOpenHelper` class. Much of the required functionality for working with databases is inherited from the `SQLiteOpenHelper` class, although some of its methods will be overridden to implement the functionality required for this app.

1. Open the project you worked on in chapter 4, or the chapter 5 project that you downloaded from the book's website.
2. Right-click **com.example.mycontactlist** in the java folder of the Package Explorer.
3. Select **New > Java Class** and enter **ContactDBHelper** as the name of the new class and click **OK**.
4. Type the code in Listing 5.4 into the new class.

Listing 5.4 Code for the Database Helper Class

```
1    import android.content.Context;
2    import android.database.sqlite.SQLiteDatabase;
3    import android.database.sqlite.SQLiteOpenHelper;
4    import android.util.Log;
5
6    public class ContactDBHelper extends SQLiteOpenHelper {
7
8        private static final String DATABASE_NAME = "mycontacts.db";
9        private static final int DATABASE_VERSION = 1;
10
11       // Database creation sql statement
12       private static final String CREATE_TABLE_CONTACT =
13           ↵"create table contact (_id integer primary key autoincrement, "
14               + "contactname text not null, streetaddress text, "
15               + "city text, state text, zipcode text, "
16               + "phonenumber text, cellnumber text, "
17               + "email text, birthday text);";
18
19       public ContactDBHelper(Context context) {
20           super(context, DATABASE_NAME, null, DATABASE_VERSION);
21       }
22
23       @Override
24       public void onCreate(SQLiteDatabase db) {
25           db.execSQL(CREATE_TABLE_CONTACT);
26       }
27
28       @Override
29       public void onUpgrade(SQLiteDatabase db, int oldVersion, int newVersion) {
30           Log.w(ContactDBHelper.class.getName(),
31               "Upgrading database from version " + oldVersion + " to "
32                   + newVersion + ", which will destroy all old data");
33           db.execSQL("DROP TABLE IF EXISTS contact");
34           onCreate(db);
35       }
36   }
```

The code is relatively standard, and all that is needed to create the SQLite database and the one table required for the MyContactList app. The code can be copied and modified for other apps. The code and its potential modifications are described as follows:

- **Line 6**—The class `ContactDBHelper` is declared as a subclass of `SQLiteOpenHelper`. Most of its functionality is inherited from this class.

- **Line 8**—A static variable is declared to name the database file. A database name is required. Use the `.db` extension.

- **Line 9**—A static variable to hold the database version number is declared and initialized to 1. This variable is important. Every time the database is accessed, the existing database version is compared to the one here. If the number is higher, the `onUpgrade` method is executed. The number is incremented by the developer when they need to upgrade an existing database.

- **Lines 12–17**—A string variable is declared and assigned to a SQL command that creates the table. It is good practice to define the table definitions in this manner, so that when a change to a table needs to be made, all you have to do is change the definition in one place and increment the version number. Declare a similar variable for each table needed in your database.

- **Lines 19–21**—The constructor method calls the super class's constructor method. Nothing else needs to be done in this method. The constructor creates a new instance of `ContactDBHelper`.

- **Lines 23–26**—The `onCreate` method is called the first time the database is opened. If the database named in the `DATABASE_NAME` variable does not exist, this method is executed. The method executes the SQL assigned to the `CREATE_TABLE_CONTACT` variable.

- **Lines 28–35**—The `onUpgrade` method is executed when the database is opened and the current version number in the code is higher than the version number of the current database. This method first deletes the contact table and then executes the `onCreate` method to create a new version of the table. Carefully planning the data needed by your app is important so that you don't have to use this method much. What happens in this method is entirely up to the developer. Care must be taken, because if a table is dropped, all the user data currently in the table is lost. If you need to add columns to the table, consider executing an `ALTER TABLE` SQL command rather than a drop, and recreate the table. The `Log` command writes a message to **LogCat**, which is a system for collecting and viewing system debug information. You can view LogCat by selecting **Window > Show View > Other... > LogCat**. This command may be eliminated if you want.

A database helper class is recommended practice in Android. The primary function of the class is to determine what must be done on creation of the database and what must be done when the database is upgraded. The next step is to create a class that does the opening and closing of the database and contains the queries used to store and retrieve data from the database.

Create the Data Source Class

Create a new class named **ContactDataSource**. Enter the code in Listing 5.5, being sure to import any objects underlined in red. Two options will display for SQLException. Pick the **java.sql version**.

Listing 5.5 ContactDataSource Code

```
1    public class ContactDataSource {
2
3        private SQLiteDatabase database;
4        private ContactDBHelper dbHelper;
5
6        public ContactDataSource(Context context) {
7            dbHelper = new ContactDBHelper(context);
8        }
9
10       public void open() throws SQLException {
11           database = dbHelper.getWritableDatabase();
12       }
13
14       public void close() {
15           dbHelper.close();
16       }
17   }
```

The required methods are quite limited and fairly self-explanatory.

- **Lines 3–4**—Variables are declared to hold instances of the SQLite database and the helper class. You will get a warning on the `SQLiteDatabase` line because you don't use it yet.
- **Lines 6–8**—The helper class is instantiated when the data source class is instantiated.
- **Lines 10–16**—Open and close methods are used to access and end access to the database.

The rest of the code in this class is dependent on the needs of the app. In the case of the MyContactsList app, the ContactActivity needs to be able to insert new contacts and update data for existing contacts. This is supported by creating a method for each operation. The data for insertion or for updating a contact is passed to these methods in a Contact object.

The `Contact` class does not exist, so the first task is to create that class. Create another new class in the **src** folder named **Contact**. Enter the code in Listing 5.6 to create the `Contact` object. The ContactActivity uses objects of this class to store data entered by the user and pass it to the data source class.

You can get significant help in creating this class from Android Studio. Once you have entered all the private instance variables, select **Code > Generate > Constructor**. Select **None**, since this constructor takes no arguments. Then type the two lines that initialize the constructor. Next, select **Code > Generate > Getters and Setters**. Select all the fields and click **OK**.

Listing 5.6 The Contact Class

```
1      import java.util.Calendar;
2
3      public class Contact {
4              private int contactID;
5              private String contactName;
6              private String streetAddress;
7              private String city;
8              private String state;
9              private String zipCode;
10             private String phoneNumber;
11             private String cellNumber;
12             private String eMail;
13             private Calendar birthday;
14
15             public Contact() {
16                     contactID = -1;
17                     birthday = Calendar.getInstance();
18             }
19
20             public int getContactID() {
21                     return contactID;
22             }
23             public void setContactID(int i) {
24                     contactID = i;
25             }
26             public String getContactName() {
27                     return contactName;
28             }
29             public void setContactName(String s) {
30                     contactName = s;
31             }
32             public Calendar getBirthday() {
33                     return birthday;
34             }
35             public void setBirthday(Calendar c) {
36                     birthday = c;
37             }
38             public String getStreetAddress() {
39                     return streetAddress;
40             }
41             public void setStreetAddress(String s) {
42                     streetAddress = s;
43             }
44             public String getCity() {
45                     return city;
46             }
47             public void setCity(String s) {
48                     city = s;
49             }
50             public String getState() {
51                     return state;
52             }
```

(continued)

Listing 5.6   The Contact Class (*continued*)

```
53          public void setState(String s) {
54                  state = s;
55          }
56          public String getZipCode() {
57                  return zipCode;
58          }
59          public void setZipCode(String s) {
60                  zipCode = s;
61          }
62          public void setPhoneNumber(String s) {
63                  phoneNumber = s;
64          }
65          public String getPhoneNumber() {
66                  return phoneNumber;
67          }
68          public void setCellNumber(String s) {
69                  cellNumber = s;
70          }
71          public String getCellNumber() {
72                  return cellNumber;
73          }
74          public void setEMail(String s) {
75                  eMail = s;
76          }
77          public String getEMail() {
78                  return eMail;
79          }
80     }
```

The Contact class is a very simple class. It declares variables for each piece of data needed for a contact and declares a method to set the value of the variable and a method to get the value of the variable (getters and setter). The only real important code is in the class constructor method. Notice that in this method the contact's ID is set to −1 by default. This is used by the app to determine if the contact is new and needs to be inserted or the contact already exists and needs to be updated. The birthday variable is also initialized to the current date. This allows the app to assume that there will always be a Calendar value in the birthday variable.

After creating the Contact class, you can now code the insert and update methods in the ContactDataSource class. Enter the code in Listing 5.7 to create these methods. Enter the code after the close() method.

Listing 5.7   Insert and Update Contact Methods

```
1    public boolean insertContact(Contact c) {
2        boolean didSucceed = false;
3        try {
4            ContentValues initialValues = new ContentValues();
5
6            initialValues.put("contactname", c.getContactName());
7            initialValues.put("streetaddress", c.getStreetAddress());
8            initialValues.put("city", c.getCity());
9            initialValues.put("state", c.getState());
10           initialValues.put("zipcode", c.getZipCode());
11           initialValues.put("phonenumber", c.getPhoneNumber());
12           initialValues.put("cellnumber", c.getCellNumber());
13           initialValues.put("email", c.getEMail());
14           initialValues.put("birthday",String.valueOf(c.getBirthday().getTimeInMillis()));
15
16           didSucceed = database.insert("contact", null, initialValues) > 0;
17       }
18       catch (Exception e) {
19           //Do nothing -will return false if there is an exception
20       }
21       return didSucceed;
22   }
23
24   public boolean updateContact(Contact c) {
25       boolean didSucceed = false;
26       try {
27           Long rowId = (long) c.getContactID();
28           ContentValues updateValues = new ContentValues();
29
30           updateValues.put("contactname", c.getContactName());
31           updateValues.put("streetaddress", c.getStreetAddress());
32           updateValues.put("city", c.getCity());
33           updateValues.put("state", c.getState());
34           updateValues.put("zipcode", c.getZipCode());
35           updateValues.put("phonenumber", c.getPhoneNumber());
36           updateValues.put("cellnumber", c.getCellNumber());
37           updateValues.put("email", c.getEMail());
38           updateValues.put("birthday",
39              ↪String.valueOf(c.getBirthday().getTimeInMillis()));
40
41           didSucceed = database.update("contact", updateValues, "_id=" + rowId, null) > 0;
42       }
43       catch (Exception e) {
44           //Do nothing -will return false if there is an exception
45       }
46       return didSucceed;
47   }
```

The two methods are very similar. The primary difference is that the updateContact method uses the Contact ID to overwrite values in the Contact table, whereas the insertContact method just inserts contact data and the database inserts the ID because the _id field was declared as an autoincrement field.

- **Line 2**—A Boolean variable is declared and assigned the value false. Both the update and insert methods return a Boolean to tell the calling code if the operation succeeded. The value is initially set to false and then changed to true only if the operation succeeds.
- **Line 4**—The ContentValues object is used to store a set of key/value pairs that are used to assign contact data to the correct field in the table.

- **Lines 6–14**—The values for the table are retrieved from the contact object, associated with the correct field, and inserted into the `ContentValues` object. Note that the date is stored as `millis`, because SQLite doesn't support storing data as dates directly.

- **Line 16**—The database's insert method is called and passed the name of the table and values to insert. The method returns the number of records (rows) successfully inserted. The value is compared to zero. If it is greater than zero, then the operation succeeded and the return value is set to true.

- **Lines 18–20**—If the method throws an exception, the return value is already set to false, so we don't have to do anything.

- **Line 27**—The update procedure needs the contact's ID to correctly update the table. This value is retrieved from the contact object and assigned to the variable `rowId`.

- **Line 41**—The database's update method is called to place the changes in the database. Just like the insert method, if the operation is a success, the method returns the number of records affected. If this number is greater than zero, the operation was successful.

The SQLite database is ready for use. An object to create and upgrade the database has been implemented. Another object to open, close, and access the database has also been created. You are now ready to save contact data!

Using the Database

The three classes, Contact, ContactDBHelper, and ContactDataSource, are used in the ContactActivity class to implement the saving of contact data to the database. This will require implementing several new methods and modifying some existing methods. Because the methods to retrieve contacts have not been implemented yet, the update functionality will be only partially implemented at this time.

The first step is to provide an association between the ContactActivity class and a `Contact` object. This is implemented by declaring a private variable in the ContactActivity class. Enter the following code after the class declaration and before the `onCreate` method:

```
private Contact currentContact;
```

Next, associate the `currentContact` variable with a new `Contact` object by entering the following code as the last line in the `onCreate` method:

```
currentContact = new Contact();
```

Notice that while you are using a new class (Contact) in the ContactActivity class, you do not have to import it. That's because you created the `Contact` class as a part of the com.example.mycontactlist package. Android already knows about this class, so it does not have to be imported.

The final step in modifying existing code is to add a line of code in the `didFinishDatePickerDialog` method to store the selected birthday in the Contact object. Add the following line of code as the last line of code in that method:

```
currentContact.setBirthday(selectedTime);
```

This code uses the `Contact` class's `setBirthday` method to assign the date selected in the custom dialog to the `currentContact` object.

Capture User-Entered Data

The first new method needed is used to capture the user data as it is typed and store it in the `currentContact` object. The method itself does not capture the data. Rather, it sets up listeners on all the EditTexts where data can be entered. If the text changes, the listener then executes the code to set the attribute that holds the code in the `currentContact` object. The method is called in the `onCreate` method of the ContactActivity, so that the listeners are ready to go when the ContactActivity is ready for input. To start, enter the following line of code after all the other init methods in the `onCreate` method (it will be red until you add the method):

```
initTextChangedEvents();
```

Next, create a new method in the ContactActivity class called `initTextChangedEvents()`. Place this method after the other init methods currently in the class. Enter the code in Listing 5.8. Note that once you get to line 3, you should get a light bulb you can click to autogenerate the methods in lines 5, 8, and 11—or they may be automatically generated just by typing the code in line 3. Be aware that the order of the methods may not be the same as shown here.

Listing 5.8 TextChanged Event Code

```
1    private void initTextChangedEvents(){
2        final EditText etContactName = (EditText) findViewById(R.id.editName);
3        etContactName.addTextChangedListener(new TextWatcher() {
4
5            public void afterTextChanged(Editable s) {
6                currentContact.setContactName(etContactName.getText().toString());
7            }
8            public void beforeTextChanged(CharSequence arg0, int arg1, int arg2, int arg3) {
9                //  Auto-generated method stub
10            }
11            public void onTextChanged(CharSequence s, int start, int before, int count) {
12                //  Auto-generated method stub
13            }
14        });
15
16        final EditText etStreetAddress = (EditText) findViewById(R.id.editAddress);
17        etStreetAddress.addTextChangedListener(new TextWatcher() {
18            public void afterTextChanged(Editable s) {
19                currentContact.setStreetAddress(etStreetAddress.getText().toString());
20            }
21            public void beforeTextChanged(CharSequence arg0, int arg1, int arg2, int arg3) {
22                //  Auto-generated method stub
23            }
24            public void onTextChanged(CharSequence s, int start, int before, int count) {
25                //  Auto-generated method stub
26            }
27        });
28    }
```

Listing 5.8 is not the complete method. A listener has to be added for all the other EditTexts in the layout. However, the code is essentially the same for each EditText. Take time to understand this code before adding the rest.

- **Line 2**—A reference to the Contact Name `EditText` is assigned to the variable `contactName`. The variable is declared as final because it is used inside the event code.

- **Line 3**—A `TextChangedListener` is added to the `EditText` by creating a new `TextWatcher` object. `TextWatcher` is an object that, when attached to a widget that allows editing, will execute its methods when the text in the widget is changed. The `TextWatcher` object requires that three methods (lines 3, 5, and 6) are implemented, even though you will use only one of these events.

- **Line 5**—The `afterTextChanged` method is a required method for the `TextWatch` object. It is called after the user completes editing the data and leaves the `EditText`. This is the event that this app uses to capture the data the user entered.

- **Line 6**—This code is executed when the user ends editing of the `EditText`. It gets the text in the `EditText`, converts it to a string, and sets the `contactName` attribute of the `currentContact` object to that value.

- **Line 8**—The `beforeTextChanged` method is a required `TextWatcher` method. This method is executed when the user presses down on a key to enter it into an `EditText` but before the value in the `EditText` is actually changed.

- **Line 11**—The `onTextChanged` method is also a required `TextWatcher` method. The method is executed after each and every character change in an `EditText`.

- **Lines 16–17**—The pattern repeats for another EditText in the layout, except that value is assigned to a different attribute of the currentContact object.

- **Line 19**—This code gets the value entered into the editAddress EditText, converts it to a string, and sets the streetAddress attribute of the currentContact object to that value. It is essentially the same as the code in number 4, except that it gets the value from a different widget and assigns it to a different attribute.

This code needs to be repeated for the remaining EditTexts in the activity_contact.xml file. This includes the remaining address EditTexts, the phone and cell number EditTexts, and the e-mail EditText. You can copy and paste the code you already entered or type it. In either case, but especially with the copy/paste approach, make sure you get a reference to the correct widget (R.id.*widget+id*) and assign the value to the correct Contact attribute.

The next step in coding the initTextChangedEvents method is to set the phone number EditTexts to autoformat the number as it's typed. Enter the following code as the last code in that method, replacing *homephoneedittextvariable* and *cellphoneedittextvariable* with the names you used previously for the two variables:

```
homephoneedittextvariable.addTextChangedListener(new PhoneNumberFormattingTextWatcher());
cellphoneedittextvariable.addTextChangedListener(new PhoneNumberFormattingTextWatcher());
```

This code adds a listener to the phone number EditTexts that calls the PhoneNumberFormattingTextWatcher object, which in turn adds the appropriate formatting as the user types.

Save User-Entered Data

The intTextChangedEvents method you just created sets all the EditTexts to update the ContactActivity's contact object with any changes users make as they make them. The next step is to pass that object to the insert or update method in the ContactDataSource class so that the changes can be stored in the database. This requires the addition of a method that initializes the Save button and executes the code that will do the save operation when the button is pressed.

The initialization of the Save button is similar to the initialization of all the other buttons you have coded so far. The only difference is what happens when the button is pressed. Enter the code in Listing 5.9 to create the method associated with the Save button. Don't forget to call the method in the onCreate method where the rest of the button initialization methods are called.

Listing 5.9   Save Button Code

```
1    private void initSaveButton() {
2        Button saveButton = (Button) findViewById(R.id.buttonSave);
3        saveButton.setOnClickListener(new View.OnClickListener() {
4
5            @Override
6            public void onClick(View v) {
7                boolean wasSuccessful = false;
8                ContactDataSource ds = new ContactDataSource(ContactActivity.this);
9                try {
10                   ds.open();
11
12                   if (currentContact.getContactID() == -1) {
13                       wasSuccessful = ds.insertContact(currentContact);
14                   }
15                   else {
16                       wasSuccessful = ds.updateContact(currentContact);
17                   }
18                   ds.close();
19               }
20               catch (Exception e) {
21                   wasSuccessful = false;
```

(continued)

Listing 5.9 Save Button Code (*continued*)

```
22                    }
23
24                    if (wasSuccessful) {
25                        ToggleButton editToggle = (ToggleButton) findViewById(R.id.toggleButtonEdit);
26                        editToggle.toggle();
27                        setForEditing(false);
28                    }
29                }
30        });
31    }
```

The only new code in this method is the code associated with the save operation. The basic save operation opens the database, checks if this is a new contact to be inserted or if it should be updated, and if the save was successful, changes the screen back to view rather than editing mode.

- **Line 7**—A Boolean variable is declared and set to false. This variable captures the return value of the `ContactDataSource` methods and is used to determine the operations that should be performed upon success or failure of the method.
- **Line 8**—A new `ContactDataSource` object is instantiated.
- **Line 10**—The database is opened. It is good practice to open the database just prior to using it and close it as soon as you are done.
- **Lines 12–17**—The current contact's id is compared to –1. Only new contacts will have a –1 value. If it is a new contact, the `insertContact` method is called and passed the `currentContact` object. Otherwise, the `updateContact` method is called to save the new data.
- **Line 18**—The database is closed as soon as possible. Do not forget to close the database! If you do not close it, strange errors can show up during execution.
- **Lines 24–28**—The return value is checked. If the save operation was successful, the `ToggleButton` is toggled to viewing mode, and the screen is set for viewing. If it was not successful, the activity remains in editing mode.

Test the code on the emulator. You may notice one discrepancy (but note that this does not happen on all devices): when you push the Save button and the screen changes to viewing rather than editing mode, the keyboard may still be displayed. If you don't have this happen, edit your **Android Virtual Device**. Look for **Hardware Keyboard Present** and uncheck it. Stop and restart the emulator. Many Android devices do not have a hardware keyboard, and if your app keeps the soft keyboard displayed when the user is clearly done, it will make the user think that the app doesn't work properly.

Correct this by adding a method that dismisses the keyboard that is called when the Save button is pressed. The code in Listing 5.10 is a method to do this.

Listing 5.10 Partial hideKeyboard() Method

```
1    private void hideKeyboard() {
2        InputMethodManager imm = InputMethodManager)getSystemService(Context.INPUT_METHOD_SERVICE);
3        EditText editName = (EditText) findViewById(R.id.editName);
4        imm.hideSoftInputFromWindow(editName.getWindowToken(), 0);
5        EditText editAddress = (EditText) findViewById(R.id.editAddress);
6        imm.hideSoftInputFromWindow(editAddress.getWindowToken(), 0);
7    }
8
```

Repeat the last two lines of code in Listing 5.7 for each EditText in the layout (changing variable names and EditTexts). The first line gets a system service that manages user input. The second line gets a reference to an Edit-Text, and the third line closes the keyboard. Every EditText must receive this treatment because there is no way of knowing which EditText users were working with when they pressed the Save button. Add a call to this method in the `initSaveButton` method just before the ContactDataSource is instantiated.

Test the modification in the emulator. Another discrepancy is exposed (again, only if you have the hardware keyboard disabled in the AVD). The keyboard hides, but the screen remains focused on the last EditText used. When the user saves the data and the screen displays in view mode, it should be focused at the top of the screen. It does not do this. Fortunately, there is an easy fix. Tell the ScrollView to focus on the top of the screen. Change the block of code that requests focus for the contact name EditText in the `setForEditing` method to the following to change the ScrollView's focus to the top of the screen when switching to viewing mode:

```
if (enabled) {
    editName.requestFocus();
}
else {
    ScrollView s = (ScrollView) findViewById(R.id.scrollView1);
    s.fullScroll(ScrollView.FOCUS_UP);
}
```

If you added the autofocus hack discussed in Chapter 4, "Android Navigation and Interface Design," you can add the second line of code just before the `s.clearFocus()` line. The focus up must be before the clear focus. Otherwise, it will override the clear, and autofocus will again occur. Test the app again. Everything should work as expected.

One last problem exists with the ContactActivity. If the user adds a new contact, presses the Save button, and then edits the data and presses Save again, another contact will be added, rather than updating the contact just entered. This is because the `currentContact` object still has an ID of –1. There are a number of approaches to fixing this problem. You could clear the screen and make users get the contact from the contact list (not yet implemented) if they want to edit it. You could retrieve the newly inserted contact and reload the screen with all the newly entered data and the id that was created by the auto increment of the ID when the contact was inserted into the database. Or you could get the new ID and set the `currentContact ContactID` attribute to that value. That is the approach used here. Open the **ContactDataSource** and create a new method using the code in Listing 5.11.

Listing 5.11   Retrieve the New Contact ID

```
1    public int getLastContactId() {
2        int lastId = -1;
3        try {
4            String query = "Select MAX(_id) from contact";
5            Cursor cursor = database.rawQuery(query, null);
6
7            cursor.moveToFirst();
8            lastId = cursor.getInt(0);
9            cursor.close();
10       }
11       catch (Exception e) {
12           lastId = -1;
13       }
14       return lastId;
15   }
```

Notice that the structure of this method is similar to the other insert and update methods. A `try` and `catch` is used to handle an error if it occurs, and a value, set to failure initially, is returned. However, because this is a method to retrieve data from the database rather than save it to the database, there are some significant differences.

- **Line 4**—An SQL query is written to get the maximum value for the `_id` field in the contact table. The last contact entered will have the maximum value because the `_id` field is set to autoincrement.
- **Line 5**—A cursor is declared and assigned to hold the results of the execution of the query. A cursor is an object that is used to hold and move through the results of a query.
- **Line 7**—The cursor is told to move to the first record in the returned data.
- **Line 8**—The maximum ID is retrieved from the record set. Fields in the record set are indexed starting at 0.
- **Line 9**—The cursor is closed. Just like with closing the database, it is best to close the cursor as soon as you are done using it. Forgetting to do so can lead to errors during execution.

Open the **ContactActivity** code. Navigate to the `initSaveButton` method. Enter the following code after the line of code that inserts a new contact (not the update):

```
if (wasSuccessful) {
    int newId = ds.getLastContactId();
    currentContact.setContactID(newId);
}
```

The first line checks if the insertion of the new contact was successful. If it was, the second line uses the newly created retrieval method to get the newly inserted contact's ID. The second line sets the `currentContact` object's ID to the retrieved value.

Use the Debugger

The Contact Activity is finished for now. We will add some functionality later after creating other activities. Now we need to test our code. However, it is difficult to test the recently added functionality because currently it does not retrieve contact data. Thus to test that the functionality you just added is working properly, you have to watch it run. This is done using the debugger.

The first step in using the debugger is to set a *breakpoint*. A breakpoint tells the debugger to halt execution at that line of code. This gives you the capability to inspect the values in the variables and step through the code line by line. To set a breakpoint, click in the **gray vertical bar** to the left of the line of code you want to stop on. A pink dot will be placed in the bar (Figure 5.3).

```
private void initSaveButton() {
    Button saveButton = (Button) findViewById(R.id.buttonSave);
    saveButton.setOnClickListener(new View.OnClickListener() {

        @Override
        public void onClick(View v) {
            hideKeyboard();
            boolean wasSuccessful = false;
            ContactDataSource ds = new ContactDataSource(ContactActivity.this);
            try {
                ds.open();

                if (currentContact.getContactID() == -1) {
                    wasSuccessful = ds.insertContact(currentContact);
                    int newId = ds.getLastContactId();
                    currentContact.setContactID(newId);
                } else {
                    wasSuccessful = ds.updateContact(currentContact);
                }
                ds.close();
            }
            catch (Exception e) {
                wasSuccessful = false;
            }

            if (wasSuccessful) {
                ToggleButton editToggle = (ToggleButton) findViewById(R.id.toggleButtonEdit);
                editToggle.toggle();
                setForEditing(false);
            }
        }
    });
}
```

Figure 5.3 Code with breakpoint set.

To check whether `currentContact` is getting a new ID, set a breakpoint in the `initSaveButton` method on the `hideKeyboard()` line (Figure 5.3). Run the program in **debug mode** by pressing the button in the top menu. Click the **Off** button to enable editing, fill in some values, and then press the **Save** button. When the breakpoint is hit during execution, the **Debug app window** will open at the bottom left of Android Studio. The line of code that stopped execution will be displayed in the editor. The app has halted on that line and is waiting for your command. To control execution during debugging, use the **Debug toolbar** buttons at the top of the Debug window (see Figure 5.4).

Figure 5.4 Debug control buttons.

Hover over each of these to find the one that says **Step Over**. This advances the execution by one line. Click this button and watch the code step line by line until you reach the `currentContact.setContactID(newId)` line. Note that if your code doesn't follow this path, you've done something wrong and need to examine the code to ensure that it matches the code in the previous listings. Locate the **Variables** portion of the Debug window (see Figure 5.5).

In the Variables section, find the `newId` variable and verify that its value is greater than −1. This number may be significantly higher than −1 if you have run the app several times already. If it is not greater than −1, review your code. Now **step** the code one more line and inspect the `currentContact` variable. You may have to expand `currentContact` to see its attributes. If you cannot find `currentContact` in the variables list, expand the variable named `this`, which represents the whole activity, so it will have all the activity variables in it. Expand it until you find `currentContact`. Check to see that the contact ID attribute is the same as the `newId` value. If it is, you have successfully created an activity that can save data to a database!

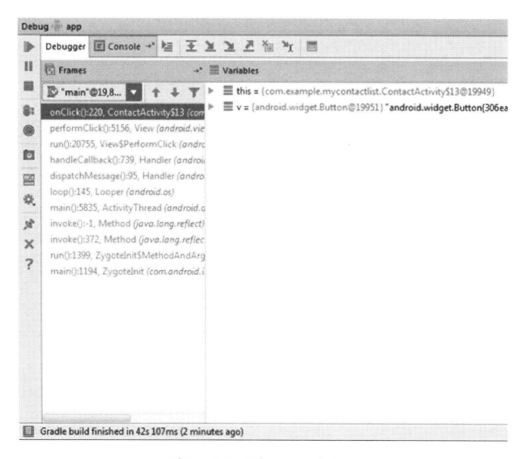

Figure 5.5 Debug app window.

The debugger can be stopped by clicking the **Stop** button. The Stop button is the one with the red square as an icon on the left side of the Debug window. You can resume execution of the code (not step-by-step) by clicking the **Resume Program** button. This button is the green triangle also on the left side of the Debug window. Resuming the program will cause it to run normally until it hits another breakpoint.

An alternative to stepping through the code with the debugger is to use logging. With this approach, you place `Log` statements in your code in places where you'd like to know the value of variables or that the method was executed. When your code executes, these statements will be written to LogCat (see the discussion of Log statement and LogCat in the "Create the Database Helper Class" section earlier in this chapter). This is a useful approach if you have to run through a significant amount of code to get to the code you are interested in.

Summary

Data that exists beyond the execution of the app is said to *persist*. In this chapter, you learned several methods to make data persist in your app. You also learned how to get that persistent data for use in the app. The first approach you learned to persist data was to use the SharedPreferences object. The SharedPreferences object is used to store primitive bits of data, such as strings and integers. You learned how to put data into a SharedPreferences object to save user choices on contact sort order, and you learned how to get those choices from the object to display the user's past choices.

The second approach you learned to implement persistent data storage was the use of a database. A SQLite database is used to store complex data. You created a class (ContactDBHelper) to create and update the database and its contents. You created a class (ContactDataSource) to access the database. Finally, you created a class (Contact) to pass a contact's data from and to the database methods.

Exercises

1. Add the choice of a background color to the settings activity. Create a couple of new color resources in color. xml. Add these choices as a RadioGroup to the settings screen. You will have to modify the layout to place all the RadioGroups in a ScrollView so that you can see them all. Make the choice persist in a SharedPreferences object. Use the following command in the `onCreate` method of the settings activity to set the chosen background color:

```
scrollviewobject.setBackgroundResource(R.color.colorresourcename);
```

2. Create a method in ContactDataSource that will only update the Contact's Address. Create a ContactAddress object to pass data to the method.

3. Modify the `Contact` table to include a field bestFriendForever that is an integer data type. Modify the `onUpgrade` method of ContactDBHelper to insert this new field without losing the data that is currently in the table.

CHAPTER 6

Lists in Android: Navigation and Information Display

Lists are very useful tools and have become ubiquitous in mobile computing. Flick scrolling a list is so common an action that my daughter once asked, after seeing my brother-in-law with a cast needed because of carpal tunnel syndrome from computer use, if she was going to get a similar disease because she does this so often. With that, she moved her index finger in the list swipe gesture. Lists are so common because they are a very useful way to organize, display, and access large amounts of data on a very small screen. This chapter explores the implementation of lists in Android. It covers simple lists that exploit the built-in list capabilities of the Android SDK and then examines the development of more complex lists, tailored specifically to the task at hand. Finally, the chapter concludes by introducing passing data between activities, using user preferences to sort a list, and changing the app's launch activity to complete the ContactListActivity.

In the MyContactList app, you will use the simple list to display the names of each of the contacts. The simple list will allow the user to click an entry in the list and go to a different activity. You will increase the functionality by displaying a more complex list that also shows the contact's phone number in a different font. This version also allows the user to delete entries and shows the full contact information in the Contact Activity. You will also see how sorting can be implemented based on the settings screen. In order to make this work properly, you will explore a new life cycle method, onResume, that runs whenever an activity becomes active.

Lists and Adapters

Two components are required for any list implementation in Android: a **ListView** widget and an *adapter*. The List-View widget is an object that can display a vertical list of items that can be scrolled through. An **Adapter** is dynamically associated with the ListView. The adapter provides access to the underlying data source for the list. In the case of a simple list, after an adapter is associated with the widget, insertion of data as a list item is handled automatically. In the case of a complex list, the developer must create a subclass of an Adapter object and code the display and behavior of the list in the new subclass.

Lists

An **AdapterView** is the super class of all views that are bound to an underlying data source. A View is the base class for all user interface components, such as the widgets used in creating layouts. The AdapterView has several subclasses, including **GridView**, **ListView**, and **Spinner** widgets. The visible component of a list is implemented with a ListView widget in an XML layout file. The widget has attributes that allow the user to configure some aspects of the display.

Adapters

Adapters act as a link between the view and the underlying data source for the list. Lists require the use of an adapter. The adapter provides access to the data items and is responsible for creating a `View` for each item. A view determines how each list item is displayed. In most cases, this display is uniform for each data item. The display does not have to be uniform, but in that case, developers must implement their own adapters to create the different views. Refer to Figure 6.1 for a visual representation of the relationship between data, adapters, and adapter views.

The super class for all adapters is **BaseAdapter**, which is an abstract class. The BaseAdapter class has three subclasses: **ArrayAdapter**, **CursorAdapter**, and **SimpleAdapter**. Table 6.1 explains these classes and their uses.

Table 6.1 Adapter Types

BaseAdapter	Abstract super class for all adapters.
ArrayAdapter	The **ArrayAdapter** is used to bind an **Array** or **ArrayList** to a view. An ArrayAdapter is always parameterized. That means it must be told what kind of data it is going to bind to a view. This data can be simple, such as **String**, or more complex, such as the Contact object created in the previous chapter.
CursorAdapter	An abstract class that binds data from a database cursor to a view. It has a concrete subclass, **SimpleCursorAdapter**, that is used to map a row layout to fields in a cursor.
SimpleAdapter	The **SimpleAdapter** class is used to bind static data to a view.

The ArrayAdapter is commonly used in list implementation. A solid understanding of how to use this class can be easily extended to other adapter types where appropriate. In this chapter the ArrayAdapter class is used to implement both a simple list and a complex list. We will begin with simple lists and move on later in the chapter to more complex list types.

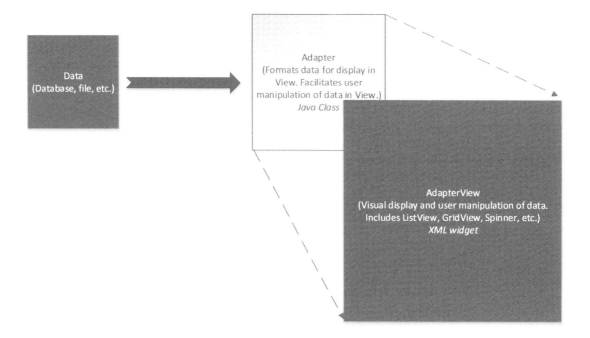

Figure 6.1   Relationship between data, adapters, and adapter views.

Simple Lists

The simple list implementation displays only the contact name of each contact in the user's contact database. For now, the user will be able to scroll through this list and click the list to open the ContactActivity, but little else.

Open the project you worked on in the previous chapter, or download the Chapter 6 project from the book website.

Create the Data Source Method

The first step to implementing the simple list is to have data. For this, you need to add a method to the Contact-DataSource class that will retrieve each contact's name. Open **ContactDataSource** and add the code in Listing 6.1 to create a method for getting this data from the database.

Listing 6.1 getContactName Code

```
1    public ArrayList<String> getContactName() {
2        ArrayList<String> contactNames = new ArrayList<>();
3        try {
4            String query = "Select contactname from contact";
5            Cursor cursor = database.rawQuery(query, null);
6
7            cursor.moveToFirst();
8            while (!cursor.isAfterLast()) {
9                contactNames.add(cursor.getString(0));
10               cursor.moveToNext();
11           }
12           cursor.close();
13       }
14       catch (Exception e) {
15           contactNames = new ArrayList<String>();
16       }
17       return contactNames;
18   }
```

Much of this method is similar to the method you wrote in the previous chapter to retrieve the last contact's ID number. The primary difference is that the query can return more than one record to the cursor, so you have to implement a loop to retrieve all the records and add them to the ArrayList.

- **Line 2**—The return value for this method is an **ArrayList**. An ArrayList is an object that acts like an array in that the data it holds can be accessed through an index. In contrast to an array, the ArrayList is not a fixed size. It can grow as data is added to it. An ArrayList is parameterized. That's the `<String>` portion of the code. This says that the values in the ArrayList are all of the String data type. Parameters for an ArrayList can be more complex objects. Later, you will parameterize an ArrayList to hold the Contact objects.

- **Line 4–5**—The SQL query is written to return the `contactname` field for all records in the contact table and then executed in Line 5. The cursur object holds the results of the query.

- **Lines 7–11**—A loop is set up to go through all the records in the cursor. The loop is initialized by moving to the first record in the cursor. Next, the while loop is set up to test if the end of the cursor's record set has been reached. Within the loop, the contact name is added to the `ArrayList`, and the cursor is advanced to the next record. Forgetting the `moveToNext()` command will leave your method in an infinite loop, because it will never reach the end of the record set.

- **Line 15**—The ArrayList is set to a new empty ArrayList in case the routine crashes partially through its filling. This way, the calling Activity can test for an empty list to determine if the retrieve was successful.

Create the Layout

Now that you have a way to get contact data, the next step is to modify the **activity_contact_list.xml** file to include a `ListView` widget. Open this file and delete the **HelloWorld TextView** if you have not already done so (see creating the layout in the "Using Preferences" section of Chapter 5, "Persistent Data in Android"). You should also add the navigation bar if you haven't done that. Be sure to delete all the `padding` attributes in the root `RelativeLayout`. In **Design** view, from the Containers folder in the Palette, drag a **ListView** to anywhere on the layout. Switch to **Text** view and modify the XML for the ListView widget to match Listing 6.2.

Listing 6.2 ListView XML

```
1    <ListView
2            android:id="@+id/lvContacts"
3            android:layout_width="match_parent"
4            android:layout_height="wrap_content"
5            android:layout_alignParentLeft="true"
6            android:layout_alignParentStart="true"
7            android:layout_alignParentTop="true"
8            android:layout_above="@+id/navbar" >
9    </ListView>
```

This XML does not include any new attributes. After you've made the XML modifications, your layout should look like Figure 6.2.

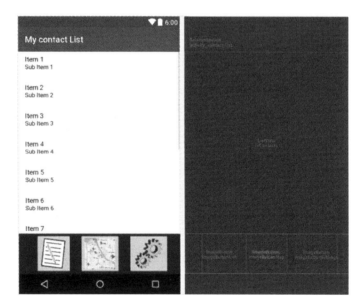

Figure 6.2 Initial list layout.

Code the Activity

After the layout is complete, open **ContactListActivity.java**. Add code to make the navigation buttons work. Be sure to disable the **List** button (see "Coding the Page's Behavior" in Chapter 5). Next, verify the class declaration line of code so that it extends `AppCompatActivity` and then enter the code in Listing 6.3 in the `onCreate` method after the calls to the button initialization methods.

Listing 6.3 Simple List Activation Code

```
1    ContactDataSource ds = new ContactDataSource(this);
2    ArrayList<String> names;
3
4    try {
5        ds.open();
6        names = ds.getContactName();
7        ds.close();
8        ListView listView = (ListView) findViewById(R.id.lvContacts);
9        listView.setAdapter(new ArrayAdapter<String>(this, android.R.layout.simple_list_item_1,
10                          ↪names));
11   }
12   catch (Exception e) {
13       Toast.makeText(this, "Error retrieving contacts", Toast.LENGTH_LONG).show();
14   }
```

Most of the code in Listing 6.3 should be familiar. The first six lines create a new `ContactDataSource` object, open the database, retrieve the contact names using the method you created, and close the database. The last line in the try clause is new. Its purpose is to associate the `ListView` widget with the `Adapter` that has the data to be displayed. To do so, it instantiates a new `ArrayAdapter` that is parameterized to hold `String` data, providing it its context (`this`), the layout to use for a list item (`android.R.layout.simple_list_item_1`), and an `ArrayList` with the data to be displayed (`names`). The layout is provided by the Android SDK, which is why the reference to the layout begins with `android` rather than `R`.

The final new line is in the `catch` statement. A `Toast` displays a message on the device screen for a brief time and then goes away. The method `makeText` configures the message. The first parameter indicates where the message should display. In this case, we want it in the current activity (`this`). The second sets the message, and the third indicates how long the message should display. Finally, `.show()` displays the message.

Run the app in the emulator and tap the **List** button in the navigation bar. Your display should look like Figure 6.3. If you have no data entered, the screen will be blank. Hit the **Back** button and enter a contact. Then tap the **List** button again. Your initial display of the list may include contacts you previously entered while testing the app in previous chapters.

Figure 6.3 Initial list running in emulator.

A list of data is much more useful if it allows the user to do something with the data. In time, you will make the tap of a contact in the list open the ContactActivity with that user's data displayed. After the following code is entered, the tap of a contact just opens the ContactActivity. Create a new method in **ContactListActivity** to initialize the clicking of an item in the list, as shown in Listing 6.4. Remember to call the method from `onCreate`.

Listing 6.4 Code to Respond to an Item Click

```
1    private void initItemClick(){
2        ListView listView = (ListView) findViewById(R.id.lvContacts);
3        listView.setOnItemClickListener(new AdapterView.OnItemClickListener() {
4          @Override
5          public void onItemClick(AdapterView<?> parent, View itemClicked, int position, long id) {
6              Intent intent = new Intent(ContactListActivity.this, ContactActivity.class);
7              startActivity(intent);
8          }
9        });
10   }
```

The pattern in this code should be starting to get familiar. A reference to the layout widget is grabbed. Next, a listener for the behavior you are interested in responding to is added to the widget. Finally, the app's response to the user's behavior is coded. Run the app on the emulator. Click any one of the contacts in the list and the ContactActivity should open.

That's all you need to code a simple list. Simple lists are useful for basic information display. To make a more interesting list that works exactly as you need for your app, you must code your own adapter and list item layout.

Complex Lists

The ContactListActivity needs to have more functionality than can be coded in a simple list. In this section, you will change the list to display the contact's name in a large blue font and the contact's phone number in a smaller black font below the name. The list item also displays an arrow indicating that tapping the contact leads to some other activity. In this case, the ContactActivity will open and the contact's data is displayed. The list also allows the deletion of one or more contacts. To get this functionality, you need to create data source methods, create your own list item layout, and create your own adapter.

Create the Data Source Method

The complex list displays and uses several bits of data about a contact. To function properly, it needs all the data for a contact. This requires a method to retrieve contact data for all contacts from the database. Open or switch to **ContactDataSource.java** to create a new method that returns that data as Contact objects in an ArrayList. Use the code in Listing 6.5.

Listing 6.5   getContacts Method

```
1    public ArrayList<Contact> getContacts() {
2        ArrayList<Contact> contacts = new ArrayList<Contact>();
3        try {
4            String query = "SELECT  * FROM contact";
5            Cursor cursor = database.rawQuery(query, null);
6
7            Contact newContact;
8            cursor.moveToFirst();
9            while (!cursor.isAfterLast()) {
10               newContact = new Contact();
11               newContact.setContactID(cursor.getInt(0));
12               newContact.setContactName(cursor.getString(1));
13               newContact.setStreetAddress(cursor.getString(2));
14               newContact.setCity(cursor.getString(3));
15               newContact.setState(cursor.getString(4));
16               newContact.setZipCode(cursor.getString(5));
17               newContact.setPhoneNumber(cursor.getString(6));
18               newContact.setCellNumber(cursor.getString(7));
19               newContact.setEMail(cursor.getString(8));
20               Calendar calendar = Calendar.getInstance();
21               calendar.setTimeInMillis(Long.valueOf(cursor.getString(9)));
22               newContact.setBirthday(calendar);
23               contacts.add(newContact);
24               cursor.moveToNext();
25           }
26           cursor.close();
27       }
28       catch (Exception e) {
29           contacts = new ArrayList<Contact>();
30       }
31       return contacts;
32   }
```

This code is very similar to the method used to retrieve the contact name. The primary difference is that it retrieves all the data for each contact and places that data in a Contact object before it adds it to the ArrayList (which is now parameterized to hold Contact objects). However, there are some notable differences:

- **Lines 10–19**—A new `Contact` object is instantiated for each record in the cursor. All the values in the record are added to the appropriate attribute in the new object. Care must be taken to get the proper field. You need to know the structure of your table for this, since the fields are only referenced by their location in the table. The first field in the table creation SQL statement is index 0 in the cursor, the second field is index 1, and so on.

- **Lines 20–22**—A new `Calendar` object is created to hold the contact's birthday. Dates are stored in millis, so the calendar object is set to the proper date using the `setTimeInMillis(long millis)` method. After the birthdate object is created, it is inserted into the Contact object.

Create the Layout

A complex list relies on the ListView widget, but also requires a custom list item layout. The list item layout is a layout like any other layout. However, it is organized so that it displays important information from one of the items in the underlying data source. It typically contains significantly fewer widgets than an activity's layout and is organized in a row-like manner. There are several steps you need to take to create the list item layout for this chapter.

1. Add some colors to the **color.xml** value file. Use **#ff0000** as the value for the color named **system_red**, **#00000000** as the value for the color named **system_transparent**, and **#0000ff** for the color named **system_blue**. Close the file.

2. Open the **dimens.xml** value file. You will need some new dimensions to set the TextView size. The following are the recommended sizes and names to add:

```
<dimen name="text_size_small">14sp</dimen>
<dimen name="text_size_medium">18sp</dimen>
<dimen name="text_size_large">22sp</dimen>
```

3. Create a new XML layout file by right-clicking the **layout** folder in the **Project** window and selecting **New > Layout resource file**. Give the file the name **list_item** and change the Root element to **RelativeLayout**. Make no other changes and click **OK**.

4. Return to **Design** view and drag two **TextViews** and one **Button** to anywhere on the layout.

5. Switch back to **Text** view and configure the XML as identified in Listing 6.6.

Listing 6.6   List Item Layout XML

```
1    <RelativeLayout xmlns:android="http://schemas.android.com/apk/res/android"
2        android:layout_width="match_parent"
3        android:layout_height="match_parent" >
4
5        <TextView
6            android:id="@+id/textContactName"
7            android:layout_width="wrap_content"
8            android:layout_height="wrap_content"
9            android:layout_alignParentLeft="true"
10           android:layout_alignParentStart="true"
11           android:layout_alignParentTop="true"
12           android:layout_marginTop="10dp"
13           android:layout_marginLeft="15dp"
14           android:layout_marginStart="15dp"
15           android:textColor="@color/system_blue"
16           android:text="Contact Name"
17           android:textSize="@dimen/text_size_large" />
```

(continued)

Listing 6.6 **List Item Layout XML** (*continued*)

```
18
19        <TextView
20            android:id="@+id/textPhoneNumber"
21            android:layout_width="wrap_content"
22            android:layout_height="wrap_content"
23            android:layout_alignParentLeft="true"
24            android:layout_alignParentStart="true"
25            android:layout_marginLeft="15dp"
26            android:layout_marginStart="15dp"
27            android:layout_below="@+id/textContactName"
28            android:text="Phone Number" />
29
30        <Button
31            android:id="@+id/buttonDeleteContact"
32            android:layout_width="wrap_content"
33            android:layout_height="wrap_content"
34            android:layout_alignParentTop="true"
35            android:layout_marginTop="10dp"
36            android:layout_alignParentRight="true"
37            android:layout_alignParentEnd="true"
38            android:layout_marginRight="10dp"
39            android:layout_marginEnd="10dp"
40            android:textColor="@color/system_red"
41            android:background="@color/system_transparent"
42            android:visibility="invisible"
43            android:focusable="false"
44            android:focusableInTouchMode="false"
45            android:layout_alignTop="@+id/textContactName"
46            android:layout_alignBottom="@+id/textPhoneNumber"
47            android:text="Delete" />
48
49    </RelativeLayout>
```

All the heights and widths of the widgets are set to `wrap_content` so that they adapt to the data that is displayed within them. Much of the XML should be familiar to you. However, a few items need to be explained.

- **Lines 5–17**—The contact name TextView is set to position itself at the top left of the list item. It is set to have a large text size, and the `textColor` attribute is set to the system resource for the blue color.
- **Lines 19–28**—The phone number TextView is positioned below the contact name TextView. It uses the default color so the `textColor` attribute is not used.
- **Lines 30–47**—The button widget introduces many new attributes. The first of these are the attributes that give the appearance desired. The attribute `textColor` sets the button text to the red color rather than the default. The `background` attribute sets the button's background color to white, which matches the background of the list item. This gives the appearance that there is no button, just text to click. The `visibility` attribute is used to hide the button until the user chooses to delete some contacts. The `alignTop` and `align-Bottom` attributes make sure the button fits between the top of the Contact Name and the bottom of the phone number. The `focusable` and `focusableInTouchMode` attributes are new, and both are set to false. This is important to the behavior of the list. By default, if a list has a widget that responds to some user event, that widget controls all clicks on the list item. In other words, if the user selected the list item, but not the widget, instead of opening the ContactActivity, the widget's method would execute and delete the contact. Setting these two attributes to false corrects that behavior.

Change the button's `visibility` attribute value to `visible` so you can see it in the layout, and switch to **Design** view. Your layout should look like Figure 6.4. If it does, switch back to **list_item.xml** and change the `visibility` attribute back to `invisible`. Note that you may see a border around the button.

Figure 6.4 List item layout.

Create the Custom Adapter

A custom list item is of little use without a custom adapter. Custom adapters are always created as subclasses of another type of adapter that is the closest fit for the behavior needed. Create a new class called **ContactAdapter** in the **com. example.mycontactlist** source folder. Modify the class by adding the code in Listing 6.7.

Listing 6.7   ContactAdapter Code

```
1    public class ContactAdapter extends ArrayAdapter<Contact> {
2
3        private ArrayList<Contact> items;
4        private Context adapterContext;
5
6        public ContactAdapter(Context context, ArrayList<Contact> items) {
7                super(context, R.layout.list_item, items);
8                adapterContext = context;
9                this.items = items;
10       }
11
12       @Override
13       public View getView(int position, View convertView, ViewGroup parent) {
14           View v = convertView;
15           try {
16               Contact contact = items.get(position);
17
18                if (v == null) {
19                  LayoutInflater vi = (LayoutInflater)
20                        ↪adapterContext.getSystemService(Context.LAYOUT_INFLATER_SERVICE);
21                  v = vi.inflate(R.layout.list_item, null);
22                }
23
24               TextView contactName = (TextView) v.findViewById(R.id.textContactName);
25               TextView contactNumber = (TextView) v.findViewById(R.id.textPhoneNumber);
26               Button b = (Button) v.findViewById(R.id.buttonDeleteContact);
27               contactName.setText(contact.getContactName());
28               contactNumber.setText(contact.getPhoneNumber());
29               b.setVisibility(View.INVISIBLE);
30           }
31           catch (Exception e) {
32               e.printStackTrace();
33               e.getCause();
34           }
35           return v;
36       }
37   }
```

It is important to understand the components of the custom adapter so that you can create your own version and have it work properly in the future.

- **Line 1**—The `ContactAdapter` class is declared as a subclass of `ArrayAdapter` that has been parameterized to hold only `Contact` objects.

- **Lines 3–4**—Two variables are declared for the class. The `items` variable holds the `ArrayList` of `Contact` objects that have been retrieved from the database. The `adapterContext` variable holds a reference to the context, in this case the `ContactListActivity`, where the list is being displayed.

- **Lines 6–10**—The constructor method for the `ContactAdapter` class is passed the context and the `ArrayList` of contacts. It calls its super class constructor method (`ArrayAdapter`), passing it the context, contacts, and layout file used for the items. It then assigns the contacts, and context that were passed in, to the `items` and `adapterContext` variables, respectively.

- **Line 13**—The `getView` method is the workhorse of this class. This method is called for every item in the underlying data source, up to the number of list items that can be displayed in the `ListView`. As the user scrolls through the list, this method is called to display contacts in the `ArrayList` as they are scrolled into view. The `ListView` passes the index of the item to be displayed and the `View`, which is the list item layout if it exists, or null if it does not. This is done so that list item views can be reused as they scroll off the screen, rather than re-creating a new view. This saves system resources.

- **Lines 18–22**—If there isn't an existing view to be reused, the `LayoutInflater` service is called to instantiate the `list_item` layout you previously created. You can use this to inflate multiple views and use them as needed based on the underlying data.

- **Lines 24–29**—References to the widgets on the `list_item` layout are acquired and used to set the widget to the proper settings for the contact it displays.

Code the Activity

Before you can test your custom adapter, you need to change the ContactListActivity code to retrieve contact objects rather than contact names, set the ListView to use the custom adapter, and code the `onItemClick` method to pass the selected contact's ID to ContactActivity. The first two changes require changing only one line of code each. Switch to the **ContactListActivity.java** file. Follow these steps to code the activity to retrieve contact objects rather than just a list of names:

1. Remove the two lines that declare and initialize the `names` variable (just before and after the `try` clause in the `onCreate` method).

2. Declare an `ArrayList` to hold the contacts as a class variable. Add this line of code after the class declaration but before the `onCreate` method:

```
ArrayList<Contact> contacts;
```

3. Initialize the `contacts` variable inside the `try` clause, just after the `ds.open()` statement:

```
contacts = ds.getContacts();
```

4. Code the activity to use the new adapter by changing this line

```
listView.setAdapter(new ArrayAdapter<String>(this, android.R.layout.simple_list_item_1, names));
```

to this

```
listView.setAdapter(new ContactAdapter(this, contacts));
```

5. Finally, modify the `onItemClick` method to pass the contact ID. Find the `onItemClick` method in the `initItemClick` method. Modify the code to match Listing 6.8.

Listing 6.8 Selected Item Click

```
1   @Override
2   public void onItemClick(AdapterView<?> parent, View itemClicked, int position, long id) {
3       Contact selectedContact = contacts.get(position);
4       Intent intent = new Intent(ContactListActivity.this, ContactActivity.class);
5       intent.putExtra("contactid", selectedContact.getContactID());
6       startActivity(intent);
7   }
```

All this method has to do is get the selected contact from the contacts `ArrayList`, get the required data from it, and pass the data to the `ContactActivity`.

- **Line 2**—The method declaration is functionally the same. However, change the name of the method parameters from the generic `arg` so that it is easier to understand what each parameter is.

- **Line 3**—Create a variable named `selectedContact` and retrieve the contact from the `ArrayList` using the position value. The position value is the index of the item tapped in the list, and it matches the index of the contact in the `ArrayList` that is displayed in that list item.

- **Line 5**—Place the contact ID in the `Bundle` that is passed to the `ContactActivity`. A Bundle is an object used in Android to pass data between Activities. The method `putExtra(key, value)` is used to put primitive data types in the Bundle in the `Intent` so that they are accessible by the activity receiving the intent. This set of key-value pairs of data is collectively known as "extras."

Save all your changes and test the adapter on the emulator. If you have properly coded these objects, your ContactListActivity in the emulator should look similar to Figure 6.5.

Figure 6.5 List with custom adapter running in emulator.

Completing the ContactList Activity

There are a few things left to complete the ContactList Activity. These things include modifying ContactActivity to use the contact ID passed to it, activating the Add Contact and Delete buttons, sorting the list using user preferences, and making the app open to the list rather than a blank contact.

Populating the ContactActivity Screen

You've learned how to get a list to respond to the selection of a contact in the list by opening the ContactActivity and passing a contact's ID value to it. The next step is to get the ContactActivity to use that ID to retrieve the contact's data and display it.

Open the **ContactDataSource.java** file and add a method to retrieve a specific contact based on the contact's ID. Use the code in Listing 6.9 to create the method. This code is essentially the same as the getContacts method, except that it returns a single contact rather than an ArrayList of all the contacts.

Listing 6.9   getSpecificContact Method

```
1     public Contact getSpecificContact(int contactId) {
2         Contact contact = new Contact();
3         String query = "SELECT  * FROM contact WHERE _id =" + contactId;
4         Cursor cursor = database.rawQuery(query, null);
5
6         if (cursor.moveToFirst()) {
7             contact.setContactID(cursor.getInt(0));
8             contact.setContactName(cursor.getString(1));
9             contact.setStreetAddress(cursor.getString(2));
10            contact.setCity(cursor.getString(3));
11            contact.setState(cursor.getString(4));
12            contact.setZipCode(cursor.getString(5));
13            contact.setPhoneNumber(cursor.getString(6));
14            contact.setCellNumber(cursor.getString(7));
15            contact.setEMail(cursor.getString(8));
16            Calendar calendar = Calendar.getInstance();
17            calendar.setTimeInMillis(Long.valueOf(cursor.getString(9)));
18            contact.setBirthday(calendar);
19
20            cursor.close();
21        }
22        return contact;
23    }
```

The pattern should look very familiar. In this method, there is no loop because only one contact is returned. Also, a Contact object is the return value rather than an ArrayList. There are three other notable differences:

- **Line 1**—The method has a parameter in its signature. The parameter is an integer that holds the ID of the contact to be retrieved.

- **Line 3**—The SQL query has a WHERE clause that is passed the value of the parameter so that only the contact with that ID value is returned to the cursor.

- **Lines 6–21**—The cursor moves to the first record returned. If a contact is found, the contact object is populated. If no contact was retrieved, the moveToFirst method will be false and the contact will not be populated.

Next, in order to populate the Contact Activity, you will need to add a new method to ContactActivity, called initContact, to retrieve the contact and populate the layout with the values of the retrieved contact. The onCreate method is modified to get the passed ID and call the method to retrieve and display the contact. Use the code in Listing 6.10 to create the new method.

Listing 6.10   Method to Load a Contact

```
1    private void initContact(int id) {
2
3        ContactDataSource ds = new ContactDataSource(ContactActivity.this);
4        try {
5            ds.open();
6            currentContact = ds.getSpecificContact(id);
7            ds.close();
8        }
9        catch (Exception e) {
10           Toast.makeText(this, "Load Contact Failed", Toast.LENGTH_LONG).show();
11       }
12
13       EditText editName = (EditText) findViewById(R.id.editName);
14       EditText editAddress = (EditText) findViewById(R.id.editAddress);
15       EditText editCity = (EditText) findViewById(R.id.editCity);
16       EditText editState = (EditText) findViewById(R.id.editState);
17       EditText editZipCode = (EditText) findViewById(R.id.editZipcode);
18       EditText editPhone = (EditText) findViewById(R.id.editHome);
19       EditText editCell = (EditText) findViewById(R.id.editCell);
20       EditText editEmail = (EditText) findViewById(R.id.editEMail);
21       TextView birthDay = (TextView) findViewById(R.id.textBirthday);
22
23       editName.setText(currentContact.getContactName());
24       editAddress.setText(currentContact.getStreetAddress());
25       editCity.setText(currentContact.getCity());
26       editState.setText(currentContact.getState());
27       editZipCode.setText(currentContact.getZipCode());
28       editPhone.setText(currentContact.getPhoneNumber());
29       editCell.setText(currentContact.getCellNumber());
30       editEmail.setText(currentContact.getEMail());
31       birthDay.setText(DateFormat.format("MM/dd/yyyy",
32               ➥currentContact.getBirthday().getTimeInMillis()).toString());
33   }
```

Again, this code should be familiar by now. It is similar to the methods used to set the ContactActivity for editing or viewing.

- **Lines 3–11**—The contact is retrieved and assigned to the Activity's `currentContact` variable.
- **Lines 13–21**—A reference to all the widgets in the layout is established so that the contact's data may be displayed in them.
- **Lines 23–30**—The widgets are set to display the values in the retrieved contact.
- **Lines 31–32**—The display of the contact's birthday requires a little more work. The time value retrieved for the birthday is converted to millis and then converted to a string value. The `DateFormat` object's format method uses this value to create a string representation of the date in the given format (`"MM/dd/yyyy"`).

The final step in populating the contact screen is to code ContactActivity to get the id passed to it and call the `initContact` method to display the contact. Scroll to the `onCreate` method and delete the `currentContact = new Contact()` line. Before the `setForEditing(false)` line, add the code in Listing 6.11.

Listing 6.11   onCreate Code to Get and Use Passed ID

```
1   Bundle extras = getIntent().getExtras();
2   if(extras != null) {
3       initContact(extras.getInt("contactid"));
4   }
5   else {
6       currentContact = new Contact();
7   }
```

This code corresponds to the code in `onItemClick` in ContactListActivity that put the selected contact ID as an extra into the bundle. Here we check the `intent` for extras. If one is found, the code gets the contact ID, retrieves the contact from the database, and displays the data in the layout. If there is no extra, it assigns a new contact object to `currentContact`, effectively setting the `currentContact` ID to −1. This takes care of coding for the click of the Add Contact button in the ContactListActivity (see the "Coding the Add Button" section that follows). The Add Contact button does not pass an extra to the ContactActivity, so the activity is ready to add a new contact's data.

Run your app. When you tap a name in the contact list, the ContactActivity should open with all the contact's data displayed. Congratulations! You have successfully learned to get data from an item selected in a list and pass that data to another activity.

The ContactListActivity is almost complete. You've got four tasks left:

1.   Code the Toolbar with the Delete and Add Contact buttons.
2.   Modify the list to sort the data according to user preferences.
3.   Modify the app to open the list activity as the first activity.
4.   Modify the `onCreate` method of list activity to check if there are any contacts saved. If there are no contacts, it will open the ContactActivity instead of the list.

First, add the toolbar and buttons to the **activity_contact_list.xml**. The code to implement the buttons is addressed later in this section. The two buttons are located at the top of the layout in a toolbar, just like in the ContactActivity. In fact, the easiest way to implement the buttons is to copy the toolbar XML and paste it into the **activity_contact_list** layout file. Whether you copy the XML or type it directly, it should look like Listing 6.12 when completed.

Listing 6.12   Toolbar XML for ContactListActivity

```
1    <RelativeLayout
2        android:id="@+id/toolbar"
3        android:layout_width="match_parent"
4        android:layout_height="wrap_content"
5        android:layout_alignParentTop="true"
6        android:layout_alignParentLeft="true"
7        android:layout_alignParentStart="true"
8        android:background="@color/toolbar_background" >
9
10       <Button
11           android:id="@+id/buttonDelete"
12           android:layout_width="wrap_content"
13           android:layout_height="wrap_content"
14           android:layout_alignParentLeft="true"
15           android:layout_alignParentStart="true"
16           android:layout_centerVertical="true"
17           android:layout_marginLeft="20dp"
```

(continued)

Listing 6.12   Toolbar XML for ContactListActivity (*continued*)

```
18                  android:layout_marginStart="20dp"
19                  android:text="Delete" />
20
21          <Button
22                  android:id="@+id/buttonAdd"
23                  android:layout_width="wrap_content"
24                  android:layout_height="wrap_content"
25                  android:layout_alignParentRight="true"
26                  android:layout_alignParentEnd="true"
27                  android:layout_centerVertical="true"
28                  android:layout_marginRight="20dp"
29                  android:layout_marginEnd="20dp"
30                  android:text="Add Contact" />
31      </RelativeLayout>
```

If you copied the XML from the ContactActivity, make sure you change the `ToggleButton` to a `Button`. The XML for the list widget also needs to be modified. In the `ListView`'s attributes, delete the line that aligns the `ListView` with the top of the parent, and add the following line in its place:

```
android:layout_below="@+id/toolbar"
```

This line positions the `ListView` below the toolbar. When complete, switch to **Design** view and verify that the layout looks like that in Figure 6.6.

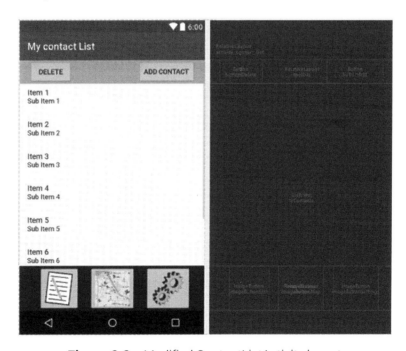

Figure 6.6   Modified ContactListActivity layout.

Coding the Add Button

Coding the Add button is just reusing code that you used before (Listing 6.13). Add this method to **ContactListActivity.java** to have the Add Contact button open the Contact Activity.

Listing 6.13   initAddContactButton() Method

```
1   private void initAddContactButton() {
2       Button newContact = (Button) findViewById(R.id.buttonAdd);
3       newContact.setOnClickListener(new View.OnClickListener() {
4           public void onClick(View v) {
5               Intent intent = new Intent(ContactListActivity.this, ContactActivity.class);
6               startActivity(intent);
7           }
8       });
9   }
```

Remember to call the `initAddContactButton()` method in the `onCreate` method.

Add Delete Functionality

The final job associated with making the list work properly is to code the capability to delete a contact from the list (and the database). This functionality is primarily implemented in the custom adapter. However, because you don't want the user to accidently delete a contact, the app provides a button to turn the delete functionality on and off. Three tasks need to be completed to implement the delete function:

1. Code a method to delete a contact from the database in ContactDataSource.
2. Code the custom adapter to delete a contact from the list and database.
3. Code the ContactListActivity to use the delete function of the adapter.

After you have the layout correct, open **ContactDataSource.java** to add a method to delete a contact. This method will be passed the ID number of the contact to delete. Refer to Listing 6.14 to code the method.

Listing 6.14   deleteContact Method

```
1   public boolean deleteContact(int contactId) {
2       boolean didDelete = false;
3       try {
4           didDelete = database.delete("contact", "_id=" + contactId, null) > 0;
5       }
6       catch (Exception e) {
7           //Do nothing -return value already set to false
8       }
9       return didDelete;
10  }
```

The `deleteContact` method is easy to understand. The method is passed the ID as the parameter contacted. A return value to indicate success or failure is set up, and the database's delete method is called. There are three parameters for the delete method. The first is the name of the table to delete from. The second is the `WHERE` clause to use to determine which records to delete. The final parameter is a string array of criteria for deletion. Only one of the last two parameters is needed. The other can be null.

Now turn your attention to the custom adapter (**ContactAdapter.java**) you created earlier. You need to add three methods to this class. The first method is used to display the Delete button in the **list_item** layout for a selected list item, and it sets a listener for the button click event. You will need to import the `OnClickListener`. It has two options. Choose **OnClickListener** in **View**. The method executed when the user clicks the Delete button removes the contact from the `ArrayList`, calls a method to hide the Delete button, and calls a method to delete the contact from the database. The second method deletes the contact from the database by calling `ContactDataSource`, and the third method hides the Delete button. The code for these methods is in Listing 6.15.

Listing 6.15 Code to Delete from List

```
1   public void showDelete(final int position, final View convertView,
2                         final Context context, final Contact contact) {
3       View v = convertView;
4       final Button b = (Button) v.findViewById(R.id.buttonDeleteContact);
5       if (b.getVisibility() == View.INVISIBLE) {
6           b.setVisibility(View.VISIBLE);
7           b.setOnClickListener(new OnClickListener() {
8               @Override
9               public void onClick(View v) {
10                  hideDelete(position, convertView, context);
11                  items.remove(contact);
12                  deleteOption(contact.getContactID(), context);
13              }
14          });
15      }
16      else {
17          hideDelete(position, convertView, context);
18      }
19  }
20
21  private void deleteOption(int contactToDelete, Context context) {
22      ContactDataSource db = new ContactDataSource(context);
23      try {
24          db.open();
25          db.deleteContact(contactToDelete);
26          db.close();
27      }
28      catch (Exception e) {
29          Toast.makeText(adapterContext, "Delete Contact Failed", Toast.LENGTH_LONG).show();
30      }
31      this.notifyDataSetChanged();
32  }
33
34  public void hideDelete(int position, View convertView, Context context) {View v = convertView;
35      final Button b = (Button) v.findViewById(R.id.buttonDeleteContact);
36      b.setVisibility(View.INVISIBLE);
37      b.setOnClickListener(null);
38  }
```

The user enables deleting by tapping the Delete button in the toolbar. This tells the list to respond to a list item selection by showing the Delete button for that list item and enabling the button's capability to respond to a click event. If the user taps a list item that is showing the Delete button but not on the button itself, the button is hidden. If the user taps the Delete button itself, the button's response to a tap event is executed, and the contact is deleted from the database and the list. This functions as essentially a two-phase commit for deleting. The user first has to choose a contact to delete and then choose to delete it. Because of this, there is no need for a warning message on the delete.

- **Lines 1–2**—The showDelete method is one of two public methods needed for the delete functionality of the custom adapter. It is called by the ContactListActivity when the user selects a list item with deleting enabled. It is passed the position of the selection in the list, the list item layout with the contact's data in it, the context where the method call originated, and the Contact object associated with the selected list item.

- **Lines 5–18**—The showDelete method checks if the Delete button is visible on the list item layout passed to it. If it is, it calls the hideDelete method. If it is not, it displays the button and enables the button click event. The click event uses the Contact object passed to the showDelete method to remove the contact from the ArrayList and remove it from the database.

- **Lines 21–32**—The `deleteOption` method is standard code for calling a method to access the database. The only new item in this method is `notifyDataSetChanged()`. This method tells the adapter that the underlying data source has changed, so that the list display will be changed to reflect the deletion.

- **Lines 34–38**—The `hideDelete` method changes the button from visible to invisible and disables the button's `onClick` event.

The final step in coding the delete functionality is to modify **ContactListActivity.java**. Open this file and insert a new method to initiate the Delete button using the code in Listing 6.16. The `adapter` variable added below will produce a syntax error until you enter the code in Listing 6.17.

Listing 6.16   initDeleteButton() Code

```
1     private void initDeleteButton() {
2         final Button deleteButton = (Button) findViewById(R.id.buttonDelete);
3         deleteButton.setOnClickListener(new OnClickListener() {
4             public void onClick(View v) {
5                 if (isDeleting) {
6                     deleteButton.setText("Delete");
7                     isDeleting = false;
8                     adapter.notifyDataSetChanged();
9                 }
10                else {
11                    deleteButton.setText("Done Deleting");
12                    isDeleting = true;
13                }
14            }
15        });
16    }
```

The code is relatively simple. It sets an `onClickListener` for the button, and when the button is clicked, it checks if the user has deleting enabled. If it is enabled, it is disabled by setting the `isDeleting` variable to false and changing the button display text to Delete. If it is not enabled, the code enables deleting by setting the `isDeleting` variable to true and changing the text of the button to Done Deleting.

This requires adding the `isDeleting` variable. Just after the `ContactListActivity` class declaration, add the line

```
boolean isDeleting = false;
```

The one new bit of code in this method is at Line 8. This code tells the adapter to update itself. This is used to set the list back to the *not deleting* mode. If the user has selected a list item and the Delete button is visible, and the user then clicks Done Deleting, this code removes the display of those buttons. Basically, the code tells the activity to update the UI when the adapter receives the message `notifyDataSetChanged()`. Be sure to call the `initDeleteButton()` method from the `onCreate` method. The `adapter` variable will be red. We will fix this after the next modification of the code.

The next step is to modify the `onItemClick` method (declared in the `initItemClick` method) to handle deleting. Modify this method to match Listing 6.17.

Listing 6.17 Modified onItemClick Method

```
1    @Override
2    public void onItemClick(AdapterView<?> parent, View itemClicked, int position, long id) {
3        Contact selectedContact = contacts.get(position);
4        if (isDeleting) {
5            adapter.showDelete(position, itemClicked, ContactListActivity.this, selectedContact);
6        }
7        else {
8            Intent intent = new Intent(ContactListActivity.this, ContactActivity.class);
9            intent.putExtra("contactid", selectedContact.getContactID());
10           startActivity(intent);
11       }
12   }
```

Just as in the `initDeleteButton` method, a variable is used that is not declared. Add the declaration to hold the adapter after the declaration of the `isDeleting` variable. Use this code:

```
ContactAdapter adapter;
```

You will also have to assign the `ContactAdapter` to this variable. In the `onCreate` method, delete this line:

```
listView.setAdapter(new ContactAdapter(this, contacts));
```

Add this code in its place:

```
adapter = new ContactAdapter(this, contacts);
listView.setAdapter(adapter);
```

Test your app. If you have properly entered this code, when you tap the Delete button and then tap one of the items in the list, you will see something similar to Figure 6.7. If you then tap the Delete button, the contact should be deleted from the list.

Android versus iOS: Creating Complex Lists

Creating a list like the one shown in this chapter is much simpler in iOS because a lot of the functionality is available in ready-made controls. In iOS, the list is called a table, and the default delete behavior is as it's described here, where the user taps a button to initiate delete mode and then is able to delete rows until the delete mode is cancelled.

Although the iOS controls provide a lot of functionality and can be customized, you do have less freedom than what is available in Android.

Figure 6.7 Deleting a contact.

You've completed the development of a custom list! The code is relatively involved, but the pattern is the basis for any future complex lists you might want to create. Complex lists are really not that difficult. Through the use of a custom adapter and layout, you can create list items with a significant amount of diverse information, including images if desired. To add an image, you would add an **ImageView** widget to the **list_item** XML. Use the `layout_alignTop` and `layout_alignBottom` attributes to position with the list item like you did with the Delete button. Loading an image will be covered in Chapter 8, "Access to Hardware and Sensors in Android."

Sort the Contacts List

The next task is to code the ContactListActivity to sort the contact list according to the preferences set by the user. The first step is to modify the `getContacts` method in ContactDataSource. The method needs to be modified to accept the sort field and sort order as parameters and use these parameters in the SQL to perform the actual sort. Switch to **ContactDataSource.java** and locate the `getContacts` method. Change the method signature from

```
public ArrayList<Contact> getContacts() {
```

to

```
public ArrayList<Contact> getContacts(String sortField, String sortOrder) {
```

Next, change the SQL statement from

```
String query = "SELECT * FROM contact";
```

to

```
String query = "SELECT * FROM contact ORDER BY " + sortField + " " + sortOrder;
```

The next step is to modify the ContactListActivity to retrieve the user sorting preferences and pass them to this modified method. Switch to **ContactListActivity.java**. There will be an error in the code because the method `get-Contacts()` no longer exists. To fix the error, you must first retrieve the stored user preferences. Enter the following two lines before the line that creates a new `ContactDataSource` object in the `onCreate` method:

```
String sortBy = getSharedPreferences("MyContactListPreferences",
    Context.MODE_PRIVATE).getString("sortfield", "contactname");
String sortOrder = getSharedPreferences("MyContactListPreferences",
    Context.MODE_PRIVATE).getString("sortorder", "ASC");
```

Now modify the call to the `getContacts` method to use these values:

```
contacts = ds.getContacts(sortBy, sortOrder);
```

Run the app. Change the sort preferences using the Settings screen. You should see the order of the contacts on the list change as you change your preferences. Try changing the sort settings and returning to the list using the list ImageButton. Now try changing the sort order and returning to the ContactListActivity using the Back button. You should notice that the list is not re-sorted when you use the Back button, but it is when you use the ImageButton. When you use the ImageButton, the flag you set (`FLAG_ACTIVITY_CLEAR_TOP`) causes the old ContactActivityL-ist activity to be destroyed, and a new one is created so the `onCreate` method is executed. When you use the Back button, the Activity still exists, so the `onCreate` method is not executed and the sort order is thus never changed.

The solution to this is to place the code that populates the list in the `onResume()` method. As you saw in Chapter 2, "App Design Issues and Considerations," the `onResume` method is executed just before the `Activity` becomes visible. This method will be executed every time the user navigates to the activity. This is an example of where you need to move some of the code from the `onCreate` method to the `onResume()` method to make sure it is executed whenever the activity becomes visible. Use the following steps:

1. After the `onCreate` method, create the `onResume` method.
2. Add a call to `super.onResume()`.
3. Cut the code from the `onCreate` method that gets the preferences, retrieves the contacts, and sets up the list, and paste it into the `onResume` method.

When complete, your code should look like Listing 6.18.

Listing 6.18   The onResume Method

```
1    @Override
2    public void onResume() {
3        super.onResume();
4        String sortBy = getSharedPreferences("MyContactListPreferences",
5            ➥Context.MODE_PRIVATE).getString("sortfield", "contactname");
6        String sortOrder = getSharedPreferences("MyContactListPreferences",
7            ➥Context.MODE_PRIVATE).getString("sortorder", "ASC");
8        ContactDataSource ds = new ContactDataSource(this);
9        try {
10            ds.open();
11            contacts = ds.getContacts(sortBy, sortOrder);
12            ds.close();
13            adapter = new ContactAdapter(this, contacts);
14            ListView listView = (ListView) findViewById(R.id.lvContacts);
15            listView.setAdapter(adapter);
16        }
17        catch (Exception e) {
18            Toast.makeText(this, "Error retrieving contacts", Toast.LENGTH_LONG).show();
19        }
20    }
```

Most of the code has been explained as you wrote it. The one new thing is the creation of the `onResume` method itself. The method overrides the `onResume` method built in to the Activity so the first line in the method calls that method, and so that all the things that need to happen when activity resumes still happen. Then your code is executed. The code you pasted into the `onResume` method should no longer be in the `onCreate` method.

Run the app again to test that sorting now works as it should when you use the back button from the Settings screen.

Set ContactListActivity as the Default Activity

The third task is to modify the AndroidManifest.xml file to open the ContactListActivity instead of the ContactAc-tivity as the initial app activity. Open **AndroidManifest.xml** by double-clicking it in the Package Explorer. Switch to the **Text** view if it is not already open. Find the code that matches Listing 6.19, and switch the name and label attributes so that the activity with the intent filter is ContactListActivity and its label, and the other activity has the name ContactActivity and its label. To do this, delete the strikeout lines (these are the original lines) in Listing 6.19 and add the new lines. Note that the manifest will also include the ContactMapActivity and the ContactSettingsActivity, so be sure to select the correct activity.

Listing 6.19   Changing the Launch Activity

```
1    <activity
2        android:name=".ContactActivity >
3        android:name=".ContactListActivity" >
4        <intent-filter>
5            <action android:name="android.intent.action.MAIN" />
6            <category android:name="android.intent.category.LAUNCHER" />
7        </intent-filter>
8    </activity>
9    <activity
10       android:name=".ContactListActivity">
11       android:name=".ContactActivity">
12   </activity>
```

Test the app. If the app does not start with the ContactListActivity, try cleaning the project to reload the manifest file. Select **Build > Clean Project**. Verify that the **MyContactList** project is selected or **Clean All Projects** is selected, and click **OK**. Run the app again. If the list still does not show as the first activity, you will have to modify your debug configuration. Select **Run > Debug Configurations**. In the window that opens, select your debug configuration if it is not already selected, and then select **Launch Default Activity**. Run the app again.

Set ContactActivity as Default Activity with no Contacts in Database

The final task is to modify the onResume method of the ContactListActivity to check if there are any contacts in the database. If there are none, the app should open the ContactActivity. Refer to Listing 6.20 to make these changes in approximately the middle of the onResume method.

Listing 6.20   Modify the onResume Method to Check for Contacts

```
1    try {
2        ds.open();
3        contacts = ds.getContacts(sortBy, sortOrder);
4        ds.close();
5        if (contacts.size() > 0) {
6            ListView listView = (ListView) findViewById(R.id.lvContacts);
7            adapter = new ContactAdapter(this, contacts);
8            listView.setAdapter(adapter);
9        } else {
10           Intent intent = new Intent(ContactListActivity.this, ContactActivity.class);
11           startActivity(intent);
12       }
13   } catch (Exception e) {
14       Toast.makeText(this, "Error retrieving contacts", Toast.LENGTH_LONG).show();
15   }
```

You are really just adding a few lines of code around an existing body of code. Add the if statement before the line that sets the adapter variable to check if there are any contacts retrieved from the database (Line 6). Close the if statement body after the setting of the onItemClickListener body of code (Line 9). Then add the else block of code to open the ContactActivity if there are no contacts.

Test the app. Delete all the contacts. Rerun the app to see if it opens to the ContactActivity. If it does, you have successfully completed this chapter. Congratulations!

Summary

Lists are an important part of almost every app. Lists can be very simple displays of relatively static data, or they can be quite complex, displaying a variety of data and having a diverse set of behaviors. Simple lists can be implemented using components provided with the Android SDK. More complex lists require the development of custom list layouts and adapters.

The ContactListActivity is finished! The activity not only displays a list of contacts, but also sorts that list according to user preferences and passes data to the ContactActivity to display a selected contact.

Exercises

1. Add the contact's cell phone number to the complex list. The list should display the contact name on the first line and *Home: the number Cell:the number* on the second line.

2. Find a small star shaped graphic and add it to the layout if the contact is a "Best Friend Forever."

3. Add another line to the list so that the list displays:

   Contact Name

   Street Address

   City, State, Zip,

   Phone number

4. Modify the custom adapter to alternately display the contact name in red and blue. For example, the first name in the list will be red, the second will be blue, the third is red, and so on.

CHAPTER 7

Maps and Location in Android

Smartphones and tablets are mobile computing devices. Both parts of that description (mobile and computing) are why location and maps are important components of many apps. Useful computation can be performed based on the device location. That location can change much faster than the location of a traditional computing device. This enables the app to very quickly change its behavior as it moves to different locations. Knowing how to capture and display location information can help you build powerful apps. This chapter describes how to take advantage of location information within your app. Location sensors can be accessed and used directly through the Android SDK. However, maps require more work. This chapter also teaches you how to set up your Android Studio environment to work with maps.

Location Sensors, Maps, and Fragments

This section begins with an overview of sensors, maps, and fragments. Sensors are hardware built in to the mobile device to allow an app to capture environmental data. Maps are used to display data that can be enhanced by a visual representation of its location. Finally, fragments are a newer approach to coding Android Activities. Fragments are a part of an Activity that represent a distinct behavior or task.

Location Sensors

Android devices typically have two location sensors. One sensor (network sensor) is based on the cell towers and/or the Wi-Fi access points your device is connected to. This sensor provides the approximate location of the device. The other sensor is based on a built-in global position system (GPS) receiver. This sensor can provide position information accurate to within a few meters, depending on conditions. However, the GPS sensor is much slower in acquiring its position information than the network sensor, and doesn't work well indoors. In addition, not all devices have a GPS sensor.

Location information is accessed within an app through the use of the **LocationManager** object. A Location-Manager is not directly instantiated. It exists as an Android system service, and is accessed through the method `get-SystemService`. The LocationManager object can request updates from either or both sensors. To get the updates, an app has to instantiate a **LocationListener**, which implements the method `onLocationChanged`. Whenever the sensor reports a location change, that change is captured by the LocationListener, which is passed a **Location** object, and the `onLocationChanged` method is executed. A Location object contains information on the new location, including GPS coordinates and altitude, which sensor provided the location, a measure of the accuracy of the coordinate estimate (usually in meters), as well as other information. The `onLocationChanged` method uses this object to perform operations based on the code the developer provided in the method. To begin receiving location information from the sensors, the LocationManager requests the updates from a specific provider and tells it what LocationListener to use to handle the updates. When the LocationManager requests updates from the GPS, the GPS is activated. However, the GPS must also be enabled by the user to be activated. If it has not been enabled, the code cannot turn it on. As a developer, you should test whether the GPS is enabled and inform the user if it is not.

Maps

Maps are implemented using the **GoogleMap** object in the source code file and a **MapFragment** in the layout file. These objects are not a part of the standard Android SDK but rather the **Google Play Services SDK**. This SDK must be installed on your development machine to implement maps in your app. Using Google Maps requires an API key, which associates your app with an attempt to access the **GoogleMap API**. This is how you, and Google, can track how often your users access the map portion of your app. The API key is free—you just have to sign up for it. Maps are implemented as a MapFragment widget in a layout. The Activity that implements the code to provide the map's behavior must be a FragmentActivity.

Fragments

Fragments were discussed in Chapter 4, "Android Navigation and Interface Design." The **FragmentActivity** is a subclass of the Activity class. An Activity that needs to implement a map must extend the FragmentActivity class rather than the Activity class. This is required because maps are encapsulated in a **MapFragment**. This allows a map to be a part of a layout rather than the only thing in a layout.

Finding Your Location

Finding a location can be performed in two ways. The first involves using the device network and/or GPS sensors to locate the device in real time. The second uses a known location (e.g., an address) and looks up the GPS coordinates via the Internet. Both approaches will be demonstrated. When working with maps, you can use the map's `getMyLocation()` method to get the device's current GPS coordinates. If you need to get the location without using a map, there is more work involved. In this section, you build and test several versions of ContactMapActivity to learn different approaches to getting location before building the final one used for the app.

Geocoding: Get Coordinates from an Address

In this first approach to getting location, the ContactMapActivity will take an entered address and look up and display the GPS coordinates of the address. This process is called *geocoding*. The first step is to create the layout in **activity_contact_map.xml**. For now, this layout will not use a map object. Refer to Figure 7.1 to code this layout. The exact layout is up to you—you've done all this before. However, to match to the code, use the following IDs for the widgets:

Get Coordinates button: `@+id/buttonGetLocation`

Latitude output TextView: `@+id/textLatitude`

Longitude output TextView: `@+id/textLongitude`

Accuracy output TextView: `@+id/textAccuracy`

Obviously, the easiest way to code the address portion of the layout is to copy the relevant XML from **activity_contact.xml**. Some minor changes need to be made to get the Address TextView to appear at the top left of the layout. The code for this section uses the same widget IDs for the address EditTexts as was used in activity_contact.xml. Note that if you haven't already, you should add the navigation buttons to the layout and code their operation in the ContactMapActivity (remember to disable the map button).

Figure 7.1 Initial layout for getting location.

After the layout has been created, open the ContactMapActivity.java file to write the code that provides the behavior for the Get Location button. The button will respond to a user tap by retrieving the data entered into the EditTexts and format them into the form required by address lookup service. It will then be sent to the service, and the resulting location will be displayed onscreen. Refer to Listing 7.1 to write this code. You will need to import multiple objects. The address will have several options. Select **Android.Location**.

Listing 7.1 Code to Look Up Address Coordinates

```
1    private void initGetLocationButton() {
2        Button locationButton = (Button) findViewById(R.id.buttonGetLocation);
3        locationButton.setOnClickListener(new View.OnClickListener() {
4
5            @Override
6            public void onClick(View v) {
7                EditText editAddress = (EditText) findViewById(R.id.editAddress);
8                EditText editCity = (EditText) findViewById(R.id.editCity);
9                EditText editState = (EditText) findViewById(R.id.editState);
10               EditText editZipCode = (EditText) findViewById(R.id.editZipcode);
11
12               String address = editAddress.getText().toString() + ", " +
13                                editCity.getText().toString() + ", " +
14                                editState.getText().toString() + ", " +
15                                editZipCode.getText().toString();
16
17               List<Address> addresses = null;
18               Geocoder geo = new Geocoder(ContactMapActivity.this);
19               try {
20                   addresses = geo.getFromLocationName(address, 1);
21               }
22               catch (IOException e) {
23                   e.printStackTrace();
24               }
25
26               TextView txtLatitude = (TextView) findViewById(R.id.textLatitude);
27               TextView txtLongitude = (TextView) findViewById(R.id.textLongitude);
28
29               txtLatitude.setText(String.valueOf(addresses.get(0).getLatitude()));
30               txtLongitude.setText(String.valueOf(addresses.get(0).getLongitude()));
31           }
32       });
33   }
```

Remember to code the call to the initialization method in the onCreate method. This code introduces a few new items.

- **Lines 12–15**—The proper format for a call to the geocoding service is the street address with the elements of the address separated by commas.
- **Line 17**—A List object variable parameterized to hold an Address object is declared. The geocoding service will return the result with this type of object.
- **Line 18**—A Geocoder variable is declared and assigned a new Geocoder object. The Geocoder object has all the information required to contact the host service (Google) via the Internet.
- **Lines 19–24**—The method getFromLocationName method is passed the address to look up as a parameter. The parameter "1" tells the service that you want one response. If you are unable to provide a specific address, you can request more responses (e.g., multiple addresses on the same street). If the service cannot find the exact location, it will return several locations with the best guess as the first entry. Because this method calls a service outside your app, it requires a try and catch to protect the app from errors produced by the service.

- **Lines 26–30**—The latitude and longitude of the first address in the returned list are displayed in the appropriate `TextView` widgets.

Switch the value in the dropdown list next to the **Run** button in the Android Studio Toolbar to **app**, and click the Run button (green triangle) to test your code on the emulator. Click the Maps button in the navigation bar to get to the ContactMapsActivity, enter an address, and click the Get Location button. The GPS coordinates should be displayed in the TextViews. Try entering a valid and an invalid address to see what happens. Using geocoding is a good way to find GPS coordinates of address information available to the app. However, it is not very useful in locating the device in real time. For that, you need to use the sensors.

Get Coordinates from the GPS Sensor

The network sensor uses cell towers and Wi-Fi access points to determine the device's location. It is not as accurate as the GPS sensor, but it is faster. Additionally, it is available on all devices, whereas a GPS sensor is not. Accessing location using the GPS sensor is discussed first. It might make more sense to begin the discussion of getting location from sensors with the network sensor, since it is less accurate. However, the network sensor cannot be tested on the emulator, whereas the GPS sensor can. In addition, the code required to use both sensors is almost identical, so learning one versus the other first does not really matter. Regardless of which is done first, the first step in using these sensors is to add the permissions required to access the sensors.

These permissions are used to alert the user during installation or upgrade what the app is allowed to access on the device. The user permits that app to use those devices, services, or data by choosing to install the app after reviewing the permissions. Permissions are set in the Android manifest file. If a permission is required by what you are trying to do, but is not in the manifest, the app will crash. Android SDK version 23 (Android 6.0 Marshmallow) changed the way permissions work. We will address that later. However, for your app to run on both older and new versions of the Android OS, you must code for both. The following is for older versions.

Open the **AndroidManifest.xml** file and enter the permissions in Listing 7.2. Put these permissions after the `<manifest` tag and before the `<application` tag.

Listing 7.2   Required Map Permissions

```
1    <uses-permission android:name="android.permission.ACCESS_COARSE_LOCATION" />
2    <uses-permission android:name="android.permission.ACCESS_FINE_LOCATION" />
```

To use the GPS sensor, you replace the geocoding code in the Get Location button with GPS listener code. You also add a method to turn off the location sensing when the app enters the Paused life cycle state. First, go to **ContactMapActivity.java** and add the following variable declarations just after the class declaration:

```
LocationManager locationManager;
LocationListener gpsListener;
```

You will have to import these classes. Use the **android.location** option, not the **com.google.android.gms** one. Next, go to the `initGetLocationButton` method and replace all the code in the `onClick` method with the code in Listing 7.3. You will also have to import some objects after entering the code.

Listing 7.3 Code to Get Coordinates with the GPS Sensor

```
1    try {
2        locationManager = (LocationManager)getBaseContext().
3                            ↪getSystemService(Context.LOCATION_SERVICE);
4        gpsListener = new LocationListener() {
5            public void onLocationChanged(Location location) {
6                TextView txtLatitude = (TextView) findViewById(R.id.textLatitude);
7                TextView txtLongitude = (TextView) findViewById(R.id.textLongitude);
8                TextView txtAccuracy = (TextView) findViewById(R.id.textAccuracy);
9                txtLatitude.setText(String.valueOf(location.getLatitude()));
10               txtLongitude.setText(String.valueOf(location.getLongitude()));
11               txtAccuracy.setText(String.valueOf(location.getAccuracy()));
12           }
13
14           public void onStatusChanged(String provider, int status, Bundle extras) {}
15           public void onProviderEnabled(String provider) {}
16           public void onProviderDisabled(String provider) {}
17       };
18
19       locationManager.requestLocationUpdates(
20           ↪LocationManager.GPS_PROVIDER,0, 0, gpsListener);
21   }
22   catch (Exception e) {
23       Toast.makeText(getBaseContext(), "Error, Location not available",
24                       ↪Toast.LENGTH_LONG).show();
25   }
```

When the user presses the button, the button gets a reference to the system's location manager and instantiates a location listener to get the GPS coordinates and accuracy from a location object each time the sensor detects a location change. Note that location can change even if the device does not move. The sensor will provide a location as soon as it can and then as it zeroes in on the exact location. Every time accuracy gets better, or worse, new GPS coordinates are produced, and this is reported as a location change.

- **Lines 2–3**—A reference to the `LocationManager` object is assigned to the `locationManager` variable. The `getSystemService` method is sent to the activity's context with a parameter that tells the context that you want the location service manager. In Android, the context of any code is the parent object or method it is placed in. The current context of the code entered in this listing is an `onClickListener`. The method `getBaseContext` is used to get the root context—in this case, an `Activity`—because an `Activity` context is required to get the system service.

- **Lines 4–12**—A new `LocationListener` is instantiated and assigned to the `gpsListener` variable. A `LocationListener` requires the implementation of four methods. However, only the `onLocation-Changed` method is needed for the purpose of reporting location. When a location change is detected, it is reported to this method as a location object. The text of the `TextViews` is set by getting the appropriate value from the location object. Note the use of the `String.valueOf` method to convert these values into strings. They are reported as double or float data types, which are not compatible with the `setText` method of the `TextView`.

- **Lines 14–16**—These three methods are required by the `LocationListener` in addition to the `onLoca-tionChanged` method. They are generally used to alert the app that the sensor status has changed. You can use these methods to alert the user to a change in the app's behavior or ability to perform a task. In this simple example, you can leave them blank as shown here.

- **Lines 19–20**—The `LocationManager` is sent the message `requestLocationUpdates` to begin listening for location changes. The parameters in this message tell the `LocationManager` to listen to the GPS sensor with no minimum time between updates and no minimum distance between locations, and to report those changes to the `LocationListener` assigned to the `gpsListener` variable. The minimum time and distance parameters are set to zero for demonstration purposes. These values should be set based on how much you expect the device to move during the app's use. Setting values higher than zero can help conserve the battery. This is especially true of the time value. The minimum time is set in milliseconds (2*60*1000 = 120000, or 2 minutes). Minimum distance is set in meters.

- **Lines 22–25**—A `Toast` is displayed if there is an error. A `Toast` is an object that displays a short message for a limited period of time on the user's display. The Toast method, `makeText`, requires a context, a message, and a period of time to display the message (`LENGTH_SHORT` and `LENGTH_LONG` are the only options). The show method displays the message.

The line `locationManager.requestLocationUpdates` will be underlined in red if the target SDK for your project is greater than 22. This is due to the new permissions model mentioned earlier. We will correct this shortly.

After the changes to the `initGetLocationButton` have been made, you need to add a method to stop the sensors if the Activity's life cycle state changes. To do this, you need to override the Activity's `onPause` method. Create a new method using the code in Listing 7.4 to do this.

Listing 7.4   onPause Method

```
1      @Override
2      public void onPause() {
3          super.onPause();
4          try {
5              locationManager.removeUpdates(gpsListener);
6          }
7          catch (Exception e) {
8              e.printStackTrace();
9          }
10     }
```

The code is straightforward. The `LocationManager` object is sent the message `removeUpdates` to end listening to the `gpsListener`. This code is within a `try and catch` block, because it is possible that the activity could pause before the user presses the Get Location button. In that case, neither the `locationManager` nor the `gpsListener` variables would have values, and the code would crash the app. You don't want this to happen. The first line of code calls the overridden method to execute the standard `onPause` routine for the activity. The `locationManager.removeUpdates` line may be underlined in red for the same reason noted previously. We will now address that issue.

The New Android Permissions Model

The old Android permissions model (prior to SDK 23) required the user to approve all permissions requested by an app prior to installation. It was an all or none prospect. If the user didn't approve all, the app was not installed. Likewise, if the user approved the permissions, the app had access to everything on the device it requested. The new model allows the user to grant permission when the app needs it. This way, the user can use the features of the app they want and still restrict what the app can do with their device in areas the user is not comfortable.

The new permissions model distinguishes between what are called normal versus dangerous permissions. Normal permissions no longer need to be declared. They are granted automatically. For example, if the app needs to access the Internet, this is termed "Normal," and the developer does not have to request the permission on devices running SDK 23 or later. However, accessing device location and device storage are termed "Dangerous," and the developer has to code the app to request the required permission when they want to access device location or storage. Once the user grants permission during app execution, that permission is granted until the user specifically rejects it by accessing the phone's settings.

To modify the code to work with the new model requires some setup. The first step is to add another dependency. To do this, complete the following steps:

1. Choose **File > Project Structure**. Note: If it is grayed out, select **app** or **MyContactList** in the Project window and try again.

2. The **Project Structure** window will open (Figure 7.2). In the window to the left, select **app** (or MyContact-List) under modules and then click on the **Dependencies** tab.

3. Click the green plus (+) sign on the top right (on Mac, select the plus below the main area). Select **Library** dependency from the pop-up window. Scroll through the list until you find **play-services (com.android. support:design:25.0.0)**. Note: The version number at the end will vary, depending on which version of Play Services is available at the time you download.

4. Select **play-services** and click **OK**. Click **OK** to close the Project Structure window. Android Studio will show a message that **Gradle Sync** started at the bottom of Android Studio. This is integrating the code into your project. When the sync is complete, you are ready to proceed.

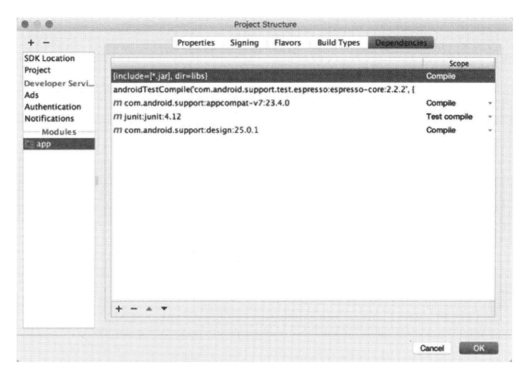

Figure 7.2   Project Structure window.

Next, create a new private method in ContactMapActivity.java with this code:

```
private void startLocationUpdates() {

    }
```

Do this before the closing curly brace of the class. Move all the code entered into the button click event (Listing 7.3) into the new method. You can cut and paste because we don't need it there anymore. Next, add the code in Listing 7.5 at the beginning of the new method.

Listing 7.5   Additional Code for startLocationUpdate

```
1   if ( Build.VERSION.SDK_INT >= 23 && v
2        ↪ ContextCompat.checkSelfPermission(getBaseContext(),
3        ↪ android.Manifest.permission.ACCESS_FINE_LOCATION) !=
4        ↪ PackageManager.PERMISSION_GRANTED &&
5        ↪ ContextCompat.checkSelfPermission( getBaseContext(),
6        ↪ android.Manifest.permission.ACCESS_COARSE_LOCATION) !=
7        ↪ PackageManager.PERMISSION_GRANTED) {
8        return ;
9   }
    --- rest of Listing 7.3 code ---
```

This new code is essentially one long `if` statement that checks if the device is running SDK 23 or higher and location permission has not been explicitly granted. If both conditions are true, the code is exited and the app will not be able to access the devices location. Note that after you add this code, the `locationManager.removeUpdates` line is no longer underlined in red. The next step is to put code in the `initGetLocationButton()` method to ask for permission to access the device's location. Enter the code in Listing 7.6 in the now-empty `onClick` method.

Listing 7.6   onClick() Method to Request Location Permission

```
1    try {
2    if (Build.VERSION.SDK_INT >= 23) {
3        if (ContextCompat.checkSelfPermission(ContactMapActivity.this,
4            ➥ android.Manifest.permission.ACCESS_FINE_LOCATION) !=
5            ➥ PackageManager.PERMISSION_GRANTED) {
6
7            if (ActivityCompat.shouldShowRequestPermissionRationale
8                ➥ (ContactMapActivity.this,
9                ➥ android.Manifest.permission.ACCESS_FINE_LOCATION)) {
10
11                Snackbar.make(findViewById(R.id.activity_contact_map),
12                    ➥"MyContactList requires this permission to locate " +
13                    ➥"your contacts", Snackbar.LENGTH_INDEFINITE)
14                    ➥.setAction("OK", new View.OnClickListener() {
15                        @Override
16                        public void onClick(View view) {
17
18                            ActivityCompat.requestPermissions(
19                                ➥ ContactMapActivity.this,
20                                ➥ new String[]{
21                                ➥ android.Manifest.permission.ACCESS_FINE_LOCATION},
22                                ➥ PERMISSION_REQUEST_LOCATION);
23                            }
24                    })
25                    .show();
26
27            } else {
28                ActivityCompat.requestPermissions(ContactMapActivity.this, new
29                    ➥ String[]{android.Manifest.permission.ACCESS_FINE_LOCATION},
30                    ➥ PERMISSION_REQUEST_LOCATION);
31            }
32        } else {
33            startLocationUpdates();
34        }
35    }else {
36        startLocationUpdates();
37    }
38    }
39    catch (Exception e) {
40        Toast.makeText(getBaseContext(), "Error requesting permission",
41                        ➥Toast.LENGTH_LONG).show();
42    }
```

When the user presses the button, the app starts location updates if the device is running an SDK less than 23 or determines if permission has been granted. If permission has not been granted, it asks for permission. The function of this code is explained as follows:

- **Line 2**—The operating system SDK is checked. If it is less than 23 the app starts the code to find the device's location.

- **Lines 3–5**—If the device is running an operating system greater than 22, this line checks if permission has been previously granted. If it has, the app starts the code to find the device's location.

- **Lines 7–9**—This statement determines if the user had previously denied a request from the app to access the device's location. If it has previously been denied, the app presents the user with a rationale telling the user why the app needs this permission. The first time the app requests a permission, a "canned" request is made that just asks for the desired permission.

- **Lines 11–25**—This code asks for permission to access location if it was previously denied. It will only show the permission request if the user previously denied this specific permission. The request for location is made with a `Snackbar`. A Snackbar is an object that implements a kind of `AlertDialog` that is run as an asynchronous task floating in the activity's layout. The user can go on using the activity; however, the Snackbar will obstruct some of the layout. The `LENGTH_INDEFINITE` code keeps the Snackbar open until the user explicitly dismisses it either by clicking the OK or Deny buttons. Finally, the code creates an OnClick listener for the OK button click event.

- **Lines 18–22**—This code requests permission for access to location. Note that it only asks for permission to access fine location. If this permission is granted, coarse location is also automatically granted. The `PERMIS-SION_REQUEST_LOCATION` will be highlighted in red. This will also be fixed later.

- **Lines 28–30**—This code is the same as described previously in Lines 3–5. It is executed if the user has not previously denied access to location.

Now we will fix the `PERMISSION_REQUEST_LOCATION` issue. Open **ContactMapActivity.java** (if not open) and put the following line of code after the `LocationListener gpsListener` line at the top of the file:

```
final int PERMISSION_REQUEST_LOCATION = 101;
```

This line declares a constant that is used to identify the permission that is being requested. Note that the code in Listing 7.6 includes this value each time it requests location permission. This is done because the user's response to any permission request is handled by the same method and we may ask for more than one permission in an activity. That method must be able to identify what permission request it is responding to, to act appropriately. The next step is to code the method required to respond to the user's response. Enter the code in Listing 7.7 after the `start-LocationUpdates()` method.

Listing 7.7 Method to Respond to Permission Requests

```
1      @Override
2      public void onRequestPermissionsResult(int requestCode,
3       ➥ String permissions[], int[] grantResults) {
4
5          switch (requestCode) {
6              case PERMISSION_REQUEST_LOCATION: {
7                  if (grantResults.length > 0 &&
8                   ➥ grantResults[0] == PackageManager.PERMISSION_GRANTED) {
9
10                     startLocationUpdates();
11
12                 } else {
13                     Toast.makeText(ContactMapActivity.this,
14                      ➥ "MyContactList will not locate your contacts.",
15                      ➥ Toast.LENGTH_LONG).show();
16                 }
17             }
18         }
19     }
```

This code is called when the user clicks one of the buttons on the permission request dialog. It is called by a response to a request for any permission.

- **Lines 2–3**—This is the method signature required to override the super class method of the same name. The request response sends the `requestCode`, which is the value you sent the request with `PERMISSION_REQUEST_LOCATION`. It is used to determine which permission request it is dealing with. The response also sends a string array with the permissions requested and an integer array with the user response to each request.

- **Lines 5–6**—A `switch` statement is used to determine which permission the method is responding to. In our activity, we only have one permission request, so there is only one `case` statement. This method can be used to deal with multiple permission requests by simply adding additional case statements.

- **Lines 7–8**—This `if` statement uses `PackageManager` to check if the permission was granted by the user. `PackageManager` is an operating system object that keeps track of what permissions were granted by the user for the apps on the device. If the permission was granted, the app starts finding the location. If it is not granted, a message explaining how the app will function without the permission is displayed.

The final step is to modify the `onPause()` method so that `locationManager.removeUpdates` line no longer creates an error. This is easy! Simply copy the code you put at the beginning of `startLocationUpdates()` method (Listing 7.5) and paste it before the `try` in the `onPause()` method. You are now ready to test finding locations!

Run the code on the emulator and press the Get Coordinates button. You should see the permission request to allow My Contact List to access the device's location (Figure 7.3). If you click Deny, you will see the Toast message that the app will not be able to locate your contacts. If you click the Get Coordinates button again, you will see the Snackbar message that the app requires the permission to locate contacts. When you click OK, you will get back to the permission dialog where you can turn the permission on to access the location functionality.

Figure 7.3 Permission request and denial message.

After giving the app permission, you will see some coordinates show up when you click the Get Coordinates button. While the button starts the location listener, until the location of the device changes, the TextViews will not change. To simulate a change to the location of the emulator, use the following steps (Figure 7.4):

1. Click the **Ellipsis** button next to the emulator.
2. Make sure the **Location** tab is selected.
3. Enter a new latitude and/or longitude value and click the **Send** button. These values should show up in your app.

Figure 7.4 Emulator location control.

To test the code on a device that has a GPS, terminate the app running on the emulator (**Run > Terminate**) and plug an Android device into the computer. (Note that the first four steps below were done in Chapter 3, "Using Android Studio for Android Development." If you did not change anything, you should be able to jump to Step 5.)

1. From the main menu, select **Run > Edit Configurations**. The **Run Configurations** window is displayed.
2. Click the **disclosure** button to the left of **Android Application** on the left side of the screen. Then click **app**.
3. Find **Deployment Target Options** on the right side of the screen and verify that **Show Device Chooser Dialog** is selected (if not, use button to select it).
4. Click **OK**. Now when you run or debug your app, a device chooser (Figure 7.5) will display all your AVDs and real devices connected to the computer. You can then choose which one you want to test on.
5. Your device must be set up to **Allow USB Debugging** before you can test the app. The location where you can turn this on varies widely among devices. It is usually in the **Settings** app under **USB Settings** or **Developer Options**. This will usually also require the device to be in developer mode, which is also done differently on different devices. You may have to do some Internet searches to determine how to change the settings for your device.
6. Make sure the device is connected to the computer and is unlocked. Select **Choose a running device** and then select your device. Click **OK**. The app will be loaded like on the emulator and begin running when finished. Note that if your device goes to sleep during this process, the app will be terminated.

After the app is running on your device, you can unplug it so that you can walk around and see the location change. If you are indoors, it may take some time to get a GPS reading. In some buildings it will not work at all, so you will have to go outside.

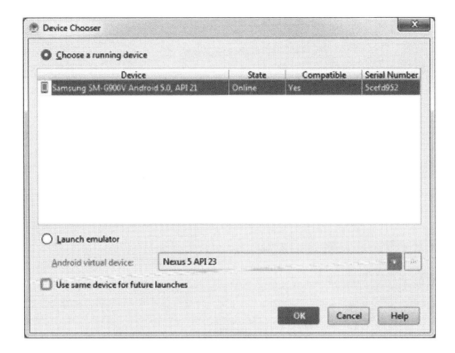

Figure 7.5 Device Chooser window.

Get Coordinates from Network Sensor

After you've gotten the GPS sensor working, changing or adding a network sensor is very easy. Add the following declaration after the `gpsListener` declaration in **ContactMapActivity.java**:

```
LocationListener networkListener;
```

Copy the code in the `startLocationUpdates()` method that begins with `gpsListener` = and ends just before the `locationManager.requestLocationUpdates` line (this includes the entire `onLocationChanged` method), and paste it back into the method just before the `locationManager.requestLocationUpdates` line. You should now have two duplicate `gpsListeners`. Change the `gpsListener` variable in the code you just pasted to `networkListener` and then add another `requestLocationUpdates` message after the one that is used to request GPS updates:

```
locationManager.requestLocationUpdates(LocationManager.NETWORK_PROVIDER,0, 0, networkListener);
```

In the `onPause` method, add the following line to turn off the network listener.

```
locationManager.removeUpdates(networkListener);
```

below the line that turns off the GPS listener.

That's all there is to it! The only real change you made was to request updates from the network sensor rather than the GPS sensor.

To test this, you must run it on a device. The emulator will not detect network sensor changes. This code will work indoors if you can get a Wi-Fi or cell signal on your device.

Often it is desirable to use both sensors, because at times one or the other is not available. Although the network sensor is not as accurate as the GPS, for some applications this may be good enough. However, if you are getting location updates from both sensors, you need some way of determining which to use. The way to do this is to write a method to take the current location and compare it to a new location to determine if it is better. To do this, add another variable to hold a location object to your set of declarations at the beginning of the ContactMapActivity class using this code:

```
Location currentBestLocation;
```

Now create a new method called `isBetterLocation` using the code in Listing 7.8.

Listing 7.8   isBetterLocation Method

```
1    private boolean isBetterLocation(Location location) {
2        boolean isBetter = false;
3        if (currentBestLocation == null) {
4            isBetter = true;
5        }
6        else if (location.getAccuracy() <= currentBestLocation.getAccuracy()) {
7            isBetter = true;
8        }
9        else if (location.getTime() - currentBestLocation.getTime() > 5*60*1000) {
10            isBetter = true;
11        }
12        return isBetter;
13    }
```

This method is an example of the types of checks that can be done to determine if a new location is better than another location.

- **Lines 2–3**—The first check determines if there is an existing location. If not, the new location is considered better.
- **Lines 6–7**—The second check determines if the new location has better accuracy than the existing location. If so, it is considered better.
- **Lines 9–10**—The last check determines how much newer the new location is. Each `Location` object gets a time stamp when it is created. In this check, if the new location is newer than the old location by more than five minutes, it is considered better, even though it may not be as accurate. This type of check is especially important if you design the app to be used when the device is in motion.

This new method should be called in the `onLocationChanged` method of both sensor listeners to determine whether you want to use the new location. For example, you could add the following code:

```
if (isBetterLocation(location)) {
    currentBestLocation = location;
    //display in location in TextViews.
}
//no else block...if not better, just ignore.
```

Android versus iOS: Location Sensors

Working with location data on iOS is similar to Android. However, although iOS devices also have both GPS and network sensors, iOS developers don't have access to the specific sensors. Instead, the developer specifies a desired accuracy of the location data, and the system chooses the appropriate sensor to provide the data. This allows the system to optimize the sensor usage for battery and performance of the device.

Setting Up for Maps

The final way to get the GPS coordinates of your device's location is through the map object. The map has built-in methods that access the sensors without you having to write any code. This makes things easier, because all sensor management is handled by the map. The drawback is that you must display a map in the layout to use these features.

There are a few things that need to be done before you can successfully add maps to your app. The first is to load the Google Play Services SDK into your workspace. Select **Tools > Android > SDK Manager**. The **SDK Manager** window opens and shows a list of available SDK Platforms. Click on the **SDK Tools** tab. Check the box next to **Google Play Services** (Figure 7.5), and click **OK**. Click **OK** in the next window that opens to begin the download and installation process. When installation is done, click the **Finish** button.

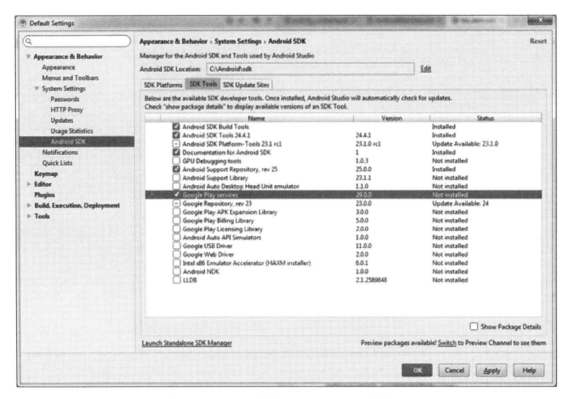

Figure 7.6 Android SDK Manager window.

Now that the Google Play Services SDK is downloaded, it must be added to your project. Select **File > Project Structure**. Refer to the instructions for adding a library dependency earlier in the chapter (Figure 7.2), but this time select the design (**com.android.google.gms:play-services:9.8.0**) library dependency. The number may be different in your installation. To use Google Maps in an app, Google requires that the app contain an API key. There are two types of keys: debug and release. The debug key can work only in debug mode and is associated with your development machine. An app compiled for release with a debug key will not run the maps portion of the app. To release the app, you need to follow a slightly different procedure to register with Google to get a release key. The API key allows you (and Google) to track how often the users of your app access the map functionality. For now, you need only a debug key.

There are several steps to getting a debug key for a maps application:

1. Get the SHA1 fingerprint for your project: Select **View > Tool Windows > Gradle**. A panel titled **Gradle projects** will open on the right side of the editor. Click the **Refresh** button (left most button, below title). Wait until your project is displayed.

2. Expand the project until you see your project name with (**root**) after it. Expand that. Expand **Tasks**. Expand **android**. Double-click **signingReport** (left side of Figure 7.7). The **Run** panel will open at the bottom of Android Studio.

3. Click **Toggle tasks/execution mode** (right side of Figure 7.7) in the Run panel. Locate **SHA1:** in the **Config: debug** portion of the report. Copy the long hexadecimal number (be careful to only copy the key and not the SHA1: header). Note the key will look similar to this: `72:27:E9:A6:AF:85:77:C2:4C:F2:22:45:72:9 8:1B:2C:50:F4:07:B1`.

4. Next, open a browser and type this URL: **https://console.developers.google.com**. If you are not logged in to Google or do not have an account, you will be prompted to get one. Note that Google Apps accounts are not eligible as developer accounts, unless enabled by the organization's App Admin. Once logged in, the first thing you have to do is create a project. Unfortunately, Google changes the layout of this site frequently, so you may have to Google "Get API Key" to find the current set of steps if the following does not work.

a. Click **Create Project** or **Create an Empty Project**. Enter **MyContactList**. Click **Create**. If you have existing projects, the new project should be given a different name. Google will work for a while. Wait until the **Google API Library** screen is displayed.

b. Find and click on the **Google Maps Android API**.

c. On the next screen, click **Enable**. You will get a message that you can't use the API until you create credentials. Click the **Create Credentials** button. Select **Google Maps Android API** in the dropdown box if it is not already displayed. Then click the **What credentials do I need** button.

d. On the next screen, click the **Done** button. The next screen will display the key name and key value. Click on the **key name**. Under **Key restrictions**, select **Android apps** and then click the **+Add package name and fingerprint button**. Fill in the package name (e.g., com.example.mycontactlist) and paste your **SHA1 fingerpint** into the appropriate box. If desired, you can change the name of the key to something other than API key 1.

d. Click **Save**. The API key is displayed. Highlight and copy it.

5. Return to Android Studio and open the **AndroidManifest.xml** file. Just before the `</application>` tag at the bottom of the file, enter the following:

```
<meta-data
    android:name="com.google.android.maps.v2.API_KEY"
    android:value="YourKeyGoesHere" />
```

The process of getting a production map key so that you can release the app to other individuals is essentially the same. However, you have to create a new keystore and get the SHA1 fingerprint from that keystore (see http:// developer.android.com/tools/publishing/app-signing.html).

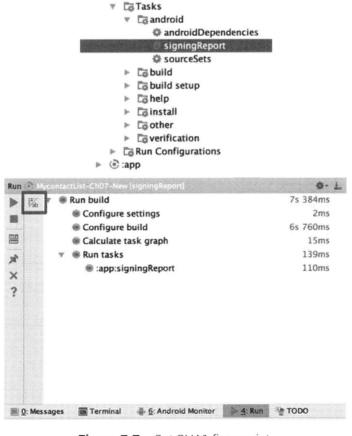

Figure 7.7 Get SHA1 fingerprint.

Android Versus iOS: Maps

Setting up your app project and development environment for using maps is significantly more difficult in Android than it is in Xcode. In Xcode, in contrast to what you've seen in this chapter, all you need to do is include the MapKit Framework in the project and you are ready to go. However, you will be using Apple Maps rather than Google Maps.

Using maps in either Android or iOS has its own unique challenges. Some things are easier in Android, such as zooming in on the map or adding annotations to the markers put on a map. Other things are easier in Xcode, such as interacting with the map with the code.

Setting Permissions for the Map

To use maps in your app, you have to give the app more permissions. Open the **AndroidManifest.xml** file and enter the permissions in Listing 7.9. Put these permissions after the `<manifest` tag and before the `<application` tag.

Listing 7.9   Required Map Additional Permissions

```
1    <permission
2        android:name="com.example.mycontactlist.permission.MAPS_RECEIVE"
3        android:protectionLevel="signature" />
4
5    <uses-permission
6        android:name="com.example.mycontactlist.permission.MAPS_RECEIVE" />
7    <uses-permission android:name="android.permission.INTERNET" />
8    <uses-permission android:name="android.permission.ACCESS_NETWORK_STATE" />
9    <uses-permission android:name="android.permission.WRITE_EXTERNAL_STORAGE" />
10   <uses-permission
11     android:name="com.google.android.providers.gsf.permission.READ_GSERVICES" />
12
13   <uses-feature
14       android:glEsVersion="0x00020000"
15       android:required="true" />
```

The permissions themselves are pretty self-explanatory with the exception of the `<uses-feature` tag. Google Maps requires access to the Open Graphics Library API to process the graphics associated with the map. This tag gives your app access to the API.

Note

Google Maps v2 often does not work well with the emulator. You must set up a new AVD that uses Google APIs as its target and select to use Hardware graphics in the Emulation options section. Using the latest version of the SDK is also helpful. However, you may still get a blank screen. There are a number of workarounds to be found on the Internet, but we have not gotten any of these to solve the problem. If you get a blank screen with the emulator, you will have to test some of this chapter's code on a real device. The instructions for running on a real device were included earlier in this chapter (see "Get Coordinates from the GPS Sensor").

Get Coordinates from the Map

Return to **activity_contact_map.xml** and delete all the widgets you put in the layout except the `navbar`. Be sure to leave the root `RelativeLayout`. Next, add a **MapFragment**. The MapFragment is not available in the Palette, so it must be added through XML. Refer to Listing 7.10 to do this.

Listing 7.10   MapFragment XML

```
1    <fragment
2        android:id="@+id/map"
3        android:layout_width="match_parent"
4        android:layout_height="match_parent"
5        android:layout_alignParentTop="true"
6        android:layout_above="@+id/navbar"
7        class="com.google.android.gms.maps.SupportMapFragment" />
```

The map object is not coded as a standard widget. Rather, a fragment is added to the layout with the standard set of attributes for size and positioning. The fragment has to be told what type of object it is. That is the reason for the class attribute. In this case, you use the **SupportMapFragment** to make the map object compatible with the earlier versions of Android targeted in this app.

The map doesn't display in Design view—just the positioning of the fragment. To see a map, you have to write code. Open **ContactMapActivity.java**. Delete the `LocationManager`, `LocationListener`, and `Location` variables. This will cause a bunch of errors. We will correct them as we modify the code to work with maps. Modify the class declaration and `onCreate` method to match Listing 7.11. Import any required classes.

Listing 7.11   Code to Set Up Google Maps

```
1    public class ContactMapActivity extends AppCompatActivity implements
2    ➥ OnMapReadyCallback, GoogleApiClient.OnConnectionFailedListener,
3    ➥ GoogleApiClient.ConnectionCallbacks {
4
5        final int PERMISSION_REQUEST_LOCATION = 101;
6        GoogleMap gMap;
7        GoogleApiClient mGoogleApiClient;
8        LocationRequest mLocationRequest;
9
10       @Override
11       public void onCreate(Bundle savedInstanceState) {
12           super.onCreate(savedInstanceState);
13           setContentView(R.layout.activity_contact_map);
14           SupportMapFragment mapFragment = (SupportMapFragment)
15               ➥ getSupportFragmentManager().findFragmentById(R.id.map);
16           mapFragment.getMapAsync (this);
17           createLocationRequest();
18
19         if (mGoogleApiClient == null) {
20           mGoogleApiClient = new GoogleApiClient.Builder(this)
21             .addConnectionCallbacks(this)
22             .addOnConnectionFailedListener(this)
23             .addApi(LocationServices.API)
24             .build();
25         }
26
27           initListButton();
28           initSettingsButton();
29           ImageButton ibMap = (ImageButton) findViewById(R.id.imageButtonMap);
30           ibMap.setEnabled(false);
31           initGetLocationButton();
32    }
```

This code uses a GoogleMap object, which is displayed in the fragment on the layout. The GoogleMap class in conjunction with the **GoogleApiClient** provides the functionality needed to get the GPS coordinates of a location in real time.

- **Lines 1–3**—The class implements several interfaces that allow it to work with the services necessary to get real-time location information from the map. First, the `OnMapReadyCallback` interface is used to notify the activity that the map has been downloaded and is ready to be used. To get real-time location updates, your activity must be connected to Google API Service. The `GoogleApiClient.OnConnectionFailedListener` and `GoogleApiClient.ConnectionCallbacks` interfaces are used to implement the functionality required to connect to the API Service. Finally, the `LocationListener` interface is used to actually capture device location changes from the map. This line will be underlined as an error until you implement the required methods for the interfaces. The easiest way to do this is to click on the reddish light bulb at the beginning of the line and selecting **Implement methods**.
- **Lines 14–15**—An instance of a `GoogleMap` is assigned to the gMap variable. Note the use of `SupportMapFragment`. As mentioned earlier, this is used to make the map compatible with earlier versions of the Android Operating System. The `SupportMapFragment` class has to be imported. Normally, this is routine—just hover over the underlined class and select import from the pop-up menu. However, in earlier versions of Android Studio, the menu often did not find this class. In this case, the import statement must be added manually. To do this, expand the import section above the class declaration and type in this statement:

```
import com.google.android.gms.maps.SupportMapFragment;
```

- **Line 16**—The map is retrieved asynchronously. Once the map has been retrieved the `onMapReady()` method is executed and we can begin working with the map.
- **Line 17**—This line calls a method that sets up the location listener. We will code this method later.
- **Lines 19–25**—Finally, the API Client is created to be used to establish a connection with API Services. If this line has an error message, go to the imports section and make sure you are importing `com.google.android.gms.common.api.GoogleApiClient`.

The next step is to code the call back methods required by the interfaces and other methods required to capture user location. If you chose to have Android Studio implement the required methods, you will see more methods in your code than in the following listing. Don't worry, we do not need those methods to get the functionality we are after, and you can just ignore them. However, the interface requires that the empty method be in the code. Refer to Listing 7.12 to code the required methods.

Listing 7.12   Methods to Capture Location

```
1   protected void onStart() {
2       mGoogleApiClient.connect();
3       super.onStart();
4   }
5
6   protected void onStop() {
7       mGoogleApiClient.disconnect();
8       super.onStop();
9   }
10
11  protected void createLocationRequest() {
12      mLocationRequest = new LocationRequest();
13      mLocationRequest.setInterval(10000);
14      mLocationRequest.setFastestInterval(5000);
15      mLocationRequest.setPriority(LocationRequest.PRIORITY_HIGH_ACCURACY);
16  }
17
18  @Override
```

(continued)

Setting Up for Maps • 137

Listing 7.12 Methods to Capture Location (*continued*)

```
19  public void onConnected(@Nullable Bundle bundle) {
20      if ( Build.VERSION.SDK_INT >= 23 && ContextCompat.checkSelfPermission(getBaseContext(),
21          ↪android.Manifest.permission.ACCESS_FINE_LOCATION)!=PackageManager.PERMISSION_GRANTED
22          ↪&& ContextCompat.checkSelfPermission( getBaseContext(),
23      ↪android.Manifest.permission.ACCESS_COARSE_LOCATION) !=
24      ↪PackageManager.PERMISSION_GRANTED)
25      {
26          return  ;
27      }
28      LocationServices.FusedLocationApi.requestLocationUpdates(mGoogleApiClient,
29      ↪mLocationRequest, this);
30  }
31
32  @Override
33  public void onConnectionSuspended(int i) {
34      if ( Build.VERSION.SDK_INT >= 23 && ContextCompat.checkSelfPermission(getBaseContext(),
35          ↪android.Manifest.permission.ACCESS_FINE_LOCATION)!=PackageManager.PERMISSION_GRANTED
36          ↪&& ContextCompat.checkSelfPermission( getBaseContext(),
37          ↪android.Manifest.permission.ACCESS_COARSE_LOCATION) !=
38      ↪PackageManager.PERMISSION_GRANTED)
39      {
40          return  ;
41      }
41      LocationServices.FusedLocationApi.removeLocationUpdates(mGoogleApiClient, this);
43  }
44
45  @Override
46  public void onConnectionFailed(@NonNull ConnectionResult connectionResult) {
47      if ( Build.VERSION.SDK_INT >= 23 && ContextCompat.checkSelfPermission(getBaseContext(),
48          ↪android.Manifest.permission.ACCESS_FINE_LOCATION)!=PackageManager.PERMISSION_GRANTED
49          ↪&& ContextCompat.checkSelfPermission( getBaseContext(),
50          ↪android.Manifest.permission.ACCESS_COARSE_LOCATION) !=
51      ↪PackageManager.PERMISSION_GRANTED)
52      {
53          return  ;
54      }
55      LocationServices.FusedLocationApi.removeLocationUpdates(mGoogleApiClient, this);
56  }
57
58  @Override
59  public void onMapReady(GoogleMap googleMap) {
60      gMap = googleMap;
61      gMap.setMapType(GoogleMap.MAP_TYPE_NORMAL);
62
63      Paste permission request code from initGetLocationButton here (Listing 7.6)
64
65  }
```

Each of these methods implements a portion of the required functionality. Their exact function is explained as follows:

- **Lines 1–4**—The method does the actually connecting of your app to API services. This happens at the onStart life cycle activity. The connection is made during onStart rather than onResume so that your app can monitor location when it is in the background. See Chapter 2, "App Design Issues and Considerations," for more description of the life cycle methods.

- **Lines 6–9**—The method disconnects your app from the API services. This happens at the `onStop` life cycle activity. The connection is made during `onStop` rather than `onPause` so that your app can monitor location when it is in the background.

- **Lines 11–16**—This method creates the parameters of your location request. It sets the standard monitoring interval (in milliseconds), the fastest interval needed, and the required accuracy level of the reported location. By using `PRIORITY_HIGH_ACCURACY`, we use the devices GPS to get the coordinates.

- **Lines 18–30**—This method starts location updates. Note the code checking for permission. Since we are requesting location of the user's device, we must check permission, as we did when using the sensors directly. The only other line of code starts the location listening through the API Client. This line will show an error that will be corrected next.

- **Lines 32–56**—The next two methods stop location updates if something happens to the connection to the API Client. The same error will be in this code as in `onConnected` method.

- **Lines 58–61**—Finally, the `onMapReady()` method is created. This method overrides a super class method, so it requires the `Override` designation. Since we want to use location in the map, we will add the permission request in this method and delete the `initGetLocationButton()` method. Be sure to copy the code before deleting the method. This code receives the `GoogleMap` object and assigns it to our `gMap` variable. The map type is also set. A map type of normal is a standard highway map. Other valid types include `MAP_TYPE_SAT-ELLITE` for satellite pictures and `MAP_TYPE_TERRAIN` for a map of the terrain features.

You can now delete the `initGetLocationButton()` and `isBetterLocation()` methods. You won't need them because the GoogleMap class provides all the functionality needed to get the GPS coordinates of a location in real time. Remember to also remove the call to `initGetLocationButton()` in `onCreate()`.

The next step is to fix the error in the line that starts the LocationListener. To do this we need to make the activity a LocationListener by implementing the correct LocationListener interface. Add the following to the end of the class declaration: `LocationListener`. Choose the **com.google.android.gms.location** option (there are two). Your class declaration should now look like this:

```
public class ContactMapActivity extends AppCompatActivity implements OnMapReadyCallback,
    GoogleApiClient.OnConnectionFailedListener, GoogleApiClient.ConnectionCallbacks,
    com.google.android.gms.location.LocationListener{
```

Android Studio will by default import the wrong LocationListener, so we do it separate from the original declaration to ensure that right one is implemented. You will have to implement the required `onLocationChanged` method after adding this interface. Whenever a change in location is detected, it causes this method to execute. Add the following code to the method to display the location when it changes:

```
@Override
public void onLocationChanged(Location location) {
    Toast.makeText(getBaseContext(), "Lat: " + location.getLatitude() +
            " Long: " + location.getLongitude() +
            " Accuracy:  " + location.getAccuracy(),
            Toast.LENGTH_LONG).show();

}
```

The next step is to change the `startLocationUpdates()` method to work with GoogleMaps, rather than the LocationManager. Delete all the code in the `startLocationUpdates()` method, following the check for permissions, and replace it with the one line of code at the end of Listing 7.13. This line enables the map to find the device location. This places a button on the map that allows the user to enable or disable the display of the small blue dot on the map, which represents the device's location.

Listing 7.13   New startLocationUpdates() Method

```
1    private void startLocationUpdates() {
2        if (Build.VERSION.SDK_INT >= 23 &&
3                ContextCompat.checkSelfPermission(getBaseContext(),
4                    android.Manifest.permission.ACCESS_FINE_LOCATION) !=
5                    PackageManager.PERMISSION_GRANTED &&
6                ContextCompat.checkSelfPermission(getBaseContext(),
7                    android.Manifest.permission.ACCESS_COARSE_LOCATION) !=
8                    PackageManager.PERMISSION_GRANTED) {
9            return;
10       }
11       gMap.setMyLocationEnabled(true);
12   }
```

You can test this code on your device or emulator. When you enter coordinates for the emulator, the map will zoom to that location. If you test it on your device, it will zoom to your current location and Toasts will begin showing your GPS coordinates. If you do not get an actual map, only a gray area where the map is supposed to be and no errors or crashes, there is likely a problem with the key you created. Go back to the API Console and check that the SHA1 key you entered exactly matches the key from the signing report and that the namespace exactly equals the name space of the app (e.g., com.example.mycontactlist). If there are no errors and it still does not work, consult the following alternative procedure.

Alternative Key Procedure

This procedure uses Android Studio to generate the map activity. You may find this easier—and it is—but if you are planning to create an app for release, you need to know the previous procedure to get a release key. The first step is to add a Google Maps Activity. Click **File > New > Google > Google Maps Activity**. On the Configure Activity window, accept all the defaults and click **Finish**. This adds the following:

- Maps Java file
- google_maps_api.xml in res/values
- activity_maps.xml

Open **google_maps_api.xml** in the editor. In the grayed-out area (commented out) there is a URL with all the necessary information as URL parameters. Copy this URL to your browser and execute it. Follow the on-screen instructions and press **Create** at the end. A key will be created, and you can paste it back into the manifest in place of your previous one. You can then delete the items just created.

Displaying Your Contacts' Locations

Now that you can find your device's location and display the real-time location on the map, it is time to show your contacts' locations on the map. The map can be accessed from any of the three other activities through the navigation bar. If the user accesses the map from either the contact list or the settings activities, the map should display all the contacts in the database on the map. If the user accesses the map from the contact activity, the map should display only that contact. Implementing the second display type requires coding the ContactActivity to pass the current contact's ID to the map.

Open **ContactActivity.java** and locate the initMapButton method. This method is modified to pass the contact's ID with the intent. Modify the code in the onClick method to match Listing 7.14.

Listing 7.14   initMapButton Modified

```
1    Intent intent = new Intent(ContactActivity.this, ContactMapActivity.class);
2    if (currentContact.getContactID() == -1) {
3        Toast.makeText(getBaseContext(), "Contact must be saved before it can be
4                ⮳mapped", Toast.LENGTH_LONG).show();
5    }
6    else {
7        intent.putExtra("contactid", currentContact.getContactID());
8    }
9    intent.setFlags(Intent.FLAG_ACTIVITY_CLEAR_TOP);
10   startActivity(intent);
```

There is no new code here. The method checks whether the contact has an ID. If not, a message is posted for the user. If there is an ID, that ID is passed to the ContactMapActivity. Switch to **ContactMapActivity.java**. The first step is to get the data for mapping. This is done by checking for any extras. If there are no extras, all the contacts are retrieved. If there is an extra, just the information for one contact is retrieved. The first step is to create two new variables for the activity. Add the following code after the `LocationRequest mLocationRequest;` line:

```
ArrayList<Contact> contacts = new ArrayList<>();
Contact currentContact = null;
```

Now add the code to retrieve the contact information after the `setContentView` line in the `onCreate` method of the ContactMapActivity. Enter the code in Listing 7.15.

Listing 7.15   Getting Data for the Map

```
1        Bundle extras = getIntent().getExtras();
2        try {
3            ContactDataSource ds = new ContactDataSource(ContactMapActivity.this);
4            ds.open();
5            if(extras !=null){
6                currentContact = ds.getSpecificContact(extras.getInt("contactid"));
7            }
8            else {
9                contacts = ds.getContacts("contactname", "ASC");
10           }
11           ds.close();
12       }
13       catch (Exception e) {
14           Toast.makeText(this, "Contact(s) could not be retrieved.", Toast.LENGTH_LONG).show();
15
16       }
```

The next step is to place markers on the map in the location of each contact. Markers can be standard pins or custom icons. Add the following code (Listing 7.16) in the `onMapReady` method after the `gMap.setMapType` line and before the permission check.

Listing 7.16 Code to Put Markers on a Map

```
1   Point size = new Point();
2   WindowManager w = getWindowManager();
3   w.getDefaultDisplay().getSize(size);
4   int measuredWidth = size.x;
5   int measuredHeight = size.y;
6
7   if (contacts.size()>0) {
8       LatLngBounds.Builder builder = new LatLngBounds.Builder();
9       for (int i=0; i<contacts.size(); i++) {
10          currentContact = contacts.get(i);
11
12          Geocoder geo = new Geocoder(this);
13          List<Address> addresses = null;
14
15          String address = currentContact.getStreetAddress() + ", " +
16                          currentContact.getCity() + ", " +
17                          currentContact.getState() + " " +
18                          currentContact.getZipCode();
19
20          try {
21              addresses = geo.getFromLocationName(address, 1);
22          }
23          catch (IOException e) {
24              e.printStackTrace();
25          }
26          LatLng point = new LatLng(addresses.get(0).getLatitude(),
27                          ➥addresses.get(0).getLongitude());
28          builder.include(point);
29
30          gMap.addMarker(new MarkerOptions().position(point).
31              ➥title(currentContact.getContactName()).snippet(address));
32      }
33      gMap.animateCamera(CameraUpdateFactory.newLatLngBounds(builder.build(),
34                          ➥measuredWidth, measuredHeight, 450));
35  }
36  else {
37      if (currentContact != null) {
38          Geocoder geo = new Geocoder(this);
39          List<Address> addresses = null;
40
41          String address = currentContact.getStreetAddress() + ", " +
42                          currentContact.getCity() + ", " +
43                          currentContact.getState() + " " +
44                          currentContact.getZipCode();
45
46          try {
47              addresses = geo.getFromLocationName(address, 1);
48          }
49          catch (IOException e) {
50              e.printStackTrace();
51          }
52          LatLng point = new
```

(continued)

Listing 7.16   Code to Put Markers on a Map (*continued*)

```
53              ↪LatLng(addresses.get(0).getLatitude(),addresses.get(0).getLongitude());
54
55          gMap.addMarker(new MarkerOptions().position(point).
56                      ↪title(currentContact.getContactName()).snippet(address));
57          gMap.animateCamera(CameraUpdateFactory. newLatLngZoom(point, 16));
58      }
59      else {
60          AlertDialog alertDialog = new AlertDialog.Builder(
61                  ↪ContactMapActivity.this).create();
62          alertDialog.setTitle("No Data");
63          alertDialog.setMessage("No data is available for the mapping function.");
64          alertDialog.setButton(AlertDialog.BUTTON_POSITIVE,
65                  ↪"OK", new DialogInterface.OnClickListener() {
66          public void onClick(DialogInterface dialog, int which) {
67          finish();
68      } });
69          alertDialog.show();
70      }
71  }
```

The code to put markers on the map uses a number of classes unique to the mapping application. These classes and their methods make up the bulk of the new code.

- **Lines 1–5**—To properly bound a group of points, the app needs to know the size of the display. This code asks the device for the dimensions of the display.

- **Line 8**—A `LatLngBounds.Builder` is used to construct the geographic boundaries of a set of GPS coordinates. This line instantiates the builder for use when the app is going to display all contacts in the database.

- **Lines 9–32**—If the contact's `ArrayList` contains `Contact` objects, the `Activity` loops through them, adding each one to the map.

- **Lines 26–28**—A `LatLng` object is instantiated with the GPS coordinates returned from the geocoding service. The `LatLng` object is a point on a map. This point is then included in the `LatLngBounds.Builder`, where it is considered in creating the map boundaries.

- **Lines 30–31**—A `Marker` is added to the map. The marker is a standard marker in the form of a pin. The `addMarker` method is a `MarkerOptions` object. The `MarkerOptions` object is used to set the `LatLng` object as the position on the map for the marker; the title of the marker that is displayed when the marker is clicked by the user; and a snippet, which is displayed under the title when the marker is clicked. A custom image can be added instead of the standard marker by setting the icon attribute of the `MarkerObject` using this form: `.icon(BitmapDescriptorFactory.fromResource(R.drawable.imagename)`.

- **Line 33**—After all the contact markers have been added, the message `animateCamera` is sent to the map to tell it to zoom in to the location of the markers. A `CameraUpdateFactory` is the object used to set the zoom level. It is passed the boundaries of the zoom through the `LatLngBounds.Builder`, the measured size of the device display, and the amount of padding to put around the bounds. If the padding is set too small, some of the contact markers will be placed so close to the edge of the screen that the user may not see all the markers.

- **Lines 37–58**—If the contacts `ArrayList` does not contain any objects, the code checks whether there is a single `Contact` object to map. If there is, the address is retrieved, and a `LatLng` object is instantiated for the contact's coordinates; the `LatLng` object is used to add a marker to the map.

- **Line 57**—The zoom level of the map is set differently with one point than with several. To zoom to a single point, the `CameraUpdateFactory` is sent the message `newLatLngZoom`. This message has the `LatLng` object and zoom level as parameters. The marker will be centered in the map and zoomed to level 16.

- **Lines 59–70**—If no contacts are available either in the `ArrayList` or the `Contact` object, the app displays an error message. In this case, an object called an `AlertDialog` is used. An `AlertDialog` displays the commonly used dialog with a title, message, and button to acknowledge that the user saw the message. This is used rather than a toast, because the user is expecting to see contacts on the map. The user may miss the toast and figure the app is not working.

Test the app. Make sure you have entered valid addresses for contacts prior to testing the mapping function.

Switching Map Type

The map is almost complete. The final touch is to add a toolbar that allows the user to select the type of map to display. Switch to **activity_contact_map.xml** and add a **toolbar**. You can do this by copying the toolbar previously created in other layouts and modifying the XML. Refer to Listing 7.17 for the modifications.

Listing 7.17   Map Toolbar XML

```
1    <RelativeLayout
2        android:id="@+id/toolbar"
3        android:layout_width="match_parent"
4        android:layout_height="wrap_content"
5        android:layout_alignParentLeft="true"
6        android:layout_alignParentStart="true"
7        android:layout_alignParentTop="true"
8        android:background="@color/toolbar_background" >
9
10       <Button
11           android:id="@+id/buttonMapType"
12           android:layout_width="wrap_content"
13           android:layout_height="wrap_content"
14           android:layout_alignParentLeft="true"
15           android:layout_alignParentStart="true"
16           android:layout_marginLeft="20dp"
17           android:layout_marginStart="20dp"
18           android:text="Satellite View" />
19   </RelativeLayout>
```

You also have to modify the map fragment position so it lays out below the toolbar you just added. To do this, delete `android:layout_alignParentTop="true"` and add `android:layout_below="@+id/toolbar"`. Next, switch to **ContactMapActivity.java** to add the code for the button. Use the code in Listing 7.18.

Listing 7.18   Toolbar Button Code

```
1    private void initMapTypeButton() {
2        final Button satelitebtn = (Button) findViewById(R.id.buttonMapType);
3        satelitebtn.setOnClickListener(new View.OnClickListener() {
4            public void onClick(View v) {
5                String currentSetting = satelitebtn.getText().toString();
6                if (currentSetting.equalsIgnoreCase("Satellite View")) {
7                    gMap.setMapType(GoogleMap.MAP_TYPE_SATELLITE);
8                    satelitebtn.setText("Normal View");
9                }
10               else {
11                   gMap.setMapType(GoogleMap.MAP_TYPE_NORMAL);
12                   satelitebtn.setText("Satellite View");
13               }
14           }
15       });
16   }
```

Remember to call the method in the `onCreate` method. The code is very simple. You are implementing this button essentially as a toggle button. When the user taps the Location button, the code tests to see what the text for the button is. If it is Satellite View, the map type is set to `MAP_TYPE_SATELLITE`, and the button's text is changed to Normal View. If the text is Normal View, the map type is set to `MAP_TYPE_NORMAL`, and the button text is set to Satellite View.

Finish the code by making the navigation buttons work. Copy the code like you did for the Settings and List Activities. Be sure to disable the Maps button and call the initialization methods in the `onCreate` method. Test the code. When testing the app, you should see a display similar to Figure 7.8. Tap the marker to have contact information displayed.

Figure 7.8 Map of contacts with marker information displayed.

Summary

Location and maps can be very useful in some apps. A device's location is acquired by listening to either the network or the GPS sensor. You can code the capability to acquire the device's location whether you use maps or not. However, if you use maps, the code for determining your location is much simpler.

Icons can be placed on a map based on their GPS coordinates. The map object has a large number of classes that facilitate the manipulation of maps. Icons on a map are called *markers*. Markers can use the standard pin icon or a custom item supplied by the developer. Icons can also be made to display information about the location through the use of a title and snippets.

Using Google Maps on the Android platform requires significantly more setup than other code you have explored in this book. However, after you have set it up, you can reuse it for other apps you want to develop.

Exercises

1. Create a layout that displays the latitude, longitude, and accuracy for the network sensor and for the GPS sensor. Add a listener for each and have it display its reported location in the appropriate onscreen widget. Run it on a device. Walk around with the app open to this screen and observe the differences.

2. Modify the layout in Exercise 1 to have a third set of latitude, longitude, and accuracy labeled *best location*. Code a method to test for the best location and put the values in these widgets. Run the app and again observe the results.

3. Modify the markers on the map to use a custom icon. You can download and use an open source graphics program such as Gimp to create your icon. You may have to work with the icon size to get it to display in a reasonable manner on the screen.

4. Add the phone number for the contact being displayed on the map.

CHAPTER 8

Access to Hardware and Sensors in Android

Mobile computing devices have hardware features that significantly distinguish them from their more stationary counterparts. Hardware features allow the device to both sense and interact with its environment. These features enable the reexamination of assumptions many developers make when developing a piece of software. The ability to sense and interact with the environment allows the developer to rethink business processes encapsulated in software. Innovative and powerful approaches to solving problems become possible. This suggests that the app developer needs to have a working knowledge of how to integrate the device's hardware features into an app. This chapter describes how to integrate hardware sensors that can provide information about the device's internal and external environment and hardware features, such as the camera and phone, provided by the Android platform that can be used independently or integrated into an app. Determining the presence of a sensor on any specific device is also addressed.

Sensors, Managers, and Other Hardware

This section covers more sensors and managers used to access sensor data. The section also covers other hardware on some devices that can be used to augment an app's functionality.

Sensors

Android devices may have any number of sensors. Two of these, the network and GPS sensors, were discussed in the previous chapter. However, other sensors may also be used in apps. In all, the Android platform supports about 12 sensors. However, there is no requirement that a manufacturer of an Android device include all of them. For this reason, it is good practice to always check for the presence of a sensor before attempting to use it. The sensors supported range from those that measure the device's ambient environment, including temperature, relative humidity, atmospheric pressure, magnetic field, and light level, to those that detect how the device is moving or rotating.

The **Sensor** class represents all types of sensors. Sensors are instantiated as a system service by the operating system and thus are not instantiated by the apps that use them. To use a sensor, the app must access it through the **SensorManager** class. The SensorManager is also a system service and not instantiated by an app. An app accesses both Sensors and the SensorManager object by creating a reference to them by calling the `getSystemService` method within an app.

Two other items are needed to work with sensors, **SensorEvent** and **SensorEventListener**. A SensorEvent is an object that is created by a Sensor when it has something to report. This object holds information about the event, including a time stamp for when the object was created, the sensor that produced the event, and data that represents the sensor's measurements at the time of the event. A SensorEventListener is an interface that is implemented by any app that wants to use sensor information encapsulated in a SensorEvent.

Managers

Android devices have hardware for processing, memory, long-term storage, and providing power. The Android OS provides objects to facilitate the monitoring of the status of this hardware. For example, the Android OS has a **BatteryManager** that can be used to monitor the battery's status, a **StorageManager** that can be used to monitor the status of long-term storage, and a **PowerManager** that can be used to monitor power consumption.

The objects used to monitor the internal environment of the device are instantiated as system services like the SensorManager. Just like with LocationManager that you saw in the previous chapter, you do not instantiate these objects. To use them in an app, you get a reference to the appropriate system service.

Other Hardware

Android devices also have other hardware features, such as a phone and a camera. These devices have an app associated with them to provide access to their functionality. In contrast to accessing the sensors and monitors, these hardware items are accessed by making calls to their **application program interface (API)**. These apps can be opened from within an app to give the user access to their functionality. In this case, the user leaves the app to interact with the device and returns to the app after completing the task. The functionality of the hardware can also be accessed by integrating the features within the app by calling the associated app's API. In this manner, the app developer can provide users with exactly the functionality they need from the device. This is how the popular flashlight apps work. Developers of these kinds of apps access and control the camera's flash from within an app to create entirely new functionality from existing hardware.

Monitoring the Battery

Typically all versions of the Android OS have some sort of battery-level monitoring display so that the user knows when to recharge the device. However, just because the battery level is displayed to the user doesn't mean that the user will pay attention and plug in the phone or tablet when needed. To avoid complications from the device shutting down during app execution, you may need to monitor the battery within the app so that the app can take necessary precautions if the level gets too low. You may also require the user to have the device plugged in to external power to carry out certain operations that might require a significant power drain.

Monitoring the battery is not crucial to the MyContactList app. However, learning how to do so is useful for understanding one approach used in Android to interact with device hardware. The Android OS has an object that monitors important measures of battery health. Some of these measures include battery temperature, voltage, charge level, and many others. To examine all available measures, review the **BatteryManager** class on the Android Developer site (search for "android batterymanager"). The BatteryManager produces a broadcast every few seconds that includes the current reading on these measures. To monitor the battery, the app has to listen for these broadcasts and respond to the measures that are important to the app.

To demonstrate monitoring the battery, you will put a small TextView in the toolbar of the Contact List activity to display the current battery level as a percentage. Begin by adding the **TextView** to the **activity_contact_list.xml** layout file. Use the code in Listing 8.1.

Listing 8.1   XML to Add a TextView to ContactListActivity Toolbar

```
1       <TextView
2           android:id="@+id/textBatteryLevel"
3           android:layout_width="wrap_content"
4           android:layout_height="wrap_content"
5           android:layout_centerHorizontal="true"
6           android:layout_centerVertical="true"
7           android:text="100%" />
```

Be sure to place this widget within the toolbar `RelativeLayout`. When complete, your toolbar should look like Figure 8.1.

Figure 8.1   Toolbar with battery level TextView.

The next step is to add code to listen for, and respond to, the battery manager's broadcasts. To do so, you have to instantiate a **BroadcastReceiver** object that will capture and respond to the broadcast. A BroadcastReceiver is an object that can receive Intents sent by other Activities both within and outside the app. Generally, you set up a BroadcastReceiver to respond only to specific types of broadcasts. The code in the BroadcastReceiver typically uses the data from the broadcast Intent to perform some action. The final step is to tell the activity to listen for broadcasts from the BatteryManager using the broadcast receiver you defined. Enter the code in Listing 8.2 in the `onCreate` method of the **ContactListActivity** class.

Listing 8.2   Monitoring the Battery

```
1    BroadcastReceiver batteryReceiver = new BroadcastReceiver() {
2       @Override
3       public void onReceive(Context context, Intent intent) {
4          double batteryLevel = intent.getIntExtra(BatteryManager.EXTRA_LEVEL,0);
5          double levelScale = intent.getIntExtra(BatteryManager.EXTRA_SCALE,0);
6          int batteryPercent = (int) Math.floor(batteryLevel / levelScale * 100);
7          TextView textBatteryState = (TextView)findViewById(R.id.textBatteryLevel);
8          textBatteryState.setText(batteryPercent + "%");
9       }
10   };
11
12   IntentFilter filter = new IntentFilter(Intent.ACTION_BATTERY_CHANGED);
13   registerReceiver(batteryReceiver, filter);
```

Not much code is needed to implement battery monitoring, because the objects provided with the Android SDK do much of the work. However, much of the code is new and needs some explanation:

- **Line 1**—A `BroadcastReceiver` variable is declared and instantiated with a new `BroadcastReceiver`. This object receives `Intents` and has the code used to respond to the `Intent`. An `Intent` is broadcast from other apps or objects executing on the device.

- **Line 4**—The `Intent` concerning battery status sent by the OS contains information about the battery as `Extras`. This line gets the extra associated with the battery's current charge level. Although the value is retrieved as an integer, it is assigned to a double variable so that it can be used as a double later.

- **Line 5**—The extra associated with the scale used for measuring the charge is retrieved and assigned to a double variable. Capturing the scale is important because different devices may use different scales for measuring charge.

- **Line 6**— The percentage of battery charge left is calculated by dividing the level by the scale. If these two variables were not defined as doubles, this calculation would produce incorrect results because a divide operation needs to produce a double value. The result of the calculation is a number between 0 and 1, which is multiplied by 100 to get a percentage. The floor function is applied to take on the integer value of the result.

- **Line 12**—A new `IntentFilter` variable is declared and assigned a new `IntentFilter`. An `IntentFilter` listens for `Intents` that have been broadcast by the system and only lets through the ones the developer is looking for. In this case, the filter looks for Battery Status changed intent. This is required because a `BroadcastReceiver` can respond to any intent. However, you want it to respond only to `Intents` sent by the battery.

- **Line 13**—The `BroadcastReceiver` is registered, which means that the app is told to listen for battery status intents and handle them with the `BroadcastReceiver` defined in the activity.

Run the app. Using the emulator will always produce the same result, and in some cases will not produce any result. However, if you test it on an actual device, you will see different percentages as the battery charges or discharges.

Using Sensors to Create a Compass

The Android OS supports a number of types of sensors. Generally, the sensors are either motion, environmental, or position sensors. Motion sensors detect how the device is moving, environmental sensors capture various measures of the device's ambient environment (e.g., the light level), and position sensors capture information that can be used to determine the physical position of the device. Not all devices have all the sensors that the OS supports. This fact has implications for how you code access to the sensors.

Accessing sensor information is not particularly important for the MyContactList app. However, understanding how these are accessed could be important for future apps you develop. In the case of the MyContactList app, you will use sensors to create a simple compass to show users what direction they are headed when they have the contact map displayed. Creating a graphical compass display is beyond the scope of this book, so you will simply add a TextView to the ContactMapActivity toolbar to display the direction in text (N, S, E, and W).

The first step is to add the TextView used to display the direction. Open **activity_contact_map.xml** and enter the **TextView** using the code in Listing 8.3.

Listing 8.3   Heading TextView

```
1    <TextView
2        android:id="@+id/textHeading"
3        android:layout_width="wrap_content"
4        android:layout_height="wrap_content"
5        android:layout_centerHorizontal="true"
6        android:layout_centerVertical="true"
7        android:text="WNW" />
```

Be sure to place this widget within the toolbar `RelativeLayout`. When complete, your toolbar should look like Figure 8.2.

Figure 8.2   Toolbar with heading TextView.

To calculate the device heading, you need to capture information from two sensors: the accelerometer and the magnetometer. The accelerometer reports device acceleration in three dimensions. The magnetometer reports the geomagnetic field in three dimensions. The math behind the heading calculation using these measures is beyond the scope of this book. Fortunately, the Android SDK again does much of the work for you. However, implementing a compass using these sensors requires a bit more work than monitoring the battery.

Open **ContactMapActivity.java** and declare four variables where you declared the GoogleMap variable (just after the class declaration). Use the following code:

```
SensorManager sensorManager;
Sensor accelerometer;
Sensor magnetometer;
TextView textDirection;
```

To monitor sensors requires a SensorManager object and Sensor objects for each sensor used. Next, add the code in Listing 8.4 to the `onCreate` method of the activity.

Listing 8.4 **Registering Sensors for Monitoring**

```
1    sensorManager = (SensorManager) getSystemService(Context.SENSOR_SERVICE);
2    accelerometer = sensorManager.getDefaultSensor(Sensor.TYPE_ACCELEROMETER);
3    magnetometer = sensorManager.getDefaultSensor(Sensor.TYPE_MAGNETIC_FIELD);
4
5    if (accelerometer != null && magnetometer != null) {
6        sensorManager.registerListener(mySensorEventListener, accelerometer,
7                                  ↪SensorManager.SENSOR_DELAY_FASTEST);
8        sensorManager.registerListener(mySensorEventListener, magnetometer,
9                                  ↪SensorManager. SENSOR_DELAY_FASTEST);
10   } else {
11       Toast.makeText(this, "Sensors not found",Toast.LENGTH_LONG).show()
12   }
13       textDirection = (TextView) findViewById(R.id.textHeading);
```

This code gets the references to the sensors and registers them to activate a SensorEventListener object when they report changes. The SensorEventListener has yet to be coded, so the references to `mySensorEventListener` will show as an error.

- **Lines 1–3**—`SensorManager` is a system service, so you get a reference to it rather than instantiate it. The `SensorManager` is used to get references to the two sensors used to measure heading.
- **Lines 5–9**—As previously noted, not all devices have all sensors. Therefore you test whether the sensor is available so that the lack of a sensor on a device does not cause the app to crash. If the sensors are present, the `SensorManager` associates each with the same event listener and passes a parameter, indicating how frequently to process sensor events.
- **Line 11**—If sensors are not available, the user is informed with a `Toast`.

The next step is to implement the SensorEventListener, which is the class that handles the actual events from the sensors and takes action on them. Code this event just as you would a method. It should be within the class body but not within any other method. Refer to Listing 8.5 to implement the listener.

Listing 8.5 **SensorEventListener Code**

```
1     private SensorEventListener mySensorEventListener = new SensorEventListener() {
2
3         public void onAccuracyChanged(Sensor sensor, int accuracy) {  }
4
5         float[] accelerometerValues;
6         float[] magneticValues;
7
8         public void onSensorChanged(SensorEvent event) {
9           if (event.sensor.getType() == Sensor.TYPE_ACCELEROMETER)
10               accelerometerValues = event.values;
11          if (event.sensor.getType() == Sensor.TYPE_MAGNETIC_FIELD)
12               magneticValues = event.values;
13          if (accelerometerValues!= null && magneticValues!= null) {
14            float R[] = new float[9];
15            float I[] = new float[9];
16            boolean success = SensorManager.getRotationMatrix(R, I,
17                                      ↪accelerometerValues, magneticValues);
```

(continued)

Listing 8.5 SensorEventListener Code (*continued*)

```
18              if (success) {
19                  float orientation[] = new float[3];
20                  SensorManager.getOrientation(R, orientation);
21
22                  float azimut = (float) Math.toDegrees(orientation[0]);
23                  if (azimut < 0.0f) { azimut+=360.0f;}
24                  String direction;
25                  if (azimut >= 315 || azimut < 45) { direction = "N"; }
26                  else if (azimut >= 225 && azimut < 315) { direction = "W"; }
27                  else if (azimut >= 135 && azimut < 225) { direction = "S"; }
28                  else { direction = "E"; }
29                  textDirection.setText(direction);
30              }
31          }
32      }
33  };
```

The sensor event listener code is relatively involved, even without needing to understand the math involved.

- **Line 3**—A `SensorEventListener` requires the implementation of two events, `onAccuracyChanged` and `onSensorChanged`. To calculate a heading, you don't need accuracy, so its method block is empty.

- **Lines 5–6**—Sensor readings are returned as a `float` array. Two variables to hold the response from each sensor are declared.

- **Lines 8–12**—The `onSensorEvent` first determines which sensor triggered the event and then captures the values it provided.

- **Lines 13–17**—If there are values available for both sensors, the `SensorManager` is asked for two rotational matrices used for orientation calculation. Discussion of the rotational matrices is beyond the scope of this book.

- **Lines 18–20**—If the matrices are successfully calculated, the `SensorManager` is asked to calculate the orientation of the device. Orientation is measured in three dimensions.

- **Line 22**—The first orientation measure is the value used to calculate the heading. It is reported in radians, so these are changed to degrees.

- **Line 23**—Convert the heading reported to eliminate negative numbers.

- **Lines 24–28**—Use degree heading to get text description. These are done in 90-degree increments. You could add more code to get finer gradations of direction, such as NW or SE.

Test the app on a device. You'll need to move the device around to get different readings. This is not possible on the emulator.

Android Versus iOS: Creating a Compass

As you have seen in the preceding section, creating a compass in Android requires accessing two sensors and manipulating the data they provide. In contrast, the device's heading is included in the Core Location framework on iOS. Heading is reported as a function of the device's location, making creating a compass in iOS significantly easier than in Android.

Using the Phone

An Android device not only provides hardware devices that can be used in an app to collect information on the device's internal and external environment; it also includes hardware capabilities that can be accessed to provide certain functionality for an app. To access data from a sensor, the app listens for a broadcast from a sensor. However, other hardware on an Android device operates only when the user or an app wants to use it. In these cases, the functionality provided by the hardware is accessed by calling the API associated with the hardware. One such piece of hardware provided by some devices is a telephone. In the MyContactList app, you will code the ContactActivity so that pressing and holding one of the contact's phone numbers will automatically call that number. This functionality requires accessing the phone's API and asking it to call the number provided.

Accessing phone functionality of an Android device requires user permission. Add the following line with the other permissions already in the **AndroidManifest.xml** file:

```
<uses-permission android:name="android.permission.CALL_PHONE" />
```

Using the phone is considered a dangerous permission, so we will also have to ask for permission to do it to make the app compatible with the newer versions of the Android OS.

The next step is to add a listener to the phone number EditTexts for the press-and-hold user action. This is done by adding a method to the **ContactActivity.java** file. Since we have to check permission, this method will call a method to check the permission. Use the code in Listing 8.6. Be sure to add the call to this activity in the onCreate method.

Listing 8.6 Initializing the LongClickListener

```
1    private void initCallFunction() {
2        EditText editPhone = (EditText) findViewById(R.id.editHome);
3        editPhone.setOnLongClickListener(new OnLongClickListener() {
4
5            @Override
6            public boolean onLongClick(View arg0) {
7                checkPhonePermission(currentContact.getPhoneNumber());
8                return false;
9            }
10       });
11
12       EditText editCell = (EditText) findViewById(R.id.editCell);
13       editCell.setOnLongClickListener(new OnLongClickListener() {
14
15           @Override
16           public boolean onLongClick(View arg0) {
17               checkPhonePermission(currentContact.getCellNumber());
18               return false;
19           }
20       });
21   }
```

The pattern in this method should be very familiar by now. A reference to the widget is created, and an event is added to the widget. Next, the widget's response to the event is coded. In this case, that is a call to another method that checks if the app has permission to use the phone. Add the checkPhonePermission method using Listing 8.7.

Listing 8.7   Check for Phone Permission

```
1      private void checkPhonePermission(String phoneNumber) {
2      if (Build.VERSION.SDK_INT >= 23) {
3          if (ContextCompat.checkSelfPermission(ContactActivity.this,
4              ↪Manifest.permission.CALL_PHONE) != PackageManager.PERMISSION_GRANTED) {
5
6              if (ActivityCompat.shouldShowRequestPermissionRationale(ContactActivity.this,
7                  ↪android.Manifest.permission.CALL_PHONE)) {
8
9                  Snackbar.make(findViewById(R.id.activity_contact),
10                     ↪"MyContactList requires this permission to place a call from the app.",
11                     ↪Snackbar.LENGTH_INDEFINITE).setAction("OK", new View.OnClickListener() {
12                         @Override
13                          public void onClick(View view) {
14                              ActivityCompat.requestPermissions(
15                                 ↪ContactActivity.this,
16                                 ↪new String[]{
17                                 ↪android.Manifest.permission.CALL_PHONE },
18                                 ↪PERMISSION_REQUEST_PHONE);
19                          }
20                      })
21                        .show();
22              } else {
23                  ActivityCompat.requestPermissions(ContactActivity.this, new
24                         ↪String[]{android.Manifest.permission.CALL_PHONE},
25                     ↪PERMISSION_REQUEST_PHONE);
26              }
27          } else {
28              callContact(phoneNumber);
29          }
30      } else {
31          callContact(phoneNumber);
32      }
33  }
```

Much of this code you saw in Chapter 7, "Maps and Location in Android." After you do all the required imports, you will still have some errors that can be corrected as follows:

- **Line 4**—The permission required to access the phone is `android.Manifest.Permission.CALL_PHONE`.
- **Line 18**—Just as in Chapter 7, we need the ability to identify which permission is being requested Open **ContactActivity** (if not open) and put the following line of code after the `Contact currentContact` line at the top of the file:

```
final int PERMISSION_REQUEST_PHONE = 102;
```

The final step to handling the permission check is to override the `onRequestPermissionsResult` method, as you did in Chapter 7. Refer to Listing 8.8 to write this code.

Listing 8.8   Handling the Phone Permission Request

```
1    @Override
2    public void onRequestPermissionsResult(int requestCode,
3        ↪ @NonNull String permissions[], @NonNull int[] grantResults) {
4
5        switch (requestCode) {
6          case PERMISSION_REQUEST_PHONE: {
7            if (grantResults.length > 0 && grantResults[0] ==
8                ↪ PackageManager.PERMISSION_GRANTED) {
9                Toast.makeText(ContactActivity.this, "You may now call from this app.",
10                       ↪ Toast.LENGTH_LONG).show();
11            } else {
12                Toast.makeText(ContactActivity.this, "You will not be able to make calls " +
13                       ↪ "from this app", Toast.LENGTH_LONG).show();
14            }
15          }
16        }
17    }
```

Notice that this follows the same pattern as in Chapter 7. There are two main differences. The first is that we check for a different permission in the switch case statement. The second is that instead of doing something, we provide a message that the functionality is now available. It is preferable to perform the action requested, as we did in the chapter on location. However, there is no way to pass the phone number to this method, so we have to be satisfied with a message.

The final step is to code the method that actually dials the phone number. Add the callContact method to **ContactActivity.java** using the code in Listing 8.9. Note that since calling the phone is considered dangerous, we have to check if permission has been granted to get it to work, just like we did in the onPause method of Chapter 7.

Listing 8.9   callContact Method

```
1    private void callContact(String phoneNumber) {
2      Intent intent = new Intent(Intent.ACTION_CALL);
3      intent.setData(Uri.parse("tel:" + phoneNumber));
4      if ( Build.VERSION.SDK_INT >= 23 &&
5          ↪ ContextCompat.checkSelfPermission(getBaseContext(),
6          ↪ android.Manifest.permission.CALL_PHONE) !=
7          ↪ PackageManager.PERMISSION_GRANTED) {
8        return ;
9      }
10     else {
11         startActivity(intent);
12     }
    }
```

Using the phone requires starting the phone app. As you have seen before, all apps are made up of activities, and to start an activity, you use an intent:

- **Line 2**—A new intent is instantiated with the parameter Intent.ACTION_CALL, which tells Android that you want to use the phone to make a call.
- **Line 3**—The telephone number to be called is passed to the intent as a uniform resource identifier (URI). A URI is similar to a uniform resource locator (URL), except that a URL identifies a location on the World Wide Web, whereas a URI can be used to identify a local resource.

Remember to call the phone call initialization method in the onCreate method.

This is all that's needed to make a phone call through an app! If you run the app now, when editing is turned on, the call function works. However, when you are in viewing mode, it does not. This is because you disabled the EditTexts in viewing mode because you didn't want any accidental changes to the user's information. To correct this, you need to modify the `setForEditing` method in ContactActivity.java.

An EditText has to be enabled to allow it to respond to a long click event. This means that you cannot ever disable them. Delete the `setEnabled` lines of code associated with the `editPhone` and `editCell` variables. The problem with doing this is that now the phone number will be editable, even in viewing mode. To correct this problem, you need to set the `inputType` of the EditText to null when in viewing mode, and set it back to accepting phone numbers when in editing mode. To do this, modify the `if (enabled)` block of code to include the following in the true block:

```
editPhone.setInputType(InputType.TYPE_CLASS_PHONE);
editCell.setInputType(InputType.TYPE_CLASS_PHONE);
```

Add the following to the false block (the `else` block):

```
editPhone.setInputType(InputType.TYPE_NULL);
editCell.setInputType(InputType.TYPE_NULL);
```

Your app can now call your contacts by pressing and holding on a phone number. Run the app. If you run the app in the emulator, the emulator will pretend to call a number, but running it on an Android Device will actually make the call.

Using the Camera

Many Android devices have a camera, which can be used independently by the user or integrated into an app. You can integrate it into an app by calling the camera API to start the camera, so that the user can take a picture using the camera app provided by Android and then return the picture to the app. You can also do it in a more sophisticated manner in which the camera's API, and thus functionality, is integrated right in the app. The former approach is similar to the way the phone functionality was used in the previous section. The latter is much more sophisticated and requires creating an activity and layout designed to provide the camera functionality desired in the app. This approach is beyond the scope of this book.

The camera will be used in the MyContactList app to capture a photo of the contact so that it can be displayed with the contact's data. To begin, there must be a place to show the image on the ContactActivity's layout. To do this, you add an ImageButton to the layout. You use the button functionality of the ImageButton to access the camera. An ImageButton must have an image associated with it, so the first step is to import the photoicon.png file (available with the resources provided with this book) into the drawable-hdpi folder. Copy the **photoicon.png** file and paste it into the **res > drawable** folder. Click **OK** on the window that opens. Next, open **activity_contact.xml** and add an **ImageButton**. Configure the button using the code in Listing 8.10. Be sure to place the widget within the **Scroll-View**—preferably after the **TextView** that displays the label **Contact**.

Listing 8.10 ImageButton Configuration

```
1    <ImageButton
2        android:id="@+id/imageContact"
3        android:layout_width="wrap_content"
4        android:layout_height="wrap_content"
5        android:layout_alignParentRight="true"
6        android:layout_alignParentEnd="true"
7        android:layout_marginRight="10dp"
8        android:layout_marginEnd="10dp"
9        android:layout_alignTop="@+id/textContact"
10       android:src="@drawable/photoicon" />
```

Modify the attributes of the `editName EditText` so it does not overrun the `ImageButton` by adding the following attribute/value pairs:

```
android:layout_toLeftOf="@+id/imageContact"
android:layout_toStartOf="@+id/imageContact"
```

When complete, your layout should look like Figure 8.3. Note that if your address EditText bleeds over the photo, you can either add the previous two attribute/value pairs to its XML or change its `margin_top` attribute value to a bigger number.

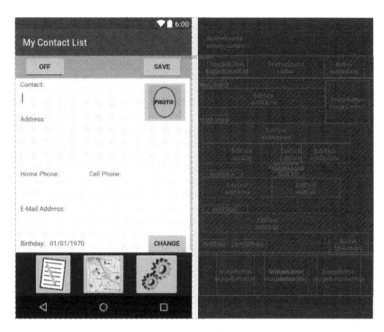

Figure 8.3 Layout with ImageButton.

The camera is outside the app, so the app needs permission to use it. As always, this is granted by entering a permission in the app's manifest. Enter the following permission after the other permissions already in the manifest:

```
<uses-permission android:name="android.permission.CAMERA" />
```

The permission to use the camera is also considered dangerous, so we will have to code the app to handle permissions in newer Android OSs. Open **ContactActivity.java** to code the camera use. This requires initializing the ImageButton to listen for an `onClick` event, writing code to have the `onClick` method check for permission to use the camera, writing a method to start the camera, and writing code to listen for the camera response to get the picture after it has been taken. Code the ImageButton initialization with the code in Listing 8.11. Again, remember to call the method in the activity's `onCreate` method.

Listing 8.11 ImageButton Initialization Method

```
1     private void initImageButton() {
2         ImageButton ib = (ImageButton) findViewById(R.id.imageContact);
3         ib.setOnClickListener(new View.OnClickListener() {
4             public void onClick(View v) {
5                 if (Build.VERSION.SDK_INT >= 23) {
6                     if (ContextCompat.checkSelfPermission(ContactActivity.this,
7                         ↪ android.Manifest.permission.CAMERA) !=
8                         ↪ PackageManager.PERMISSION_GRANTED) {
9                         if (ActivityCompat.shouldShowRequestPermissionRationale
10                            ↪ (ContactActivity.this, android.Manifest.permission.CAMERA)) {
11                            Snackbar.make(findViewById(R.id.activity_contact,
12                                ↪ "The app needs permission to take pictures.",
13                                ↪ Snackbar.LENGTH_INDEFINITE)
14                                ↪.setAction("Ok", new View.OnClickListener() {
15                                    @Override
```

(continued)

Listing 8.11   ImageButton Initialization Method (*continued*)

```
16                              public void onClick(View view) {
17
18                                  ActivityCompat.requestPermissions
19              ↪ (ContactActivity.this, new String[]
20                                      ↪ { android.Manifest.permission.CAMERA},
21                                      ↪ PERMISSION_REQUEST_CAMERA);
22                                  }
23                              })
24                          .show();
25                  } else {
26                      ActivityCompat.requestPermissions(ContactActivity.this,
27                          ↪ new String[]{android.Manifest.permission.CAMERA},
28                          ↪ PERMISSION_REQUEST_CAMERA);
29                      }
30                  }
31              else {
32                  takePhoto();
33              }
34          } else {
35              takePhoto();
36          }
37      }
38   });
39   }
```

Find the `setForEditing` method and add this code to enable and disable the picture button with the rest of the widgets in the layout:

```
ImageButton picture = (ImageButton) findViewById(R.id.imageContact);
picture.setEnabled(enabled);
```

Now you have to add the identifier for the permission result. Add this line to the top of the file where you declared the other identifier:

```
final int PERMISSION_REQUEST_CAMERA = 103;
```

Add code to the `onRequestPermissionsResult` method to handle the request for permission to access the camera. Add the code in Listing 8.12 after the closing } of the `case (PERMISSION_REQUEST_PHONE)` statement.

Listing 8.12   Handling the Camera Permission Request

```
1   case PERMISSION_REQUEST_CAMERA: {
2       if (grantResults.length > 0 && grantResults[0] == PackageManager.PERMISSION_GRANTED) {
3           takePhoto();
4       } else {
5           Toast.makeText(ContactActivity.this, "You will not be able to save
6               ↪ contact pictures from this app", Toast.LENGTH_LONG).show();
7       }
8       return;
9   }
```

Next, add the code to access the camera and get the returned picture. The camera app is, of course, an activity, so it must be started with an `Intent`. Use the code in Listing 8.13 to create the `takePhoto` method and the method to capture the picture.

Listing 8.13   Starting the Camera and Capturing the Result

```
1    public void takePhoto(){
2        Intent cameraIntent = new Intent(android.provider.MediaStore.ACTION_IMAGE_CAPTURE);
3        startActivityForResult(cameraIntent, CAMERA_REQUEST);
4    }
5
6    protected void onActivityResult(int requestCode, int resultCode, Intent data) {
7        if (requestCode == CAMERA_REQUEST) {
8            if (resultCode == RESULT_OK) {
9                Bitmap photo = (Bitmap) data.getExtras().get("data");
10               Bitmap scaledPhoto = Bitmap.createScaledBitmap(photo,144,144,true);
11               ImageButton imageContact = (ImageButton) findViewById(R.id.imageContact);
12               imageContact.setImageBitmap(scaledPhoto);
13               currentContact.setPicture(scaledPhoto);
14           }
15       }
16   }
```

Not much code is required to implement the camera functionality, because the objects in the Android SDK do most of the work.

- **Line 2**—A new intent is instantiated with a parameter that tells the system to open the camera in image capture mode. You do not have to check whether the camera is present. The permission you added in the manifest would not let your app run on the device if it did not have a camera.

- **Line 3**—The Activity is started in a different way than you have seen before. In this case, you want the activity to return a value to the app after it has completed, so you use the startActivityForResult method. The parameters are the new Intent and a static variable called CAMERA_REQUEST. The variable CAMERA_REQUEST is identified as an error because it has not been defined. This variable is an integer that is used to identify the response from the camera when it finishes. The value is not fixed by the SDK but should be given a large integer so it is not confused with other built-in responses. Add this line after the class declaration to fix the error:

```
final int CAMERA_REQUEST = 1888;
```

- **Line 4**—The onActivityResult method is declared. This method receives a request code that was sent to the camera, a result code, and an intent that includes the data (the picture in this case) from the intent you started. This method is executed when the camera finishes.

- **Line 7**—The returned request code is checked to see if it is the one sent to the camera.

- **Line 8**—Check if the camera returned with a picture.

- **Line 9**—The data from the Intent is assigned to a variable declared as a Bitmap. The method .get("-data") doesn't specify a type of data to get from the extras, so it must be cast into a Bitmap. After the photo is captured, it is displayed in the ImageButton, and the contact object's picture attribute is set to hold the photo.

- **Line 10**—The picture is scaled so that a consistent-sized photo is displayed in the ImageButton. The parameters of this method are the picture to be scaled, the height and width to scale to in pixels, and whether a filter should be applied during the scaling operation. Generally, when scaling down, this filter has no effect but can change the result when scaling up.

The setPicture method must be added, along with a Bitmap variable to the Contact object. Open **Contact. java** and add a variable to the class using the following code:

```
private Bitmap picture;
```

Next, add the setters and getters with the code in Listing 8.14. Close the file.

Listing 8.14   Picture Variable Setter and Getter

```
1    public void setPicture(Bitmap b) {
2        picture = b;
3    }
4    public Bitmap getPicture() {
5        return picture;
6    }
```

Now that you have a picture to save, the method to display a contact must be modified to display the saved contact picture, the ContactDataSource methods to save and retrieve contacts must be modified to store and retrieve the picture, and the database must be modified to have a field in the table to hold the picture. First, open **ContactDB-Helper.java** to add the field to the database. The first step is to tell the app that the database has changed. Locate the following line and increase the version number by 1.

```
private static final int DATABASE_VERSION = 2;
```

Next, add a picture field with a data type of blob to the contact table. The blob data type can hold any type of binary data and is typically used for picture, audio, and video objects. The data type, blob, is an acronym for "binary large object." Change the last line in the CREATE_TABLE_CONTACT string to the following:

```
+ "email text, birthday text, contactphoto blob);";
```

The last step is to modify the onUpgrade method. Technically, you would not have to modify this to get the change to the database. It is currently written to delete the current table and create a new one when the database is updated. However, there is one big drawback: all the user's contacts will be deleted! If you are in the development stage prior to release of the app, this is OK. If the app has been released, this is not an option. To handle a change to the database structure without losing all the user data, modify the onUpgrade method to match the code in Listing 8.15.

Listing 8.15   onUpgrade Modifications

```
1    @Override
2    public void onUpgrade(SQLiteDatabase db, int oldVersion, int newVersion) {
3    // Log.w(ContactDBHelper.class.getName(), "Upgrading database from
4    // version " + oldVersion + " to "
5    // + newVersion + ", which will destroy all old data");
6    // db.execSQL("DROP TABLE IF EXISTS contact");
7    // onCreate(db);
8        try {
9            db.execSQL("ALTER TABLE contact ADD COLUMN contactphoto blob");
10        }
11        catch (Exception e) {
12            //do nothing
13        }
    }
```

The modifications comment out the deletion and re-creation of the table and add an SQL statement to add the new field to the table. This line is surrounded by a try and catch statement, so that if the field has already been added, it doesn't crash the app.

After the ContactDBHelper.java file has been modified, the **ContactDataSource.java** file needs to be modified to save and retrieve the picture. The code in Listing 8.16 must be added to both the insertContact and updateContact methods. The code must be placed prior to the call to update or insert the contact. Note that in the updateContact method, you need to use updateValues.put("contactphoto", photo) instead of initialValues.put("contactphoto", photo).

Listing 8.16 Saving a Picture to the Database

```
1    if (c.getPicture() != null) {
2
3        ByteArrayOutputStream baos = new ByteArrayOutputStream();
4        c.getPicture().compress(Bitmap.CompressFormat.PNG, 100, baos);
5        byte[] photo = baos.toByteArray();
6        initialValues.put("contactphoto", photo);
     }
```

To store a bitmap to the database, it must first be converted to a byte array. This code uses standard objects in the Android SDK to do this conversion. After the photo is converted, it is placed into the values to be updated like any other value. Next, modify the getSpecificContact method to load the Contact object with the picture. This does not need to be done in the getContacts method because the picture is not used by any activity that uses the whole set of contacts. Returning the picture from the database is essentially the reverse process from saving to the database (Listing 8.17).

Listing 8.17 Getting a Picture from the Database

```
1    byte[] photo = cursor.getBlob(10);
2    if (photo != null) {
3        ByteArrayInputStream imageStream = new ByteArrayInputStream(photo);
4        Bitmap thePicture= BitmapFactory.decodeStream(imageStream);
5        contact.setPicture(thePicture);
6    }
```

Again, the objects supplied by Android do most of the work. The byte array is retrieved from the database and is then tested to determine if a picture has been stored. The 10 in the getBlob method is the index of the contact-photo field in the contact table. The conversion from byte array to Bitmap will cause a crash if no picture is stored. After the data has been converted, it is set in the Contact object.

The last step is to modify **ContactActivity.java** to display the retrieved picture along with the rest of the contact's data. This is done in the initContact method. Place the code in Listing 8.18 where appropriate in that method.

Listing 8.18 Display the Photo

```
1    ImageButton picture = (ImageButton) findViewById(R.id.imageContact);
2    if (currentContact.getPicture() != null) {
3        picture.setImageBitmap(currentContact.getPicture());
4    }
5    else {
6        picture.setImageResource(R.drawable.photoicon);
7    }
```

The code gets a reference to the ImageButton on the layout and checks if the contact has a picture. If there is a picture, it sets it as the button's image. If not, the default image resource is displayed.

Test the app on an Android device. The camera display you see will depend on the device you are running the app on. After taking a picture, the ContactActivity should look similar to Figure 8.4.

Figure 8.4 Contact with a picture.

Summary

An Android device provides many hardware features that enable the creation of innovative apps or enhance the capabilities of more traditional apps. The approach used to access these features is dependent on the hardware device. However, regardless of the type of hardware to be accessed, the developer must always include a permission to use the item in the app's manifest file. Sensors that may be used to detect the environment that the device is currently in or how the device is moving are accessed by enabling methods in your code that listen for status changes of the sensor. The app can then use those status changes to do something useful for the user.

Hardware features provided by the Android system that may be used through an app (such as the phone) may also be accessed through other apps or integrated into apps. These features are accessed via calls to the device's API. Through API calls, the developer can ask the hardware feature to perform functions for the app.

Exercises

1. Modify the toolbar of the ContactActivity to display the proximity sensor readings. Add the proximity sensor service so that this works.
2. Modify the app so that when the user long-clicks the cell number of a contact, the text messaging service is opened instead of the phone service. You will have to have a permission in the manifest to send text (SMS) messages.
3. Modify the app to open a dialog to enter a text message that will be sent from the app instead of opening the text message service.
4. Modify the app to display an incoming text message as a Toast. You will have to register your app with a permission to read text (SMS) messages and set up a listener for text messages.
5. Modify the compass to report NW, NE, SW, and SE, in addition to the N, S, E, and W headings.

PART III

DEVELOPING THE iOS APP

CHAPTER 9

Using Xcode for iOS Development

This part of the book covers how to create iOS apps. You learn to use the powerful Xcode development environment. In this first chapter, you learn to build a simple but complete iOS app—a variation on the traditional "Hello World" app—and run it on the simulator and a physical iOS device (iPod, iPhone, or iPad).

Creating the Xcode Project

You're no doubt eager to get started creating your first iOS app, so jump right in and launch Xcode. You should find it in the Applications folder on your Mac. After Xcode starts, you should see the screen shown in Figure 9.1. Creating a new Xcode project requires going through a series of screens and making decisions about the kind of project you will be creating.

1. Select the **Create a New Xcode Project** option. If you don't have Xcode installed on your Mac, simply go to the App Store and search for it—it's a free download.

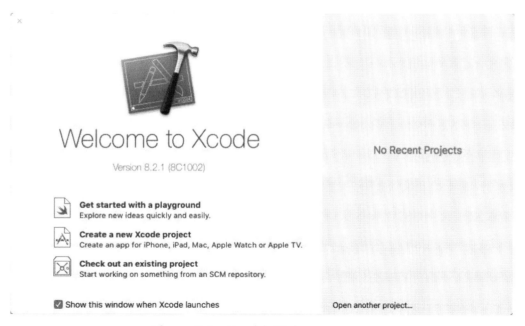

Figure 9.1 Xcode's Welcome screen.

2. Next, you're given a number of options for creating projects based on various templates, as shown in Figure 9.2. You'll notice in the tab bar at the top of the window that you can create projects for both iOS and OS X. Our focus here is on iOS applications, so choose that tab. You will see several templates that will make creating a new app simpler. For your first app, choose **Single View Application**, and click **Next**.

Figure 9.2 Choose the Single View template for the first project.

3. On the next screen (Figure 9.3), you choose a **Product Name** for your app, which is the name that will show up in the App Store. Type "**Hello World!**" The **Team** entry allows you to specify a development team that the app will be developed with. The team controls how you will be able to distribute the app (see Chapter 16, "Publishing Apps") and allows for testing the app on a physical device (which is covered at the end of this chapter). The **Organization Name** will show up in the App Store, so should be the same for all your apps. The **Organization Identifier** is your organization's reverse domain name (e.g., com.company), and this becomes part of the **Bundle Identifier**, which will uniquely identify an app in the App Store. Be sure to set the **Language** to **Swift.**

On this screen, you can also choose which **Devices** to target (iPhone, iPad, or Universal). Universal creates a single app but with a different user interface for iPhone and iPad, enabling the same app to be installed on both types of devices. In this app, you will only build the user interface for iPhone, so choose **iPhone** as the option here.

We will not use Core Data, Unit Tests, or UI Tests in this project, but it doesn't hurt to leave the checkmarks at their default. Later in the book, you will see Core Data functionality, and in this chapter, you will see some of the files generated by leaving this checkmark on.

Swift or Objective-C?

Prior to 2014, all native development for iOS was done in the programming language Objective-C. This is a fairly old language whose roots trace to Smalltalk and the time that Steve Jobs was ousted from Apple, during which he spent time at NeXT. The language was used as the default language for programming the NeXT workstations, and when Steve jobs returned to Apple in 1996, he brought the language along. Objective-C is a solid object-oriented language, but it has a very peculiar syntax that makes it difficult for beginners to learn. Swift, by contrast, is much more user friendly and looks much more familiar to those with experience with Java and C#. It is clear by now that Swift will be the language of choice for all development on Apple's platforms (iOS, WatchOS, tvOS, and macOS). However, there are a lot of apps still being developed and maintained in Objective-C.

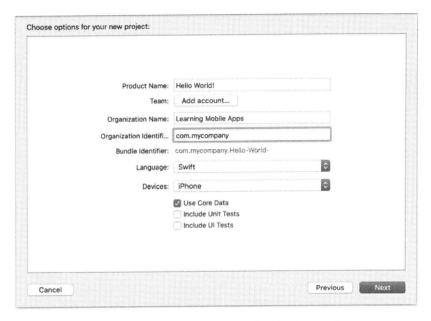

Figure 9.3 Choosing options for the iOS project.

4. Click **Next,** and you will have to choose a location to save your project. You can navigate to an appropriate place on the disk to create the project files. Click **Create.**

Xcode Project Folder

The Xcode project is created in a folder and consists of a file with the extension .xcodeproj and a number of other files and folders. You can easily move the entire project between computers by copying the directory that contains the .xcodeproj file and any subfolders as well. We have found that when we work on our regular computers (office, home, and so on), using Google Drive or Dropbox works well to keep all the files of a project in sync. But we often find ourselves compressing the project folder and e-mailing or copying to a thumb drive to make sure we have a good copy of the project. To reopen a project that has been moved, you can double-click the .xcodeproj file. You also have the option of using version control systems by taking advantage of Xcode's built-in support of Git.

After creating the project, you're now looking at the main Xcode workspace window. Figure 9.4 shows an overview of the Xcode workspace, which you should familiarize yourself with. Generally, you work from left to right in the IDE. Choosing an item in the Navigator Area displays the item in the Editor Area, and the Utility Area displays detailed information about the item in the Editor Area. Each main area has a Selector Bar that allows for choosing the specific information shown in that part of the IDE. For example, the Inspector Selector Bar allows for choosing between six different kinds of information about the document, shown in the Editor Area.

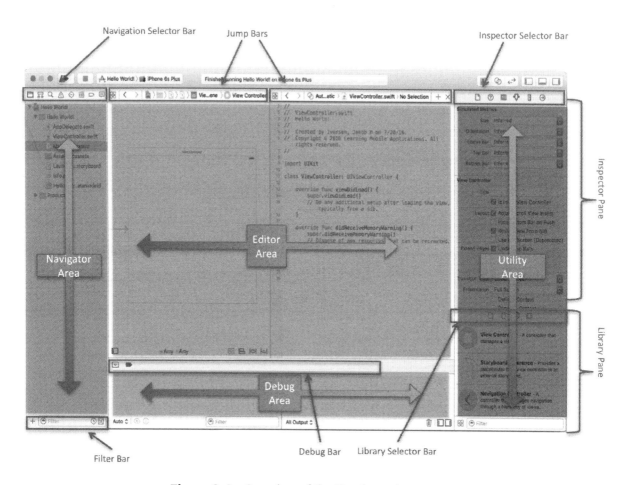

Figure 9.4 Overview of the Xcode workspace.

Xcode is a very powerful development environment with a lot of functionality. If you decide to do any serious development for iOS, you should take some time to figure out how everything works. You can find a detailed description of the Xcode workspace in the documentation (**Help > Xcode Overview**). We won't go into a lot of detail now, but you will discover some of the Xcode functionality as you need it. However, if you take some time to look through the documentation, you will likely save a lot of time later on.

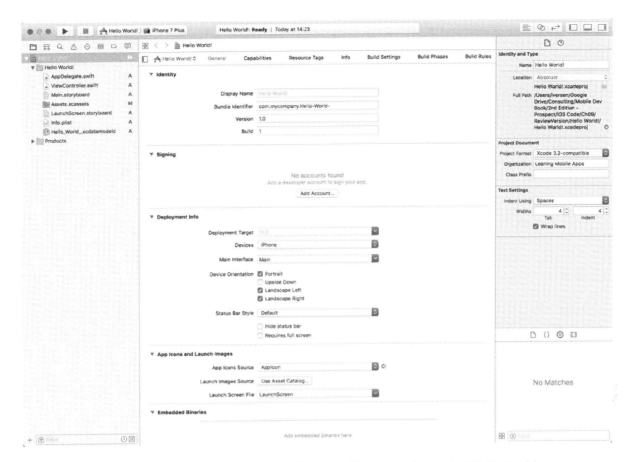

Figure 9.5 Overview of the Xcode workspace with our newly created Hello World app.

Project Settings

After you've created the Hello World project, you should see the view of Xcode, as shown in Figure 9.5. In the center of the workspace is a summary of the app and several app-wide settings. The first section enables you to specify the version and build for the app. The version is used when the app is published to the App Store. Anytime an app with a higher version number is published, all your users will be prompted to download a new version. The build number is for internal use by the developer. You can choose which device types to target, as well as which version of iOS you want to target. As of this writing, the current version of iOS is 10.2. This setting determines the minimum version of iOS your users have to be running in order to run your app. This is just a signal within the app store. Apps are typically built using the latest available base SDK, so if you use features in a later SDK than your deployment target, you will need to insert checks in your code to make sure your app doesn't crash on devices with older versions of iOS.

This is also where you can specify which device orientations are supported. By default, iPhone apps support portrait and landscape, left and right, but not upside down. (iPad default is to support all four orientations.)

On the left, in the navigation area, you can see the files that Xcode created for you. Figure 9.6 shows a closer look at what it should look like. The exact number and types of files created depends on which choices you made when creating the project. Here's an overview of some of the files and folders created in this project:

- **AppDelegate.swift**—The App Delegate manages issues related to the entire app and are primarily used to manage the life cycle of the app—how it is started, what happens when it goes to the background, and so on. This life cycle is covered in more detail in Chapter 2, "App Design Issues and Considerations," and in Chapter 11, "Persistent Data in iOS." All Swift code files have the extension .swift.

- **Main.storyboard**—The storyboard is used to design the interaction between multiple screens in your app, as well as designing the layout of the individual screens.

- **ViewController.swift**—The view controller contains the code that controls the user interactions with the app. Most of the programming we do in this book will be in this file.

- **Assets.xcassets**—This folder contains all the images, including icons, needed for your app.
- **LaunchScreen.storyboard**—When your app launches, the launch screen should contain a simplified view of the app user interface that can be loaded quickly, so the user gets a better experience when starting the app.
- **info.plist**—This file contains a few app-specific settings. Most of these are controlled in other parts of Xcode.
- **HelloWorld.xcdatamodeld**—This file contains information about the Core Data model for the app, which is where you can save data for the app. More details in Chapter 11, "Persistent Data in iOS."
- **Products**—This is your compiled app file.

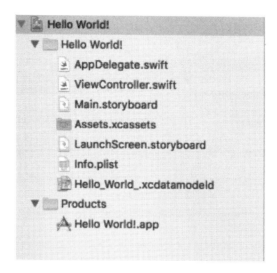

Figure 9.6 Contents of the Hello World project.

Creating the User Interface

In this section, you will see how to create a very simple user interface in Xcode. To open a file for editing in Xcode, you need to click it only once. Double-clicking will open it in a separate window.

1. Click once on the **Main.storyboard** file. This opens the file in Interface Builder (see Figure 9.7), where you can easily create the user interface for your app. With the storyboard open, you can drag user interface elements from the utility pane on the bottom right and control a range of settings in the top of the utility pane. Note that to get the exact same view as in Figure 9.7, you may have to expand the items on the left-hand side of the storyboard and select **View Controller.**

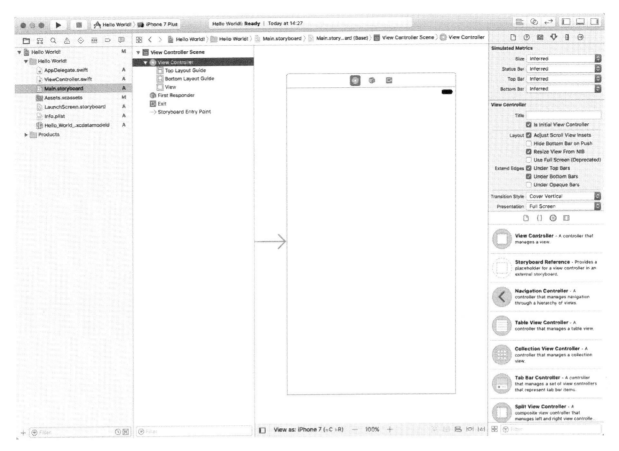

Figure 9.7   Interface Builder.

2. In the lower right of the utility area, you should see the Object Library, which contains all the user interface elements you can use in your app. If you don't see the Object Library, click the square in a circle icon highlighted in blue in Figure 9.7.

   Start by dragging a **Label** onto the user interface canvas (see Figure 9.8). You may have to scroll down the list of controls to find the Label. You can also use the Search bar below the controls and type in **label**. Notice that you get blue dotted guidelines as you drag the label around. Drag it to the middle of the screen.

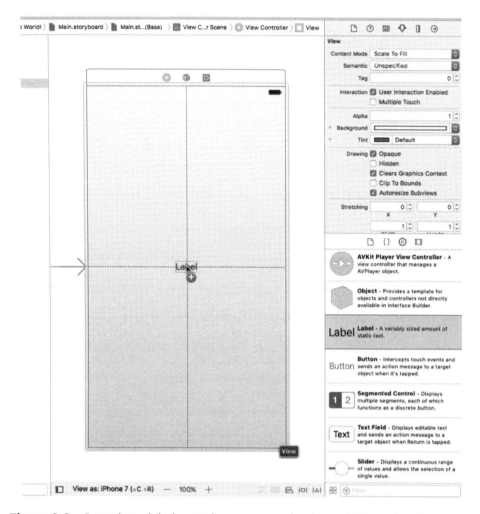

Figure 9.8 Dragging a label onto the canvas and using guidelines for placement.

3. Double-click the **label** to change the text of it to **Hello World!** and then press **Enter**. We want the label to be centered on the screen when you run the app. To do this, click on the **Align** button at the bottom right of the Interface Builder window and check the last two options, which will center the control horizontally and vertically in the container (see Figure 9.9). Then click **Add 2 Constraints**.

This adds two rules for the control that will center the control, regardless of which screen size and orientation is used when running the app. In Chapter 10, "iOS Navigation and Interface Design," you will learn more about Auto Layout, which is the name for the technology used to control placement of controls in an iOS app.

The label isn't centered anymore in the designer, but this can be fixed by clicking the **Update Frames** button, which is located two buttons to the left of the Align button. This will update the designer to match any constraints added for the item you currently have selected. Clicking it with the label selected should place it back in the center of the screen.

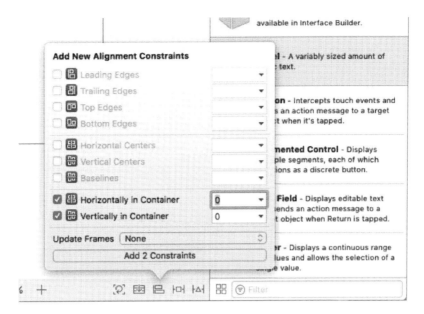

Figure 9.9 Centering a control in a container.

4. Above the utility area on the right, you have a little menu bar of five items. The fourth one from the right should be selected. This is the **Attributes Inspector**, which enables you to set many properties for the currently selected user interface element. For the label, you can change its appearance quite a bit. Feel free to play around, but you just need to change the font size to **24**. After you have changed the font size, the label caption may not be entirely visible. You can use the Update Frames button to make sure the text shows up.

Figure 9.10 Changing the Font using the Attributes Inspector.

Running the App in the Simulator

Launching the app in the built-in simulator that comes with Xcode is quite simple. In the top-right corner of Xcode, you will see a big Run button, and next to that is something called a Scheme, which allows you to choose which device is targeted (see Figure 9.11). Click the right side of the **Scheme** and choose one of the iPhone simulators. If you have a physical device connected to your computer, it will also show up in this list. You'll see later in this chapter how you set up to run your app on a physical device.

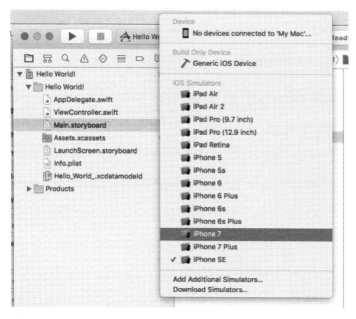

Figure 9.11   Choosing an iPhone Simulator to run the app.

Click the **Run** button on the top left of the Xcode toolbar and wait a few seconds for the Simulator to launch with your app (see Figure 9.12). You can control how the Simulator looks and behaves in the Hardware menu. If you choose a device with a high-resolution screen, it may not fit on your computer screen comfortably. In that case, you can go to **Window > Scale** and choose a zoom level.

Figure 9.12   iOS Simulator with the Hello World! app.

Creating Advanced Layout

The Hello World! app you created is very simple. This section will show you how to create a more advanced app with some real functionality. First, you will set up the user interface using the AutoLayout system, where you add constraints to each of the user interface controls, describing the placement of the control relative to the screen and other controls. You already saw how you can use constraints to center a control on the screen. Next, you will also see that you can place controls a number of pixels below another control. The next chapter will contain much more detail on how to use constraints to construct a much more sophisticated user interface.

1. Switch back to Xcode and make sure the storyboard is open. Then double-click the **Hello World label** and change it to **Please enter your name:** and drag it to the top of the screen.

2. Drag a **Text Field** (scroll or search for it in the Object Library) onto the canvas and place it below the label. The exact placement doesn't matter, because you will use constraints to place it relative to the label a little later.

3. Drag a **Button** below the text field. Double-click the button and change its text to **Tap Here!**

4. The final control to add is a Label, which you can place below the button. Delete its text, and specify its color as **blue** and the alignment to be **Centered** using the **Attributes Inspector.**

    To finish the layout of the app, you will need to add some constraints to the controls you added. As you go through the following steps, you will have errors and warnings about the constraints not being correct. These errors will resolve when you get to Step 10.

5. Select the original **label** and remove the constraint to center vertically. Constraints are removed in the sidebar by expanding the **View** and then the **Constraints**. Select the **centerY = centerY** constraint and press the **Delete** key (see Figure 9.13).

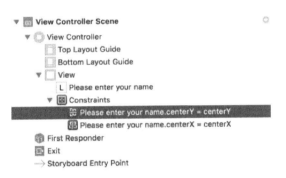

Figure 9.13 Deleting a constraint.

6. Add a constraint to place the original label control 20 pixels below the top of the screen by selecting the label and then clicking the **Add New Constraints** button at the bottom right of the Interface Builder. Then enter **20** in the top box, making sure that the line between the top box and the center square is highlighted. Then click **Add 1 Constraint** (see Figure 9.14).

Figure 9.14 Adding a constraint 20 pixels below the top of the screen.

7. Select each of the three new controls and add the constraints to center them horizontally in the container (see Figure 9.9). You may find it easier to select the last label in the sidebar, since its content is empty.

8. Select the text field and add a constraint, setting the width to **200**.

9. Add constraints to each of the three new controls to place them **15** pixels below the previous control.

10. Once all the constraints are added, you can select View in the sidebar; then click the **Update Frame** button in the bottom right of the Interface Builder.

Select the text field and look in the **Attributes Inspector** at some of the settings available. Change the Capitalization to **Words**, and then look at the Keyboards option. You can specify a keyboard that will show up on screen that is suited to the kind of data being input (for instance, if you need to have the user input only numbers, you can specify a Number Pad). This would be a good time to try out the different keyboards. You need to run the Simulator to test the effect each time you choose a different one. If the keyboard doesn't show up in the Simulator when you select the text field, go to **Hardware > Keyboard > Toggle Software Keyboard**.

Before moving on, make sure the keyboard is set to Default. Figure 9.15 shows sidebar with all the constraints added, as well as the completed UI in both the Interface Designer and the iOS simulator with the default keyboard activated.

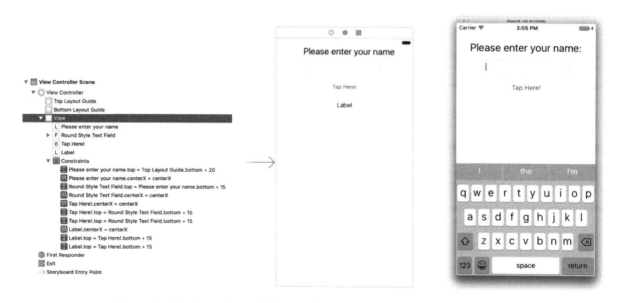

Figure 9.15 Completed UI in Interface Designer and the iOS simulator.

Adding App Behavior

Having created the user interface, your next task is to add some action to the app. The action you want is to have the app take the name entered and say Hello to the user by name.

1. Return to Xcode and click **Stop** to quit the simulator. Then make sure **Main.storyboard** is open in the editor.

2. Click the **Show Assistant Editor** button in the top-right corner of the Xcode window. (It's the second button from the left; see Figure 9.16.)

Figure 9.16   Creating an outlet for a user interface element.

This opens an extra editor that by default contains the file that best matches what is displayed in the main window. For the storyboard, that should be the corresponding **ViewController.swift**. If this file isn't showing up in the Assistant, click the **Related Items** icon at the top left of the editor (it's the one with four small squares).

3. We will need to create what are called *outlets* for those user interface elements we want to be able to access from the code. This includes the text field, where we need to be able to read the text the user entered and the bottom label that will be updated to contain our own text string based on the two text fields. To create the outlets, control-drag from the **text field** to the view controller below the `class` line. Then let go, and you should see the situation as shown in Figure 9.17.

Figure 9.17   Creating an outlet for a user interface element.

4. Enter **txtName** in the Name field and click **Connect**. You should now have this line of code in ViewController:

```
@IBOutlet weak var txtName: UITextField!
```

For more detail on what this code means, you can look in Appendix C, "Introduction to Swift." For now, all you need to know is that this has provided a name for the text field that we can reference in our code as `txtName`.

5. Do the same for the bottom label, naming it **lblOutput**. You can control-drag from the sidebar to create this outlet, since the label doesn't have any content.

6. Next, you'll add the code for the button. The first step is the same: control-drag from the **button** to the view controller below the properties for the text fields and label. However, this time, in the top drop-down choose **Action** instead of Outlet (see Figure 9.18). Give it the name **showOutput**. For the Event, we will use the default **Touch Up Inside**, but take a moment and look through the list of all the possible events that this button will respond to. Touch Up Inside means that the button responds to events where users touched the button and then released their fingers while still inside the button. The convention in iOS is that to cancel a touch, you would drag your finger outside the target and then let go (try it on your own device to see how it works). Leave the Arguments as **Sender**. Click **Connect**.

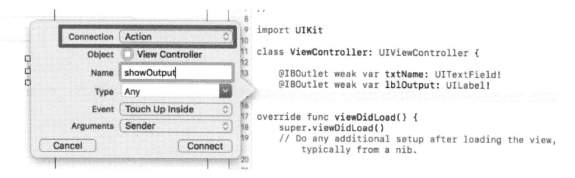

Figure 9.18 Creating the action for the button.

Connecting Code to UI—iOS versus Android

In both Android and iOS, the user interface (UI) and the code that makes the UI work are stored in different files. This means that both types of app coding require that the code has to link to the UI in some way. In iOS, this is often referred to as "wiring up" the user interface. However, in Android, connecting the UI to the code is done entirely in the code itself.

If you've ever created a program with a UI on a different platform, you're probably used to having to provide variable names for all UI elements. In iOS and Android, we just provide names to those UI elements we will need to access in code. Thus, the static label at the top of our UI isn't given a name. The same goes for the button, where we will need to intercept the event that happens when the user taps the button but we really don't care about the button itself.

In Android, whenever some code needs a reference to a control, we use a special command that will find it by its ID. This requires extra coding but provides great flexibility. Forgetting to connect the code to the UI widget needed in either operating system will result in a runtime error.

7. You will now have a method called showOutput. Between the curly braces of this method, enter the code shown in Listing 9.1.

Listing 9.1 The showOutput: Method

```
1   @IBAction func showOutput(_ sender: Any) {
2       let name = txtName.text
3       let output = "Hello " + name!
4       lblOutput.text = output
5   }
```

The following is a brief explanation:

- The first line is the method declaration. (Appendix C, "Introduction to Swift," has more detail on how Swift methods are declared.)

- Line 2 declares a constant called name and assigns the value in the text field (txtName) by calling the text field's text property.

- Line 3 declares a constant called output that is initialized with a string that combines the string "Hello" with the name constant.

- The last line assigns the result to the text property of the output label (lblOutput).

8. Run the app and test it by entering different names and touching the Tap Here! button.

UI Design—iOS versus Android

Both iOS and Android uses relative positioning when creating a layout. iOS uses a system called AutoLayout. This enables creation of UI designs that are independent of the physical screen of the device. This means that app developers don't have to worry (too much) about screen sizes of different devices. However, relative positioning also means that the position of one control affects other controls.

The two systems are similar in that they don't rely on the actual grid of pixels on the screen. But whereas Android mostly relies on the relationships between the controls, iOS uses a system of equations that describe a control's relationship to the screen and other controls.

Dismissing the Keyboard

As you may have noticed when using the app, the keyboard doesn't go away by itself when a text field loses focus. To get the keyboard to disappear, you have to add a little code to the program. Listing 9.2 shows the code to add to `viewDidLoad` in **ViewController.swift** and a new method called `dismissKeyboard`.

Listing 9.2   Code to Dismiss the Keyboard

```
1    override func viewDidLoad() {
2        super.viewDidLoad()
3        // Do any additional setup after loading the view, typically from a nib.
4        let tap: UITapGestureRecognizer = UITapGestureRecognizer(target: self,
5                                          action: #selector(self.dismissKeyboard))
6        view.addGestureRecognizer(tap)
7    }
8
9    func dismissKeyboard() {
10       //Causes the view (or one of its embedded text fields) to resign the first responder status.
11       view.endEditing(true)
12   }
```

- Line 4 creates a constant called `tap` of the type `UITapGestureRecognizer`. This object listens for taps, and when it recognizes a tap, it calls the method identified in the `#selector` section. In this case, it will call the `dismissKeyboard` method.
- Line 6 adds the `tap` object to the `view`, which means that it will listen to any taps that occur anywhere in the view.
- Line 11 inside the `dismissKeyboard` method simply calls the `endEditing` method, which looks at the current view and any subviews looking for textfields. If it finds any, those text fields are forced to end what is called first responder status, which in effect means that it loses focus and the keyboard disappears.

App Icons and Launch Images

The Assets.xcassets folder is called the Asset Catalog and was introduced with Xcode 5 as a way to manage all the images needed for your app, including app icons and launch images.

App Icons are graphical images that are used to indicate your app on the home screen of the iOS device your app is running on. When you create the icon for your app, you should be prepared to create it in a number of resolutions so that it looks great on different devices, and for various uses within the app as well. The icon is used in several places:

- On the home screen, to give the user an easily recognizable image of your app.
- In Spotlight results when the user is searching on the device.
- In the Notification area, when a new notification is displayed.
- In the Settings app, where the user can change various settings for your app.

In each of these areas, the icon is supplied in different resolutions, and the resolutions also differ between iPad and iPhone, in addition to depending on whether the device is a regular display or a retina display. There can also be differences depending on whether your app is targeting iOS 7 or versions of iOS earlier than that. In all, a Universal app targeting both iPhone and iPad and made available for both iOS 6 and iOS 7 may have to have as many as 17 versions of the app icon.

Fortunately, the asset catalog makes it relatively simple to find out what you need. Click the **Assets.xcassets** folder and then AppIcon (Figure 9.19). On the right, you see eight spots for icons. For this app, the icons will be supplied only for iOS 7+ and iPhone. To determine the resolution you need to supply, you look at the number in the last line under each spot (20pt, 29pt, 40pt, and 60pt). This is how many logical points the image takes up. However, if you look just below each of these images, it says either 2x or 3x, indicating that the real pixel count is either double or triple in each direction (a 40pt image in 2x would be 80x80 pixels and in 3x would be 120x120 pixels). The 2x designation is for retina displays and 3x for retina HD, which is used on the iPhone Plus models.

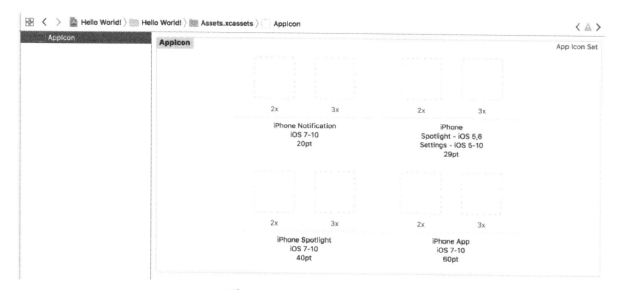

Figure 9.19 Asset catalog.

Manually creating all the proper resolutions for an icon is a lot of work. Fortunately, there are templates available for various image programs and online services that can handle some of the tedium. One example is the website MakeAppIcon, where you can upload a single high-resolution image and then download a compressed file with all the image sizes you need—including for Android and Apple Watch apps. The book includes a zip file with such a set.

Once you have uncompressed the downloaded file, you can get it into the Asset catalog, simply by dragging the entire folder of icons into the Asset catalog below AppIcon. This will create a new entry called AppIcon-1, with all the slots populated with icons, as shown in Figure 9.20. You can just delete the original AppIcon entry and rename the new one to AppIcon.

You can test how the icon looks by running the app in the simulator and then clicking the Home button (**Hardware > Home**) to get to the home screen, where the app icon will be shown along with the app name. You can see the Spotlight icon in the simulator if you click the home screen and drag down. This will pull down a search field. Type **Hello** into the resulting search field, and the icon will show up in the search results.

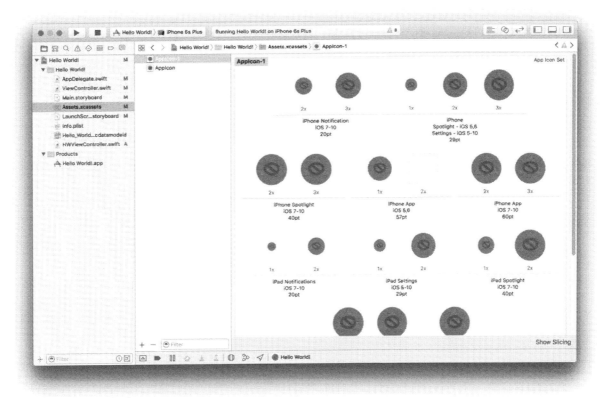

Figure 9.20 Populated AppIcon asset.

To have your app listed in the app store, you also need to supply icons in sizes of 512x512, 1024x1024, and 1536x1536 pixels.

The other option that is available in the asset catalog is launch images. A launch image is shown as the app is launching. Apple recommends that your launch image is a blank version of the app's first screen. This way, the user will quickly see the app and what it looks like before it is filled in with data. Launch images are also supplied in different resolutions, depending on the device. Table 9.1 shows the possible resolutions for launch images.

Table 9.1   Typical Launch Image Dimensions

Device	Portrait	Landscape
iPhone Plus	1080 x 1920 pixels	1920 x 1080 pixels
iPhone 6 and 7	750 x 1334 pixels	1334 x 750 pixels
iPhone 5, SE	640 x 1136 pixels	1136 x 640 pixels

iPhone Screen Sizes and Resolutions

When the first iPhone was released, the resolution was set to 320x480 pixels. Programmers would use this coordinate grid to arrange their user interface. When the iPhone 4 was released, it sported a retina display with double the resolution (640x960), also known as retina or 2x. However, from the perspective of the programmer, the original 320x480 grid was still used to position everything on the screen, so apps didn't have to be updated to handle the higher resolution. But all the UIKit controls were rendered in higher resolution, and all images could now be supplied in retina versions with double the resolution.

With the iPhone 5 and iPod touch 5, Apple again changed the resolution, this time increasing the vertical size to 1136 pixels (giving a grid of 320x568). The iPhone 5 increased the physical size of the screen from 3.5 to 4 inches, so when you see references to a 4-inch screen, this is the screen introduced with the iPhone 5 (and iPod touch 5).

The trend continued with the introduction of iPhone 6, which sported a 4.7 inch screen and a 750 x 1334 pixel resolution and the iPhone 6 Plus, which had a 5.5 inch screen and 1080 x 1920 pixel resolution.

With this many screen sizes, it has become unwieldy to manually create all the different sizes needed for image assets, so app developers turn to various tools like Sketch and Photoshop to help automate the process.

With the increasing number of screen sizes, Apple has also moved from absolute positioning of user interface elements to a system of relative layout that uses constraints on each element to describe its location relative to the other controls on the screen, as well as its parent container.

Testing iOS Apps on Physical Devices

The iOS Simulator is very powerful and allows for doing most of the testing you need for most business apps. In a classroom situation, you can do a lot of interesting and worthwhile things without using real devices. However, students get excited about seeing their creations running on a real device, and there are certain features where it is necessary to test on a device. The following are some limitations of the simulator, requiring you to test on a real device:

- No phone or messaging—The Simulator can toggle the in-call status bar, but doesn't make or receive calls.
- Access to camera
- Realistic access to network (perhaps to test for network coverage in a specific location)
- Access to gyroscope and altimeter (perhaps for developing game controls)
- Realistic user touch interactions

A few years ago, it was a fairly complicated process to set up and manage physical devices for testing. However, Apple has greatly simplified the process. There are really just a few simple steps involved:

1. Create an Apple ID at https://appleid.apple.com. If you already have one, you can skip this step. You do not have to sign up for Apple's developer program to be able to run your app on a device. However, if you want to publish your app to the App Store (see Chapter 16, "Publishing Apps"), you will need to sign up and pay.

2. Add your Apple ID to Xcode by choosing **Xcode > Preferences… > Accounts > + > Add Apple ID…** (see Figure 9.21).

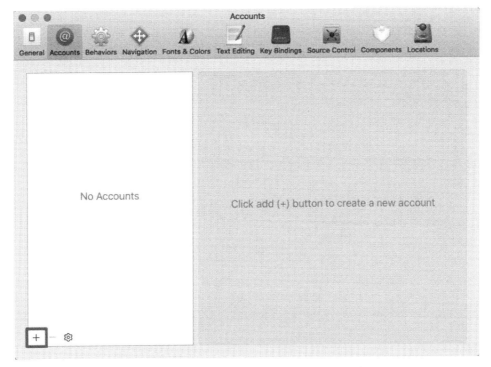

Figure 9.21 Adding an account to Xcode.

3. Enter your Apple ID user name and password and click **OK**.

4. Connect a physical device.

5. Select your physical device in the Scheme list where the Simulator model is listed:

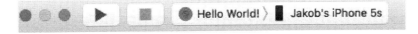

6. Click the **Run triangle button**. The first time you do this, it may take a while for the app to run, as the device needs to process symbol files (Figure 9.22). You will need to make sure the device is unlocked before the app can be installed and run.

Figure 9.22 Waiting for symbol files to be processed on physical device.

Xcode will automatically sign the app and install the necessary profiles on the device in order to run the app. You can check the status of the signing process, and switch between development teams if you have multiple teams or multiple Apple IDs in the Project Summary under Signing (see Figure 9.23).

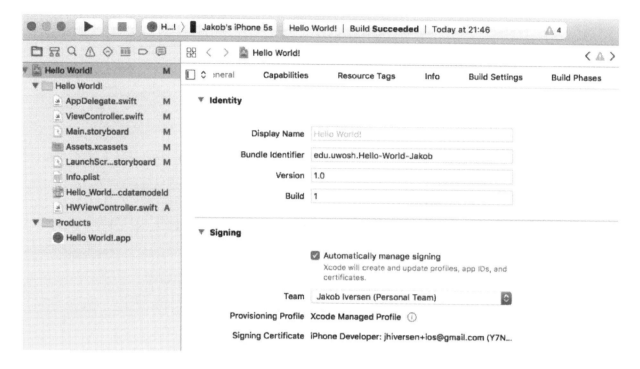

Figure 9.23 Signing an app.

As you run your app on the device, you may find it helpful to view the Devices window. Go to **Window > Devices**. This will show you the currently running device and any simulators available, and allows for viewing device logs and taking screenshots (Figure 9.24).

Figure 9.24 Devices window.

Apple offers an iOS University Developer Program for free to qualified higher education institutions. This program used to be the best way to allow students to test on physical devices. However, with the recent changes to Xcode allowing anyone with an Apple ID to test on a physical device, there isn't much of an advantage to the University Developer Program, and we recommend having students just create an Apple ID.

Summary

Congratulations! You have built your first iOS app. You created an Xcode project, designed and coded a user interface, and finally made the app do something. Along the way, you learned the process of iOS app development, the Xcode development environment, the components of an iOS app, and how to run the app on a physical device.

Exercises

1. Split the name field into first and last name. Then make sure both first and last names show up when tapping the button.
2. Change the functionality of the `showOutput` method so that if no text has been entered, the output changes to Hello World!
3. Explore the properties for the text fields, buttons, and labels within Xcode. Change the label to green and bold text. Change the border style for the text field, and add a clear button that will reset the UI back to its initial state.
4. Add a new button to the app, with a method that will change the `lblOutput` text to Hello World!
5. Rotate the simulator while running the app, and observe the results.
6. Run the app in the iPad simulator. Then change the project's Device's setting to Universal (under Deployment info) and run again in the iPad simulator. Observe the results.
7. Add several new text fields to enter a number, a phone number, an e-mail address, and so on, and set the keyboard to the appropriate type. Be sure that the keyboard dismisses appropriately from each of the new fields.

iOS Navigation and Interface Design

Because the screens are small on mobile devices, as a developer, you have to pay careful attention to how you use that space and set up a logical navigation structure in your app. Many mobile apps use multiple screens with carefully arranged navigation between these screens. In iOS, several built-in controllers can help you create a logical flow in your app. It's very important to understand how these controllers work and how you can take advantage of them. In this chapter, you create the basic user interface for the MyContactList app and learn how to use two important means of navigating around an iOS app: the Tab Bar Controller and the Navigation Controller. You also learn how to use *AutoLayout* to adjust the placement of controls and how to use many of the built-in user interface components available for iOS apps, as well as how to create the user interface for the app using the Storyboard feature in Xcode.

Views and Controllers

The user interface classes in iOS are contained in the UIKit framework. The UIKit framework contains a large number of classes that you can take advantage of in your apps. The classes are arranged in an inheritance hierarchy, with the top class being **UIView**. This class describes a basic rectangle with width, height, background color, and so on. It can contain subviews and may also have a parent view. One of the subclasses of UIView is **UIWindow**, which has been restricted to set its origin to the top left of the screen. Each iOS app has one UIWindow object that is created when the app launches. All other screens are subviews of UIWindow. Other subclasses of UIView include **UILabel**, **UIScrollView**, **UINavigationBar**, **UITableCell**, and **UIControl** (which is the parent class for most of the regular controls used for creating apps, such as **UIButton**, **UITextField**, and **UISlider**). Figure 10.1 shows the relationships between some of the common UIKit classes.

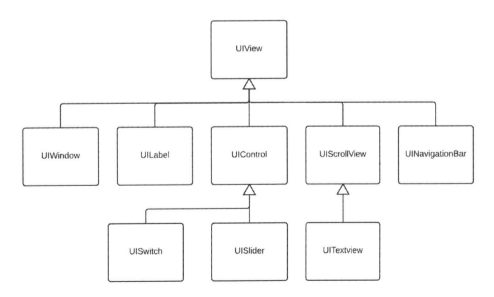

Figure 10.1   Relationships between some of the common UIKit classes.

View Controller

When you create iOS apps, you often need to create multiple screens for each app. Each screen is managed by an instance of the **UIViewController** class, where other **UIView** objects for the various user interface elements are added. As you saw in the previous chapter, the screens can be designed using Interface Builder to add the various user interface elements needed for the app. In this situation, the View Controller is managed in two files: a .storyboard file that specifies the layout of user interface elements and a .swift view controller file that contains all the code that manages the user interactions. In some situations, there is no storyboard file for a view controller. You will see an example of this in Chapter 12, "Tables in iOS: Navigation and Information Display," where the user interface is described entirely in code.

After the View Controller has been set up, it can be added to the application in different ways. It can be added as a root view, as you saw in the Hello World app in the previous chapter, as one of the tabs in a tabbed interface, as a page in a page layout, or as part of a navigation hierarchy. You will see examples of both tabs and navigation hierarchy in the following sections.

Tab Bar Controller

The Tab Bar Controller shows up at the bottom of iPhone apps and allows the user to choose between different screens in the app. This user interface is used in many common apps, including the built-in News app (see Figure 10.2).

Figure 10.2 Tab Bar Controller shown at the bottom of the built-in News app.

Navigation Controller

The Navigation Controller is used to allow the user to drill down through multiple screens while keeping track of the path so the user can later go back the same way. This pattern is also used very frequently in iPhone apps, including the built-in Contacts app, as shown in Figure 10.3. When the user taps one of the contacts listed in the screen on the left, the app navigates to the screen on the right, but the button at the top left allows the user to navigate back to the list of all users.

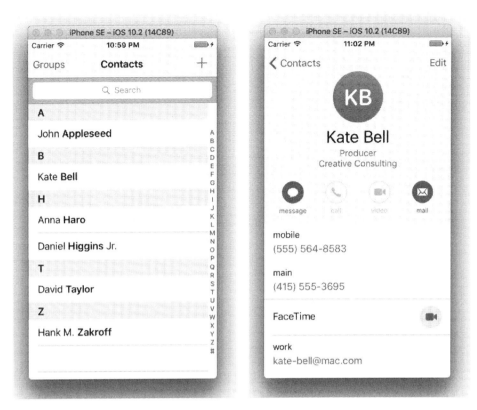

Figure 10.3 Navigation Controller in the built-in Contacts app.

Creating the Interface

In this section, you see how to create the project and the user interface for the MyContactList app that will be the example for the next few chapters.

Creating the Project

Create a new project in Xcode (**Shift-Command-N**) using the following settings in the first two steps in the wizard, leaving all other settings at their defaults:

- **Template**—Tabbed Application
- **Product Name**—My Contact List
- **Team**—Leave blank or add an account as described in Chapter 9, "Using Xcode for iOS Development." If you don't add an account, you will have a signing status error once the project is created. This will not cause any issues until you need to run the app on a physical device.
- **Organization Name**—Learning Mobile Apps
- **Organization Identifier**—com.company.lma
- **Language**—Swift
- **Devices**—iPhone

Creating the Views

As described in more detail in Chapter 2, "App Design Issues and Considerations," MyContactList will have three basic screens: displaying and editing the contacts, a map view of one or more contacts, and a settings screen. The contacts screen will also have an associated screen to edit the birthdate of the contact. Your first task is to create views for each of these four screens. Because you chose the Tabbed template when creating the project, two of the view controllers and the tab bar have already been created for you in the storyboard. When you open **Main.storyboard**, you will see the Tab Bar Controller and two View Controllers (Figure 10.4).

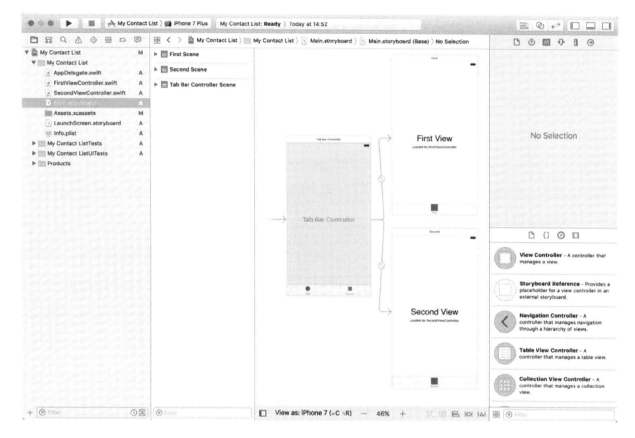

Figure 10.4   Tab Bar Controller and two View Controllers.

Because the tab bar needs three scenes, start by adding a new View Controller for the third scene.

1. Drag a **View Controller** into the Storyboard from the Object Library on the lower right-hand side of the Xcode screen (see Figure 10.4).

2. Select the **Tab Bar Controller**.

3. Control-drag from the **Tab Bar Controller** to the new **View Controller**, and then let go (hold down the control key then click on the Tab Bar Controller and drag). You will use this technique to accomplish a number of tasks when building user interfaces for iOS.

4. Choose **view controllers** in the dialog that pops up (Figure 10.5). This will add an arrow from the Tab Bar Controller to the new View Controller and add a third element to the actual tab bar (Figure 10.6).

5. To help distinguish among the three View Controllers, copy the label that says **First View** onto the new **View Controller** by selecting it and pressing **Cmd-C**; then select the new **View Controller** and press **Cmd-V**. You may have to zoom in a little to be able to select the label.

6. With the label selected, click the **Align** button at the bottom of the editor and select to center it both horizontally and vertically in the container. Then click **Add 2 Constraints**. The label will now have some orange lines attached to it, but the location didn't change. If you were to run the app now, it would be positioned properly, but the storyboard doesn't always update automatically. To fix any discrepancies, you can click the **Update Frames** button at the bottom of the editor.

7. Double-click each of the three labels and change the text to **Contacts**, **Map**, and **Settings**, as shown in Figure 10.6.

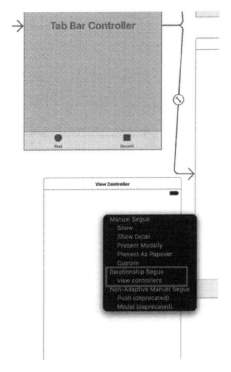

Figure 10.5 Adding a new View Controller.

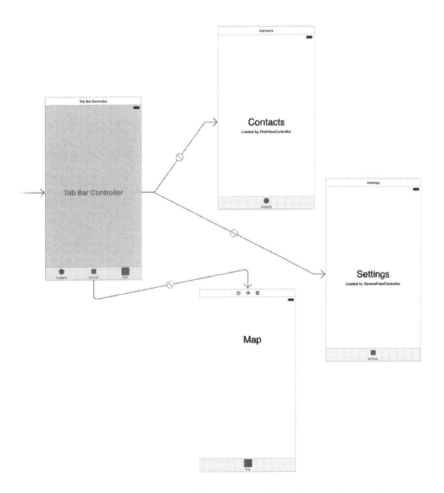

Figure 10.6 Completed interface of the Tab Bar Controller.

If you run the app now, you will see the Contacts screen come up, and then the three tabs at the bottom, named First, Second, and Item. Here's how to change the tabs to have the proper names:

1. Open **Main.storyboard** and select the **First View Controller** in the **Document Outline**.
2. Make sure the **Attributes Inspector** is selected and then change the **Title** to **Contacts** (Figure 10.6). This will change both the name of the scene and the view controller in the **Document Outline**.
3. Select the Tab Bar item (it says "First") at the bottom of the Contacts View Controller, and change the **Title** in the Attributes Inspector to **Contacts** (Figure 10.8).
4. Repeat for the **Map** and **Settings** screen.

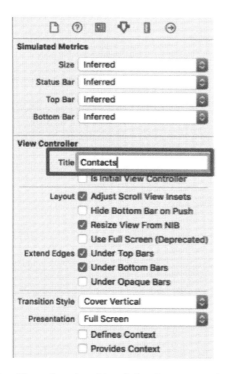

Figure 10.7   Changing the title of the Contacts View Controller.

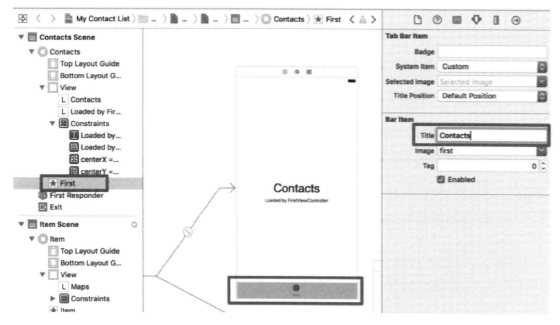

Figure 10.8   Changing the title of the Tab Bar Item.

The last step in setting up the tab bar and its views is to make sure the code files for each view is set up properly. Each view has an associated code file called a view controller that handles all events for the view. When the Tab Bar was created from the template, it automatically created two view controller code files, named FirstViewController.swift and SecondViewController.swift. Unfortunately, support for refactoring has not yet been extended to Swift, so the easiest way to get the code files to match up with the views is to create new code files and delete the autogenerated ones:

1. Right-click the **My Contact List folder** in the Project Navigator and select **New File…**.

2. Select **Cocoa Touch Class** and click **Next**.

3. Name the class **ContactsViewController** and make sure the **Subclass…** is set to **UIViewController**. This means that the class you are creating will be named ContactsViewController and will be a subclass of UIViewController.

4. Verify that the **Language** is **Swift**, and then click **Next** to see where the file will be created (which should be in the root folder of the project). Click **Create**.

7. Repeat for the other two views, creating **MapViewController** and **SettingsViewController**.

Once you have the three files created, you need to associate them with each view in the storyboard. Using the Document Outline, select the Contacts scene and open the Identity Inspector. Then change Class to **ContactsViewController** (see Figure 10.9). Rather than trying to find the class in the dropdown list, you can just start typing the name. Repeat for the other two views, and then delete **FirstViewController.swift** and **SecondViewController.swift** by selecting them and pressing **Delete**. Select **Move to Trash**.

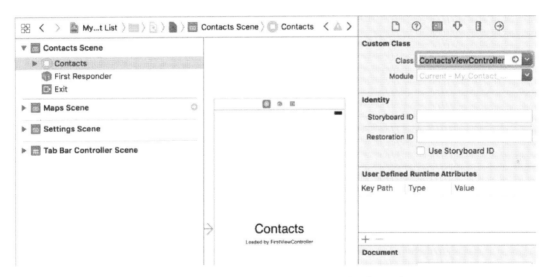

Figure 10.9 Setting the ViewController for a view.

The tab bar allows for having both a title and an image (icon). These images have to be around 20x20 pixels for regular screens and about 40x40 pixels for retina screens. iOS comes with a set of standard icon symbols you can use, but there are only 12 of them, so chances are they won't cover what you need. Instead, you can design your own using a graphics program, or you can license a set of icons from someone who has already created them. One such source is Glyphish (www.glyphish.com), which provides several sets of icons, either free or at a low cost. The paid version provides both regular and retina sizes, whereas the free version has only a single size.

For the My Contact List app, we have included a sample set from Glyphish with the download files for the book. After you download it, open **Assets.xcassets** in Xcode and drag the following files to the left side of the Assets.xcassets window: **sample-881-globe** and **sample-834-bolt**. These both have @2x in the file name as well, indicating that they are retina files. If you select one of them, you will see that on the right side of the asset catalog, there are slots for 1x, 2x, and 3x icons. The sample set provided isn't complete, but there are two different versions of the globe, so if you select sample-881-globe, you can then drag **sample-401-globe** into the 1x slot for that icon (Figure 10.10). Because you won't need them anymore, you can delete the images named first and second. (Right-click the image name and select **Remove Selected Items**.)

Figure 10.10 Adding images to the Asset Catalog.

The images are now available for use anywhere in your code. The icons are licensed under a Creative Commons attribution-only license, which means they can be used in any of your projects, as long as you put a note in your code with a reference to the Glyphish website. However, if you intend to create an app for use with real customers, you'll want to have the high-resolution versions that are available in the paid version of the icon set—or create your own set of icons for a custom look in your app.

With the images imported, you now need to have them show up in the tab bar. You probably noticed that no image was added for the Contacts tab. That's because there is a built-in image for Contacts that you will use instead. This does mean that the icons will end up not having the same look and feel, which is not something you should do for a real app. Here it is done to show you both approaches.

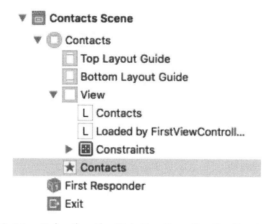

Figure 10.11 Selecting the Tab Bar Item for the Contacts Scene

1. Open **Main.storyboard** and select the Tab Bar Item for the **Contacts Scene** (Figure 10.11).

2. Make sure the **Attributes Inspector** is open, and then change the **System Item** to **Contacts**. As you do that, you'll notice the other default options that you can use, such as Search, Bookmarks, History, and so on. Note: this will remove the title you entered. The title will now match the default option selected but will be displayed in the title text field.

3. Select the **Tab Bar Item** for the **Map Scene**.

4. In the **Attributes Inspector**, use the Image drop-down list to change the **image** to **sample-881-globe**.

5. Use the same technique to change the **Settings image** to **sample-834-bolt**.

Run the app and you should see the three tabs with the text show up. Tap on each tab to make sure the proper View Controller shows up (see Figure 10.12).

Figure 10.12   The completed Tab Bar with three view controllers.

Auto Layout

Auto Layout is Apple's approach to designing a scene for multiple size displays. Auto Layout uses constraints to position the controls in a scene relative to the container they are in. The container can be the main view for the screen, other views in the main view, or special views (StackView) used solely to position controls in a scene. A StackView is used to position a set of controls relative to one another either vertically or horizontally. Controls can also be constrained to other controls in a view. Auto Layout requires a minimum of two constraints for each control. One constraint identifies the horizontal position of the control and the other the vertical position. Constraints are added after the control is placed in the scene. Figure 10.13 shows the buttons used to add constraints. These buttons are located at the bottom right of the Interface Builder window.

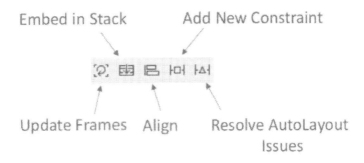

Figure 10.13   Interface Builder AutoLayout buttons.

To accommodate significantly different screen sizes (such as iPhone vs. iPad), Auto Layout uses Trait Variations. Essentially this allows you to modify individual constraints for different size screens. For example, the size of a label may need to be much larger for an iPad so you add a size variation for iPad screens. Since this book only focuses on iPhone, trait variations will not be covered further.

Auto Layout can be confusing and frustrating at times. Inadvertently or incorrectly placed constraints can totally alter the look of the interface. Take your time working through the next section. Read all the steps for a section before performing any action.

Design the Contacts Screen

Now it's time to set up the user interface for the most complicated user interface in the app, the Contacts scene. Refer to the completed design in Figure 10.16 as you create the screen.

1. Open **Main.storyboard** and remove the labels from the **Contacts** scene by clicking each and pressing **Delete**.

2. Drag a **Segmented Control** to the canvas and place it in the center of the screen toward the top. A Segmented Control can have multiple segments, only one of which can be activated at a time. This is the iOS equivalent of a radio button. Double-click the text **First** and change to **View**; then change **Second** to **Edit**. You can also change these in the **Attributes Inspector** by choosing the **Segment** and then changing the **Title**.

3. Drag a **Label** to the left side of the screen below the Segmented Control and change its text to **Contact:**.

4. Drag a **Text Field** to the right of the label.

5. Select the **label** and **text field** and click the **Embed in Stack** button at the bottom of the Interface Builder (refer to Figure 10.13). This puts a Horizontal Stack View around the two controls and allows you to position the two together. The text field is going to become very narrow—don't worry, this will be fixed later.

6. Select the **stack view** in the Document Outline and change the **Spacing** in the **Attributes Inspector** to **10**. This puts a little space between the label and text field.

7. Select the **Contact:** label and change its **Horizontal Content Hugging Priority** in the **Size Inspector** to **251**. By making this value higher than the text field, the label will hug closer to the left edge than the text field, making the text field stretch to fill the remaining space.

8. Select the **stack view**, hold down the option key and drag down to make a copy of the stack view. Then change the label to **Address:**. This keeps all the settings you made to Spacing and Content Hugging intact. You can do the same for the Email Address field.

9. For the row with City, State, and Zip code, drag three text fields into the scene and place them horizontally next to each other. Use the **Attributes Inspector** to change the **Placeholder Text** in each of them to **City**, **State**, and **Zip code**, respectively. Select all three text fields and embed them in a Stack View, and set its **Spacing** to **10**.

10. Select the **State** text field and then set a constraint for a width of 50 by clicking the **Add New Constraints** button, typing **50** into the **Width** text field, and clicking **Add 1 Constraint** (Figure 10.14).

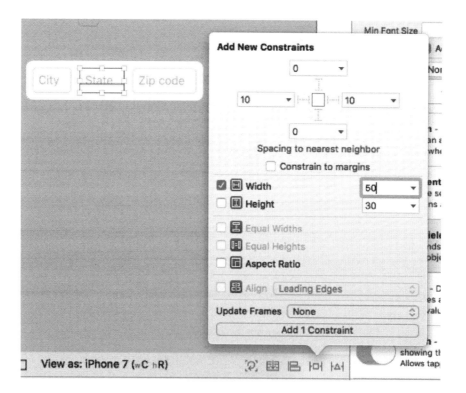

Figure 10.14 Adding a Width constraint.

11. Select the **City** field and change its **Horizontal Content Hugging Priority** to **249**. This will let the city text field expand while keeping the State and Zip code fields constant.

12. For the **Cell Phone** and **Home Phone** fields, place the label and text field above each other before embedding each pair in its own vertical stack view. Then select the two stack views and place in a horizontal stack view. Keeping the two stack views selected, click **Add New Constraints** to set the widths equal for the two stack views (**Add New Constraints > Equal Widths > Add 1 Constraint**). If you have trouble selecting the stack views in Interface Builder, you can select them in the Document Outline.

13. Select the new horizontal stack view containing the phone number controls and set its **Distribution** to **Fill Proportionally** and **Spacing** to **30**. The controls in this stack view will look too small—but this will also be fixed later.

14. For the last row, add two Labels and a Button next to each other horizontally and embed them in a horizontal stack view, and set the stack view's **Distribution** to **Fill Proportionally** and **Spacing** to **30**. Change the label texts as shown in Figure 10.16, and the set the **Horizontal Content Hugging Priority** for the **Birthday** label and the **date** label to **251** to keep them on the left side.

15. You now have one segmented control and six horizontal stack views at the highest level of the screen. Your next step is to arrange all the stack views in a vertical stack view. Make sure they are lined up in the order shown in Figure 10.16, and then embed them in a stack view. It is easiest to select all the stack views from the Document Outline rather than the screen prior to embedding. Embedding in the stack view will change the display and compress all the controls. This will be fixed in the following steps.

16. Set the **Spacing** of the new vertical stack view to **15**, and the **Alignment** and **Distribution** both to **Fill**.

17. Use the **Attributes Inspector** to change the **Capitalization** to **Words** for the **Contact**, **Address**, and **City** fields. Change **Capitalization** for the **State** field to **All Characters**.

18. Use the **Attributes Inspector** to change the **Keyboard** type for the **Zip code** field to **Number Pad**, to **Phone Pad** for the two **phone** fields, and to **E-mail Address** for the **Email** field.

You now have all the controls in the scene, and in the next steps you will place the high-level controls—the segmented control and the stack view. What you will need to do is pin the segmented control to the top of the screen, and then pin the stack view 15 points below the stack view. Then you will fix the left and right edges of the stack view to the outer edges of the screen.

1. Select the **segmented control**; then click the **Add New Constraints** button and add a constraint of 0 at the top of the control. (Enter **0** in top text field if it is not already 0. If it is, just click the vertical bar below it so it turns solid red, and click **Add 1 Constraint**.)

2. Click the **Align** button and add a constraint to center **Horizontally in Container**.

3. Select the **Stack View** in the left **Document Outline**, and control-drag to the **segmented control** and select **Bottom** from the pop-up menu. This will fix the stack view right at the bottom of the segmented control.

4. To add some distance between the two, expand the Constraints area in the Document Outline and find the constraint that you just created. It will say something like *Stack View.top = Edit, View.bottom*. If it says *Stack View.bottom = Edit, View.bottom*, use **Attributes Inspector** to change **First Item** to **Stack View.top**. What this is doing is ensuring that the top of the stack view is aligned with the bottom of the segmented control. Set the **Constant** to **15**, as shown in Figure 10.14, to put some distance between the two controls.

Figure 10.15   Changing constraint properties.

5. Select the **stack view** and click **Add Constraints**, and add constraints of **0** on both the left and right. This makes the left and right side of the stack view stick to the edges of the superview (which is the entire screen).

If the layout of the controls still doesn't look quite right, you can select the top-level view in the Document Outline, and then click the **Update Frames** button at the bottom of the Interface Builder. This will make the layout look closer to what it will be at runtime.

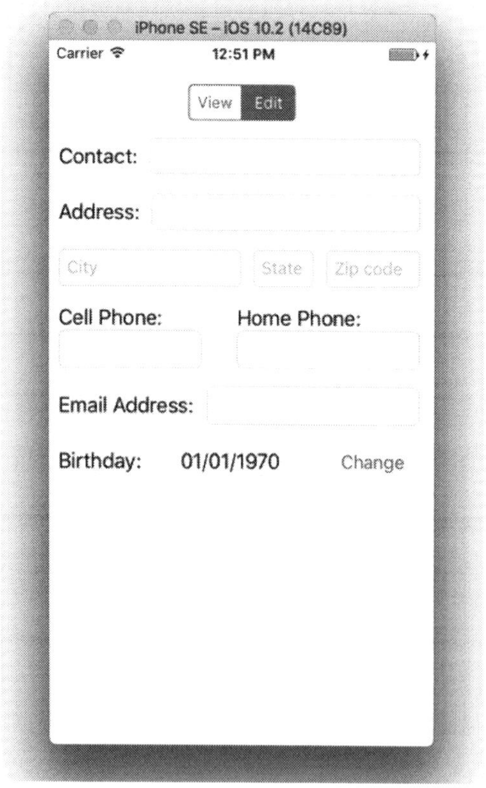

Figure 10.16   Designing the Contacts screen.

Run the app to see if things work as expected. You'll notice that you can't dismiss the keyboard, and that some of the controls are hidden behind the keyboard. Both of these problems can be fixed by using a scroll view control, which will allow for scrolling the screen up and down so everything is visible even on a small screen. One of the features of the scroll view is that it also allows for dismissing the keyboard when the scrolling is activated.

1. Select the **top-level stack view** in the **Document Outline**.
2. Select **Editor > Embed In > Scroll View**. This will embed the stack view in a Scroll View. The next steps will show you how to set the stack view and scroll view up properly.
3. First, set up the scroll view similarly to how you positioned the stack view:
   a. Control-drag from the **scroll view** to the **segmented control**, and set the constraint's **Constant** to **15** points. Again, make sure it's the top of the scroll view that is pinned to the bottom of the segmented control.
   b. Add constraints to set the left, right, and bottom to **0** to pin the remaining three sides to the super view's margins.
4. Next, pin the stack view inside the scroll view:
   a. Select the **stack view**; then add constraints to set all four sides (top, left, right, and bottom) to **0** to pin all sides to the scroll view's edges.
   b. Select both the **scroll view** and **stack view**. This is best done in the **Document Outline**. Then press the **Add New Constraints** button and select **Equal Widths** to ensure the two controls have the same width.
   c. If the left edge of the stack view extends beyond the screen, you can change the constant for the constraint for the width. I had to subtract 20 to make it look right. See Figure 10.17.

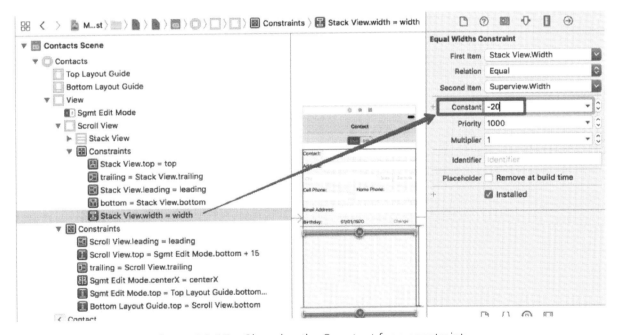

Figure 10.17   Changing the Constant for a constraint.

   d. Select the **Stack View.leading = leading** constraint and change the **Superview.leading** entry to be **Relative to margin**. (The constraint will change to **Stack View.leading = leadingMargin**.) See Figure 10.18.

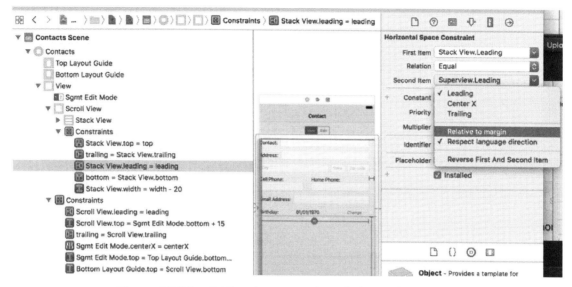

Figure 10.18 Setting the constraint relative to the margin.

Figure 10.19 shows the document outline of the completed Contacts scene. You can reference this to see if there are any discrepancies to the constraints and structure of the controls in your layout. There are many opportunities to make a mistake when setting up a user interface.

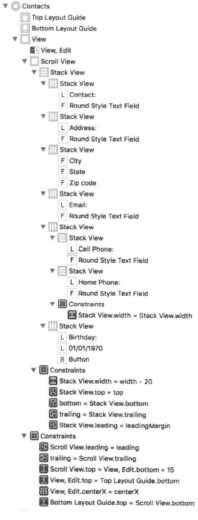

Figure 10.19 Document outline for the completed Contacts scene.

The final step in configuring the scroll view is to have it dismiss the keyboard. Select the Scroll View in the Storyboard and Keyboard setting in the Attributes Inspector (Figure 10.20). There are two ways to dismiss the keyboard. The first option, Dismiss on Drag, will dismiss the keyboard as soon as the user starts dragging the scroll view. Dismiss Interactively will dismiss the keyboard as the user scrolls down and starts to scroll into the space where the keyboard is; the keyboard will slide down with the scrolling, which is a very nice effect. You can try out both of them to see which you think works best. But since the primary purpose for having the scrolling is to bring controls up from underneath the keyboard, the best approach here is **Dismiss Interactively**.

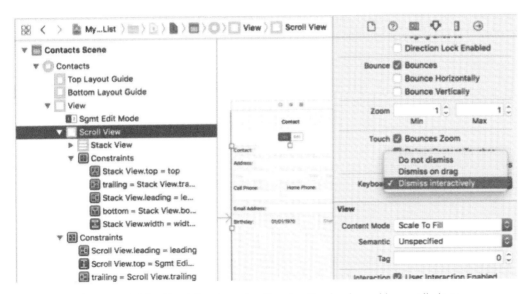

Figure 10.20 Deciding how to dismiss the keyboard in scroll view.

If you run the app and enter information, you will notice a problem. When you tap in a text field near the bottom of the screen, the keyboard will cover up the field, making it difficult to enter data correctly. Unfortunately, avoiding the keyboard is not a built-in function, so you will have to code it yourself. The first step is to make an outlet for the ScrollView in ContactsViewController.swift. Switch to **Assistant Editor**; then control-drag from **Scroll View** in the **Document Outline** to **ContactsViewController.swift** and name the outlet **scrollView**. The next step is to enter the code in Listing 10.1. The basic function of this code is to detect if the keyboard has been displayed and then move the scroll view and its contents enough so that the selected control is not covered. When the keyboard is dismissed, it then moves the content back to its original position.

Listing 10.1   ContactsViewController.swift

```swift
1    override func viewWillAppear(_ animated: Bool) {
2        super.viewWillAppear(animated)
3        self.registerKeyboardNotifications()
4    }
5
6    override func viewWillDisappear(_ animated: Bool) {
7        super.viewWillDisappear(animated)
8        self.unregisterKeyboardNotifications()
9    }
10
11   func registerKeyboardNotifications() {
12       NotificationCenter.default.addObserver(self, selector:
13           #selector(ContactsViewController.keyboardDidShow(notification:)), name:
14           NSNotification.Name.UIKeyboardDidShow, object: nil)
15       NotificationCenter.default.addObserver(self, selector:
16           #selector(ContactsViewController.keyboardWillHide(notification:)), name:
17           NSNotification.Name.UIKeyboardWillHide, object: nil)
18   }
19
20   func unregisterKeyboardNotifications() {
21       NotificationCenter.default.removeObserver(self)
22   }
23
24   func keyboardDidShow(notification: NSNotification) {
25       let userInfo: NSDictionary = notification.userInfo! as NSDictionary
26       let keyboardInfo = userInfo[UIKeyboardFrameBeginUserInfoKey] as! NSValue
27       let keyboardSize = keyboardInfo.cgRectValue.size
28
29   // Get the existing contentInset for the scrollView and set the bottom property to
30   //be the height of the keyboard
31       var contentInset = self.scrollView.contentInset
32       contentInset.bottom = keyboardSize.height
33
34       self.scrollView.contentInset = contentInset
35       self.scrollView.scrollIndicatorInsets = contentInset
36   }
37
38   func keyboardWillHide(notification: NSNotification) {
39       var contentInset = self.scrollView.contentInset
40       contentInset.bottom = 0
41
42       self.scrollView.contentInset = contentInset
43       self.scrollView.scrollIndicatorInsets = UIEdgeInsets.zero
44   }
```

The code is a standard posted solution but needs some explanation:

- **Line 3**—When the scene is about to be displayed, a method is called to register the code to listen for notifications that the keyboard has been displayed.

- **Line 8**—Similarly, when the view disappears, a method is called to stop the keyboard from listening for notifications.

- **Lines 11–18**—This method registers the code for notifications and tells the system to execute the appropriate method when the event occurs.

- **Lines 20–22**—This method removes the listener.

- **Lines 25–27**—Information is collected from the notification to get the size of the keyboard displayed. This is needed to move the content the appropriate amount.

- **Line 31–32**—Content Insets are the distance of the scroll view's content from the scroll view's edges. The insets collection is retrieved and the bottom inset is set to the height of the keyboard so that the content will be above the keyboard.

- **Line 34–35**—The scroll view is then set to use the new content insert values.

- **Lines 38–44**—When the keyboard disappears, the scroll view's content insert values are set back to the original values.

The scroll view is used extensively throughout iOS. It would be worthwhile for you to spend some time understanding how it works, to create very powerful user interfaces for your own apps. In addition to scrolling up and down, as you have seen here, **UIScrollView** also allows for scrolling horizontally as well as zooming. So, for instance, if you want to display an image and allow the user to zoom in and then scroll around the image, you would use a UIScrollView to support both the zooming and scrolling.

If you have gotten to this point and your user interface doesn't look exactly like what is shown here (or nothing like it!), don't be afraid to start over. It takes significant practice to become familiar with AutoLayout, so going through these steps a couple times will definitely be a benefit to you. You should also not be afraid to play around with the interface and try out how different settings affect the layout. To start over, simply delete all the controls in the scene and start dragging them in again.

Add Navigation Controller for the Date Screen

The Birthday on the Contacts screen is changed by tapping the Change button, which will cause a new screen to appear where the date can be chosen. This illustrates several new elements, including the use of the DatePicker control and the use of the Navigation Controller to move between related screens in the app. It takes a little work to get this set up, so be careful as you go through these steps.

A Navigation Controller is a special control that allows users to drill down through several screens and then return the way they came by tapping a button in the top left of the screen to navigate back to the previous screen. In MyContactList, you implement this by adding a Navigation Controller to the Contacts Controller, so the Tab Bar will actually be connected to the Navigation Controller, which in turn is connected to the View Controller (see Figure 10.21).

1. Select the Contacts Scene and then choose **Editor > Embed In > Navigation Controller**. This adds a Navigation Controller between the Tab Bar Controller and the Contacts Scene (Figure 10.20). It also adds a gray bar to the top of the Contacts Scene. This is the navigation bar, which will contain the title of the screen, the button for navigating back, and possibly some other controls.

2. Set the title of the navigation bar by selecting the Contacts Scene's Navigation Item in Document Outline, and then use the Attributes Inspector to set the Title to **Contact** (Figure 10.22).

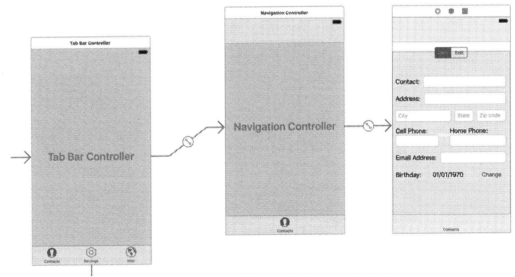

Figure 10.21 Adding a Navigation Controller.

Figure 10.22   Setting the navigation bar Title.

If you run the app, you should see the navigation bar show up on the Contact screen, but otherwise, everything else should function as before. The next step is to add a View Controller for the Date screen and add that to the Navigation Controller as well.

1. Drag a new **View Controller** onto the **Storyboard**, and place it to the right of the **Contacts** Scene.

2. Use the **Attributes Inspector** to change the new View Controller's **Title** to **Birthdate**.

3. Control-drag from the **Change** button on the **Contacts** Scene to the new **Birthdate View Controller**, and pick **Show** in the action menu that comes up. This will create a segue between the two screens that is activated when the user taps the Change button. (Note that the connections between the various view controllers are called *segues*, as they define how the various screens will transition back and forth.)

Run the app and tap the Change button, and you should see the Birthdate screen (Figure 10.23). The Contact button will take the user back to the Contacts screen. The text for the Contact button is the Title setting in the Navigation Item for the Contacts Scene. You can set an alternative text for the button here by adding text to the Back Button setting for the Navigation Item.

The last step in setting up the user interface and navigation is to add the capability to choose a date on the Date screen.

1. Open **Main.Storyboard** and drag in a **Date Picker** from the toolbox and place it at the top of the **Date View Controller**.

2. Add constraints of **0** to the top, left, and right edges of the **date picker** to keep it at the top of the screen.

3. Click the **Update Frames** button to display it properly in the Interface Builder.

The Date Picker can be configured to work with both time and date. However, in this app, it is only relevant to use dates, so open the Attributes Inspector and change the Mode to Date. As you can see, you can also set the default date, as well as constrain the picker between specific dates. You don't have to change these settings for this app. Run the app and make sure the Date Picker shows up as expected. Figure 10.23 shows the completed navigation control hierarchy for the Contacts and Date Scenes. In the next chapter, you will see how to bring the date chosen back to the Contacts screen.

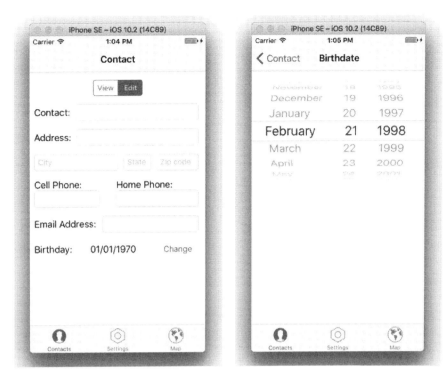

Figure 10.23   The completed navigation interface for the Contact and Date screens.

Activating the Interface

The next chapter is dedicated to implementing most of the functionality of saving data from the Contacts screen, but for now, we will implement the capability to switch between the view and edit modes. The code for this is quite simple but somewhat tedious. The edit mode is controlled by the Segmented Control. When the user changes to View, all the controls will be disabled so they can't be edited. And when the user changes back again, they will be reactivated.

However, before jumping into setting it up, let's take a look at a part of the Xcode interface that will be very helpful to understand. This is the area at the top right of the screen where you will find six buttons that allow you to customize what is displayed in Xcode (see Figure 10.24). The first three buttons will switch between what is shown in the middle section of Xcode:

- **Standard Editor**—Shows a single editing pane. This is the default.
- **Assistant Editor**—Displays two editing views side by side. The Assistant will try to automatically select the best view in the right-hand view. For instance, if you select a Scene in storyboard, the Assistant will show its corresponding View Controller Swift file.
- **Version Editor**—Shows versions of documents you're working on. This is particularly useful when the project is under source control.

The right-most buttons will turn on/off display of the three sections on the left, right, and bottom of Xcode. This is particularly helpful when working on smaller screens. For instance, if you use the Assistant to work on both the Storyboard and a corresponding code file, it can be very helpful to turn off the Navigator and Utilities areas:

- **Navigator Area**—The area on the left of Xcode where you navigate the file in the project, see error messages, and so on.
- **Debug Area**—This is at the bottom of the screen and contains the console and the debugger.
- **Utilities Area**—Shows up on the right side of the screen and contains the various Inspectors, such as Attributes and Identity.

Figure 10.24 The completed navigation interface for the Contact and Date screens.

With that description, here's how to activate the interface:

1. Select the **Contacts** scene in **Main.storyboard** and turn on **Assistant Editor** mode. This should open ContactsViewController.swift next to the Storyboard. Control-drag from the **Segmented Control** in the Contacts scene to the body of the ContactsController.swift file.

2. Add an action named **changeEditMode** (see Figure 10.25). Click **Connect**. The `changeEditMode` method is called anytime the value of the Segmented Control is changed, but the method call doesn't indicate the current value of the control, so you need to add an outlet to be able to reference and read the value.

3. Control-drag again from the **Segmented Control** to the first line in the ContactsViewController class. Add an outlet named **sgmtEditMode**. Click **Connect**.

4. You will also need to reference all the text fields and buttons in the interface. You do this by control-dragging from each of the controls. However, because they are inside several other controls, it may be easier to drag from the Document Outline. See Listing 10.1 for the names to give the text fields, the Birthdate label, and the Change button.

5. Implement the `changeEditMode` method, as shown in Listing 10.2.

6. Run the app and switch between view and edit modes.

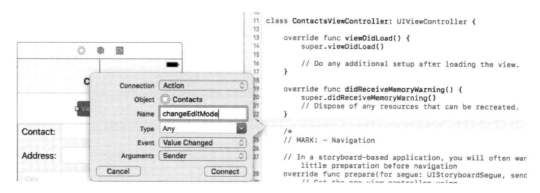

Figure 10.25 Adding an action to change the edit mode.

Listing 10.2 ContactsViewController.swift

```swift
1   import UIKit
2
3   class ContactsViewController: UIViewController {
4
5       @IBOutlet weak var sgmtEditMode: UISegmentedControl!
6       @IBOutlet weak var txtName: UITextField!
7       @IBOutlet weak var txtAddress: UITextField!
8       @IBOutlet weak var txtCity: UITextField!
9       @IBOutlet weak var txtState: UITextField!
10      @IBOutlet weak var txtZip: UITextField!
11      @IBOutlet weak var txtCell: UITextField!
12      @IBOutlet weak var txtPhone: UITextField!
13      @IBOutlet weak var txtEmail: UITextField!
14      @IBOutlet weak var lblBirthdate: UILabel!
15      @IBOutlet weak var btnChange: UIButton!
16
17      override func viewDidLoad() {
18          super.viewDidLoad()
19          // Do any additional setup after loading the view.
20          self.changeEditMode(self)
21      }
22
23      override func didReceiveMemoryWarning() {
24          super.didReceiveMemoryWarning()
25          // Dispose of any resources that can be recreated.
26      }
27
28      @IBAction func changeEditMode(_ sender: Any) {
29          let textFields: [UITextField] = [txtName, txtAddress, txtCity, txtState, txtZip, txtPhone,
30                                          txtCell, txtEmail]
31          if sgmtEditMode.selectedSegmentIndex == 0 {
32              for textField in textFields {
33                  textField.isEnabled = false
34                  textField.borderStyle = UITextBorderStyle.none
35              }
36              btnChange.isHidden = true
37          }
38          else if sgmtEditMode.selectedSegmentIndex == 1{
39              for textField in textFields {
40                  textField.isEnabled = true
41                  textField.borderStyle = UITextBorderStyle.roundedRect
42              }
43              btnChange.isHidden = false
44          }
45      }
46  }
```

The code is relatively straightforward, but still deserves some description.

- **Lines 5–15**—These are the properties for each of the controls that you need to be able to reference in the code.
- **Lines 28–45**—The `changeEditMode` method is called whenever the segmented control changes state and will change the controls as needed to reflect the state of the control.
- **Line 20**—Calls the `changeEditMode` method to ensure that the controls are set properly when the view loads.

- **Lines 29–30**—All the properties are changed in the same way for each of the text fields, so you set up an `Array` object containing all the text fields by separating the list of objects with commas and surrounding the entire list with square brackets.
- **Line 31**—Check the value of the Segmented Control. Viewing is 0, and Editing is 1.
- **Line 32**—Use a fast enumeration loop to go through all the text fields in the array.
- **Lines 33–34**—In view mode, the text fields are disabled, and the border is set to not be there (`UITextBorderStyle.none`).
- **Line 36**—The Change button should not be shown in view mode.
- **Lines 38–43**—When switching to edit mode, the code is similar, but the values are opposite. The text fields are enabled and the border is set to the Rounded Rect mode (the default). The button is hidden.

Run the app and enter some data into the text fields, and then try switching back and forth between View and Edit.

Troubleshooting Connections

If you make a mistake in connecting the fields and the outlets, you may have some strange results when running the app. It's always a good idea to check the connections if something doesn't work as expected. You can see all the connections made on a View Controller by selecting the Connections Inspector in the Utilities area. To bring up the Connections Inspector, select the control, and then click the right-most button in the Utilities area. Figure 10.26 shows both the Connections Inspector, as well as what it looks like when you right-click a control. Both of these approaches will allow you to manage the connections for a control.

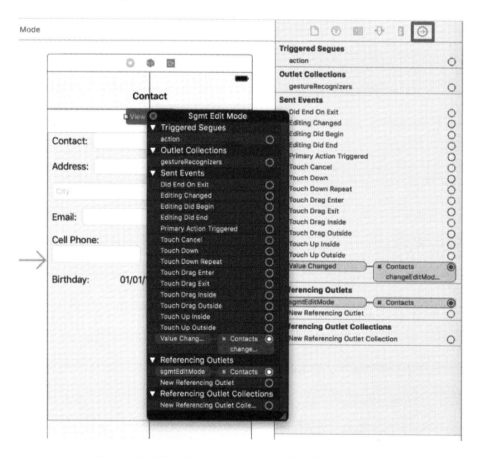

Figure 10.26 Managing connections for a control.

One common mistake that can be difficult to troubleshoot is if you delete an outlet or action method in the code without deleting the corresponding connection. If you do this, it will look like everything is working until you go to run the app, and it will crash with a message like this:

```
2017-01-19 11:02:54.250 My Contact List[27142:1468815] *** Terminating app due to uncaught
exception 'NSUnknownKeyException', reason: '[<My_Contact_List.ContactsViewController
0x7f9dfc403f00> setValue:forUndefinedKey:]: this class is not key value coding-compliant for
the key lblTest.'
```

In this case, an outlet was added called lblTest, and then the code was deleted but the outlet still existed. If you see this error, look for the control that the outlet had been connected to, and then use one of the two approaches in Figure 10.26 to inspect the connections and delete it by clicking the x in the box on the right.

Summary

Creating a user interface in iOS is relatively straightforward using the Interface Builder and the stack views. However, there are subtle complexities in ensuring a good layout that functions across all device sizes and screen rotations. And as you saw, you still need to know how to write code to make some things work.

Navigation between screens can be tricky to get set up right, especially when both tab bars and navigation controllers are involved.

Exercises

1. Add a new tab to the tab bar with an associated view controller.
2. Change the Segmented Control to a Switch.
3. Split the Contact field into first and last name fields.
4. Set the Date Picker to start on your birthday, and limit the range to be from January 1, 1980, to January 1, 2000.

CHAPTER 11

Persistent Data in iOS

Storing data that the user will need to run the app is an important part of developing for the mobile platform. In addition to the regular purposes for saving data, the mobile platform also presents unique challenges regarding the life cycle of an app that requires special consideration to saving data. Because the app can become inactive and be closed down at any point, it's important to save enough of the app's state on a regular basis to allow the user to continue working in a meaningful way when the app becomes active again.

In this chapter, you will see several ways that you can save data on iOS. Most of the attention is going to be on a system called **Core Data** that provides strong support for a database-backed persistence solution for iOS apps, but you will also see how to save to files directly, as well as how to save app settings.

User Defaults

When you need to save a little bit of data in your app, the **UserDefaults** object is a very simple and easy way to do so. UserDefaults is a front-end to a key-value file (often referred to as Plist files because of the .plist extension) that is stored in the app's Preferences directory. There's only one file, but in this file, you can store as many values as you want. When storing values in the file, you have to supply a key string to identify the value when retrieving it later. You can store many data types in UserDefaults, including all primitive types as well as **Data**, **String**, **Date**, **Dictionary**, and **Array**. Other data types can be archived and stored as a Data object.

File Data Storage

Like most other operating systems, iOS enables saving data in files, either in regular text files or by archiving (what's known as *serialization* in Java and C#). The techniques for working with files are similar to many other programming languages, but it's worth noting that on iOS, apps are sandboxed, which means that each app is isolated from the other apps and from the operating system. One of the consequences is that each app has only a very simple file system that by default consists of a few standard directories: Documents, Library, and tmp. As a developer, you can store files in the Documents and tmp directories. The Documents folder is backed up when the device is backed up. The tmp folder is not. By storing data in files, you can quickly store user data and can even take advantage of Apple's iCloud to allow the user to sync documents between their devices. This is a powerful service, but it works only between devices for a single user. iCloud will not allow you to let your users exchange data.

Core Data

Core Data is a powerful data persistence solution developed by Apple to provide object-oriented storage. Core Data is an object-wrapper on top of a data store—typically a SQLite database. This allows the developer to work with objects that map to entities in the database without worrying too much about the underlying database design and queries. For apps that need business data stored, Core Data is a strong solution to meet this need.

Figure 11.1 shows an overview of the Core Data framework. The framework stores data in files. The default is a SQLite database, but you can also choose to use XML or binary data. The Persistent Object Store wraps around the data file and presents a common interface to the rest of the stack. You will not need to interact with the Persistent Object Store, except to choose which file format to store the data in. The Persistent Store Coordinator allows for having multiple data stores in the same app, and will then coordinate access to those stores. However, it is very rare for iOS apps to have multiple data stores, and you should never have to directly interact with the Persistent Store Coordinator.

The Managed Object Model is the description of the layout of the data. This is where you describe the structure of your data. The design of the data structure is similar to relational database design, in that data is organized into entities that are related through relationships.

When you need to access the data, you will not directly interact with the data store. Instead, you will work with the Managed Object Context, which allows you to access the objects that are stored in the data file. The Managed Object Context can keep track of multiple changes to the objects, and will periodically, or when instructed, save the changes to the persistent store.

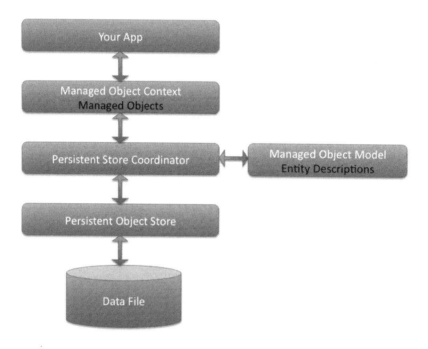

Figure 11.1 Overview of the Core Data framework.

Using SQLite Directly in iOS Apps

Just like Android, iOS apps can also work with SQLite databases directly. If you are developing an app to be available on both platforms, you might consider eschewing Core Data for shipping a regular SQLite database with your app. You can design and populate the database outside of the app and add it to the app bundle before shipping the app. The techniques used to work with SQLite on iOS are quite similar to those used on Android. However, one thing to be aware is that the SQLite libraries used to interact with the database on iOS are written in C and not Swift, so the method calls are going to look different from what you have seen here.

Storing the Settings

In the settings part of the app, the user is able to change the sort order of the displayed contacts. The contacts can be sorted in either ascending or descending order by Name, City, or Birthday (Figure 11.2). Although the user interface for this screen might more logically be set up using Segmented Controls, you will get a chance to work with two new controls, the Picker View and the Switch. The user's preference for sorting will be stored in a UserDefaults object. The data will be stored in the Settings screen and read in the Contacts section of the app.

Figure 11.2 The completed Settings scene.

Creating the Settings Interface

In this section, you will create the interface for the Settings screen. Use Figure 11.2 as a guide in completing the following steps:

1. Open **Main.storyboard** and delete the **labels** from the Settings Scene.
2. Drag a new **label** to the top of the screen and change its text to **Sort Order:**.
3. Drag a **Picker View** and place it below the label.
4. Drag a **Label** below the Picker and change its text to **Ascending Sort:**.
5. Drag a **Switch** and place it to the right of the label.
6. Put the Ascending Sort: label and the Switch in a **horizontal stack view** with spacing **10**.
7. Select the Sort order: label, the Picker, and the horizontal stack view and add them to a **vertical stack view**.
8. Select the vertical stack view and add **constraints** to center it both horizontally and vertically. Click the **Update Frames** button to see the controls displayed properly.

Now you need to set up outlets and actions for the Settings Scene.

1. Open **Main.storyboard** and display the **Settings** scene on the left and **SettingsViewController.swift** in the Assistant editor on the right (which should happen automatically when you view the Settings scene and activate the Assistant Editor).
2. Control-drag from the Picker View and Switch to immediately inside the class declaration to create outlets named **pckSortField** and **swAscending**, respectively. Note that because the controls are inside the stack view, it may be easier to control-drag from the Document Outline on the left instead. You can check that you did it right when the Type is UIPickerView and UISwitch, respectively, for the two controls.
3. Control-drag from the switch to add an action called **sortDirectionChanged**. Place this at the end of the class (but inside the curly brace).

If you run the app now, you will get a blank Picker View, so you will need to initialize it with the field names to sort by. You'll populate it in code in the next section. When working with a Picker View, you need to conform to two protocols in the View Controller: `UIPickerViewDataSource` and `UIPickerViewDelegate`. The former has methods to specify the data source for the contents of the Picker View, whereas the latter has methods that allow you find out which row the user has chosen in the Picker. Add the two protocols in the class declaration line, as shown in line 1 of Listing 11.1. Then modify the class as shown in the rest of Listing 11.1.

Listing 11.1   Implementing the Picker View Protocols SettingsViewController.swift

```
1    class SettingsViewController: UIViewController, UIPickerViewDataSource, UIPickerViewDelegate   {
2
3        @IBOutlet weak var pckSortField: UIPickerView!
4        @IBOutlet weak var swAscending: UISwitch!
5
6        let sortOrderItems: Array<String> = ["ContactName", "City", "Birthday"]
7
8        override func viewDidLoad() {
9            super.viewDidLoad()
10
11           // Do any additional setup after loading the view.
12           pckSortField.dataSource = self;
13           pckSortField.delegate = self;
14       }
15
16       override func didReceiveMemoryWarning() {
17           super.didReceiveMemoryWarning()
18           // Dispose of any resources that can be recreated.
19       }
20
21       @IBAction func sortDirectionChanged(_ sender: Any) {
22       }
23
24       // MARK: UIPickerViewDelegate Methods
25
26       // Returns the number of 'columns' to display.
27       func numberOfComponents(in pickerView: UIPickerView) -> Int {
28           return 1
29       }
30
31       // Returns the # of rows in the picker
32       func pickerView(_ pickerView: UIPickerView, numberOfRowsInComponent component: Int) -> Int {
33           return sortOrderItems.count
34       }
35
36       //Sets the value that is shown for each row in the picker
37       func pickerView(_ pickerView: UIPickerView, titleForRow row: Int, forComponent component: Int)
38                       -> String? {
39           return sortOrderItems[row]
40       }
41
42       //If the user chooses from the pickerview, it calls this function;
43       func pickerView(_ pickerView: UIPickerView, didSelectRow row: Int, inComponent component: Int) {
44           print("Chosen item: \(sortOrderItems[row])")
45       }
46   }
```

To have a fully functioning Picker View, you need to set up a data source, and implement several methods that display the data, and respond to the user making a selection in the Picker.

- Line 6 adds an array to store the items that will show up in the Picker View. This needs to be declared at the class level, because it will be accessed in several methods in the class.

- In `viewDidLoad`, set up SettingsViewController as the data source for the Picker View (line 12). This works because the View Controller conforms to `UIPickerViewDataSource`.

- Set the View Controller as the delegate for the Picker View (line 13), so whenever actions are taken on the Picker View, specific methods are called in the view controller. This works because the View Controller conforms to `UIPickerViewDelegate`.

- The `//MARK:` notation in line 24 is used for documentation. You can see this show up in Xcode if you click the right-most item in the selector bar above the SettingsViewController.swift file (Figure 11.3). The dash right after the colon is what gives the horizontal line. Using this notation can be a good way to easily navigate long source files.

- The Picker View can be configured to show multiple components, or columns, that can be selected independently. The `numberOfComponents` method in lines 27–29 returns the number of columns to display. This example only has one column, so the method just returns 1.

- The `pickerView(_:numberOfRowsInComponent:)` method in lines 32–34 specifies how many rows or elements to display in the Picker. By returning the number of elements in the array, we allow for just that many rows in the Picker.

- The `pickerView(_ :titleForRow: forComponent)` method in lines 37–40 is the most crucial method for setting up the Picker View, because it is the one that makes the data show up in the Picker View. When the Picker is displayed on the screen, the system will make repeated calls to this method, passing in the row number and getting the corresponding text for the row back. In this case, the method uses the row number to return the corresponding item from the array.

- Whenever the user chooses a row in the Picker View, the method `pickerView(_:didSelectRow:inComponent:)` in lines 43–45 will be called. For now, the method simply prints a message to the console indicating which item was chosen. In the next section, you will use this method to update the stored data. Notice the backslash followed by a parenthesis in line 44. This allows for the integer to be converted to a string representation for printing, and is a common way in Swift to embed variable values in strings.

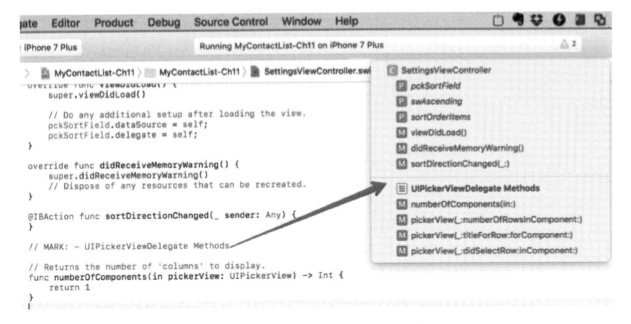

Figure 11.3 Drop-down menu on the right showing the result of #pragma mark in the code.

Run the app to make sure the Picker View shows up correctly, and the selected item is printed to the console at the bottom of Xcode every time a selection is made. In the next section, you will see how to store the values.

Working with the UserDefaults Object

The `UserDefaults` object is used to store data values for an app in a key-value list on the disk. Working with `UserDefaults` is very simple. You start by getting a reference to the standard `UserDefaults` object with this line of code:

```
var settings = UserDefaults.standard
```

To store a value in the settings object, you use code like this:

```
settings.set("City", forKey: "sortField")
```

This saves the value "City" with the key "sortField". Every value must have a unique key. There are also versions of the set methods that can be used to store scalar values such as `Bool` and `Int`. Here's an example:

```
settings.set(true, forKey: "sortDirectionAscending")
```

Retrieving the data is equally simple. Using the reference called `settings` to the `UserDefaults` object, you would retrieve an object using this call:

```
var sortfield = settings.string(forKey: "sortField")
```

The data is periodically saved, but to force saving, you can call the synchronize method:

```
settings.synchronize()
```

This will save any changes you've made to the file.

iOS versus Android: User Settings

The functionality provided by `UserDefaults` in iOS is provided by `SharedPreferences` in Android. In both cases, these objects are used to store single bits of information. However, whereas Android can store only simple data types in `SharedPreferences`, iOS has the capability to store more complex objects.

Activating the Settings Interface

Now that the Settings scene is set up with a Picker View and a switch, it's time to work on storing the data for the user preferences. For the settings to work consistently, they should be set to some default values when the app first launches. The place to do that is in the app delegate, so open **AppDelegate.swift** and add the code in Listing 11.2 to the `application(_ :didFinishLaunchingWithOptions):` method.

Listing 11.2 Saving Default Settings in AppDelegate.swift

```
1   func application(_ application: UIApplication, didFinishLaunchingWithOptions launchOptions:
2   [UIApplicationLaunchOptionsKey: Any]?) -> Bool {
3       // Override point for customization after application launch.
4       let settings = UserDefaults.standard
5
6       if( ettings.string(forKey: "sortField") == nil {
7           settings.set("City", forKey: "sortField")
8       }
9       if settings.string(forKey: "sortDirectionAscending") == nil {
10          settings.set(true, forKey: "sortDirectionAscending")
11      }
12      settings.synchronize()
13      print("Sort field: \(settings.string(forKey: "sortField")!)")
14      print("Sort direction: \(settings.bool(forKey: "sortDirectionAscending"))")
15      return true
16  }
```

By putting this code in AppDelegate.swift, it will be executed anytime the app launches.

- The method starts in line 4 by getting a reference to the standard `UserDefaults` object. In this case, it's named `settings`. Since `settings` will refer to the same object throughout its lifetime, it is declared as a constant with the `let` keyword.
- The bulk of the method is two `if` statements that check whether a value is already stored with two specific keys in the settings object. The first one (line 6) checks if the `sortField` has been set. If not, it stores `City` as the value in `sortField` in line 7. This approach ensures there is a value in the field, but also avoids overwriting any existing value.
- The second `if` statement in lines 9–11 repeats the same check for the sort direction. If no value is stored, it defaults to `true`.
- Line 12 ensures that any changes are saved back to the settings file, and lines 13 and 14 write the values of the two settings fields to `NSLog`. This shows how to retrieve a Boolean value using the `bool(:ForKey:)` method and retrieve a string by using `string(:ForKey:)`.

Next, we need to make sure the UI controls on the Settings screen get updated when the view is loaded. We do this in the `viewWillAppear` method in **SettingsViewController.swift**, as shown in Listing 11.3.

Listing 11.3 Setting the User Controls Based on the Stored Values

```
1   override func viewWillAppear(_ animated: Bool) {
2       //set the UI based on values in UserDefaults
3       let settings = UserDefaults.standard
4       swAscending.setOn(settings.bool(forKey: "sortDirectionAscending"), animated: true)
5       let sortField = settings.string(forKey: "sortField")
6       var i = 0
7       for field in sortOrderItems {
8           if field == sortField {
9               pckSortField.selectRow(i, inComponent: 0, animated: false)
10          }
11          i += 1
12      }
13      pckSortField.reloadComponent(0)
14  }
```

- This code reads the values from the standard `UserDefaults` object (line 3) and updates the UI with those values. Line 4 sets the value of the switch based on the value in the `sortDirectionAscending` key by calling the `setOn:` method on the switch.

- The Picker View is a little more complex to set. First, read the `sortField` value into a constant in line 5. Then the Picker View is updated by telling it which number row to select, so the `for` loop in lines 7–12 goes through the `sortOrderItems` array, which is where you stored the items that are displayed in the Picker View. If a match is found, the Picker View is told in line 9 to select that row. There's only one component, or column, so that is set to 0. The selection can be animated so the Picker View spins to the selection, but this is not appropriate here, because the selection is already made before the user opens the Selection screen, so we set `animated` to `false`.

- To have the Picker View change, you call `reloadComponent`. (You could also have called `reloadAll-Components` and not needed to specify which component to reload.)

- To store the values chosen by the user, implement `sortDirectionChanged:` as shown in Listing 11.4 to store the value of the switch, and update the implementation of `pickerView(:didSelectRow:inComponent:)` as shown in Listing 11.5. There's no new code in either of those two listings.

Listing 11.4 Storing the Value of the Switch

```
1   @IBAction func sortDirectionChanged(_ sender: Any) {
2       let settings = UserDefaults.standard
3       settings.set(swAscending.isOn, forKey: "sortDirectionAscending")
4       settings.synchronize()
5   }
```

Listing 11.5 Setting the User Controls Based on the Stored Values

```
1   func pickerView(_ pickerView: UIPickerView, didSelectRow row: Int, inComponent component: Int) {
2       let sortField = sortOrderItems[row]
3       let settings = UserDefaults.standard
4       settings.set(sortField, forKey: "sortField")
5       settings.synchronize()
6   }
```

If you run the app, you should be able to make a selection in the Settings screen and have those settings stored for later. If you try stopping the execution of the app in Xcode and relaunching the app, you should see that the settings persist.

Global Constants

The code you wrote previously uses literal string values to identify the key fields used in UserDefaults. This can be a problem, because if they aren't spelled the same everywhere you use them, you will get some very strange error messages. One solution to this problem is to create an object to hold global constants, and then define the string keys in that object. Here's how to update the code to be more robust.

1. Select **File > New > File**, and select **Swift File**. Click **Next**.

2. Name the class **Constants** and click Create.

3. Open the **Constants.swift** file and add the code shown in Listing 11.6. This declares a `struct` that contains the two keys as static strings that are globally available. A struct in Swift works in many ways like a class, in that you can declare methods in a struct, but because structs are always copied and passed as values rather than as references, they are particularly well suited to simple data structures that contain scalar values.

4. Open **AppDelegate.swift** and replace all occurrences of the literal strings with the keys to the constant variables in `application(:didFinishLaunchingWithOptions:)`. The relevant lines of code are shown in Listing 11.7 in bold.

5. Update the keys in **SettingsViewController.swift** by updating `viewWillApeear`, `sortDirection-Changed` and `pickerView(_ :didSelectRow:inComponent:)` to use the constant string variables instead of the literal string values. The updated methods are shown in Listing 11.8. The relevant lines are bolded.

Run the app and make sure the saving and retrieving of the settings still work as expected.

Listing 11.6   Constants.swift

```
1    import Foundation
2    struct Constants {
3        static let kSortField = "sortField"
4        static let kSortDirectionAscending = "sortDirectionAscending"
5    }
```

Listing 11.7   Using the Constant Variables as Keys in AppDelegate.swift

```
1    func application(_ application: UIApplication, didFinishLaunchingWithOptions
2                         launchOptions: [UIApplicationLaunchOptionsKey: Any]?) -> Bool {
3        // Override point for customization after application launch.
4        let settings = UserDefaults.standard
5
6        if settings.string(forKey: Constants.kSortField) == nil {
7            settings.set("City", forKey: Constants.kSortField)
8        }
9        if settings.string(forKey: Constants.kSortDirectionAscending) == nil {
10            settings.set(true, forKey: Constants.kSortDirectionAscending)
11        }
12        settings.synchronize()
13        NSLog("Sort field: %@",  settings.string(forKey: Constants.kSortField)!)
14        NSLog("Sort direction: \(settings.bool(forKey: Constants.kSortDirectionAscending))")
15
16        return true
17    }
```

Listing 11.8   Using the Constant Variables as Keys in SettingsViewController.swift

```
1    override func viewWillAppear(_ animated: Bool) {
2        //set the UI based on values in UserDefaults
3        let settings = UserDefaults.standard
4        swAscending.setOn(settings.bool(forKey: Constants.kSortDirectionAscending), animated: true)
5        let sortField = settings.string(forKey: Constants.kSortField)
6        var i = 0
7        for field in sortOrderItems {
8            if field == sortField {
9                pckSortField.selectRow(i, inComponent: 0, animated: false)
10            }
11            i += 1
12        }
13        pckSortField.reloadComponent(0)
14    }
15
16    @IBAction func sortDirectionChanged(_ sender: Any) {
17        let settings = UserDefaults.standard
18        settings.set(swAscending.isOn, forKey: Constants.kSortDirectionAscending)
19        settings.synchronize()
20    }
21
22    func pickerView(_ pickerView: UIPickerView, didSelectRow row: Int, inComponent component: Int) {
23        let sortField = sortOrderItems[row]
24        let settings = UserDefaults.standard
25        settings.set(sortField, forKey: Constants.kSortField)
26        settings.synchronize()
27    }
```

Using Files

As noted in the Android section of the book, the MyContactList app does not really have a need to store data in a file. Accessing and storing contacts in a database is a better solution than in a file. One possible use for a file in the app could be to export the contacts in the database for export to another app or for backup. This is beyond the scope of the book at this point. However, we will discuss some of the options.

First, an app can store data in the standard file storage on the device in a location that is only accessible by the app. However, there are two storage locations available in this private location. The first is the Documents directory, which is backed up whenever the device is backed up. The second is the tmp directory, which is not backed up. You will need to decide which directory to use based on the use of the data once it is saved.

The process of storing data in a file starts with converting the data to text (if it is not already). The next step is to get a path to the file in the selected directory. For example,

```
let documentDirectoryURL = try FileManager.default.url(for: .documentDirectory,
                                    in: .userDomainMask,
                                    appropriateFor: nil,
                                    create: true)
let fileDestinationUrl = documentDirectoryURL.appendingPathComponent("contact.txt")
```

The first statement gets the path as a URL to the Documents directory in the app's private storage. The second statement appends the desired file name to the Document's directory path. This may now be used to store data in that file. The following line writes the data stored in the string `exportData` to the file:

```
try exportData.write(to: fileDestinationUrl, atomically: false, encoding: String.Encoding.utf8)
```

To read the data back into a string, you must get the path to the file in the same way as above, but then use the following to store it in a string. In this case, the path to the file is held in `fileImportUrl`.

```
let inString = try String(contentsOf: fileImportUrl)
```

For more details on file storage, you can reference Apple's developer site, which provides plenty of information on how to do this.

Setting Up Core Data

As stated earlier, the recommended way to work with structured data in an iOS app is to use Core Data. When you work with Core Data, you have to design the structure of the data. But before we can get on with designing the database, we need to do a little bit of setup in the **AppDelegate** file. The code required is in Listing 11.9. This code is standard for most iOS apps, so one easy way to get this code is to copy it from a project that has the Core Data functionality included. In fact, the code in Listing 11.9 was copied from such a project. You can also just type in the code in Listing 11.9 at the end of the AppDelegate class. You also need to add this line after the other import statement:

```
import CoreData
```

Listing 11.9   Setting up CoreData in AppDelegate

```
1    // MARK: - Core Data stack
2
3    lazy var persistentContainer: NSPersistentContainer = {
4        /*
5         The persistent container for the application. This implementation
6         creates and returns a container, having loaded the store for the
7         application to it. This property is optional since there are legitimate
8         error conditions that could cause the creation of the store to fail.
9        */
10       let container = NSPersistentContainer(name: "MyContactListModel")
11       container.loadPersistentStores(completionHandler: { (storeDescription, error) in
12           if let error = error as NSError? {
13               // Replace this implementation with code to handle the error appropriately.
14               // fatalError() causes the application to generate a crash log and terminate. You should
15               // not use this function in a shipping application, although it may be useful during
16               // development.
17
18               /*
19                Typical reasons for an error here include:
20                * The parent directory does not exist, cannot be created, or disallows writing.
21                * The persistent store is not accessible, due to permissions or data protection when
22                * the device is locked.
23                * The device is out of space.
24                * The store could not be migrated to the current model version.
25                Check the error message to determine what the actual problem was.
26                */
27               fatalError("Unresolved error \(error), \(error.userInfo)")
28           }
29       })
30       return container
31   }()
32
33   // MARK: - Core Data Saving support
34
35   func saveContext () {
36       let context = persistentContainer.viewContext
37       if context.hasChanges {
38           do {
39               try context.save()
40           } catch {
41               // Replace this implementation with code to handle the error appropriately.
42               // fatalError() causes the application to generate a crash log and terminate. You should
43               // not use this function in a shipping application, although it may be useful during
44               // development.
45               let nserror = error as NSError
46               fatalError("Unresolved error \(nserror), \(nserror.userInfo)")
47           }
48       }
49   }
```

The code has two parts:

- First, a variable called persistentContainer is set up in line 10 as a wrapper around the actual data store. The container set up in line 10 contains the name of the CoreData datamodel ("MyContactListModel"), which you will create in the next section.

- The saveContext method in line 35 will be called whenever data changes need to be saved to the persistent container. Most of the rest of the code is for handling errors. In the default code, the error handling is very crude, in that it crashes the app and writes an error message to the log. As the comments in the code explain, this is not an appropriate approach in a shipping app.

What about Linking Binaries?

In past versions of Xcode, it was necessary whenever you imported a framework such as CoreData, CoreMotion, and so on that you also had to link the corresponding binary file to the project. This process has been automated in the current version so you only have to add the import statement to the code, and Xcode will automatically link the binaries for you. In fact, if you have experience with iOS development, you will see that Apple's engineers are continually working on automating as many tasks as possible for you.

Designing the Data Structure

The data structure is designed in a Core Data model. You add this by selecting **File > New File**. Select **Data Model** in the Core Data section. Click **Next** and enter **MyContactListModel** as the file name. Click **Create**.

The data structure for the app is very simple with just a single entity. For the following steps of actually designing the data structure, refer to Figure 11.4.

1. Select the **data model** you just created.
2. Click the **Add Entity** button at the bottom and then double-click the word Entity to rename the new entity to **Contact** (entity names must begin with an uppercase letter).
3. Click **Add Attribute** and name the first attribute **contactName** (attribute names must begin with a lower-case letter) and give it the type **String**.
4. Add the remaining attributes as shown in Figure 11.5. Each of the attributes are of type **String** except birthday, which is **Date**.

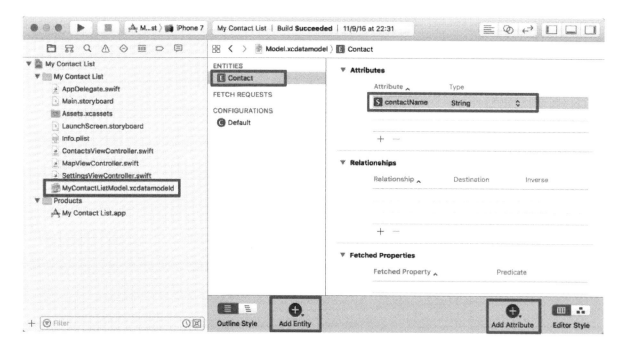

Figure 11.4 Using the Core Data Model editor.

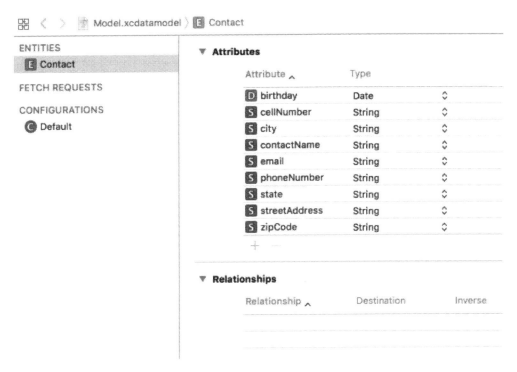

Figure 11.5   Attributes of the Contact entity.

What about NSManagedObject Subclass?

If you have experience with previous versions of Xcode and iOS, you would have expected at this point to go to Editor > Create NSManagedObject Subclass. However, starting with Xcode 8, this class is automatically generated, so you don't have to explicitly create this class. In fact, if you do, you will get error messages saying that the generated class is a duplicate—even if you have no other class by that name in your project. If you want the previous behavior where you explicitly generate the class, select the Entity and then use the Data Model Inspector to change Codegen to Manual/none.

Saving Contact Data

Once you have the data structure designed, the next step is to be able to save the data to the database. To do this, you will add listeners to each of the text fields on the Contacts screen, so that whenever the user is done making changes to one of them, the contact object is updated. Switch to **ContactsViewController.swift** and modify the beginning of the class as shown in Listing 11.10.

Listing 11.10   Modifying ContactsViewcontroller for Saving Data

```
1    import CoreData
2
3    class ContactsViewController: UIViewController, UITextFieldDelegate {
4
5        var currentContact: Contact?
6        let appDelegate = UIApplication.shared.delegate as! AppDelegate
7
```

- Line 1 adds an import for CoreData.
- Line 3 adds the interface declaration, `UITextFieldDelegate`, to the class declaration.
- Line 5 sets up a variable, `currentContact`, to hold information about the `Contact` entity being edited. The question mark means that the variable is optional (as there may not be a value associated with it). In Swift, optional variables can be set to `nil`. However, unlike in most object-oriented programming languages, `nil` is not a pointer to a nonexistent object. It is the absence of a value, which means it can also be used with tuples and struct values, which are simpler data structures than classes.
- Line 6 sets up a reference to the App Delegate that will be used to access the Core Data functionality.

If you get a syntax error that Contact isn't found, you can try doing a Clean of the project (**Product > Clean**) and then a Build (**Product > Build**). If this doesn't fix it, you can try restarting Xcode or restarting the computer.

You may wonder why you aren't supposed to get a syntax error when adding a variable of type Contact, since you haven't added a Contact class to the project. This is because, starting with Xcode 8, a class is automatically generated behind the scenes for every entity you create in the data model. By default, the name is the same as the entity, but you can control this in the Data Model Inspector when looking at the entity in the data model.

Next, add lines 6–11 in Listing 11.11 to the `viewDidLoad` method.

Listing 11.11   Adding Listeners to the Text Fields

```
1    override func viewDidLoad() {
2        super.viewDidLoad()
3        // Do any additional setup after loading the view.
4        changeEditMode(self)
5
6        let textFields: [UITextField] = [txtName, txtAddress, txtCity, txtState, txtZip,
7                                         txtPhone, txtCell, txtEmail]
8        for textfield in textFields {
9            textfield.addTarget(self,
10                        action: #selector(UITextFieldDelegate.textFieldShouldEndEditing(_:)),
11                        for: UIControlEvents.editingDidEnd)
12       }
13   }
```

- Line 6 puts all the text fields into an array, similar to how it was done in Chapter 10, "iOS Navigation and Interface Design..
- Line 8 sets up a loop to go over all the text fields in the array.
- Line 9–11 is where the real action is. Each time this is executed, it adds a listener (called a target in iOS) to the text field. The first parameter, `self`, specifies the object that contains the method that is called when the event occurs that the listener is listening for. In this case, the method will be in the current class, so we use `self`. The second argument, `action`, specifies the name of the method to call when the event occurs. In this case, the method is a standard method from the `UITextFieldDelegate` protocol, called `textFieldShouldEndEditing`. This method is called just as the text field is done editing the text and is a method that can be used for text validation, among other things. The third argument, `for`, is the actual event to listen for. This is `editingDidEnd`, which occurs after the user leaves the text field.

Next, you need to add the `textFieldShouldEndEditing` method that is to be called when the event occurs. Add the method immediately below `viewDidLoad`. The code for this method is in Listing 11.12.

Listing 11.12 Populating currentContact from Text Field Values

```
1    func textFieldShouldEndEditing(_ textField: UITextField) -> Bool {
2        currentContact?.contactName = txtName.text
3        currentContact?.streetAddress = txtAddress.text
4        currentContact?.city = txtCity.text
5        currentContact?.state = txtState.text
6        currentContact?.zipCode = txtZip.text
7        currentContact?.cellNumber = txtCell.text
8        currentContact?.phoneNumber = txtPhone.text
9        currentContact?.email = txtEmail.text
10       return true
11   }
```

This method updates the `currentContact` object with the values in all the text fields. Line 10 then saves the data to the context, ensuring that it is inserted into the underlying database. You can run the app at this point, and by inserting a breakpoint in the `textFieldShouldEndEditing` method, you can see that every time you leave a text field, all the values in the `currentContact` object are updated.

currentContact Object

The code in Listing 11.12 updates the values in the `currentContact` object; however, it does not save the object to the database. To do this, you'll need to add a Save button to the interface and code an event associated with the button to save to the database. The button will actually be a special button called a **UIBarButtonItem** that is used in the navigation bar.

Follow these steps to add the button and implement the save functionality:

1. Add the following method to **ContactsViewController.swift**:

    ```
    func saveContact() {
            if currentContact == nil {
                let context = appDelegate.persistentContainer.viewContext
                currentContact = Contact(context: context)
            }
        appDelegate.saveContext()
        sgmtEditMode.selectedSegmentIndex = 0
        changeEditMode(self)
    }
    ```

    If there is no `currentContact` object, the code first uses the `appDelegate` variable to get a reference to the Managed Object Context (which is essentially the file that stores the data). This is used in the next line, which instantiates the `currentContact` variable by inserting it as a new object into the context. The `appDelegate.saveContext()` line saves the object to the database. The final two lines change the scene from editing to viewing mode.

2. Add the following line to the `changeEditMode` method just after the `btnChange.isHidden = true` line to ensure there is no button in View mode:

    ```
    navigationItem.rightBarButtonItem = nil
    ```

3. Add this statement just after the `btnChange.isHidden = false` line to create a UIBarButtonItem in the left spot of the navigation bar with the text Save, and associate it with the `saveContact` method you just created:

    ```
    navigationItem.rightBarButtonItem = UIBarButtonItem(barButtonSystemItem: .save,
                                            target: self,
                                            action: #selector(self.saveContact))
    ```

Later, we will add functionality to display the saved entities.

Modifying the Data Model

If you change the data model after the app has run the first time, your app is going to give an error message that the data model no longer matches the database created for the app. Core Data provides functionality for migrating your data model. There are several approaches to changing the data model design, but they are all based on providing different versions of the data model. Whenever you need to make a change, you add a new version by selecting Editor > Add Model Version. The new version starts out as a copy of the old version, and you can then make your changes in the new version. After you have created the new version, you create a mapping model that lets you specify how each entity and attribute in the old version maps to the new version.

The mapping model is then used in code when the app starts to check for changes and migrate the database to the new version of the model. If your changes are minor, such as adding or removing attributes and entities, the system may be able to infer the mapping model, and you can simply ask it to do the conversion without setting up an explicit mapping model. This process is called Lightweight Migration.

This mapping process can be used both during development and after your app has been released. During development, you also have the option of deleting the database file from the app's sandbox. Then Core Data will automatically create a new blank copy of the database the next time the app launches.

For more detail on how to migrate between data models, you should refer to the Core Data documentation on Apple's Developer Portal.

Running the app right now will not provide any feedback as to what data was saved, but you can check that the database was created by opening up a Finder window and navigating to the location of the files for your app. It takes a bit of work to get to the folder.

1. In Xcode, select **Window > Devices** and then locate the Simulator you ran the app on. Copy the **Identifier** for this Simulator by triple-clicking it (see Figure 11.6).

2. Open a Finder window and select **Go > Go To Folder**.

3. Enter **~/Library/Developer/CoreSimulator/Devices/{DEVICE IDENTIFIER}/data/Containers/Data/ Application**, but replace {DEVICE IDENTIFIER} with the Identifier you copied in Step 1.

4. You will see a folder for each app on the Simulator. Unfortunately, they are only named with a long string of letters and numbers, so the only way to find the app you're looking for is to open each folder and look for the .app file, which will have the name of the app. The easiest way to do this is to sort by Date Modified. Your app should be one of the most recently modified.

4. After you find the correct app, you can open up its Library directory, and then Application Support. You should see a file named MyContactListModel.sqlite. Although you can't open it directly, you can convince yourself that it is being modified by looking at the file size and latest modified time stamp. If you want to look inside the database file, there are many free tools available to examine SQLite files if you want to take a closer look. An easily accessible option is a Firefox extension called SQLite Manager. You can also download DB Browser for SQLite at http://sqlitebrowser.org.

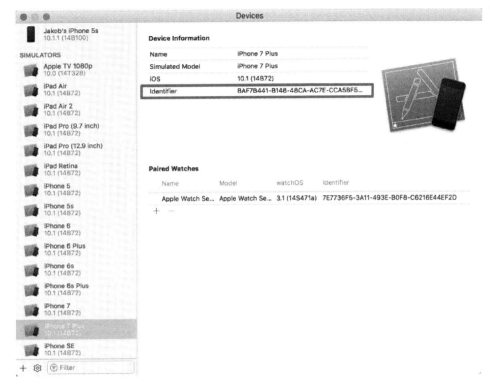

Figure 11.6 Finding the Simulator Identifier.

In the next chapter, you learn how to retrieve the data in the database and display it in the app.

Passing Data between Controllers

In this section, you will see how to pass data between screens. The Birthday label on the Contacts screen is changed on the Date screen. When the user taps the Change button next to the birthday, the Date screen is opened with a Date Picker, where the user can choose the desired date. Tapping the Save button brings the user back to the Contact screen and changes the Birthday label to what was chosen in the Date Picker. Since each screen is managed by a view controller, we will be passing data between controllers.

The standard way to pass data back from a View Controller is to use the *delegate pattern*. With this pattern, you will have a reference in the Date Controller back to whatever controller called it (allowing for the Date Controller to be used in many contexts), as well as one or more methods that the Date Controller knows exist in the calling controller. The delegate pattern is used widely in iOS, so you should spend some time to make sure you understand it well.

Figure 11.7 shows how the delegate pattern is set up in this example. The key is to create a protocol called **DateControllerDelegate**. A Swift protocol is very similar to an interface in languages like C# and Java. However, instead of implementing an interface, a class can *adopt a protocol*, and then is said to *conform* to that protocol. So, in this example, the ContactsViewController adopts the DateControllerDelegate protocol, and then must implement all the specified methods in the protocol. The Delegator, in this case DateViewController, holds a reference called delegate to an object that conforms to the delegate protocol. The delegator will then be able to call on all the methods in the protocol and know that they are available.

The delegate pattern is often used to allow for passing data between a main and sub view controller in a navigation hierarchy. In that case, the delegator is the sub view controller and the delegate is the main view controller. By giving the sub view controller a reference back to the main view controller, the sub view controller will always be able to pass data back to where it was called from. This allows the sub view controller to be used by different kinds of main view controller—as long as they implement the delegate protocol.

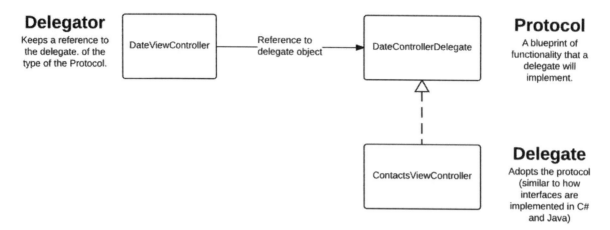

Figure 11.7 Delegate pattern.

There are several steps to set up this pattern:

1. Define a delegate protocol in the sub view controller (the one being opened from another controller—in our case the Date Controller).
2. Set up a property called delegate in the sub view controller to hold a reference to the main view controller.
3. Specify that the main controller should implement the delegate protocol.
4. Implement the methods specified in the protocol in the main controller.
5. Set up the main view as a delegate of the sub view.
6. Call the delegate methods from the sub view.

In the next sections, you see how to do each of these steps in detail, but first, you need to add a view controller for the Date screen.

1. Select **File > New File**… or press Command-N.
2. Select **Cocoa Touch Class** and click **Next**.
3. Enter **DateViewController** for the Class name and **UIViewController** for the Subclass… field. Don't create a XIB file, and make sure the Language is set to **Swift**. Click **Next**.
4. Ensure that MyContactList is checked as a Target and click **Create**.
5. Open **Main.storyboard** and select the **Birthdate** Scene. In the Identity Inspector, change the Class to **DateViewController** to connect the scene to the code-behind-file.

You now have a new file in your project, DateViewController, which will be used to manage any actions on the Birthdate scene. This file will contain the `DateControllerDelegate` interface, as well as a reference to a delegate that it can use to specify the date that was picked.

Step 1: Set Up Delegate Protocol

Switch to **DateViewController.swift** and add lines 3–5 in Listing 11.13.

This sets up the delegate protocol and specifies that any class adopting this protocol must also implement the `dateChanged` method. What the class chooses to have the `dateChanged` method do is up to the developer. In this case, the Date Controller calls this method on its delegate anytime the date changes. Note that the protocol uses the `class` keyword to specify that it only is available to be applied to classes—not to structs and enumerations.

Step 2: Add Delegate Property

For the sub view to call back to the main view, it needs a reference to the main view. You do this by setting up a property that will have a reference to the main view. Add line 10 in Listing 11.13. The `delegate` property is of the same type as the protocol you just created. This will allow any kind of controller (or other object) to take advantage of the Date

Controller to set a date. In some instances, a main controller may not set itself as a delegate of the Date Controller, so the delegate variable is set to `weak`, and the type is optional as specified by the question mark. See Appendix C for more description of how to declare variables in Swift.

Listing 11.13   Setting Up the Delegate Pattern in DaveViewController.swift

```
1    import UIKit
2
3    protocol DateControllerDelegate: class {
4        func dateChanged(date: Date)
5    }
6
7    class DateViewController: UIViewController {
8        //Delegate may not always be set, so it's weak, and the type is optional (?)
9        //Optional types are set to nil by default - no need for init methods.
10       weak var delegate: DateControllerDelegate?
11
12   [... Rest of DateViewController class...]
```

Step 3: Specify That Main View Will Implement Delegate Protocol

Switch to **ContactsViewController.swift** and specify that the class will conform to `DateControllerDelegate` by adding it to the list of interfaces in the class declaration:

```
class ContactsViewController: UIViewController, UITextFieldDelegate, DateControllerDelegate {
```

Step 4: Implement the Methods of the Delegate Protocol

Having specified that the Contacts Controller adopts `DateControllerDelegate`, you now have to implement the required methods—in this case, just the `dateChanged` method, as shown in Listing 11.14.

Listing 11.14   Implementing the dateChanged Method in ContactsViewController.swift

```
1    func dateChanged(date: Date) {
2        if currentContact != nil {
3            currentContact?.birthday = date as NSDate?
4            appDelegate.saveContext()
5            let formatter = DateFormatter()
6            formatter.dateStyle = .short
7            lblBirthdate.text = formatter.string(from: date)
8        }
9    }
```

There are several things going on here that deserve explanation:

- The method starts by checking if the `currentContact` variable is populated, since `currentContact` is optional.
- Line 3 then sets the date that was passed in from the calling controller to the `birthday` property in `currentContact`. Note that the date has to be cast to `NSDate`. This is because the automatically generated Core Data class uses `NSdate`, whereas the date picker provides a `Date`. `NSDate` is the original type from Objective C, whereas `Date` was added with Swift. There is no functional difference between the two, and at some point Apple may very well decide to switch to `Date` for the Core Data generated classes.
- Line 4 saves the context, so the date is saved with the contact.
- Lines 5 and 6 set up a date formatter and format the date using the short style (MM/DD/YYYY in the US locale). You can option-click the DateFormatter class name to see the class reference for more detail on how to format in other styles.
- Finally, the formatted date is set on the label on the Contacts screen.

Step 5: Set Up Main Controller as Delegate

The delegate property in the sub view needs to be set up at the time the sub view is called by the main view. In this case, the sub view is called when the user taps the Change button. However, because the segue controls make the Birthdate screen active, no code is being called directly. Instead, you can implement the `prepare(for segue: sender:)` method, which is called anytime a segue is executed in the app. Listing 11.15 shows how this method is implemented to set the delegate of the Date screen to be the Contact screen. You add the code to **ContactsController.swift**. It is a very typical pattern that a class that adopts a delegate protocol will set itself as the delegate.

Listing 11.15   Adding the Delegate Reference in ContactsViewController.swift

```
1    override func prepare(for segue: UIStoryboardSegue, sender: Any?) {
2        if(segue.identifier == "segueContactDate"){
3            let dateController = segue.destination as! DateViewController
4            dateController.delegate = self
5        }
6    }
```

- The method first checks to see which segue initiated the call to the method (line 2). The string `"segueC-ontactDate"` is a unique identifier of the segue, which will be entered into storyboard shortly.

- Line 3 gets a reference to the destination View Controller, which is the `DateViewController` in this case.

- Line 4 sets the delegate for the Date Controller to be the Contacts Controller (self). This allows the Date Controller to call the `dateChanged` method in the Contacts Controller.

To set the identifier for the segue, open **storyboard** and select the **segue** between the Contact and Date scenes. Use the Attributes Inspector to set the Identifier to **segueContactDate** (see Figure 11.8).

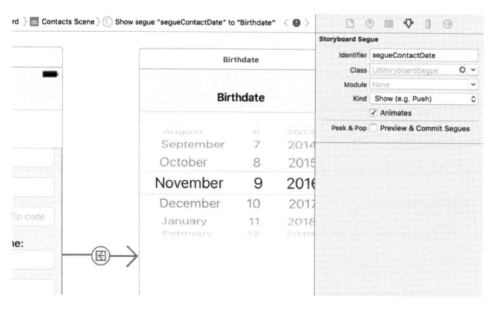

Figure 11.8   Setting the identifier for the segue.

Step 6: Call the Delegate Methods from the Subview

When the date is picked, the user taps a Save button on the toolbar to save the date and be brought back to the previous screen. The Contact button acts as a cancel, where the date will not be changed on the main controller.

To be able to reference the Date Picker on the Date scene, you need to add an outlet for it. Open the **Storyboard** with the Assistant Editor, and control-drag from the **Date Picker** to **DateViewController.swift** to create an outlet named **dtpDate**.

Implement the `viewDidLoad` and `saveDate` methods, as shown in Listing 11.16.

Listing 11.16 Calling the Delegate Methods in DateViewController.swift

```
1   override func viewDidLoad() {
2       super.viewDidLoad()
3
4       // Do any additional setup after loading the view.
5       let saveButton: UIBarButtonItem =
6           UIBarButtonItem(barButtonSystemItem: UIBarButtonSystemItem.save,
7                                                 target: self,
8                                                 action: #selector(saveDate))
9       self.navigationItem.rightBarButtonItem = saveButton
10      self.title = "Pick Birthdate"
11  }
12
13  func saveDate(){
14      self.delegate?.dateChanged(date: dtpDate.date)
15      self.navigationController?.popViewController(animated: true)
16  }
```

This code sets up the Save button and connects it to the method to save the date.

- Lines 5–8 sets up a `UIBarButtonItem` for the Save button. Many standard system buttons can be used. Here we used `UIBarButtonSystemItem.save`, but you should spend some time looking through the list of the options using code completion. The action parameter is important as well. This contains the method name for the method that will be called when the button is tapped.
- Line 9 adds the Save button on the right in the navigation bar.
- Although you already set the title of the View Controller in storyboard, line 10 demonstrates how to set the title of a View Controller in code. This can be useful to do when the title might be different for different controllers that would use this date picker controller. In this case, we use it to pick a birthdate, but other controllers might use it for other kinds of dates.
- The `saveDate` method in lines 13–15 is the one that is called when the button is tapped. The method calls the `dateChanged` method in the delegate, passing the chosen date from the date picker. Then it pops the View Controller off the stack, which returns the user to the previous view controller, which in this case is the contacts controller. You will get a warning on this line, because the `popViewController` method returns the view controller that you left, but this isn't used for anything. You can safely ignore the warning.

You can now run the app, change the date, and have it show up on the main contacts screen. Remember to put the screen in Edit mode to have the Change button show up.

iOS versus Android: Delegates versus Listeners

This pattern of using a delegate to pass data between controllers has a parallel in Android. In Chapter 4, "Android Navigation and Interface Design," you set up a custom dialog to capture the birthday of a contact. That custom dialog is implemented as a class, which declared a `SaveDateListener` interface (the delegate protocol in iOS) with the `didFinishDatePickerDialog` method (required delegate method). In the `ContactActivity`, you tell the class to implement the SaveDateListener (set up main controller as delegate) and implement the `didFinishDatePickerDialog` method (implement the methods of the delegate protocol). In that method, you write code to handle the new birthday. After the user changes the date in the dialog and taps the OK button, the dialog calls the `didFinishDatePickerDialog` method, passing it the selected date (call the delegate methods in main controller).

Summary

Being able to store data in an app is very important to almost all apps. You have seen two important ways to do this in this chapter. Core Data is a very powerful object-oriented wrapper around a persistent data store (SQLite by default), which allows you to store any kind of data in a relatively simple way. In the next chapter, you will see how to retrieve the data and display multiple contact records. You also saw how to store simple pieces of data like that used for the settings in the app. It is common for both these approaches to coexist in the same app.

Along the way, you gained some experience with additional user interface controls, allowing you to learn how to use a Picker View and a Switch. Finally, you saw how to use a struct to keep global constants to reduce possible errors from using literal strings to access keys in the UserDefaults object.

Exercises

1. Add a few more items to the Picker View for sort fields.
2. Store the array with the values for the Picker View in UserDefaults.
3. Experiment with adding `// MARK:` notations to a few more of the source code files and observe the effects.
4. Change the Picker View and the Switch on the Settings screen to segmented controls.
5. Add a new item to the Settings screen to store a default state. This state should be filled in when a user starts editing a new contact. Let the user type in the default state in a textfield.
6. Add a new scene with a picker with all 50 states. Use a delegate to pass data back to the Settings screen to fill in the default state.
7. Add an additional attribute to the Core Data model to store a home e-mail address. Update the Contact scene to allow the user to enter the e-mail address.
8. Add the home e-mail address to the possible sort fields.
9. Add the sort fields to Constants.swift and pull them from there as needed.
10. Add another Entity to Core Data to store the settings. Change the app to store the settings in the new entity.
11. Add an indicator on the Contacts screen to show whether the contact has been saved or not.

CHAPTER 12

Tables in iOS: Navigation and Information Display

One of the big innovations on the small screen is the introduction of structured content that can be scrolled up and down and that allows for drilling down for more detailed content. On Android, this pattern of navigation is called Lists, as described in Chapter 6, "Lists in Android: Navigation and Information Display." In iOS, it is called Tables and has a number of built-in but very customizable layouts and controls. The Tables layout is used in many apps you use every day and in many of the built-in apps that come with iOS devices.

Anytime you see data presented in a single-column format, whether it's in the Settings app, the list of music in the iTunes app, or the list of e-mails in the Mail app, those are examples of using a Table configured in different ways.

There are project templates in Xcode that have table views included, but because the data for the MyContactList app is from a database, it is just as easy to generate the table and associated view programmatically. Right now, MyContactList doesn't have a way to show all the contacts in the database. So far, you have only enabled saving contacts. In this chapter, you will see how to set up a table and populate it with data from MyContactList. You will also learn how to use the table features to modify the data directly from the table, such as deleting records.

Overview of Tables

A table in iOS is a single-column table where each cell contains data to be displayed to the user. The user can scroll-flick through the content by flicking a finger up and down the screen. The individual cell objects are reused when they scroll off the screen, and then they show up at the other end of the screen. This saves tremendous amounts of memory on the device by not having to create an object for every entry in potentially very long tables.

Tables are often used as navigation controllers to allow users to select content in a cell in the table and get more detailed information and/or take action on the data on a separate view controller. You will see the important role that navigation controllers play when you are working with tables.

The cells in a table can be set up with several standard style options: **Default**, **Subtitle**, **Value1**, and **Value2**. These can be set in either code or in Interface builder. **Default** has a single title and an optional image, whereas **Subtitle** adds the option of a subtitle below the title (Figure 12.1 uses the subtitle style). **Value1** does not permit images and right-aligns the subtitle in blue, and **Value2** puts the title in blue and aligns the title and subtitle against each other down the middle.

Table cells can also be adorned with various accessories on the right edge of the cell to indicate what functionality is available when the user taps the cell. You can choose from three standard accessories, as shown in Figure 12.1, in addition to supplying your own image as an accessory.

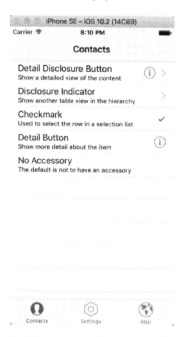

Figure 12.1 Cell Accessory Views and their typical uses.

Setting Up Tables

Open your project from Chapter 11, "Persistent Data in iOS," or open the Chapter 12, "Tables in iOS: Navigation and Information Display," project that comes with the book. The first step is to create a new View Controller to hold the table. For the table to show up, you need to insert it in the tab controller. It replaces the controller that allows for editing and viewing a single Contact, which will then be called from the Table Controller instead of directly from the Tab Controller.

1. Open the **Storyboard** and drag a **Table View Controller** onto the canvas.

2. Select the **Navigation Controller** that is between the Tab Bar Controller and the ContactsView Controller, and control-drag from the yellow **Navigation Controller icon** in the bar above the Navigation Controller scene to the new **Table View Controller**. Select **root view controller** in the menu that pops up when you release the mouse. This makes the new Table View Controller the first controller in the Navigation Controller hierarchy, and it shows the Table View instead of the Contact editing screen. Later in the chapter, you will connect the Contact screen to the Table View. You can rearrange the storyboard to clearly show the new Table View Controller between the Navigation Controller and the Contact scene.

3. To create the code file used to control the Table View Controller, select **File > New > File**. Choose **Cocoa Touch Class**, and click Next.

4. Change the Subclass Of field to **UITableViewController**, and change the Class to **ContactsTableViewController**. Make sure the check box for XIB file is **unchecked** and the language is set to **Swift**; then click **Next**. On the next screen, verify that the file is being saved in the top-level folder of the project and that the **Target for MyContactList Core Data** is checked. Click **Create**.

5. Switch back to **Storyboard** and select the **Table View Controller**. Use the Identity Inspector to change the Class to **ContactsTableViewController**. This ties the code file to the scene.

Try running the app. You should see a lined screen above the tab bar, as shown in Figure 12.2. If you click and drag on the screen in the simulator, you will notice that you can drag the lines up and down, as you would with a regular table.

Figure 12.2 App with empty table.

Populate the Table with Data

A table without data isn't very exciting, so the next task is to have some data show up in the table. Switch to **ContactsTableViewController.swift** and scroll down until you see several premade methods related to the table. These are all methods that are declared in **UITableViewDelegate** and **UITableViewDataSource**. The Table Controller is a subclass of **UITableViewController**, which conforms to these two protocols, so the template added all the required methods from those protocols.

The system will make calls to the delegate methods as it needs to work with the table, so most of your work in setting up a table is to implement the methods in the two protocols. Throughout the rest of this chapter, you will see how to use several of the delegate methods. To see the rest of them, you can look up the documentation on the two protocols by opening the Documentation (Help > Documentation and API reference) and searching for UITableViewDelegate and UITableViewDataSource.

Before you can get started using these methods, you need to create some data. Initially, the data is stored in a simple array, so you can easily see what's going on. Declare an array to hold the data by adding this line in ContactsTableViewController.swift right after the class declaration:

```
let contacts = ["Jim", "John", "Dana", "Rosie", "Justin", "Jeremy", "Sarah", "Matt", "Joe", "Donald", "Jeff"]
```

This creates an array with static data that can be displayed in the table as a quick demonstration of how the table works. Later, you can switch to working with the full Contact objects. At that point, the contact data will be editable as well. To have the data actually show up in the table, you modify some of the autogenerated methods. Locate the `numberOfSections(in tableView:)` method. This method returns the number of sections (or groupings) in a table. For this table, there's a single section. See the built-in Settings app for an example of multiple sections in a table. Change the method to return a value of 1 and remove the line that begins with `#warning`.

Just below is the `tableView(_ tableView:numberOfRowsInSection:)` method. This returns the number of data rows a particular section has, so that iOS knows how many table cells to present. In this case, the number of rows will equal how many names are in the array given previously (later, it will return how many Contact objects are in the database). Remove the `#warning` line and replace the return line with this line:

```
return contacts.count
```

This returns the number of elements in the contacts array.

The `tableView(_ tableView:cellForRowAt indexPath:)` method is the workhorse method when it comes to tables. This method is called by the system to generate the data for a particular cell, so it is passed the section and row as the `indexPath` parameter. You use this to configure the actual cell. Listing 12.1 shows the content for this method, which is already in the class; it just needs to be uncommented by removing the /* and */ surrounding it and slightly edited as shown.

Listing 12.1   Populating the Table with Data

```
1   override func tableView(_ tableView: UITableView, cellForRowAt indexPath: IndexPath) ->
2   UITableViewCell {
3       let cell = tableView.dequeueReusableCell(withIdentifier: "ContactsCell", for: indexPath)
4
5       // Configure the cell...
6       cell.textLabel?.text = contacts[indexPath.row]
7       return cell
8   }
```

This code is fairly standard when working with tables, so it's important to understand what's going on.

- Line 3 creates the cell object. The only thing you need to change in this line is the identifier, ContactsCell. This is a unique identifier for all cells in the table that are set up in the same way so the objects can be reused when the cell scrolls off the screen. If you created an app where some rows need to look different, you would also use different reuse identifiers for the different types of cells. In all, only enough cell objects will end up being created in the system to be displayed on the screen at any given time. (Thus devices with larger screens will have more cells created.)

- In line 6, you use the textLabel property of the cell to set the text that will show up on screen. The data is pulled from the contacts array using the requested row number as the index.

In order to connect the code to the Storyboard, you also need to enter the identifier on the prototype cell in the Storyboard. Open **Storyboard** and select the **Table View Cell** (which may be easiest to select in the sidebar), and then use the **Attributes Inspector** to change the Identifier to **ContactsCell** (see Figure 12.3).

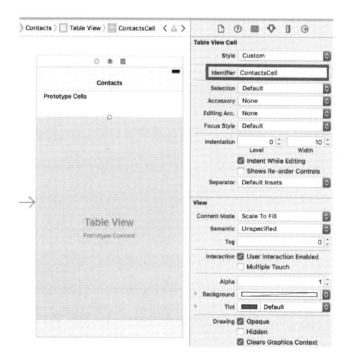

Figure 12.3   Setting the Table View Cell Identifier.

Now you can run the app and see the names from the Contacts array show up in the table. You can scroll up and down and see the cells scroll off the screen. (If you chose a device with a large screen, they may all fit on the screen.) One thing missing, though, is the title of the screen. It should say Contacts in the navigation bar at the top. This is an easy fix. You select the **Navigation Item** under the Table View Controller in the Document Outline and change the Title to **Contacts**. Figure 12.4 shows the app with the title set and the static names from the array.

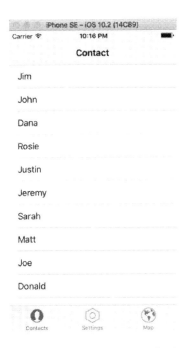

Figure 12.4 Table with static data.

Now that you've seen how to work with the table using the delegate methods to configure the table and populate the table cells, it's time to retrieve the data from the database and display real Contacts objects.

Retrieve Data from Core Data

In the previous chapter, you saw how to save data to Core Data by inserting a Contact object into the managed object context. Retrieving data is similar, but instead of inserting objects, you will fetch them, and then specify some action to take on the retrieved objects. Before moving on to the code changes, you will change the look of the cells to the Subtitle style, which shows two labels in the cell. Go to **Storyboard** and select the **prototype cell**, and then use the Attributes Inspector to change the Style to **Subtitle**.

Switch back to **ContactsTableViewController.swift** and make the changes shown in Listing 12.2 to have the data show up from the database.

Listing 12.2   Retrieving Data from Core Data in ContactsTableViewController.swift

```
1    import UIKit
2    import CoreData
3
4    class ContactsTableViewController: UITableViewController {
5
6        // let contacts = ["Jim", "John", "Dana", "Rosie", "Justin", "Jeremy", "Sarah", "Matt", "Joe",
7    "Donald", "Jeff"]
8        var contacts:[NSManagedObject] = []
9        let appDelegate = UIApplication.shared.delegate as! AppDelegate
10
11       override func viewDidLoad() {
12           super.viewDidLoad()
13           loadDataFromDatabase()
14       }
15
16       override func didReceiveMemoryWarning() {
17           super.didReceiveMemoryWarning()
18           // Dispose of any resources that can be recreated.
19       }
20
```

(continued)

Listing 12.2   Retrieving Data from Core Data in ContactsTableViewController.swift (*continued*)

```
21        func loadDataFromDatabase() {
22            let context = appDelegate.persistentContainer.viewContext
23            let request = NSFetchRequest<NSManagedObject>(entityName: "Contact")
24            do {
25                contacts = try context.fetch(request)
26            } catch let error as NSError {
27                print("Could not fetch. \(error), \(error.userInfo)")
28            }
29        }
30
31        // MARK: - Table view data source
32
33        override func numberOfSections(in tableView: UITableView) -> Int {
34            return 1
35        }
36
37        override func tableView(_ tableView: UITableView, numberOfRowsInSection section: Int) -> Int {
38            return contacts.count
39        }
40
41        override func tableView(_ tableView: UITableView, cellForRowAt indexPath: IndexPath) ->
42                        UITableViewCell {
43            let cell = tableView.dequeueReusableCell(withIdentifier: "ContactsCell", for: indexPath)
44
45            // Configure the cell...
46            let contact = contacts[indexPath.row] as? Contact
47            cell.textLabel?.text = contact?.contactName
48            cell.detailTextLabel?.text = contact?.city
49            return cell
50        }
51    }
```

The code is relatively simple, but spread out over several places in the file.

- Line 2 imports the CoreData functionality needed to load the data for the table.
- Line 8 changes the contacts array to hold NSManagedObject instances. This allows us to hold the Contact objects that will be retrieved from CoreData.
- Line 9 simply creates a reference to the appDelegate. Eventually it will be necessary to access the appDelegate from multiple places in the code, so this line sets up a class variable for the app delegate.
- When the view controller is first loaded into memory, the contacts array is populated with data by calling the loadDataFromDatabase method in line 14. This method is defined in lines 21–29. Line 23 defines what data is to be pulled from CoreData by creating a NSFetchRequest object specifying that Contact entities will be retrieved. Line 25 then executes the fetch and stores the results in the contacts array. Because the fetch may fail, it is placed in a do block. If any errors occur, they can be handled in the catch block. In this case, we simply print an error message to the console.
- Lines 46–48 are also changed to reflect the changes to the contacts array. First, an entire Contact object is retrieved in line 46, and then the entire object is available to be retrieved. Line 47 sets the textLabel to the contactName, and line 48 sets the detailTextLabel to the city for the contact. The detailTextLabel shows up below the textLabel in smaller text when the Table View Cell's style is set to Subtitle.

If you run the app, you should see whatever data you entered and saved when testing the app in the previous chapter. If the table shows up blank, the most likely explanation is that you didn't save any data in the previous chapter. You will enable the app to add data again in the next section.

Adding Contact Data

To be able to add a new Contact, you need to add the Contact editing screen back into the Storyboard. You will add a special Add button with a plus sign that will display the Contact editing screen.

1. Open **Main.Storyboard** and select the **Table View Controller**.
2. Drag a **Bar Button** item from the Object Library to the navigation bar and drop it to the right of the text Contacts. Before dropping it, you should see a blue rectangle appear on the navigation bar. Drop it into this rectangle.
3. Use the **Attributes Inspector** to change the **System Item** to **Add**. This changes the button to a plus sign.
4. Control-drag from the **Bar Button** item to the **Contact** editing screen and select **Show**. This sets up a segue between the Table View Controller and the Contact editing screen, and pushes the Contact editing screen onto the navigation stack, so the proper buttons for navigating back to the table view will be set up in the navigation bar (see Figure 12.5).
5. Select the **segue** and change its **Identifier** to **AddContact**.

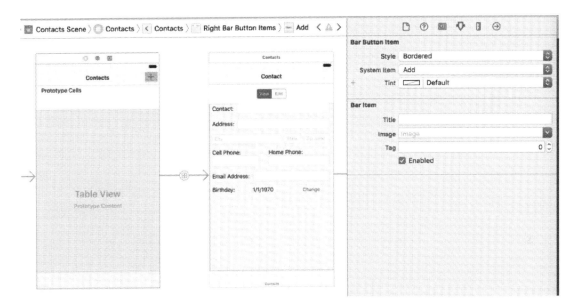

Figure 12.5   Setting up the navigation from the table view to the Contact screen.

You can run the app now and click the plus button on the table to have the Contact editing screen show up with the proper navigation buttons on it.

Display Detailed Data

The next step is to allow the user to select an entry in the table and have the full Contact object displayed on the Contact screen. As shown in Figure 12.1, when a table cell has more data than can be displayed, the convention is to add a Detail Disclosure accessory to that cell. So, you will see how to do that in this section and have that disclosure button trigger the segue that populates the Contact screen with the corresponding Contact object.

First, you'll need to set up a segue from the Prototype cell to the Contact screen.

1. Control-drag from the **Prototype** cell to the **Contact** screen and select **Accessory Action > Show** (see Figure 12.6). This creates a second segue between the two screens that is activated when the user taps an accessory button on the cell. You will create the accessory a little later in this section. It may be easier to drag from ContactsCell in the Document Outline rather than directly from the Prototype Cell.
2. Select the new segue and use the **Attributes Inspector** to change the **Identifier** to **EditContact** (see Figure 12.7). This identifier will be used to uniquely identify the segue.

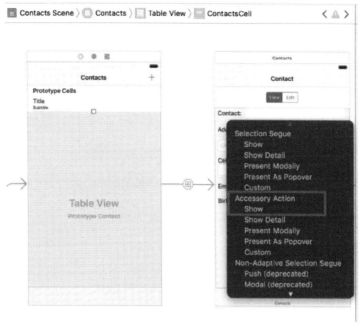

Figure 12.6   Setting up the navigation from the table view to the Contact screen.

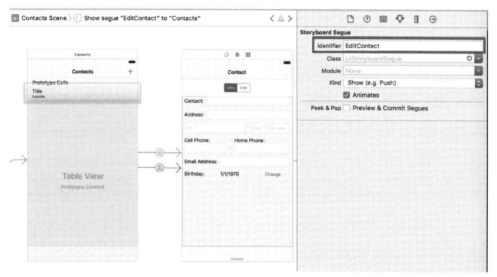

Figure 12.7   Setting up the navigation from the table view to the Contact screen.

Switch to **ContactsTableViewController.swift** and add the following line to the `tableView(_tableView:-cellForRowAt:)` method just before the return statement:

```
cell.accessoryType = UITableViewCellAccessoryType.detailDisclosureButton
```

This adds the accessory button to the cell. The other options for adding accessories are `none`, `disclosureindicator`, `checkmark`, and `detailButton`. Figure 12.1 shows how each of them looks and how they are typically used. When adding the accessory type, you can omit the `UITableViewCellAccessoryType` class, and just write the line like this:

```
cell.accessoryType = .detailDisclosureButton
```

The compiler will infer that `detailDisclosureButton` is a property of `UITableViewCellAccessoryType`. This is a general feature of Swift that you can often omit the class name like that.

To pass the selected Contact from the table, you implement the `prepare(for:sender:)` method in ContactsTableViewController.swift, as shown in Listing 12.3.

Listing 12.3   Passing Cell Data to Detail Screen

```
1    override func prepare(for segue: UIStoryboardSegue, sender: Any?) {
2        if segue.identifier == "EditContact" {
3            let contactController = segue.destination as? ContactsViewController
4            let selectedRow = self.tableView.indexPath(for: sender as! UITableViewCell)?.row
5            let selectedContact = contacts[selectedRow!] as? Contact
6            contactController?.currentContact = selectedContact!
7        }
8    }
```

This is similar to the code you saw previously for passing data from the Contact editing screen to the Date screen.

- Line 2 checks to see if the segue matches the identifier we set up in Storyboard.
- If so, line 3 gets a reference to the Contact editing screen view controller, because that is the destination for the segue.
- Line 4 finds out which row was selected in the table, and line 5 gets a reference to the corresponding Contact object from the contacts array.
- Line 6 assigns the selected contact to the currentContact property in ContactsViewController, which will allow that controller to populate the user interface with the selected Contact.

If you run the app now, you will see the detail disclosure buttons, and you will be able to select a row in the table and have the detailed view controller show up. But the data from the Contact object doesn't show up. Listing 12.4 shows the code you need to add to the viewDidLoad() method in **ContactsViewController.swift** to populate the fields in the user interface.

Listing 12.4   Populating the User Interface

```
1    override func viewDidLoad() {
2        super.viewDidLoad()
3        // Do any additional setup after loading the view.
4
5        if currentContact != nil {
6            txtName.text = currentContact!.contactName
7            txtAddress.text = currentContact!.streetAddress
8            txtCity.text = currentContact!.city
9            txtState.text = currentContact!.state
10           txtZip.text = currentContact!.zipCode
11           txtPhone.text = currentContact!.phoneNumber
12           txtCell.text = currentContact!.cellNumber
13           txtEmail.text = currentContact!.email
14           let formatter = DateFormatter()
15           formatter.dateStyle = .short
16           if currentContact!.birthday != nil {
17               lblBirthdate.text = formatter.string(from: currentContact!.birthday as! Date)
18           }
19       }
20       changeEditMode(self)
21
22       let textFields: [UITextField] = [txtName, txtAddress, txtCity, txtState, txtZip,
23                                        txtPhone, txtCell, txtEmail]
24       for textfield in textFields {
25           textfield.addTarget(self,
26                               action: #selector(UITextFieldDelegate.textFieldShouldEndEditing(_:)),
27                               for: UIControlEvents.editingDidEnd)
28       }
29   }
```

The new code is in lines 5–19. This code should be fairly self-explanatory, but a few notes are necessary:

- The `if` statement in line 5 checks to make sure the `currentContact` object is instantiated. The following statements populate all the text fields.
- The exclamation marks are needed because `currentContact` is optional. Since we know at this point that `currentContact` contains an object, we can use the exclamation mark to implicitly unwrap the value.
- Lines 14–15 set up a `DateFormatter` to format the date to short format.
- Line 16 checks that the `birthday` property is set to a value before line 17 formats and assigns to the label.

With these changes, if you run the app, the Contact controller interface will populate when the user selects a row.

Reloading Table Data

You may have noticed when running the app and creating or making changes to a Contact on the detail editing screen and going back to the table screen that the contact isn't updated. But stopping and re-running the app makes the data show up properly. The reason for this is that we load the database data in the `viewDidLoad()` method. This method is executed once when the controller is first instantiated. Moving to the detail screen to make changes and back again to the table doesn't execute the `viewDidLoad()` method again. However, you may recall from Chapter 2, "App Design Issues and Considerations," that the `viewWillAppear()` method is executed just before the view is displayed.

For the data to be loaded reliably every time the view becomes active again, we will use `viewWillAppear()` to load the data from the database. Listing 12.5 shows the method, which you will need to type in after the `viewDid-Load()` method in **ContactsTableViewController.swift**. As you start typing, you may notice that code completion in Xcode is smart enough to also help you write an entire method header.

Listing 12.5   Reloading the Data for the Table

```
1    override func viewWillAppear(_ animated: Bool) {
2        loadDataFromDatabase()
3        tableView.reloadData()
4    }
```

This ensures that the data is reloaded from the database in line 2. Line 3 reloads the data in the table itself. It basically redraws all the visible cells for the table, so that the data from the database is also displayed in the table after being refreshed. After adding this method, you can comment out the call to `loadDataFromDatabase()` in `viewDidLoad()`.

Deleting Records

If you've been running the app to test it along the way, you probably have a long list of contacts that cannot be deleted. This is not an ideal situation, so now it's time to add the capability to delete records from both the table and the database.

The pattern here is slightly different from what you did to be able to add records. You still need to create a button for the navigation bar that will put the table in edit mode. In edit mode, the user can tap a row to delete it from both the table and data source. This requires implementing a UITableViewDataSource delegate method that is called when the user selects a row for deletion.

Start by adding this line to the end of `viewDidLoad()` in **ContactsTableViewController.swift**:

```
self.navigationItem.leftBarButtonItem = self.editButtonItem
```

This will put a button with the word *Edit* in the left part of the navigation bar. If you run the app now and tap the Edit button, each row will get a Delete icon in front of it. If you tap that, a red Delete button will show up on the right side of the row. Tapping this button would delete the row without further warning, which isn't necessary because the user has already confirmed the intent by tapping three distinctly different areas of the screen (see Figure 12.8). You might be tempted to use Storyboard to add the Edit button, but doing so doesn't set up the three-step process of deleting the row.

Figure 12.8 Deleting records.

If you run the app now, nothing happens when the Edit button is tapped. For this, you need to implement `tableView(_ tableView:commit:forRowAt:)`, which is already included in ContactsTableViewController. swift. You just need to add the lines of code shown in Listing 12.7.

Listing 12.6 Deleting Rows from the Table

```
1    override func tableView(_ tableView: UITableView,
2                        commit editingStyle: UITableViewCellEditingStyle,
3                        forRowAt indexPath: IndexPath) {
4        if editingStyle == .delete {
5            // Delete the row from the data source
6            let contact = contacts[indexPath.row] as? Contact
7            let context = appDelegate.persistentContainer.viewContext
8            context.delete(contact!)
9            do {
10               try context.save()
11           }
12           catch  {
13               fatalError("Error saving context: \(error)")
14           }
15           loadDataFromDatabase()
16           tableView.deleteRows(at: [indexPath], with: .fade)
17       } else if editingStyle == .insert {
18           // Create a new instance of the appropriate class, insert it into the array,
19           //and add a new row to the table view
20       }
21   }
```

This method is called for both insert and delete operations; however, in this app you use only the delete operation here, because the insert was already coded in a different way.

- Line 4 retrieves the object for the row that the user tapped on, and line 8 deletes the object from the context.

- Saving the context (line 10) can cause errors, so this is surrounded by `try/catch`. Forcing the context to save changes causes the object to be deleted from the data store immediately.

- Line 15 reloads the data from the database into the contacts array. You could also redefine the contacts variable to be of type NSMutableArray, in which case you would be able to delete the individual object directly from the array.

- Finally, line 16 removes the row from the table. In this case, it is done with an animation. You can option-click the method name to see more options for fading the row out.

You can now run the app and delete records by tapping the Edit button. However, after you have implemented tableView(_ tableView:commit:forRowAt:), you get an additional way to delete rows by swiping across the row. To try this in the simulator, use the mouse and click one end of a row and drag toward the other, and you will get a Delete button for that row. This way, you don't even need the Edit button set up.

Alert Controller

When you need to provide feedback to the user, you often want to have a message pop up that the user needs to take action on. This could be to provide information, input data, or to confirm an action. This is done using an Alert Controller (**UIAlertController**). An Alert Controller pops up a message on the screen with one or more buttons for the user to click, and can also be configured to allow for user input. In this example, when the user taps the actual cell, you will show a message indicating which contact was selected and allow the user to show more details about the contact or dismiss the message. In this case, a Cancel button dismisses the alert, and the Show Details button takes the user to the Contacts Controller to see all the data for the contact (Figure 12.9).

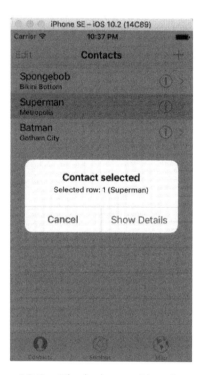

Figure 12.9 Displaying an Alert Controller.

Capturing which row was selected is done by implementing tableView(_ tableView:didSelectRowAt:), as shown in Listing 12.9 to show the Alert Controller when a row is tapped.

Listing 12.7   Showing an Alert Controller When User Selects a Row

```
1   override func tableView(_ tableView: UITableView, didSelectRowAt indexPath: IndexPath) {
2       let selectedContact = contacts[indexPath.row] as? Contact
3       let name = selectedContact!.contactName!
4       let actionHandler = { (action:UIAlertAction!) -> Void in
5           self.performSegue(withIdentifier: "EditContact", sender: tableView.cellForRow(at: indexPath))
6       }
7
8       let alertController = UIAlertController(title: "Contact selected",
9                                           message: "Selected row: \(indexPath.row) (\(name))",
10                                          preferredStyle: .alert)
11
12      let actionCancel = UIAlertAction(title: "Cancel",
13                                      style: .cancel,
14                                      handler: nil)
15      let actionDetails = UIAlertAction(title: "Show Details",
16                                      style: .default,
17                                      handler: actionHandler)
18      alertController.addAction(actionCancel)
19      alertController.addAction(actionDetails)
20      present(alertController, animated: true, completion: nil)
21  }
```

- The method starts by getting the contact object associated with the selected row in line 2, and assigning the contact name to a constant in line 3.

- Lines 4 and 5 sets up an action handler that contains the code to execute when the user taps the Show Details button. The code is in a Closure, which is a Swift concept for a code block that can be passed as a parameter. The code here shows how to programmatically execute a segue by using the Storyboard identifier. The `sender` object is important, as it has to match up with the type of object that the segue is set up for, which is a `UITableCell` in this case.

- Lines 8–10 set up the `UIAlertController` with a title and message. The preferred style can either be `.alert` (which we are using) or `.actionsheet`. The action sheet is used when more than two or three options are needed, as it stacks the buttons on top of each other.

- Lines 12–17 set up two `UIAlertAction` objects, one for each of the buttons. The first one is for Cancel and is very simple. Notice that the style is set as `.cancel`. Only one button an alert controller can use the cancel style. The second one uses the default style, but more interestingly, it has the reference to the `actionHandler`, so when the user taps the Show Details button, the code in `actionHandler` is executed.

- Lines 18 and 19 add the two buttons to the Alert Controller, and line 20 displays the controller. When you run the app, you should now be able to tap a cell in the table and see the alert. Taping Show Details should bring up the Contact editing screen.

There is an alternative approach to accomplishing the previous step of programmatically showing a different controller. This approach offers some additional flexibility, as it doesn't rely on a predefined segue between controllers. Instead it allows you to instantiate a controller directly and insert it into the navigation hierarchy. The following shows how to implement this alternative approach.

First, replace the body of the action handler in Listing 12.8 (line 5) with the code in Listing 12.9.

Listing 12.8   Instantiate View Controller and Display in Navigation Hierarchy

```
1   let storyboard = UIStoryboard(name: "Main", bundle: nil)
2   let controller = storyboard.instantiateViewController(withIdentifier: "ContactController")
3                   as? ContactsViewController
4   controller?.currentContact = selectedContact
5   self.navigationController?.pushViewController(controller!, animated: true)
```

The code is fairly straightforward.

- Line 1 gets a reference to the storyboard named `Main`, as there may be more than one storyboard in a project. Note that the `name` is a string, so you have to be careful with spelling as the compiler can't check it for you.

- Next, line 2 instantiates an instance of the view controller using an identifier. This also needs to be entered into the storyboard, which you will do shortly. The controller is cast as a `ContactsViewcontroller`, because you need to set the selected contact, which happens in line 4.

- Finally, line 5 uses the navigation controller to push the view controller onto the navigation stack. This ensures that the controller has the Back button to allow the user to go back to the table view controller.

To set the identifier for the Contact Controller, open **Main.Storyboard** and select the **Contact** scene's view. In the **Identity Inspector,** set the **Storyboard ID** to **ContactController** and check **Use Storyboard ID** (see Figure 12.10). Now you can run the app, and the alert view should work just like it did before.

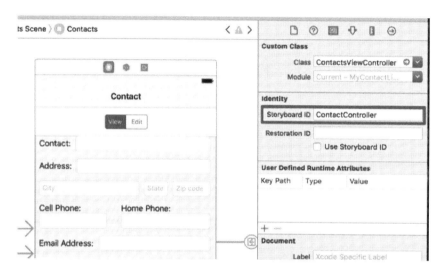

Figure 12.10   Setting the Storyboard ID for the view controller.

iOS versus Android: Creating Tables

Creating a table like the one shown in this chapter takes quite a bit more work on Android, because much more of the design and coding has to be done manually. On Android, there isn't a ready-made table with editing capability as you have seen here. Instead, the Android developer needs to design and create similar functionality from scratch.

Although the iOS controls provide a lot of functionality, and can be customized, you do have less freedom than what is available in Android.

Sort the Table

One of the features of MyContactList is to be able to sort the table by different criteria, as specified on the Settings screen. The code changes to enable sorting are relatively minor because the Core Data framework handles the heavy lifting. You need to make changes to `loadDataFromDatabase()` in **ContactsTableViewController.swift**, as shown in Listing 12.9.

Listing 12.9   Enable Sorting of the Table

```
1    func loadDataFromDatabase() {
2        //Read settings to enable sorting
3        let settings = UserDefaults.standard
4        let sortField = settings.string(forKey: Constants.kSortField)
5        let sortAscending = settings.bool(forKey: Constants.kSortDirectionAscending)
6        //Set up Core Data Context
7        let context = appDelegate.persistentContainer.viewContext
8        //Set up Request
9        let request = NSFetchRequest<NSManagedObject>(entityName: "Contact")
10       //Specify sorting
11       let sortDescriptor = NSSortDescriptor(key: sortField, ascending: sortAscending)
12       let sortDescriptorArray = [sortDescriptor]
13           //to sort by multiple fields, add more sort descriptors to the array
14       request.sortDescriptors = sortDescriptorArray
15       //Execute request
16       do {
17           contacts = try context.fetch(request)
18       } catch let error as NSError {
19           print("Could not fetch. \(error), \(error.userInfo)")
20       }
21   }
```

- The code starts by reading from the default settings file in line 3, and then in lines 4 and 5 retrieves the sort field and sort direction using the keys defined in Constants.swift.

- The sorting is specified in line 11. NSSortDescriptor is a class that contains instructions on how to order objects. By passing in the sort field and whether to sort in ascending or descending order, the fetch request will use these instructions to do the actual sorting.

- Line 12 adds sortDescriptor to an array that is passed to the request in line 14. You can create multiple sort descriptors, which will then be applied in the order listed in this array. This would allow for sorting by one field first and then another field (e.g., sort by name within city). In this case, there's only one sort field, so the array contains only one object.

- The execution of the request in lines 16–20 is unchanged from before.

This is all the code you need to be able to sort the data based on the user selections on the Settings screen. However, if you run the app now, it will promptly crash with a message like this:

```
*** Terminating app due to uncaught exception 'NSInvalidArgumentException', reason: 'keypath
City not found in entity <NSSQLEntity Contact id=1>'
```

The reason for this is that when we stored the sort fields in the previous chapter, they were stored with uppercase initial letters (hence "City" in the error message). However, attributes in Core Data are always stored with lowercase. To fix this, you need to make sure that everywhere there's code to store the sort fields that they are stored in lowercase. There are two places to make the fix: First, in the declaration of the sortOrderItems array in **SettingsViewController.swift**, the sort fields were also added. Change these to lowercase, like this:

```
let sortOrderItems: Array<String> = ["contactName", "city", "birthday"]
```

Second, in application(_ application:didFinishLaunchingWithOptions) in **AppDelegate.swift**, there's a check for whether the sort field is nil, and if not, the sort field is stored as City. Change this to lowercase:

```
If settings.string(forKey: Constants.kSortField) == nil {
    settings.set("city", forKey: Constants.kSortField)
}
```

These are all the code changes needed. However, the app still crashes with the same error message, because the value in the Plist file wasn't changed. There are a couple of ways to fix it:

1. Delete the app from the device. The next time you run the program, it will be reinstalled and the settings file recreated. If you do this, all your contacts previously entered will also be deleted.

2. The settings are stored in a Plist file in the app's directory in the simulator (see Chapter 11, "Persistent Data in iOS," for instructions on how to locate the app's directory). The Plist file is in the app's */Library/Preferences* folder. If you delete it, it will be re-created with default values on the next launch. You can edit it by right-clicking and selecting **Open With > Xcode**. Then you can click the **sortField** entry and change its value.

3. Comment out the line of code in `loadDataFromDatabase()` that applies the sort descriptor to the fetch request (lines 11–14 in Listing 12.9). Then run the app and change the settings so the proper value is stored in the file. Then uncomment the sorting again in code and launch the app again. While requiring a bit of work, this may be the easiest approach.

You can choose whichever approach you prefer. Run the app and check that the sorting works as intended.

Summary

Congratulations! You have mastered one of the most important parts of developing apps for the iPhone: navigation using tables. In addition, you saw how to integrate tables with data stored in Core Data. Like so many other aspects of iOS development, it is crucial to know which methods to override to make the built-in functionality work to do what you want it to do.

Exercises

1. Change the cell layout to use the other two styles.

2. Expand the settings screen to allow for specifying two sort fields. Then have the sorting be done by first one and then the other field.

3. Choose different fields from the Contact class to display in the table.

4. Change the display in the table to look like this instead:

   Main label: Superman from Metropolis.

   Detail Label: Born on: April 18, 1938.

5. Change the app so when the user taps the + button to add a new Contact, the Contact screen is put into edit mode and the cursor placed in the first text field.

6. Add a Delete button to the Alert Controller, and implement the functionality to delete the chosen contact. Use the destructive style for the button.

7. Add the ability to sort by a secondary field (e.g., sort by name within the city).

8. Find a way to have the picker for the sort field display the fields with uppercase words and the name as Contact Name, rather than contactName.

CHAPTER 13

Maps and Location in iOS

To truly realize the benefits of mobile computing, you will often want to take advantage of the device's capability to know where it is located and display maps of information to the user. Knowing the location of the device can be useful to many types of apps, but the precision needed for the location will be very different for various types of apps. For instance, an app used to let users track the route of their exercise run will need much more detailed location data than an app showing a user the nearest movie theater.

This chapter examines some of the powerful tools that the iOS platform provides to help you work with location and map data. The chapter covers how to expand the app to find the current location of the user, do both forward and reverse geocoding (translate between coordinates and addresses), and plot multiple locations on a map.

Overview of Location and Mapping

iOS has very strong and integrated support for location and mapping. This support includes several hardware sensors, such as GPS, Wi-Fi, and cellular radios, as well as software frameworks that make it easy for you as a programmer to access the information from the hardware.

Hardware and Sensors

Different devices running iOS will have different hardware sensors to provide location data. The most accurate sensor for outdoor use is the GPS, which can provide accuracy down to a few meters, but it isn't available on iPod touch or the Wi-Fi iPad versions. The iPhone and 3G iPad can also take advantage of cell tower triangulation, and all devices can use the location of Wi-Fi access points to provide location data. Some devices also have a GPS and altimeter built in to provide data on where the device is headed and how high it is above or below sea level. Whenever a location or heading is reported, it also reports an accuracy that you can use to understand the quality of the data received.

As an iOS developer, you don't decide which sensors to use, but you should understand that different devices may not provide the same level of accuracy, which may impact the way your app works. Further, the user also has the option of turning off location services entirely. And because this is a device setting that can be controlled by Parental Controls, some users may not be able to turn on location services. Tracking and using location also has an impact on battery life of the device. In fact, some location tracking modes are only available when a device is plugged into power. You should design your app to take all these things into account, and provide a good experience to the user.

Core Location

Apple provides two frameworks for working with location: **Core Location** and **MapKit**. Core Location allows for finding and working with current location and heading information. In addition, Core Location also lets you set up geographic regions (called *geofences*) to help you take action when the device enters or leaves a region. The framework uses the available hardware sensors to provide location data as close as possible to the accuracy you have requested. In addition, Core Location also handles geocoding, which allows for translation between a geographic point and an address, or vice versa. Geocoding requires an active Internet connection, because the lookup between address and coordinate is done by Apple's servers. All Core location classes are prefixed with CL.

MapKit

For displaying a map, Apple provides the MapKit framework, which uses Apple's mapping service and lets you very easily display a map, detect the user's location, add overlays, and plot any location on the map using different kinds of pins and callouts. The map can also perform reverse geocoding. All the MapKit classes are prefixed with MK.

---

iOS versus Android: Setting Up to Use Maps

There's quite a bit more work in setting up to work with maps on Android. Whereas iOS comes bundled with all the necessary frameworks and libraries, on Android, the developer needs to download the Google Play SDK and register for a Google Maps API key.

By registering for an API key, any hits to the Google Maps API can be associated with a particular app. With its integrated set of offerings, Apple has made it simpler for developers to get started with development. However, in the end, the result is the same, because all iOS apps have to be digitally signed, and thus Apple can associate any hits to its map API to a particular app.

To take advantage of this ease of use, you have to use the Apple Map data, which was often criticized after its initial launch but has improved significantly since then. If you would rather use Google Maps as the engine for mapping in your apps, you can download the Google Maps SDK for iOS and sign up for an API key in the same way as described in Chapter 7, "Maps and Location in Android."

Adding Location Information to the App

Working with location data and maps on iOS is relatively simple. By tapping into the provided frameworks, you can build powerful apps very quickly that take location data into account. In this chapter, you will expand the MyContactList app with a map that shows all your contacts as well as the user's location on a map.

To better understand the capabilities available when working with location, the first step is to build a temporary screen to explore the location functions before building the final app. The Map Screen controller is used to provide the location information until it is replaced later in the chapter with an actual map.

Finding Location—Forward Geocoding

When working with maps, you need to use coordinates, expressed in latitude and longitude degrees. You can find the device's location from the sensors (GPS, cell towers, and Wi-Fi), which give you latitude/longitude coordinates directly. However, the coordinates are not very people-friendly, so it's important to be able to convert between addresses and coordinates. This process is called *geocoding*, and comes in two flavors: *forward* and *reverse* geocoding. Forward geocoding lets you take a human-readable address and convert it to a set of coordinates, whereas reverse geocoding is the opposite process that lets you go from coordinates to an address. In this chapter, you will see how to do forward geocoding.

To demonstrate how geocoding works, you add a screen to show location data in the MyContactList app you worked on in the previous screen. Open the project from the previous chapter or the project for this chapter that comes with the book. Then, open the **Storyboard** and drag a new **View Controller** into the Storyboard. Change the **user interface** to match that shown in Figure 13.1. The text fields enable the user to type in a street, city, and state. When the user taps the Address to Coordinates button, the address information will be converted to a coordinate, and the latitude and longitude will be output to the corresponding labels. Tapping the Device Coordinates button will get the location of the device and output the information to all the labels. The gray boxes, where the output will go, are labels and have been given a gray background so they are visible without content.

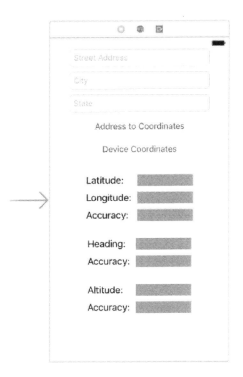

Figure 13.1 User interface for exploring Core Location.

Here are the steps to set up the user interface:

1. Drag **text views** in and set the **placeholder text**.
2. Add **Constraints** to the text views for a **width** of **250**.
3. Drag the **buttons** in and change the text for each of them.
4. Embed the text views and buttons in a **stack view** with **Spacing** set to **10**.
5. Drag two labels in below the stack view and change the text of one to **Latitude:**, and for the other, set the **Background** to **Light Gray Color**. For the gray label, delete the text "Label" and replace it with a space. If you just delete all the text, the width of the label becomes essentially undefined, and it becomes very difficult to work with in Interface Builder.
6. Add a **constraint** to set the **width** of the gray label to **100**.
7. Embed the two **labels** in a stack view.
8. Option-drag from the **stack view** with the labels to create a copy of it. Repeat this until you have seven stack views with labels. Change the heading labels as shown in Figure 13.1.
9. Embed the first **three sets of labels** (latitude, longitude, and accuracy) in a stack view, the next two in a stack view, and the last two in a stack view. Each of these stack views should have a spacing of **10**.
10. Embed all the **stack views** in a **stack view** with spacing **30** and Alignment **Center**.
11. Set the top constraint for the stack view to **0**, constrained to the **margin**, and center it **horizontally**.

Drag the **entry arrow** that points to the left side of the Tab Bar controller to the new scene. This will make the app start with the new scene and ignore all other controllers in the app. This will cause a warning that some scenes are unreachable. You can ignore this warning as you work on the temporary scene.

After building the UI in Interface builder, you need to add a code file for the view controller.

1. Select **File > New > File**.
2. Select **Cocoa Touch Class** and click **Next**.
3. For **Class**, enter **LocationDemoViewController**, and for **Subclass of** enter **UIViewController**. Don't create a XIB file and select **Swift** as the language. Click **Next**.

4. Make sure the **Target** for MyContactList is selected, and then click **Create**.

5. In **Main.storyboard**, select the new view controller, and change the **Class** in the **Identity Inspector** from UIViewController to **LocationDemoViewController**. Be careful to select the top-level view controller, and not the View inside that. You should see the entire scene have a blue frame. It may be easier to select in the Document outline.

Now you can wire up the scene. Use the **Assistant Editor** to control-drag from the controls on the screen to **LocationDemoViewController.swift** to add outlets for the three text fields with these names: **txtStreet**, **txtCity**, and **txtState**. Then add outlets for the output labels with these names (from top to bottom): **lblLatitude**, **lblLongitude**, **lblLocationAccuracy**, **lblHeading**, **lblHeadingAccuracy**, **lblAltitude**, and **lblAltitudeAccuracy**. Next, add actions for the two buttons named **addressToCoordinates** and **deviceCoordinates**.

Listing 13.1 shows the outlets and actions, as well as the code to dismiss the keyboard as described in Chapter 9, "Using Xcode for iOS Development."

Listing 13.1 Outlets and Actions in LMALocationDemoViewController.swift

```
1    import UIKit
2
3    class LocationDemoViewController: UIViewController {
4        @IBOutlet weak var txtStreet: UITextField!
5        @IBOutlet weak var txtCity: UITextField!
6        @IBOutlet weak var txtState: UITextField!
7        @IBOutlet weak var lblLatitude: UILabel!
8        @IBOutlet weak var lblLongitude: UILabel!
9        @IBOutlet weak var lblLocationAccuracy: UILabel!
10       @IBOutlet weak var lblHeading: UILabel!
11       @IBOutlet weak var lblHeadingAccuracy: UILabel!
12       @IBOutlet weak var lblAltitude: UILabel!
13       @IBOutlet weak var lblAltitudeAccuracy: UILabel!
14
15       func dismissKeyboard() {
16           // Causes the view (or one of its embedded text fields) to resign the first responder status.
17           view.endEditing(true)
18       }
19
20       override func viewDidLoad() {
21           super.viewDidLoad()
22           // Do any additional setup after loading the view.
23           let tap: UITapGestureRecognizer = UITapGestureRecognizer(target: self,
24                                                 action: #selector(self.dismissKeyboard))
25           view.addGestureRecognizer(tap)
26
27       }
28
29       override func didReceiveMemoryWarning() {
30           super.didReceiveMemoryWarning()
31           // Dispose of any resources that can be recreated.
32       }
33
34       @IBAction func addressToCoordinates(_ sender: Any) {
35       }
36
37       @IBAction func deviceCoordinates(_ sender: Any) {
38       }
39   }
```

Now the user interface is set up, and it's time to start working on geocoding the address. The Core Location framework first needs to be added to your project. There are two elements to this. First, you need to import the framework by adding this line:

```
import CoreLocation
```

Next, you'll need to implement the forward geocoding functionality. Start by adding this line just below the outlets:

```
lazy var geoCoder = CLGeocoder()
```

This sets up a variable to hold a `CLGeocoder` object, which is the one doing the heavy lifting of interfacing with the geocoding web service. The keyword `lazy` indicates that while the line indicates that the `CLGeoCoder` object should be created immediately, instantiation will be deferred until the object is actually needed. This is called lazy instantiation and allows the system to conserve resources. This is especially useful for objects that have the potential for consuming a lot of memory and/or battery. See Appendix C, "Introduction to Swift," for more discussion of lazy instantiation.

Now you can implement the `addressToCoordinates(_ sender:)` method as shown in Listing 13.2.

Listing 13.2 Forward Geocoding

```
1    @IBAction func addressToCoordinates(_ sender: Any) {
2        let address = "\(txtStreet.text!), \(txtCity.text!), \(txtState.text!))"
3        geoCoder.geocodeAddressString(address) {(placemarks, error) in
4            self.processAddressResponse(withPlacemarks: placemarks, error: error)
5        }
6    }
7
8    private func processAddressResponse(withPlacemarks placemarks: [CLPlacemark]?, error: Error?) {
9        if let error = error {
10            print("Geocode Error: \(error)")
11        }
12        else {
13            var bestMatch: CLLocation?
14            if let placemarks = placemarks, placemarks.count > 0 {
15                bestMatch = placemarks.first?.location
16            }
17            if let coordinate = bestMatch?.coordinate {
18                lblLatitude.text = String(format: "%g\u{00B0}", coordinate.latitude)
19                lblLongitude.text = String(format: "%g\u{00B0}", coordinate.longitude)
20            }
21            else {
22                print("Didn't find any matching locations")
23            }
24        }
25    }
```

This code shows several interesting things, not only about location data, but also about multithreaded programming in iOS. It uses the `geoCoder` object to send a simple string representation of the address to a web service and then handles the results of the search asynchronously and displays the best location in the labels on the screen.

- Line 2 constructs a single string containing the address information from the three text fields. The geocoding can handle strings similar to what you would type into an online mapping website like Google Maps. It is also possible to create a more structured entry, called a Dictionary, to use for the lookup, but for many situations, a simple string will do just fine.

- Line 3 calls the method `geoCodeAddressString(_addressString:completionHandler:)` to do the actual geocoding. This method sends the string to an Apple service across the Internet. The results come back in an array containing `CLPlacemark` objects. The completion handler is new. Since this method can take a while to complete depending on Internet speeds, the completion handler will finish the work of dealing with the results while the rest of the program continues. This ensures that the app remains responsive during the call to the geocoding service. The parenthesis at the end of line 3 contains parameters to the completion handler, and the completion handler itself follows the `in` keyword. In this case, it is just a single line that calls a separate method, `processAddressResponse(placemarks: error:)`, which is declared in lines 8–25.

- Lines 9–11 check if there was an error in geocoding and simply prints this error to the console. In a real app, you should probably notify the user as well. In this app, you can force an error by leaving all the input fields blank before activating the geocoding.

- If no error was detected, line 13 declares a `CLLocation` object called `bestMatch`, and line 14 checks if any results come back. This line requires a bit of extra explanation. The `if let` notation is called optional binding and allows for only assigning a value to `placemarks` if the conditions on the right side of the equal sign result in non-nil or true. In this case, the optional `placemarks` array is non-nil and has at least one element. In that case, line 15 assigns the location of the first placemark to the `bestMatch` variable. Sometimes results can be ambiguous and multiple results are returned. You could set up a loop to go through all the results, but here we keep it simple and assume that the first result is good enough.

- Lines 17–20 are where the results are actually used and the coordinates are assigned to the corresponding labels. We use optional binding to get the coordinate portion of the `bestMatch` location. The `CLPlacemark` object contains a large amount of information (such as state, city, points of interest) for the location, but the actual coordinates are also stored in there. The code `\u00B0` is the Unicode for a degree symbol that is added to the end of the numerical value. The placeholder `%g` is used to format a decimal number with six significant digits.

If you run the app now, you can type in an address, tap the Address To Coordinates button, and get a set of coordinates. You can check the accuracy by typing the coordinates into Google Maps to get a map of the point.

Finding the Device Location

It can be very useful in many apps to find the location of the device. The location is available through a **CLLocationManager** object, which acts as an interface to the sensors that measure both location and heading (compass) information. However, before you can get to any of the location information about the device, you have to ask for permission, since location data is considered private, and something the user needs to explicitly allow your app to access.

Asking for Permission

There are a couple steps involved in setting up permissions on iOS. First, you need to make an entry in the app's **Info. plist** file. Open the file and select the **Information Property List** entry (the first line in the file). Then select **Editor > Add Item**. You can also click the little plus symbol next to Information Property List. In the new entry, you choose the appropriate key. For location, there are two options to choose from:

- *Privacy - Location When in Use Usage Description.* This key is used to request permission for apps that use location for the current task only.

- *Privacy - Location Always Usage Description.* This key also requests permission for an app to use location, even when the app is not in the foreground.

In this app, we are not going to request location when the app is in the background, so go ahead and pick **Privacy - Location When in Use Usage Description**. You can use the up and down arrows to search for this or begin typing and pick it from the dropdown list. For either of the keys, you also have to provide a description. This description will be shown to the user as a way of describing why your app needs to know the location of the device. See Figure 13.2.

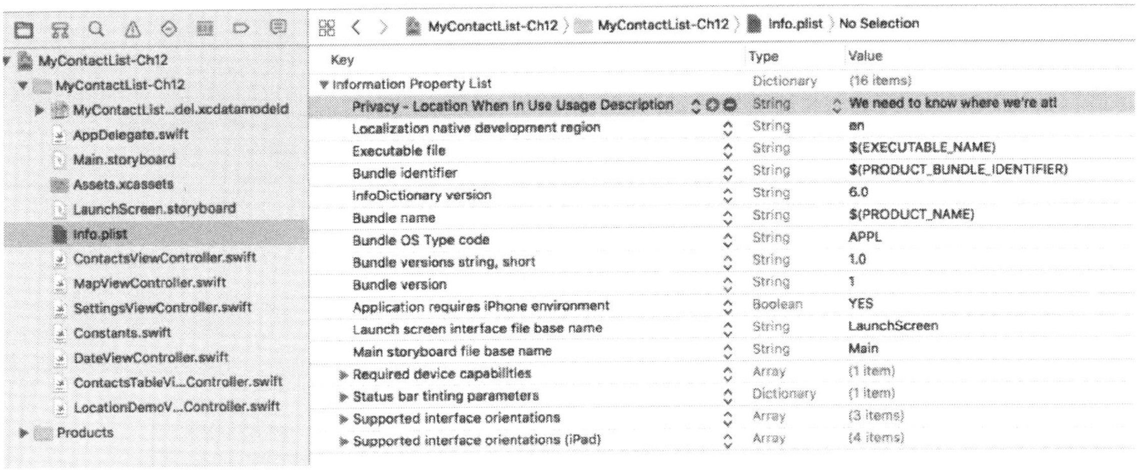

Figure 13.2 Adding keys to request location permission in Info.plist.

There are a number of frameworks that require asking for permission in iOS. These include Calendar, Contact, Reminder, Photo, Bluetooth, Sharing, Microphone, Camera, Location, HealthKit, HomeKit, Media Library, Motion, CallKit, Speech Recognition, SiriKit, and TV Provider. You will see a couple more of these later in the book, but the principles for requesting permissions is the same as you will see here.

Next, open **LocationDemoViewController.swift** and implement CLLocationManagerDelegate in the class declaration line:

```
class LocationDemoViewController: UIViewController, CLLocationManagerDelegate {
```

Then declare a class variable below the geoCoder variable to reference the location manager instance:

```
var locationManager: CLLocationManager!
```

Listing 13.3 shows the changes you need to make to viewDidLoad() to set up the locationManager and check that the authorization is granted by the user.

Listing 13.3 Setting Up Location Manager

```
1    override func viewDidLoad() {
2        super.viewDidLoad()
3        // Do any additional setup after loading the view.
4        let tap: UITapGestureRecognizer = UITapGestureRecognizer(target: self,
5                                                    action: #selector(self.
6    dismissKeyboard))
7        view.addGestureRecognizer(tap)
8        //Set up location manager
9        locationManager = CLLocationManager()
10       locationManager.delegate = self
11       locationManager.requestWhenInUseAuthorization() //ask for permission to use location
12   }
13
14   //Called when the location permission status changes
15   func locationManager(_ manager: CLLocationManager,
16                   didChangeAuthorization status: CLAuthorizationStatus) {
17       if status == .authorizedWhenInUse {
18           print("Permission granted")
19       }
20       else {
21           print("Permission NOT granted")
22       }
23   }
```

- Lines 8–10 are new in `viewDidLoad`, but the only one that requires explanation is line 10, which calls `requestWhenInUseAuthorization()` on the location manager. This is a required call to request that the user grants permission to use location for the app. Note that this call has to match the permission you requested in the Plist. If you had chosen Privacy - Location Always Usage Description in the Plist, you would have had to call `requestAlwaysAuthorization` instead.

- Line 13 declares the delegate method `locationManager(_ manager:did didChangeAuthorization status:)`, which is called whenever the authorization status changes (e.g., if the user grants or revokes the app's permission to use location).

- Line 16 shows how to check for what the permission was changed to. In this case, we just print a status message to the console to announce the change. At this point you can run the app and observe how the permission is requested from the user. Figure 13.3 shows that you can control the message that is displayed asking the user for permission. Apple's guidelines specify that the message should explain why your app needs to use location data. If the user changes his or her mind later, the setting can be changed in the Settings app under Privacy > LocationServices.

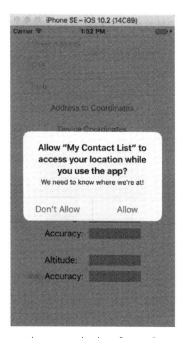

Figure 13.3 Requesting permission from the user to use location.

With the permission set up, you can turn your attention to getting the location from the location manager. To start and stop the location manager, implement the `deviceCoordinates` and `viewDidDisappear` methods as shown in Listing 13.4.

Listing 13.4   Starting the Location Manager

```
1    @IBAction func deviceCoordinates(_ sender: Any) {
2        locationManager.desiredAccuracy = kCLLocationAccuracyHundredMeters
3        locationManager.distanceFilter = 100
4        locationManager.startUpdatingLocation()
5        locationManager.startUpdatingHeading()
6    }
7
8    override func viewDidDisappear(_ animated: Bool) {
9        locationManager.stopUpdatingLocation()
10       locationManager.stopUpdatingHeading()
11   }
```

The Location Manager is started when the user presses the Device Coordinates button and is stopped anytime the view disappears, to conserve battery. Line 2 sets the desired accuracy. Table 13.1 lists the possible values to choose from. It's always best to choose the least accurate option your app can use and still do what needs to be done. This lets the system conserve battery power as much as possible.

Another battery saving feature is to set up a distance filter, as shown in line 3. This indicates the distance in meters the device has to move before an update location event is generated. Here the device has to move 100 meters before an update happens. Line 4 starts the location manager running and updating the location, and line 5 tells the location manager to also report on changes to heading (compass) information.

The `viewDidDisappear` method is called when another view moves to the foreground. There's no need to keep the Location Manager running when the view is no longer visible, so these two statements simply stop the updates from the location manager.

Table 13.1 Overview of Accuracy Options for Location Services (All Indicators Are Prefaced with "kCLLocationAccuracy".)

Distance Indicator	Precision
BestForNavigation	Use for navigation apps. Combines the highest level of accuracy with additional sensor data. Intended for use only when the device is plugged in.
Best	Highest level of accuracy
NearestTenMeters	10 meters
HundredMeters	100 meters
Kilometer	1 kilometer
ThreeKilometer	3 kilometers

To take advantage of the Location Manager, you need to implement some of its delegate methods. The first will be called whenever the device location is updated, and is shown in Listing 13.5.

iOS versus Android: Access to Hardware Location Sensors

Android developers can choose which specific location sensor to use (GPS or network sensor), giving some additional flexibility. In iOS, by contrast, you have seen how you can specify an accuracy and a distance filter, but you can't request that location data has to come from the GPS. Instead, the operating system decides how to best achieve the desired accuracy while balancing performance and battery usage.

In both systems, you have to be mindful of how much you use the location sensors and remember to turn off location services when not needed anymore, because they do use extra battery.

Listing 13.5 Getting Location Updates

```
1   func locationManager(_ manager: CLLocationManager, didUpdateLocations locations: [CLLocation]) {
2       if let location = locations.last {
3           let eventDate = location.timestamp
4           let howRecent = eventDate.timeIntervalSinceNow
5           if Double(howRecent) < 15.0 {
6               let coordinate = location.coordinate
7               lblLongitude.text = String(format: "%g\u{00B0}", coordinate.longitude)
8               lblLatitude.text = String(format: "%g\u{00B0}", coordinate.latitude)
9               lblLocationAccuracy.text = String(format: "%gm", location.horizontalAccuracy)
10              lblAltitude.text = String(format: "%gm", location.altitude)
11              lblAltitudeAccuracy.text = String(format: "%gm", location.verticalAccuracy)
12          }
13      }
14  }
```

Whenever the Location Manager updates the location of the device, it calls the `locationManager(_ manager:didUpdateLocations:)` method. Because some time may have passed since the last call to the method, several locations may be available in the locations array. The most recent location is in the last position in the array that is passed to the method.

- Line 2 gets the most recent location from the array. In order to ensure that the location is actually recent, the next few lines ensure that the location was recorded less than 15 seconds ago.

- To do this, you get a time stamp for the location in line 3, and then check the time interval between now and then in line 4.

- Because the `howRecent` variable is of type `TimeInterval`, line 5 converts it to a Double and checks that it is less than 15 seconds. This ensures that old data isn't used to update the UI. Of course, exactly how old the location data is that is useful depends on the purpose of the app.

- Lines 6–8 simply update the labels in the UI with the coordinates as you have seen before.

- Accuracy is reported in much the same way as the coordinates in line 9. It gives you the radius in meters of the circle within which the device may be found. The coordinates indicate the center of the circle.

- The Location Manager also reports altitude in meters above or below sea level, as well as vertical accuracy in meters to this number, as shown in lines 10–11.

To get the heading (compass) information for the device, you implement the `locationManager(_ manager:didUpdateHeading:)` method, as shown in Listing 13.6.

Listing 13.6 Getting Heading Updates

```
1   func locationManager(_ manager: CLLocationManager, didUpdateHeading newHeading: CLHeading) {
2       if newHeading.headingAccuracy > 0 {
3           let theHeading = newHeading.trueHeading
4           var direction: String
5           switch theHeading {
6           case 225..<315:
7               direction = "W"
8           case 135..<225:
9               direction = "S"
10          case 45..<135:
11              direction = "E"
12          default:
13              direction = "N"
14          }
15          lblHeading.text = String(format: "%g\u{00B0} (%@)", theHeading, direction)
16          lblHeadingAccuracy.text = String(format: "%g\u{00B0}", newHeading.headingAccuracy)
17      }
18  }
```

This method works in the same way as the location updates and is called whenever the heading information for the device is updated.

- In this case, the accuracy is checked to see if it's valid (line 2). The heading information can be invalid if the device isn't calibrated or if there is strong interference from local magnetic fields.
- The CLHeading object contains information about both the magnetic heading and the true heading. In this case, we use the true heading in line 4.
- Lines 5–14 use a switch statement to set a compass heading (N, S, E, W) based on the heading in degrees. This uses Swift's ability to switch on a range of values. The less than sign means that the interval goes from exactly the lower value up to but not including the upper value in the range.
- Lines 15 and 16 update the labels with the heading and accuracy. The accuracy is reported as the number of degrees the heading may be off in either direction. (For example, if the heading is reported as 300 degrees and accuracy as 10 degrees, the actual heading may be anywhere from 290 to 310 degrees.)

The last delegate method to implement deals with error conditions, and is shown in Listing 13.7.

Listing 13.7 Handling Errors from the Location Manager

```
1   func locationManager(_ manager: CLLocationManager, didFailWithError error: Error) {
2       let errorType = error._code == CLError.denied.rawValue ? "Location Permission Denied" :
3       "Unknown Error"
4       let alertController = UIAlertController(title: "Error Getting Location: \(errorType)",
5           message: "Error Message: \(error.localizedDescription))",
6           preferredStyle: .alert)
7       let actionOK = UIAlertAction(title: "OK",
8                                    style: .default,
9                                    handler: nil)
10
11      alertController.addAction(actionOK)
12      present(alertController, animated: true, completion: nil)
13  }
```

The locationManager(_ manager:didFailWithError:) method is called if the location manager encounters an error situation. In this case, the app shows an Alert Controller, but in a more realistic app, you would want to deal with this in a more intelligent way.

The most common error situation is that the user has turned off Location Services. You can check for this by looking at error._code. If this is set to CLError.denied, then Location Services is turned off for the app or the entire device. This statement gets the actual raw value for the denied property, which is a Boolean, and then uses a conditional assignment statement to assign one of two literal strings to the errorType variable.

Lines 4–6 create the alert view with the error type as the title and the raw error message in the message parameter. Line 7 simply displays the alert controller.

Now you can run the app and test that it can find the location of the device. The location information can be tested in the simulator by selecting **Debug > Location** and choosing one of the options for locations. The default is Apple, which is the location of Apple's headquarters in Cupertino, California. Custom Location lets you enter a set of coordinates yourself. The remaining options simulate a moving device at various speeds. Try them out and see what they do. Unfortunately, none of the options provide heading or altitude information. These need to be tested on an actual device.

This section showed the standard Location Services, but you can also use the significant-change location service, which relies only on cell tower placement to provide location updates when the user has moved a significant distance. This option uses much less battery and also allows the app to monitor locations in the background.

Adding a Map

Next, you see how to add a map and display the user's location as well as that of the contacts in the database on the map. As with most of the frameworks in iOS, MapKit handles a lot of the heavy lifting for you. You will also see the location manager again, helping to show the user's location on the map. You will implement this in the main MyContactList app.

Start by opening **storyboard** and moving the **start arrow** for the app back to the **Tab Bar**, thus ignoring the temporary location scene you created in the previous section. As an exercise, you can add it back as a new tab in the app.

Next, delete the **label** and then drag a **Map Kit View** onto the **Map** scene; then set constraints to set the Map Kit View to fill the screen by setting constraints at **0 pixels** from each of the margins. If the constraints end up being set relative to the margin, select each one and use the Identity Inspector to uncheck *Relative to margin* for each one. You may choose to keep the top constraint relative to the margin of the superview, as this will keep the map from showing under the status bar with the network indicator, time, and battery status. Click the **Update Frames** button to update the design view.

Next, use the **Assistant Editor** mode and control-drag from the Map Kit View to create an outlet called **mapView** in **MapViewController.swift**. If you don't create the outlet, the app will crash on startup. You also need to import the `MapKit` framework.

You can now run the app, and the map shows up in the map screen, but it is zoomed out very far. However, you can interact with the map just like the regular Maps app, by pinching to zoom, scrolling, and the like. To zoom using the Simulator, hold down the Option key while clicking on the map, and you will get two gray dots that simulate a user with two fingers on the screen.

Display the User's Location on the Map

Having removed the Location Demo screen from the app, you will need to implement the authorization code again in **MapViewController.swift**. To do this, implement `CLLocationManagerDelegate`, set up a reference to a `CLLocationManager` object, and add these three lines of code to `viewDidLoad`:

```
locationManager = CLLocationManager()
locationManager.delegate = self
locationManager.requestWhenInUseAuthorization()
```

If you continued from the past section, this part wouldn't make any difference when running the app, since the permission was already granted to the app installed on the device you're testing on. However, if you installed the app on a different device at this point, not including this code would cause it to not ask for permission, so the user tracking wouldn't work.

The absolute simplest way to show the user's location on the map is to go back into the **Attributes Inspector** for the map and check the box to **Show User Location**. If you run the app again, you will see a blue dot where the user is located (by default at Apple in California). Try zooming in close enough to see city streets and then select **Debug > Location > Freeway Drive**. You will now see the blue dot moving as the device movements are simulated.

Although it is very easy to show the user's location on the map like this, it is also very limited, because you won't be able to do anything with it beyond showing the location. For instance, later in the chapter you learn how to add a description of the user's location to the map, which requires more coding than what you can get with this method.

Another simple approach to display the user's location on the map is to enable user tracking. This is one line of code that will show the user's location and keep the map centered and zoomed in on that location until the user interacts with the map:

```
mapView.setUserTrackingMode(.follow, animated: true)
```

This could go in `viewWillAppear`, and then as soon as the map is displayed, it will zoom in on the user's location. A common approach is also to add a button to the user interface that enables the tracking of the user. Remove the **Show User Location** on the `mapView` control, and the `viewWillAppear` method if you added that to MapViewController.swift. Here's how to set up the custom user tracking:

1. Drag a **button** on top of the map view, and change its text to **Find me!**.
2. Set **constraints** for the **top** and **left** side of the button of **20** pixels each to place the button in the top left of the screen.
3. Using the **Assistant Editor**, control-drag from the **button** to **MapViewController.swift** and create an action function called **findUser**. Add the code as shown in Listing 13.8. This enables showing the user location and thus not relying on the setting in the storyboard, and then starts tracking the user.

Listing 13.8   Showing the User's Location on the Map

```
1   @IBAction func findUser(_ sender: Any) {
2       mapView.showsUserLocation = true
3       mapView.setUserTrackingMode(.follow, animated: true)
4   }
```

Run the app and then tap the Find Me! button, and you should see the screen zoom in on the user location. If you have the Simulator set to show the Freeway Drive, you should see the map moving as the simulated device moves around the interstate highways around California, as shown in Figure 13.4. If you move the map or zoom, it will stop moving the map to track the user, but pressing the Find Me! button will start the tracking again.

Figure 13.4   User's location displayed on the map.

For more sophisticated operations, you need to implement the `MKMapViewDelegate` protocol, which allows you to be notified of updates to the map, including the user's location. To display a map that's zoomed in on the user's current location, follow these steps:

1. Specify that `MapViewController` should implement the `MKMapViewDelegate` protocol by adding `MKMapViewDelegate` to the end of the class declaration line.
2. In `viewDidLoad`, set the delegate of the map view to be the map view controller:

    ```
    mapView.delegate = self
    ```

3. Implement `mapView(_ mapview:didUpdate userLocation:)` as shown in Listing 13.9.

When running the app, you can see that it shows the user's location and zooms in to where you can see the city level. If it doesn't seem to be working, go to **Debug > Location** in the Simulator and make sure it isn't set to **None**.

Listing 13.9   Display the User's Location on the Map

```
1   func mapView(_ mapView: MKMapView, didUpdate userLocation: MKUserLocation) {
2       var span = MKCoordinateSpan()
3       span.latitudeDelta = 0.2
4       span.longitudeDelta = 0.2
5       let viewRegion = MKCoordinateRegionMake(userLocation.coordinate, span)
6       mapView.setRegion(viewRegion, animated: true)
7   }
```

Line 6 sets the map view to display a specific region, `viewRegion`, which is created in line 5 based on the user's location and a `span`. The span is used to indicate how many degrees are visible on the map. This is used to specify the zoom level. The lower the span numbers, the farther the map is zoomed in. You may very well need small fractional numbers to see a city-street level map. There are several other ways you can set the zoom level of the map. One common approach is to use a statement like this to define the visible region:

```
let viewRegion = MKCoordinateRegionMakeWithDistance(userLocation.coordinate, 5000, 5000)
```

This sets the view region to 5,000 meters on either side of the user's location. You can read Apple's Location Awareness Programming Guide for more detail on how to work with location data. Running the app will zoom to the user's location similar to before, but you can now specify the zoom level of the map. Because this method is called any time the user's location changes, it essentially disables the ability to zoom and pan the map when the device is being moved.

Adding Annotations to the Map

One of the nice features of MapKit is the capability to show an exact location on the map with a pin. These pins are called annotations, and you can add as many as you need to the map. Annotations are created in a class that implements the **MKAnnotation** protocol, so start by adding a new Swift file called **MapPoint.swift**. Open the new file and change it as shown in Listing 13.10.

Listing 13.10   MapPoint.swift

```
1     import Foundation
2     import MapKit
3
4     class MapPoint: NSObject, MKAnnotation{
5         var title: String?
6         var subtitle: String?
7         var latitude: Double
8         var longitude: Double
9
10        var coordinate: CLLocationCoordinate2D {
11            return CLLocationCoordinate2D(latitude: latitude, longitude: longitude)
12        }
13
14        init(latitude: Double, longitude: Double) {
15            self.latitude = latitude
16            self.longitude = longitude
17        }
18    }
```

This sets up the `MapPoint` class, which will be used to store the annotation for a single point on the map.

The class imports `MapKit` (line 2), is a subclass of `NSObject`, and implements the `MKAnnotation` protocol (line 4). This protocol specifies three properties, used to describe the annotation, `title`, `subtitle`, and `coordinate`. It's important to spell the names of the properties correctly, as they are defined in the protocol. The only required property is coordinate, so this is the only one the compiler will complain about if you misspell it. If either of the other two is misspelled, the annotation just won't show up. Fortunately, in recent versions, Xcode has started showing a warning if you are close enough. In the first edition of this book, we spent a lot of time trying to figure out why the subtitle didn't show up. As it turned out, we had written it subTitle with an uppercase T instead of lowercase.

This implementation of the class uses `latitude` and `longitude` as helper variables, and the init method also takes `latitude` and `longitude` (lines 14–17). The `coordinate` property is set up as read-only and then handles the conversion in line 11.

Now, to have the annotation for the user's location show up on the map, you need to add a few lines of code to `mapView(_ mapView:didUpdate userLocation:)` in **MapViewController.swift**, as shown in Listing 13.11.

Listing 13.11   Adding an Annotation for the User's Location to the Map

```
1    func mapView(_ mapView: MKMapView, didUpdate userLocation: MKUserLocation) {
2        var span = MKCoordinateSpan()
3        span.latitudeDelta = 0.2
4        span.longitudeDelta = 0.2
5        let viewRegion = MKCoordinateRegionMake(userLocation.coordinate, span)
6        mapView.setRegion(viewRegion, animated: true)
7        let mp = MapPoint(latitude: userLocation.coordinate.latitude,
8                          longitude: userLocation.coordinate.longitude)
9        mp.title = "You"
10       mp.subtitle = "Are here"
11       mapView.addAnnotation(mp)
12   }
```

You need to add lines 7–11. This sets up a `MapPoint` object with the user's location in lines 7–8 and two literal string values for `title` and `subtitle` in lines 9–10. Line 11 adds the annotation to the map.

You can run the app, and you should see the result in Figure 13.5 (with the simulated location set to Apple, and after clicking Find me! and clicking the pin).

Figure 13.5   Map with an annotation for the user's current location.

Removing Annotations

If you run the app with the device moving, you will notice that multiple annotations are added to the map, which will ultimately result in pins being displayed along the entire path the device traveled. To clean up annotations, you can use this line of code:

```
self.mapView.removeAnnotations(self.mapView.annotations)
```

The annotations are in an array so you could also remove all but the last annotation added with this bit of code:

```
if let mp = self.mapView.annotations.last{
    mapView.removeAnnotations(self.mapView.annotations)
    mapView.addAnnotation(mp)
}
```

Display Contacts on the Map

The last piece of functionality to add to the app is the capability to plot the contacts on the map. To do this, you will need to do the following:

1. Add a property to the map controller to hold the array of all the contacts in the database.
2. Populate the array from the database.
3. Use a loop to look up the location of each contact and annotate locations for them on the map.

This section goes through each of those steps. First, open **MapViewController** and add an `import` statement for `CoreData`. Then add the following line after the `mapView` outlet:

```
var contacts:[Contact] = []
```

This creates the property to hold an array of all the contacts to be displayed. To populate the array, add the `viewWillAppear` method, as shown in Listing 13.12.

Listing 13.12   Adding Annotations for All Contacts

```
1   override func viewWillAppear(_ animated: Bool) {
2       //Get contacts from Core Data
3       let appDelegate = UIApplication.shared.delegate as! AppDelegate
4       let context = appDelegate.persistentContainer.viewContext
5       let request = NSFetchRequest<NSManagedObject>(entityName: "Contact")
6       var fetchedObjects:[NSManagedObject] = []
7       do {
8           fetchedObjects = try context.fetch(request)
9       } catch let error as NSError {
10          print("Could not fetch. \(error), \(error.userInfo)")
11      }
12      contacts = fetchedObjects as! [Contact]
13      //remove all annotations
14      self.mapView.removeAnnotations(self.mapView.annotations)
15      //go through all contacts
16      for contact in contacts { //as! [Contact] {
17          let address = "\(contact.streetAddress!), \(contact.city!) \(contact.state!)"
18          //geocoding
19          let geoCoder = CLGeocoder()
20          geoCoder.geocodeAddressString(address) {(placemarks, error) in
```

(continued)

Listing 13.12   Adding Annotations for All Contacts (*continued*)

```
21              self.processAddressResponse(contact, withPlacemarks: placemarks, error: error)
22          }
23      }
24  }
25
26  private func processAddressResponse(_ contact: Contact, withPlacemarks placemarks: [CLPlacemark]?,
27                                      error: Error?) {
28      if let error = error {
29          print("Geocode Error: \(error)")
30      }
31      else {
32          var bestMatch: CLLocation?
33          if let placemarks = placemarks, placemarks.count > 0 {
34              bestMatch = placemarks.first?.location
35          }
36          if let coordinate = bestMatch?.coordinate {
37              let mp = MapPoint(latitude: coordinate.latitude, longitude: coordinate.longitude)
38              mp.title = contact.contactName
39              mp.subtitle = contact.streetAddress
40              mapView.addAnnotation(mp)
41          }
44          else {
45              print("Didn't find any matching locations")
46          }
47      }
48  }
```

There's no new code here. You've seen all of it in previous listings, so just a high-level description of what's going on here follows.

- Lines 3–11 pull in all the contacts from the database.
- Line 12 converts the array of `NSManagedObject` to an array of `Contact` objects.
- Line 14 removes all previous annotations from the map. This ensures that if a contact has been removed or changed, the annotation is placed correctly.
- Line 16 sets up a loop to go through all the contacts. Note that the array is cast to an array of `Contact` objects instead of `NSManagedObjects`. This allows us to work with the content in the contacts.
- After creating an address string, line 18 geocodes the address and passes off the handling to the private method `processAddressResponse`.
- The method indicated in lines 26–48 processes the results of the geocoding. Notice that this method includes both the original contact as well as the results of the geocoding. You may be tempted to move the instantiation of the `geoCoder` outside the loop, so a new object isn't created for each time through the loop. However, if you do this, the geocoding doesn't work and only looks up the first contact.
- Lines 36–40 add the actual annotations to the map using the name and street address of each contact.

The processing of the results of geocoding is very similar to what you did in the previous section, except an annotation is added to the location. The annotation uses the name and street address for the contact.

If you run the app, be sure to have a few contacts in the database with the address, city, and state included. You should then see a pin for each contact on the map, and tapping the pin should bring up the contact's name and street address.

Zooming to Show Annotations

One issue with the app at this point is that the map is zoomed out very far when displaying the annotations. There is a very simple fix for this. You can simply add this one line of code to display all annotations on the map:

```
mapView.showAnnotations(mapView.annotations, animated: true)
```

If you replace the code in the findUser method with this line, you can tap the Find me! button and have the map zoom in to show all the annotation pins. It doesn't work to add this method in viewWillAppear, as that will be called before the geocoding is complete and the annotations have been added to the map.

Switching between Map Types

You can display the map as standard, satellite, or hybrid. To demonstrate how to set the map type, you add a segmented control to the bottom of the display to allow the user to choose which map type to display.

1. Open **Storyboard** and add a **segmented control** to the bottom of the map screen. You can add it right on top of the map, which would allow you to programmatically hide it at some point and then have the map take up more of the screen. Rename the segments **Standard, Hybrid, and Satellite**, as shown in Figure 13.6. To add a third segment, select the **segmented control** in Interface Builder, and then go to **Attributes Inspector** and set the Segments attribute to **3**.

2. Add **constraints** to center the **segmented control** and be **0** points from the bottom of the container.

3. Add an outlet for the segmented control, named **sgmtMapType**.

4. Add an action for the segmented control, named **mapTypeChanged**.

5. Implement the mapTypeChanged() method in MapViewController as shown in Listing 13.12.

Figure 13.6 Segmented control to choose map type.

Listing 13.13 Changing the Map Type

```
1    @IBAction func mapTypeChanged(_ sender: Any) {
2        switch sgmtMapType.selectedSegmentIndex {
3        case 0:
4            mapView.mapType = .standard
5        case 1:
6            mapView.mapType = .hybrid
7        case 2:
8            mapView.mapType = .satellite
9        default: break
10       }
11   }
```

Summary

Maps and location are very important for many mobile applications, so having a solid understanding of how to integrate these features into your apps is crucial to becoming a professional mobile developer. In this chapter, you saw many of the techniques and learned the skills necessary to create location-aware apps. However, there's much more to learn in this area, so you should keep studying Apple's documentation on maps and location programming.

Exercises

1. Add a control to allow the user to change the accuracy setting for the sensor, and notice how the output changes when moving about using different settings.

2. The app now has database access code in several view controllers. To support a cleaner design, add a database access class that controls all access to Core Data and provides useful methods and properties to the rest of the app.

3. Turn off the user's permission to access location for the App (in the Simulator, go to Settings > Privacy > Location). Run the app again and observe what happens. Is this appropriate behavior? How could it be improved?

4. What would happen if the code in Listing 13.10 was placed in `viewDidLoad` instead of `viewWillAppear`?

5. Change the text displayed on the pin to include the City for the contact.

CHAPTER 14

Access to Hardware and Sensors in iOS

A big part of the promise of mobile computing is that the mobile devices today offer features that aren't available in any other general-purpose computing devices. Besides mobility, the availability of hardware sensors on the device is what makes it possible to create truly innovative solutions that would not be possible otherwise.

This chapter demonstrates several approaches to interacting with the hardware on the device.

- You can use **UIDevice** to get basic information about the device, including OS Version and its current orientation (Landscape, Portrait, and so on).
- The Notification Center can be used to get regular updates on the state of the battery, including charge level and whether the device is plugged in.
- A simple approach to taking a picture is to use a ready-made view controller that allows for taking still pictures or videos.
- The phone and messaging (SMS) system can be opened using a URL that will send data to a default app for a variety of functions on the phone (including the browser and e-mail).
- Finally, you can use the powerful Core Motion framework to detect and work with a range of sensors on the device, including accelerometer, magnetometer, and gyroscope.

Knowing how to interact with the hardware on the device is an important step toward being able to create apps that take advantage of the full promise of mobile computing. This will allow you to create systems that could not have been possible without a capable mobile device.

Getting Device Information

One of the basic ways to interact with the hardware on the device is to retrieve data about the device itself. In iOS, the device is represented by the **UIDevice** class, which contains information about the device itself, such as its assigned name, operating system version, and device model (iPad, iPhone, iPod touch). The class also can tell you the orientation of the device (portrait and landscape) and provide status on the battery and the proximity sensor (whether the phone is close to the face of the user).

Listing 14.1 shows some of the ways you can use the `UIDevice` class. Later sections in this chapter contain other examples of interacting with this data.

Listing 14.1   Getting Information about the Current Device

```
1    override func viewDidAppear(_ animated: Bool) {
2        let device = UIDevice.current
3        print("Device Info:")
4        print("Name: \(device.name)")
5        print("Model: \(device.model)")
6        print("System Name: \(device.systemName)")
7        print("System Version: \(device.systemVersion)")
8        print("Identifier: \(device.identifierForVendor!)")
9
10       let orientation: String
11       switch device.orientation {
12       case .faceDown:
13           orientation = "Face Down"
14       case .landscapeLeft:
15           orientation = "Landscape Left"
16       case .portrait:
17           orientation="Portrait"
18       case .landscapeRight:
19           orientation = "Landscape Right"
20       case .faceUp:
21           orientation = "Face Up"
22       case .portraitUpsideDown:
23           orientation = "Portrait Upside Down"
24       case .unknown:
25           orientation = "Unknown Orientation"
26       }
27       print("Orientation: \(orientation)")
28   }
```

You can implement `viewDidAppear()` in **SettingsController.swift** and then add this code to it, so that it runs every time the Settings screen is selected. The code gets several pieces of information about the device and prints it to the console to demonstrate what you can find out about the user's device.

- **Line 2**—This gets a reference to the current device object. Notice that you can't instantiate the object; you just get a reference to it.
- **Line 4**—This is the name the user has given to the device. You could use this if your app might run on several of the user's devices and you need to provide an easy way for the user to distinguish among them.
- **Line 5**—The model of the device, such as iPhone and iPad.
- **Line 6**—The name of the OS, such as iPhone OS.
- **Line 7**—OS Version number.
- **Line 8**—Unique identifier of the app for the vendor. All apps from the same vendor running on one device will have the same value. But the same app on different devices owned by the same user will have different values. You can use this identifier to uniquely identify the devices your app is running on. If a user deletes all your apps and then installs one again, the value will change.
- **Lines 10–29**—The orientation of the device. A switch statement is used to identify all the ways the device can be oriented. Note that the value of this property is of the physical device, regardless of whether your app supports a given orientation.

If you run the app and switch to the Settings screen, you will get output like this for running on the Simulator (time stamps removed for better readability):

```
Device Info:
Name: UWO407210
Model: iPhone
System Name: iOS
System Version: 10.2
Identifier: 0A1698F4-7984-45AC-90C4-C8811C6006BC
Orientation: Portrait
```

The simulator reports the device name as the name of the computer that is controlling the device.

Monitoring Battery Status

One of the hardware devices available through UIDevice is the battery. Although the user always has a battery meter in the status bar of the device, you can use access to the battery information in various ways in your app, such as not starting certain operations if the battery is really low or requiring the device to be plugged in to execute something that is likely to drain the battery significantly.

The pattern for checking the battery is instructive and is used in other situations when developing for iOS. To access the battery information, you set up an **NSNotificationCenter** object, which provides a mechanism for broadcasting information within a program. In this case, you will set up a view controller to be an observer to changes in either the charge level of the battery or its charging state (full, plugged in, or unplugged). When either of these events occur, a method is called in the view controller and you can take appropriate action.

It isn't particularly relevant to MyContactList to monitor the battery status, but to demonstrate how it works you will add a simple battery indicator to the Settings screen, showing the battery charge level and state (see Figure 14.1). You will need a physical device to test this code, because the simulator doesn't simulate a battery. As you can see in the screenshot, the battery percentage doesn't match the one listed in the status bar.

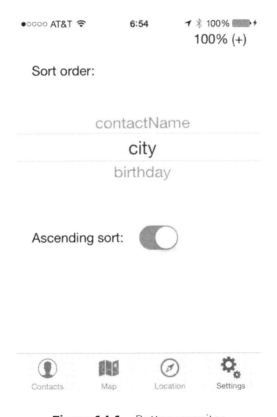

Figure 14.1 Battery monitor.

Start by setting up the user interface. Open **Main.storyboard** and add a label to the top-right corner of the **Settings scene**. Add constraints to place it **0** pixels from the **top** and **right** margins. Use the **Attributes Inspector** to right-align the text in the label. Add an outlet for the label called **lblBattery**. To start monitoring the battery, and update the label with the battery information, change `viewDidLoad`, as shown in Listing 14.2.

Listing 14.2   Start Monitoring the Battery Status

```
1    override func viewDidLoad() {
2        super.viewDidLoad()
3
4        // Do any additional setup after loading the view.
5        pckSortField.dataSource = self;
6        pckSortField.delegate = self;
7
8        UIDevice.current.isBatteryMonitoringEnabled = true
9        NotificationCenter.default.addObserver(self,
10                                  selector: #selector(self.batteryChanged),
11                                  name: Notification.Name.UIDeviceBatteryStateDidChange,
12                                  object: nil)
13       NotificationCenter.default.addObserver(self,
14                                  selector: #selector(self.batteryChanged),
15                                  name: Notification.Name.UIDeviceBatteryLevelDidChange,
16                                  object: nil)
17       self.batteryChanged()
18   }
```

Line 8 starts by enabling monitoring of changes to the battery. This includes changes to the level of the battery charge as well as to the state of charging (whether the device is plugged in or not). To be notified on an ongoing basis, you add an observer to the default notification center. Here you add notifications for two events: Changes to the state of the battery (lines 9–12), and changes to the charge level (lines 13–16). The two statements are otherwise identical, but it's important to understand each of the four parameters:

- `self`: The first parameter is the object that will be notified when the event occurs. Using `self` means the current object will be notified.

- `selector`: This has the name of the method that will be called when the event occurs. The method is shown in Listing 14.3. The method is the same for both events in this case, but it could obviously be two different methods.

- `name`: The name of the event being observed. In this case, it is the notification that the battery level and the state changed.

- `object`: This indicates the object where the notification is coming from. We don't worry about this, so we use `nil`.

Taken together, this method sets up a notification that when the level of the battery changes in the device, an event is generated that calls the `batteryChanged` method in the current class.

Line 17 sets the text on the label by calling the method `batteryChanged` (Listing 14.3). Notifications about changes in battery level occur only when it changes a full percentage point, so rather than relying only on the notification to update the status, this call updates it immediately.

After you have entered the code in Listing 14.2, you will see several warnings and errors in Xcode, because you still need to code the two `batteryChanged` method that actually handle the changes to the status. This is shown in Listing 14.3.

Listing 14.3 Handling Changes to the Battery Status

```
1    func batteryChanged(){
2        let device = UIDevice.current
3        var batteryState: String
4        switch(device.batteryState){
5        case .charging:
6            batteryState = "+"
7        case .full:
8            batteryState = "!"
9        case .unplugged:
10           batteryState = "-"
11       case .unknown:
12           batteryState = "?"
13       }
14       let batteryLevelPercent = device.batteryLevel * 100
15       let batteryLevel = String(format: "%.0f%%", batteryLevelPercent)
16       let batteryStatus = "\(batteryLevel) (\(batteryState))"
17       lblBattery.text = batteryStatus
18   }
```

The `batteryChanged` method is called whenever notification is sent for either a change in battery level or battery state to actually get the values from the battery and create a formatted display for the label. The method is straightforward and doesn't contain much new functionality. A switch statement in line 4 checks the status and converts it into a text symbol. Line 14 calculates the percentage value for the battery level, and lines 15 and 16 format and combine the two values into a single string that is assigned to the label in line 17.

If you run the app, you should see the battery information on the Settings screen. The Simulator doesn't include battery information, so you will need to run the app on a physical device. In the Simulator, the display shows up as **–100% (?)**.

If you want to just check the battery status to see if an operation can proceed rather than monitor the status, you don't need to set up the notifications, but you do need to enable battery monitoring as shown in line 8 in Listing 14.2. When you are done checking the battery, you should turn off the monitoring. In this app, you should turn off monitoring in `viewDidDisappear` with the following line:

```
UIDevice.current.isBatteryMonitoringEnabled = false
```

Controlling the Camera

There are a couple different ways to capture images within an iOS app. The simplest method involves using a built-in navigation controller that contains all the necessary controls to take a picture and return it to your app.

To expand the MyContactList app to allow for taking a picture, you have to carry out the following steps:

1. Add an entry in info.plist to request permission to use the camera.
2. Make room in the UI for the image and a button to take an image.
3. Implement code to bring up camera control.
4. Handle the data returned from the camera controller
5. Change Core Data design to store the picture.
6. Save the image to Core Data.
7. Make sure the image is brought back to the UI when view control is loaded.

Using the camera requires permission from the user, so start by adding the *Privacy – Camera Usage Description* key as an entry in **Info.plist**, and then add a description to show to the user for why the app needs to use the camera. If you want to allow the user to access the photo library, you would also have to add an entry for *Privacy – Photo Library Usage Description*.

The next step is to change the UI layout in the Contacts editing screen. You can simply add another stack view at the bottom of the screen to hold an image and a button.

Start by opening **Main.storyboard** and drag an **Image View** and place it below the Birthday label. Then drag a **button** and place it to the right of the image. Select the two controls and embed them in a **stack view**. Check in the Document Outline on the left that it is inside the top-level stack view (one level below the scroll view). If it isn't, drag it to the correct spot.

Select the image view and add constraints to set both the **height** and **width** to **100** pixels. Create an outlet for the image view called **imgContactPicture**. Change the text on the button to Take Picture and create an action function called **changePicture**. Figure 14.2 shows the completed layout.

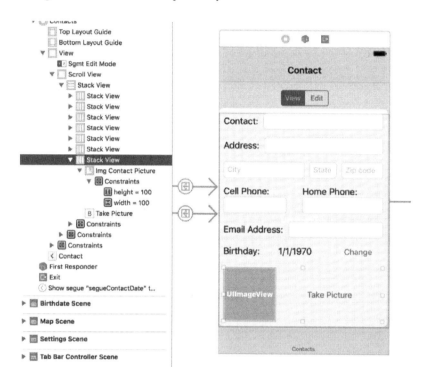

Figure 14.2   User interface for adding an image to a Contact.

Next, you implement the button's action method, as shown in Listing 14.4. This method requires implementing `UIImagePickerControllerDelegate` and `UINavigationControllerDelegate`, so add both of these to the class declaration line.

Listing 14.4   Launching the Image Picker

```
1    @IBAction func changePicture(_ sender: Any) {
2        if UIImagePickerController.isSourceTypeAvailable(.camera){
3            let cameraController = UIImagePickerController()
4            cameraController.sourceType = .camera
5            cameraController.cameraCaptureMode = .photo
6            cameraController.delegate = self
7            cameraController.allowsEditing = true
8            self.present(cameraController, animated: true, completion: nil)
9        }
     }
```

This code is executed when the user taps the camera button to bring up the camera controller.

- Note with line 2, not all iOS devices have a camera, so to avoid the app crashing if the camera isn't present, you should always check for the presence of hardware sensors. It doesn't seem very logical to ask `UIImage-PickerController` whether a camera is available, but that is the recommended pattern.

- Line 3 creates the controller for the camera, and then a few properties are set. The source type can be either camera, photo library, or saved photos album. The default is photo library, so we set it to `.camera` in line 4.

- The controller can be used to capture video as well as stills. The `cameraCaptureMode` property can be used to restrict to only one of them, as it is done here, because only the still camera option will work for this app. If you set the `allowsEditing` property to `true`, as shown in line 7, the user will be allowed to move and scale the image after it has been taken.

- Finally, line 8 presents the `cameraController` to the user.

With `changePicture` implemented, the camera control now comes up when the camera button is tapped, and the user can take a picture. Figure 14.3 shows the camera user interface for taking the picture and editing after it has been taken. However, nothing happens with the image when the user returns to the app. The picture was supposed to show up in the image view.

Figure 14.3 Camera controller interface.

To actually do something with the image, you need to implement a delegate method, `imagePickerController(_ picker:didFinishPickingMediaWithInfo:)`, that the camera controller will call when it is done with its work (see Listing 14.5).

Listing 14.5 Handling the Image Picker Returned

```
1   func imagePickerController(_ picker: UIImagePickerController,
2                         didFinishPickingMediaWithInfo info: [String : Any]) {
3       if let image = info[UIImagePickerControllerEditedImage] as? UIImage {
4           imgContactPicture.contentMode = .scaleAspectFit
5           imgContactPicture.image = image
6       }
7       dismiss(animated: true, completion: nil)
8   }
```

The camera controller is a `UIImagePickerController` that returns its data in a String array called `info`.

- Line 3 conditionally assigns the returned image to an `image` constant. In this case, the edited image is used (i.e., the one the user zoomed and moved before tapping Use).

- If you want to disregard any edits made by the user, you can retrieve `UIImagePickerControllerOriginalImage` instead. The image is then assigned to the `imgContactPicture` control in line 5.

- Line 4 ensures that the image keeps the proper aspect ratio when it's assigned to the control.

- Line 7 handles dismissing the camera control so the regular app becomes visible again. If you forget this step, the camera control won't disappear when the user taps Use, so this is a very important step.

Now you can run the app, take a picture, and see how it shows up in the user interface in the proper place, as shown in Figure 14.4. Remember that this will not work on the Simulator because it does not have a camera.

Figure 14.4   Image showing up in the user interface.

To save the image to the database, you first have to make a few changes to the Core Data Model to include the image in the Contact entity:

1. Open **MyContactListModel.xcdatamodeld** in the project, and click the **+** under the list of attributes.

2. Add a property named **image** with a type of **Binary Data**. Be careful if you use the mouse to add the data type in, because the list of attributes is automatically sorted as soon as you enter the name, so you may end up changing the type of the birthday attribute and leaving the image type as undefined. If this happens, you will get compiler errors when you try to run or build it, but they can be fixed by making the birthday a Date type and the image a Binary Data type.

3. With the image attribute selected, open **Data Model Inspector** and check **Store in External Record File**. This allows Core Data to store the image as a file outside the database and just keep an index pointer to the actual file (see Figure 14.5). This is a good practice when storing images that could be quite large.

4. Make sure that the image is saved and retrieved from the database. To save the image, you add this code at the end of the `if` statement in Listing 14.5 (after line 5):

```
if currentContact == nil {
        let context = appDelegate.persistentContainer.viewContext
        currentContact = Contact(context: context)
    }
    currentContact?.image = NSData(data: UIImageJPEGRepresentation(image, 1.0)!)
```

This creates a `Contact` object if `currentContact` hasn't been set, and then converts the image to a JPEG image with no compression. (Lower the 1.0 value to compress the image.) Because Core Data stores binary data as NSData, the image needs to be converted to NSData before being assigned to the `currentContact`.

5. To retrieve the image from the database, add these lines along with the other lines for populating the user interface with data from the contact object in `viewDidLoad`:

```
if let imageData = currentContact?.image as? Data {
    imgContactPicture.image = UIImage(data: imageData)
}
```

This takes an image that's stored as `NSData` and turns it into a `UIImage` that can be displayed, and assigns it to the `image` property of the Image View control.

Figure 14.5 Allowing images to be stored in external record file.

Try running the app on a device with a camera. If the app crashes with a problem related to versions of the Core Data model store, something went wrong with the automatic lightweight migration. This is prone to happen in development environments. One simple solution is to uninstall the app and launch it again. This will, of course, remove the entire database of contacts, so it isn't a good solution in production environments. A discussion of the migration of data models is beyond the scope of this book. You can find more detail about migrating Core Data models in Apple's Core Data Model Versioning and Data Migration Programming Guide (https://developer.apple.com/library/content/documentation/Cocoa/Conceptual/CoreDataVersioning/Articles/Introduction.html).

You should now be able to add a picture to a contact and have it be saved to the database and show up again in the user interface. As you have seen, taking a picture is quite easy (Listing 14.4 and 14.5), but handling the image takes a little more work. The controller used to take pictures here is easy to use but not very flexible; it uses a lot of memory and is rather slow. But if you don't need a lot of sophistication, it works well. If you do require more power, you can look at the **AVFoundation** framework, which allows for very customizable and powerful image solutions.

Calling a Phone Number

One of the most important hardware features of most mobile devices is the phone. You can integrate the phone functionality into your app by letting the user call relevant numbers from within the app. Calling a phone number launches the Phone app on the phone, but control is returned to your app when the call is done.

Calling a phone number from within your app is very simple and requires only two lines of code:

```
let url = NSURL(string: "telprompt://1234567894")
UIApplication.shared.open(url as! URL, options: [:], completionHandler: nil)
```

This tells the phone to launch the URL. Any URL starting with telprompt:// will be treated like a phone number. You can also use tel:// as a prefix. The difference is that telprompt:// gives the user a prompt that the number will be called, whereas tel:// will just call the number. In most cases, you should use telprompt://. Other URL schemes open other apps. For instance, http:// opens Safari, and sms:// opens the Message app.

Long Press Gesture

In MyContactList, calling a phone number is a very useful feature. It will be implemented to allow the user to long press on the label above the phone number field on the Contact screen to call the number. A *long press* means that the user holds a little longer than a regular tap—about one second. To set this up, you first need to add an outlet named **lblPhone** for the label. Because a label normally doesn't respond to user interaction, you need to open the **Attributes Inspector** and set the **Interaction** for the label to **User Interaction Enabled**.

Then you add these two statements to the end of viewDidLoad in **ContactsViewController.swift**:

```
let longPress = UILongPressGestureRecognizer.init(target: self,
                                       action: #selector(callPhone(gesture:)))
lblPhone.addGestureRecognizer(longPress)
```

The first statement sets up a gesture recognizer, which is a special object that is designed to recognize a long press. The gesture recognizer is given the view controller (self) as a target meaning that any long presses will be sent to the view controller, and the action to take when that happens is specified in the action selector. In this case, the callPhone method is called. The second statement adds the gesture recognizer to the lblPhone field so that long presses on this control are recognized. It would be convenient to also add the gesture recognizer to the cell phone field; however, only one view can be associated with a gesture recognizer at a time. If you want to have multiple controls recognize a long press, you would have to create a gesture recognizer for each of them.

Next, you need to implement callPhone(gesture:), which is shown in Listing 14.6.

Listing 14.6   Method to Call Phone Number on Long Press

```
1   func callPhone(gesture: UILongPressGestureRecognizer) {
2       if gesture.state == .began {
3           let number = txtPhone.text
4           if number!.characters.count > 0 { //Don't call blank numbers
5               let url = NSURL(string: "telprompt://\(number!)")
6               UIApplication.shared.open(url as! URL, options: [:], completionHandler: nil)
7               print("Calling Phone Number: \(url!)")
8           }
9       }
10  }
```

This method illustrates several important features:

- The long press gesture is recognized many times by the system as long as the user keeps holding the finger, so to avoid handling all those events, you should always use an if statement to check the state of the gesture as shown in line 2. Here we check for the .began state, which is only called once for an entire gesture press, and this statement will be true only the first time through this method.

- Line 4 checks that the phone number in the corresponding text field isn't blank, which would make it difficult to call.

- Line 5 creates a NSURL object that holds the phone number to call by concatenating the protocol prefix (telprompt://) with the phone number from the txtPhone field.

- Line 6 calls the number, and line 7 prints a status message to the console. Since the simulator doesn't show the phone call, this print statement is included to give some feedback that the long press gesture was recognized.

Now you can run the app. If you have an iPhone to run this on, it will prompt you with an Alert View asking you to call the number (see Figure 14.6). If you run the app on the simulator, you need to watch the console for the Long Press message when you click and hold the phone number.

Figure 14.6 Calling a phone number after long press gesture is recognized.

Checking OS Version Number

As Apple makes changes to Swift and iOS, you may find yourself in a situation where you have to write code that is specific to certain operating systems versions. In this section, you will see how to check which version of iOS the device is running and use that to call specific statements. In this case, we will check if the user has allowed the camera to be accessed, and if not, ask her to go to the settings to enable the camera before proceeding.

Start by adding an `import` statement to **ContactsViewController.swift** for `AVFoundation`. Then make changes to `changePicture` and add `openSettings` as shown in Listing 14.7.

Listing 14.7 Finding the iOS Version Number

```
1    @IBAction func changePicture(_ sender: Any) {
2        if AVCaptureDevice.authorizationStatus(forMediaType: AVMediaTypeVideo) !=
3                                              AVAuthorizationStatus.authorized
4        {   //Camera not authorized
5            let alertController = UIAlertController(title: "Camera Access Denied",
6                                            message: "In order to take pictures, you need to
7    allow the app to access the camera in the Settings.",
8                                            preferredStyle: .alert)
9            let actionSettings = UIAlertAction(title: "Open Settings",
10                                      style: .default) {action in
11               self.openSettings()
12           }
13           let actionCancel = UIAlertAction(title: "Cancel",
14                                     style: .cancel,
15                                     handler: nil)
16           alertController.addAction(actionSettings)
17           alertController.addAction(actionCancel)
18           present(alertController, animated: true, completion: nil)
19       }
```

(continued)

Listing 14.7 Finding the iOS Version Number (*continued*)

```
20        else
21        {   // Already Authorized
22            if UIImagePickerController.isSourceTypeAvailable(.camera){
23                let cameraController = UIImagePickerController()
24                cameraController.sourceType = .camera
25                cameraController.cameraCaptureMode = .photo
26                cameraController.delegate = self
27                cameraController.allowsEditing = true
28                self.present(cameraController, animated: true, completion: nil)
29            }
30        }
31    }
32
33    func openSettings(){
34        if let settingsUrl = URL(string: UIApplicationOpenSettingsURLString) {
35            if #available(iOS 10.0, *) {
36                UIApplication.shared.open(settingsUrl, options: [:], completionHandler: nil)
37            } else {
38                UIApplication.shared.openURL(settingsUrl)
39            }
40        }
41    }
```

- Line 2 checks if the user has granted permission to use the camera. If so, lines 21–29 are executed as before.

- However, if permission is not granted, an alert controller with two actions is created and presented in lines 5–18.

- In lines 9–12, the action for opening the settings is created. This calls the `openSettings()` method if the user selects the Open Settings option.

- Line 34 retrieves the `UIApplicationSettingsURLString`, which can be used to pass to the open method to launch the Settings app for your app.

- Line 35 checks to see that the device is at least running iOS 10. If so, line 36 calls the open method with `settingsURL` to open the app's settings.

- However, in versions prior to iOS 10, the method was called `openURL` and is called as you can see in line 38.

You can run the app and then quit it by pressing the Home button. Then launch Settings and scroll down until you find the entry for MyContactList. At this point, turn off the camera (left side of Figure 14.6). Go back to My Contact List (which can be done by double-tapping the Home button and then selecting My Contact List). Now when you tap the Change Picture button, you will get the message about the permissions (right side of Figure 14.6).

Using Core Motion for Accelerometer Data

Included in iOS is a framework called Core Motion, which provides access to several sensors, including a gyroscope, a magnetometer, and an accelerometer. In this section, you learn how to access the data from the accelerometer to move an object around the screen of the device by tilting the device.

The accelerometer provides data about the velocity that the device is moving in three dimensions. If the device is held vertically in front of you, the x-axis measures movement left and right, the y-axis measures movement away from and toward you, and the z-axis measures movement up and down. When working with the accelerometer, you create an object of the class `CMMotionManager`. It's important to create only a single instance of this class in your app to avoid performance issues. After the `CMMotionManager` is created, you set up a block of code to execute asynchronously anytime motion data is updated. You can set an update interval to make sure the app receives all the data it needs without causing too much performance drain. To keep battery drain to a minimum, it's important to also remember to stop the accelerometer updates when they are no longer needed.

Device movement is not relevant to MyContactList, so you will do something a little silly and have the battery display you added previously move around the Settings screen when the user tilts the device.

To make sure that only a single instance of CMMotionManager is created, the instantiation is handled in the application delegate, and any other class that needs accelerometer data will then get a reference to the single object. Start by adding an import statement for CoreMotion and this line just after the class declaration in **AppDelegate.swift**:

```
lazy var motionManager = CMMotionManager()
```

This sets up a property with an object that is only instantiated when it's needed.

Next, open **SettingsViewController.swift** and add an import statement for CoreMotion and the method in Listing 14.9 to retrieve the motion manager from the app delegate as needed.

Listing 14.8 Retrieving the Motion Manager and Starting Motion Detection

```
1   func startMotionDetection(){
2       let appDelegate = UIApplication.shared.delegate as! AppDelegate
3       let mManager = appDelegate.motionManager
4       if mManager.isAccelerometerAvailable {
5           mManager.accelerometerUpdateInterval = 0.05
6           mManager.startAccelerometerUpdates(to: OperationQueue.main) {
7               (data: CMAccelerometerData?, error: Error?) in
8               self.updateLabel(data: data!)
9           }
10      }
11  }
```

This method starts by getting a reference to the app delegate and then to the motion manager.

- Line 3 checks if the device has an accelerometer, and if so, sets the update interval in seconds. This interval corresponds to updates 20 times per second. The interval of updates can be set for updates as frequently as 100 times per second.
- Line 6 starts the updates to the accelerometer with a completion handler that will be executed each time the accelerometer's update interval occurs. The accelerometer provides its results in the data parameter as a CMAccelerometerData object, which contains the x, y, and z velocities. The completion handler simply calls the updateLabel method (Listing 14.10) to update the label's movements around the screen.

Before implementing Listing 14.10, add an outlet named **settingsView** for the top-level View in the **Settings Scene** and control-drag to **SettingsViewController.swift**.

Listing 14.9 Update Label to Be Moved around the Screen

```
1   func updateLabel(data: CMAccelerometerData){
2       let statusBarHeight = UIApplication.shared.statusBarFrame.height
3       let tabBarHeight = self.tabBarController?.tabBar.frame.height
4       let moveFactor:Double = 15.0
5       var rect = lblBattery.frame
6       let moveToX = Double(rect.origin.x) + data.acceleration.x * moveFactor
7       let moveToY = Double(rect.origin.y + rect.size.height) - (data.acceleration.y * moveFactor)
8       let maxX = Double(settingsView.frame.size.width - rect.width)
9       let maxY = Double(settingsView.frame.size.height - tabBarHeight!)
10      let minY = Double(rect.size.height + statusBarHeight)
11      if(moveToX > 0 && moveToX < maxX){
12          rect.origin.x += CGFloat(data.acceleration.x * moveFactor)
13      }
14      if(moveToY > minY && moveToY < maxY){
15          rect.origin.y -= CGFloat(data.acceleration.y * moveFactor);
16      }
```

(continued)

Listing 14.9   Update Label to Be Moved around the Screen (*continued*)

```
17          UIView.animate(withDuration: TimeInterval(0),
18                         delay: TimeInterval(0),
19                         options: UIViewAnimationOptions.curveEaseInOut,
20                         animations: {self.lblBattery.frame = rect},
21                         completion: nil)
22      }
```

This method is called 20 times per second with new accelerometer data and moves the label to its new position based on data in the accelerometer. In this case, only movement along the x- and y-axes are used, and not the z-axis. This method has a lot of things going on, but is fairly typical of moving things around on a screen. For many business applications, this is an unusual kind of programming, but for games and simulations, this kind of thing is quite common.

- Lines 2 and 3 get the height of the status bar at the top of the screen (where the time and network indicators are) and the tab bar at the bottom of the screen, so we can avoid moving the label into those areas.

- The `moveFactor` declared in line 4 is a multiplier that decides how far the label is moved with each update. Changing this value will make the label move faster or slower. Line 5 gets a rectangle based on the frame around the label. The rectangle is used in the calculations of where to move the label. Lines 6 calculates the next position along the x-axis by multiplying the `moveFactor` with the acceleration along the x-axis and adding it to the original x-axis location of the label. The accelerometer data is reported between −1 and 1, with 0 being at rest. Line 7 repeats for the y-axis.

- To keep the label from moving off the screen, the dimensions of the screen are calculated, taking the width of the label (line 8), the height of the tab bar (line 9), and the status bar (line 10) into account.

- Line 11 checks to see if the new position will move the label off the screen along the x-axis, and if not, updates the x value for the position of the label. Line 12 repeats this for the y-axis.

- The final statement (lines 17–21) updates the display by animating the movement from the old to the new location. By setting `duration` and `delay` to 0, the animation is carried out immediately (and thus not really animated), but if you had an object you wanted to animate from one location to another, you could set the duration to some value in seconds, and it will then be animated from one place to another on the screen. The `options` parameter is a way to specify how the animation is done. In this case, the label is moved a small distance each time, so no transition is needed. The `animations` parameter is where you specify the code that will run to update the display. In this case, it is the animation of moving the label from its original location to the newly calculated one. If you wanted to run code after the animation was done, you could add a similar block in the `completion` parameter.

The only thing left is to start the collection of accelerometer data and then stop it again. In this case, the animation should keep going as long as the user is viewing the Settings screen, but stop as soon as the user leaves it. The ideal place to achieve this is to start in `viewDidAppear` and stop in `viewDidDisappear`. Add the following line to the end of `viewDidAppear` to start the motion detection:

```
self.startMotionDetection()
```

Then add lines 3 and 4 to `viewDidDisappear`, as shown in Listing 14.10, to stop the motion detection when the user leaves the Settings screen.

Listing 14.10   Stop Motion Detection

```
1    override func viewDidDisappear(_ animated: Bool) {
2        UIDevice.current.isBatteryMonitoringEnabled = false
3        let appDelegate = UIApplication.shared.delegate as? AppDelegate
4        appDelegate?.motionManager.stopAccelerometerUpdates()
5    }
```

The method is very simple; it gets the motion manager from the app delegate and stops the updates of accelerometer data. If you run the app, you should now be able to tilt the device and have the label move around the screen.

Summary

With the skills you have learned in this chapter, you have the foundation to start taking advantage of using the hardware features of the user's device in your own apps. When you do so, be careful to check for the availability of sensors on the device and turn off sensors when not needed to avoid draining the battery. For most of the examples in this chapter, it is necessary to have a physical device for testing, because the Simulator doesn't simulate most of the hardware sensors.

Exercises

1. Add functionality to the app to detect orientation change and place the current orientation of the device on a label.
2. Make sure the camera button shows up only on devices that support a camera.
3. Make sure the camera button is shown and hidden appropriately when the user changes between edit and view modes.
4. Implement a long-press recognizer for the cell phone field, but instead of calling the number, send a message.
5. Add a check to see if permission is granted for location when the user taps the Find Me! button, and then direct them to change the Settings to allow the functionality.
6. Create a new Single-View project and use the accelerometer data to create a simple game where the player gets points by tapping a button that can be moved around the screen by tilting the device.
7. Add three sliders and use them to display the accelerometer data in all three dimensions in real time.

PART IV

BUSINESS ISSUES

CHAPTER 15

Monetizing Apps

The market for apps is big and getting bigger. Vision Mobile has estimated that there are 2 billion global smartphone users in 2015 and there were 180 billion app downloads in that year. The State of the App Economy 2017 report issued by the App Association finds that app revenues reached $51 billion in 2016 in the United States and predicts that number will reach $100 billion by 2020. How do you get a piece of that pie? You've created and tested a great app. Now you want your efforts to pay off. What is the best way to do this? What options do you have to make money from apps? What do you have to do to start? In this chapter, you explore the various avenues for monetizing apps.

App Monetization Strategies

Making money from apps is possible but difficult. There are hundreds of thousands of apps available. The revenue generated from an individual app is typically very small, and the app stores take a 30% cut of all the revenue that your app generates. How do you get people to pay you to use yours? What are the different ways you can collect money for the use of your apps? More importantly, how can you get a lot of people to pay you to use the app so that the revenue generated enough to fund further development or expansion? These are some of the questions that many developers are asking. Some questions have concrete answers. Others are still very much open for debate.

Paid Apps

The simplest approach to monetizing an app is to charge for the download. The price is advertised in the app store, and the user decides, based on your description of the app, whether to buy it. If the user buys the app, you get the money. No need to worry about getting clicks or designing features to be purchased. The problem is getting enough customers to generate significant income. One approach to solving this problem is to raise the price of the app. However, as the price of the app goes up, the number of downloads goes down. As mentioned before, the market is very price sensitive. You will need a very enticing description of your app to get downloads. Additionally, after users have purchased the app, future updates are free. You would need to add a new app to charge again.

A significant problem for all strategies, which is exacerbated with paid apps, is getting the potential customer to find your app among the thousands of apps in the app stores. If the user searches the app store using keywords, and your app is displayed along with a number of free apps, the user will often not even read your app's description, focusing only on the free ones. To attempt to remedy this, you need to advertise. Advertising is a double-edged sword. It costs money! Even a limited Google ad campaign where you pay Google to display an ad whenever someone searches on a set of keywords costs hundreds of dollars. It takes a lot of $.99 app sales to cover this cost.

An up-and-coming paid app approach is to build apps for business use. An app such as Bossy (described in Chapter 1, "Why Mobile Apps?") is designed to solve a business problem. A Bossy download costs $24.99. However, if your app solves a business problem, a business will be happy to pay the cost. This approach does require marketing. It is unlikely that businesses will search the Play Store for a solution to their business problems. This approach requires a much larger commitment than is typical for many app developers. It requires a business plan, establishing a target market, and directly contacting the market with information about your product. It also requires a potentially significant monetary investment.

Ad Supported Apps

The app market is very price sensitive. Free apps get downloaded at a much greater rate than any paid app. However, a totally free app is hard to make money with. That is why, although many apps appear to be free, they often have a way to make money built within the app. The most common approach to making money from a free app is to embed ads within the app screens. Ads take up screen real-estate, so you will have to plan and code the user interface with this in mind.

While there are several different companies that provide the ability embed ads in your apps, AdMob from Google is well integrated with Android and therefore probably the easiest for the beginner. AdMob is included in Firebase. Firebase is a collection of backend development tools. Once you become adept at developing, learning more on how to use the tools provided in Firebase to enhance your app would be a good idea. Because setting up for supporting ads in your app mostly involves registering for the ads with either Google or Apple, as well as submitting bank account information (so you can be paid) and a W-9 tax form (so you can pay taxes on your ad revenue), it isn't feasible to have a tutorial in this chapter on setting up ads. Instead, here are the basic steps you need to follow to embed ads in an Android app, after you have properly registered for AdMob with Google:

1. Open the Firebase assistant by clicking **Tools > Firebase**.
2. Find **AdMob** in the list of services and click **Add a banner to your app**.
3. Follow the instructions carefully.

You can also use AdMob in an iOS app, either directly using the SDK or with Firebase (https://firebase.google.com/docs/admob/ios/quick-start). Download the SDK from https://developers.google.com/mobile-ads-sdk/download#downloadios. The process to add an ad to an iOS project is a bit lengthy to discuss here, but in essence you add the AdSupport Framework from the unzipped download file to your project, and then add the ad view where needed to your xib files. A complete description of the process is located at https://developers.google.com/mobile-ads-sdk/docs/.

To use AdMob to make money from ads on your app, as well as test the ads, you need to sign up with AdMob (http://www.google.com/ads/admob/). Ads generate money for you only when they are clicked. Each click generates only a few cents, so you need a lot of clicks to make any real income. For example, we have a free card game on Android that is ad supported. It has been downloaded by nearly a thousand people. The money it generates is measured in dollars per month. In contrast, we have an app that costs $1.99. It gets only a couple of downloads per month but generates as much money as the more frequently downloaded and used ad-supported app.

In-App Purchases

Making enough money from ad-supported apps to support a business is difficult. You need a very popular app to generate a significant amount of money. Another approach for monetization is to release a free app that is supported by in-app purchases. The basic theory for an in-app purchase monetization strategy is that you generate downloads with the free app, get the users hooked, and then allow them to add features by advertising the feature in the app. The sale is made during use of the app. This is a very popular approach among app developers. In fact, more than 75% of the revenue going to iPhone developers in February 2013 came from in-app purchases. Another advantage over the basic paid app is that in-app purchasing opens up the possibility of a regular revenue stream from the same user, instead of relying on a single purchase up front.

In-app purchasing is one way to establish a *freemium* business model, where most of your users use the free version, but a small percentage becomes heavily invested in your app and service and convert to paying for the service, thus underwriting the free experience for everyone else.

You can use several approaches to create products for in-app purchase. Most are dependent on the type of app and its designed use. Game apps often limit the user to only a few game levels and then provide an in-app purchase option for moving to the next level. Other games have consumables that can be purchased during game use. For example, a number of lives are purchased and used up. If users want to continue playing, they have to buy more. Other apps include features that can be unlocked with an in-app purchase. For example, an app may have a mapping feature, such as in the MyContactList app. The button opens the map screen but rather than display the contact, it presents the user with a message that the feature needs to be purchased before the contacts will be displayed. Another approach is to limit the amount of data that can be saved or the number of times the app can be used before the user needs to pay for it. Finally, if your app includes access to content, that content could be purchased on a subscription basis. For example, services that provide weather information cost the developer money, depending on the number of times the weather service is accessed. If the user wants that information in the app, the developer could charge a subscription fee to cover the cost and generate revenue for themselves. Often an in-app purchase strategy is combined with an ad-supported strategy. The free version includes ads that are eliminated as a bonus for an in-app purchase.

To implement in-app purchases in Android, you have to get the Google Play Billing Library from the Android SDK Manager. It is found in the extras folder in the SDK manager. Import the **IInAppBillingService.aidl** file into the **src** folder of your project. Also, import the files in the **util** folder of the example app included in the library. Complete information on implementing in-app purchases in Android is available here: http://developer.android .com/google/play/billing/index.html.

Implementing in-app purchases in iOS is easier, because all you have to do to get the code is add the **StoreKit** framework to your project. Products that can be purchased in the app are set up in iTunes Connect and then made available in the app. The complete process is too detailed to cover here, but complete information is available at https:// developer.apple.com/library/content/documentation/NetworkingInternet/Conceptual/StoreKitGuide/Introduction .html.

Subscriptions

Selling your app outright and then collecting no revenue from a customer as long as they use the app often does not create enough sustainable revenue to keep the developer in business. Offering subscriptions to all or some portion of the app may be a good choice to counter this problem. Both Google and Apple offer this approach for their apps. However, the challenge becomes keeping the app's content relevant or the app useful enough to get customers to keep renewing their subscriptions. This approach requires coding similar to in-app billing, where the app checks its subscription status during use of the app to ensure the customer is up-to-date.

Understanding the Economics of App Stores

Often developers are surprised that they have to pay Google and Apple 30% of any sales made in the app stores (whether from paid apps or in-app purchases). We have often heard from clients that paying 30% to Google and Apple makes it impossible to do business, because they don't have 30% margins in the rest of their business to give away. To the extent that a mobile app sale replaces a regular sale of the same product, this argument makes sense. However, if the sale of the mobile app is incremental to the rest of the business, the additional revenue could be lower.

You have to remember that you pay Apple and Google to set up an entirely new sales channel. They run and operate the stores, so you don't have to worry about setting up a new infrastructure to handle sales of mobile apps.

If you wanted to avoid giving 30% of your sales to Google and Apple, you can carry out the sales outside of the app stores. For instance, you could set up your own website where users register for an account, and then any sales made on your website could be made accessible to the app with a login in the app. This is the model that Amazon uses with the Kindle app. If you want to read a Kindle book on a mobile device, you buy the book on Amazon's website, and then you log in to the Kindle app and your content from Amazon is available to you.

Apple is particularly strict about restrictions on the purchasing of content outside the app store, so Amazon isn't even allowed to have a link in its app that takes users to their store where they can buy the books.

If you wanted to avoid the need to register users, you could also create a system where you e-mail an unlock code to users who have made a purchase. The app could then unlock specific functionality based on the unlock code. However, you have to be careful in designing the system for the unlock codes, both technically and because of the workload involved. And depending on how you set it up, you may also run afoul of Apple's App Store rules for in-app purchases. You might find that the work involved makes in-app purchasing more appealing.

Owning Your Own Business

If you are going to sell apps, you should have a business. This is not an absolute requirement. The Play and App Stores will let you sell apps as an individual. However, it is good practice because you can cleanly separate your individual life, income, and assets from your business income and assets. This is important for both tax and liability purposes. The vehicle for setting up your own business is in most cases a limited liability corporation, or LLC.

Create an LLC

An LLC is a legal entity that is organized by registering the business with a state. The process should take no more than an hour or so and cost under $200. The basic process is as follows:

1. Establish the business name. Some form of *limited liability corporation*, or *LLC*, should be in the name. Check your proposed name against the database of names maintained by your state to make sure it has not been used.
2. Download the Articles of Organization form from your state and fill it out.
3. Identify a registered agent. This is the individual who will receive legal documents for the business. It can be you.

4. Create an operating agreement that details the financial and management responsibilities of the members of the LLC (owners are called members). This is not required by every state but is good practice.

5. File the forms with your state and pay the registration fee.

That's it. You now own a business! The LLC shields your personal assets in the event your app causes a problem that you get sued for. If you are found liable, they can take your business assets but not touch your personal assets. An LLC is also useful for tax purposes. The expenses you have incurred during app development, distribution, and marketing can be subtracted from the revenue you receive. The final number, whether it is positive or negative, is then transferred to your personal income taxes. If the number is positive, you will pay taxes through your personal income. If the number is negative, it reduces the amount of personal income taxes you pay.

Plan Your Business

If you plan to sell your app, you should get an LLC. However, you do not necessarily have to plan your business. If the app is a passion for you and you don't necessarily want to run a business, don't worry about it. Just put it on the market and keep it up-to-date. However, if you want to try to make real money in the app development business, you should develop a business plan.

The details of developing a business plan are not covered here. There are many resources available on the web to help you do this. The Small Business Administration (http://www.sba.gov) is an excellent resource. The purpose here is to encourage you to do so. There are many benefits to the act of developing a business plan. Developing the plan will help you think about what the mission of your organization is, who the market is, who the competitors are, and how you want to run your business. Making a significant amount money from apps requires money for marketing and development. A good business plan is a necessary condition for attracting enough capital to develop and test the app and begin establishing demand for your products.

Other Income Possibilities

Making money from selling apps or advertising in apps is possible. However, your income is very dependent on how successful your app is in terms of number of downloads. In fact, only a limited number of app development organizations get the lion's share of the billion-dollar market place described earlier in this chapter. The rest of the market is divided up by thousands of developers. Even so, you should create, publish, and attempt to monetize an app in at least one of the markets. This will give you the knowledge and "street cred" to make money in other ways from app development. Although the authors of this book have several apps available in both markets, we make far more money doing training and consulting than we do from the monetization of our apps.

One of the surest ways to make money from app development is to get paid to do it for someone else. This way, you get paid whether the app sells or not. App developers are a very hot commodity in the business world. The average salary for an app developer employed by an organization is around $100K/year. You have to sell a lot of $.99 apps each year to make this kind of money. Vision Mobile estimates that 43% of enterprise app developers earn at least $120,000 per year, while only 19% of consumer app developers earn the same amount. If you establish your ability by publishing apps for both iOS and Android, you can greatly increase your marketability. This is true if you intend to work for a corporation, or if you want to work for yourself as an independent developer.

You can approach independent development as a consultant or a contract developer. Developing a consulting business requires business planning. You need to identify your potential market, get your business name out to potential customers, and develop marketing materials to sell your ability to perform the job they need done. Another approach is to become a freelancer. There are sites that post small jobs that businesses need done (e.g., http://www.freelancersoutpost.com). You find a job that you are interested in and place a bid. If the organization accepts your bid, you develop the app for them and get paid when you're done. The advantage to this approach is that you can do it as a sideline business to pick up extra income. The disadvantage is that most projects have fairly small price tags, so it is much more difficult to make a significant income as your only business.

Choosing a Platform

Should you develop for Android or iOS? Both? There are advantages and disadvantages to all three options. You will have to consider your app audience, market size, how committed you are to making a successful app, and what your goals are in publishing an app. Each of the three options will be considered in this section.

> ## What about Windows Phone and Blackberry?
>
> If you're a whiz at ASP.NET development, or you really enjoy the experience of a great physical keyboard available on a Blackberry, you may ask yourself, why not develop for Windows Phone or Blackberry as well? Although it may be easy to start developing apps for Windows Phone if you're very comfortable with Visual Studio, C#, and .NET, the market share of the Windows Phone operating system means that you will not have very many potential customers for your apps. Blackberry and Windows Phone are both below 5% market share, so your efforts are likely better spent making sure you have developed great iOS and Android apps.

Android has the biggest market share in terms of devices sold. Therefore, it also has the biggest potential for app sales. However, much of the market growth is outside the United States. Your app would have to have universal appeal to take advantage of the growth. A second problem with the Android smartphone market is that although the market is big, many of the owners of these phones primarily use them as "dumb phones." They are not a likely market for your app. Finally, Android app users are much less willing to pay for an app than their iPhone compatriots are. Studies have shown that each iOS user spends about three times as much on apps as an Android user. On the other hand, some industry segments you might target may have a tendency to use Android devices at a much greater rate than iOS devices. In particular, small businesses, such as the fence builder industry discussed in Chapter 1, "Why Mobile Apps?," are primarily Android users, and the potential to develop apps for these industries is very large.

Android has an advantage in that the barrier to entry is lower for the casual developer than it is for iOS. The fee to be a developer is a one-time fee, and all the tools are free. You can develop Android apps on either Windows or Mac computers. Finally, publishing an app is relatively easy. If you want to publish apps for fun, for bragging rights, or to demonstrate your credentials as a developer, Android is a good choice.

Although the iOS market is smaller than the Android market, people get iPhones because they want to use the apps. They are much more likely to look for apps to use, and iPhone users are also much more willing to pay for an app. This makes selling an app using the simple paid approach, as well as the in-app purchase approach discussed earlier, much more feasible. Whereas Android has a higher market share overall, iOS has about 65% market share in the enterprise market, and several large providers like IBM, SAP, and Cisco Systems have made significant investments in enterprise apps for iOS. On the other hand, Apple charges a higher annual fee to be a developer; the publishing process is more complicated, and is in no way guaranteed. Finally, you must have a Mac to use Xcode to create your app. You cannot create an iOS app on a Windows machine.

Why not publish on both? If you are trying to make money from apps, this is probably the way to go. You get access to a larger market and thus more potential revenue generation. In addition, after you've gone through the effort of designing a user experience, user interface, and logic to create an app for one platform, you can leverage that effort by creating an app for the other environment. You will have to completely recode the app, but coding is much easier if you already know what you want the app to do. Also, many of the control structures are almost identical on the two platforms (e.g., a `for` loop), so much of the code structure can be copied directly between the code files. You will have to learn both development environments in depth, but you've got a good start from what you have learned by completing this book. The primary problem with targeting both markets is that you will have to keep your app current on both platforms. This means more work just to keep the lights on.

Summary

You can make money from mobile apps in several ways. Revenue can be generated through monetization of the app itself using ads, in-app purchase, or charging for the download. If you choose to generate revenue from your apps, you should create a limited liability corporation for both tax and liability purposes. You can also make money by coding apps for other people or organizations as a consultant or freelancer. Finally, money can be made by getting hired as an app developer in a larger company. This is a much more reliable source of income than any of the other approaches.

Exercises

1. Add an ad to the ContactListActivity in the Android version of MyContactList. Be sure to set the test device id if you want to test it. Try this in the iOS version as well.

2. Write a brief business plan for MyContactList. How would you monetize the app? Who is the market?

3. What kind of app do you want to make? Who is the target audience? How will you monetize it? Why would somebody want your app? How difficult would it be to make?

CHAPTER 16

Publishing Apps

Creating an app can be a fun and challenging exercise, but for most developers, this is not enough. The finished app has to be available for someone to use to complete the process. Apps are made available to their audience by publishing them. The manner of publication is dependent on the target audience and the platform. The two primary audiences are typically the employees of an organization for which the app was developed or the public. Many aspects of publishing are the same for both audiences. However, some important differences exist that the developer needs to be aware of. Likewise, publishing Android versus iOS apps can be very similar, but with some significant differences. One of the most important differences from publishing traditional desktop software is that the ways to publish mobile apps are much more restricted. For consumer apps, there are gatekeepers in the form of app stores that you will have to interact with to distribute your app. In this chapter, you learn the basics of publishing apps for both consumer and enterprise audiences and both platforms.

App Distribution through the App/Play Stores

Both Apple and Google provide a marketplace where developers can sell their apps. To publish an app in either of these stores, a developer must configure the app and conform to the requirements established by their sponsors. A significant amount of the work required to publish the app should be done during development. Both Google and Apple have requirements and guidelines for apps that should be incorporated during development. You should read through these guidelines prior to development so that you are not doing a lot of rework just to get the app published. Apple is especially meticulous about these rules. Every app is reviewed before it is published, and if your app does not conform, it will be rejected. The guidelines for Apple's app review are available at https://developer.apple.com/app-store/review/guidelines/, and Google's are at https://play.google.com/about/developer-content-policy/. Google may publish an application that does not meet its store requirements, but will remove the app from the store later if it finds that the app violates its rules.

When you are confident your app meets publication requirements of the marketplace you are targeting, the process of publishing requires several steps in either marketplace and is greatly facilitated by preparing prior to beginning the process. The preparation is similar for both stores. You will need to prepare an icon for your app. Android requires an app icon sized to 512x512, whereas iOS requires the icon to be 1024x1024 pixels. Both platforms require at least one screenshot of your app.

For iOS, you can supply screenshots at the highest resolution your app supports, but taking differences in user interface into account. For instance, if your app supports split screen on iPhone 7 or 7 Plus, you may need to provide a separate screenshot at that resolution in addition to lower-resolution images for the iPhone SE. The exact dimensions of the screenshots also depend on a number of factors, such as whether the app shows status bars.

If you are targeting tablets, you also will need to provide screenshots. You can provide up to eight screenshots for each targeted Android device and up to four screenshots for each targeted iOS device. For iOS apps, you also have to supply a launch image that matches the resolution for the devices that the app will run on. The launch image is displayed while the app is loading and is intended to help give the impression that the app is launching quickly. It should thus include a blank screen of what the first screen in the app would look like. The launch screen can be set up as a storyboard inside Xcode—in fact, the default project types include a default launchScreen.storyboard for this exact purpose. Using the storyboard, you can create an actual user interface for the launch image, or you can use a static graphic image.

In addition to preparing screenshots, you should also prepare a description of your app. This narrative is presented to potential customers, so you should be as clear as possible in describing exactly what the app is designed to do and why it is advantageous for the customer to buy the app. For iOS apps, you will also have to provide a description of any specific conditions or requirements that the tester will need to know to adequately review your app.

Other considerations prior to beginning the publication process include determining what price you want to charge for the app. In Android, you enter this price. In iOS, you will be prompted to select from a set of pricing tiers. You should also determine what general category best describes the app (e.g., game, sports, tool, and so on) because you will have to indicate this during the publishing process. Finally, you will need to determine in which countries your app should be made available. And if your app is truly international, you should also consider adding internationalization support to the app, including translation, support for different currencies, number formatting, units of measurements, and so on.

After you have completed the previous steps, you are ready to publish. Although there are many similarities, each store has its own process and requirements. Additionally, these processes change frequently. You should study the specific description of the procedure in the developer documentation for each platform. To get access to these resources for iOS, go to http://developer.apple.com. To access Android resources, go to http://developer.android.com/distribute.

Android Play Store Distribution

The Google Play Store does not provide any copy protection for your app. Instead, Google provides a Licensing Library, which allows developers to add copy protection to their apps. The Licensing Library needs to be added to the workspace just like the Google Play Services library was added (Chapter 7, "Maps and Location in Android"). After the library is added, search the developer site for detailed instructions for adding licensing to your app. When you add licensing to an app, each time the user opens the app, the Play Store is queried to determine whether the user bought the app. If the user did not buy the app, the developer can have the app close or take whatever action is deemed appropriate. If you do not use licensing, your app can be copied to other devices quite easily.

After you have added licensing (if you want to), the app needs to be compiled into a signed Android application package (APK) file. Prior to compiling the app, you need to go through the code and remove any logging operations, all debug breakpoints, and address as many of the warnings identified by Android Studio as you think necessary. To create a signed APK (which is required by the Play Store), you need to set a private key. Fortunately, you can create your private key while completing the process to generate a signed APK.

1. Click **Build** > **Generate Signed APK…** If you do not have a release key, you can create one here. If you do, you must select it here (Figure 16.1). Click **Create new…**

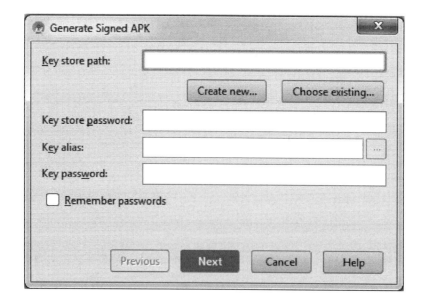

Figure 16.1   Generate a signed APK for release.

2. The **New Key Store** window will open (Figure 16.2). Click the **…** button after the **Key store path** field. In the window that opens, navigate to the folder where you want to store the keystore and then enter a name for the keystore at the bottom of the window. Click **OK**. You will return to the **New Key Store** window with the

keystore name and path entered. Enter and confirm a **password**. Next, for the alias, use the **keystore name you entered concatenated with alias**. For example, the alias for the keystore named mykeystore would be mykeystorealias. Enter another **password** for the alias. Enter the number of **years** you want this key to be valid. Finally, fill in any company information you want and click **OK** (see Figure 16.2).

Figure 16.2 Creating a new keystore.

3. The **New Key Store** window closes and the **Generate Signed APK** window is displayed filled in with the key information (Figure 16.3).

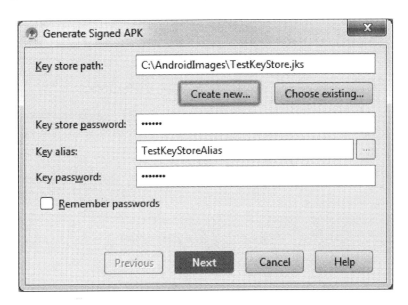

Figure 16.3 Configured key.

4. Click **Next**. By default, the generated APK is saved in the same location as the project (Figure 16.4). Use the ... button if you wish to change this. Click **Finish**. The signed APK can be created and stored in the specified location. This APK will be uploaded to the Play Store during the publishing process.

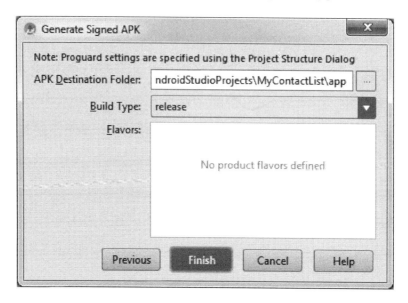

Figure 16.4 Select APK location.

An app is published through the Developer Console (https://play.google.com/apps/publish/). To publish apps, you need to sign up as a Google developer. The cost is a one-time fee of $25, which must be paid from a Google Wallet account. If you are going to sell your apps, you will need this account for payments. The account can be set up through the console. After you have set up all your accounts, you are ready to publish!

After setup, the Developer Console displays all the apps you have published. To start, click the + Add New Application button at the top of the screen. You will be prompted to choose the default language and title of your app. Then you can choose to either Upload APK or Prepare Store Listing. It doesn't matter which one you do first. You have to do both eventually.

The left side of the console has a menu with five choices: APK, Store Listing, Pricing & Distribution, In-app Products, and Services & APIs. You have to complete the first three to publish your app. The steps in each are fairly self-explanatory but very detailed, so we will not explain them line by line. The APK menu item is where you upload your app APK. You can upload it for production, or for alpha or beta testing. Alpha testing is usually done by your developers, and beta testing is performed after alpha test by real users. To use either of these features you have to set up a Google Group or Google+ Community. If you upload for testing, it will not be available to the public, but you, your developers, or selected users can test its performance as a user would experience it. The Store Listing menu item is where you provide product details, such as its description and screenshots. You must also categorize the app and provide contact details for you or your company. Finally, in the Pricing and Distribution area, you provide the price for the app and specify the countries where you want to sell it.

When you've completed all three of these items, a green check mark will appear next to each one. You can publish it using the button at the top right of the console. The publishing process takes a few hours before your app appears in the Play Store. Congratulations! You are now in the Android business.

iOS App Store Distribution

The Apple App Store provides strong controls over illegal copying of your app. As a developer, unlike in Android, you don't have to worry about setting up any licensing. However, the built-in copy protection requires other additional work to get your app published. The first step is to set up your Distribution Certificate and Distribution Provisioning Profile (Chapter 9, "Using Xcode for iOS Development"). The next step is to set up an entry for your app in iTunes Connect (https://itunesconnect.apple.com). You will have to use your developer ID to sign in. iTunes Connect is the website that is used to manage many aspects of your app, including seeing reports on how the app is performing.

In iTunes Connect, you provide information about the app, pricing, and screenshots prior to being able to upload the app. To start, click Manage Your Apps in the console. In this section, you can add iOS or Mac OS X apps, depending on your developer license. Click Add New App. If you have a Mac Developer account, you will be asked to select either iOS App or Mac OS X app. Select iOS app.

The App Information screen requires selecting the default language of the app, entering the app name, entering a SKU number, and selecting the Bundle ID. The SKU number is a unique number used to identify your app. A standard approach is to concatenate the year of publication, the number of the app in your stock, and the version number. For example, your first app could be 201700010001. For Bundle ID, it is best to select Xcode iOS Wildcard AppID and then enter the app name in Bundle ID Suffix. The Bundle ID Suffix must match the name that is entered as the last part of the Bundle Identifier in the Project Summary in Xcode. For the MyContactList app, the Bundle ID you used was com.mycompany.MyContactList. The Bundle ID Suffix is MyContactList for this app. When it's complete, click the Continue button.

The next section is too detailed to go through in depth here. In this section, you provide an app description, screenshots, icon, rating and categorization, and specific review information, much like you did for your Android app. Once it is complete and you click the Save button, you will get a summary screen for the app. The app status should be listed as Prepare for Upload. Click View Details below the app icon, and then click Ready to Upload Binary at the top right of the next screen. You will be asked to verify that your app is compliant with export laws if it contains any cryptography. Choose the answer that fits your app and click Save, and then Continue. Your app status is now Waiting for Upload. Open your app in Xcode to complete the process.

When your app is open in Xcode, do the following to upload the app to iTunes Connect:

1. Change the active scheme from the simulator to **iOS Device** in the upper-left corner of Xcode (see Figure 16.3).

Figure 16.5 Changed scheme to iOS Device.

2. Select **Product > Archive** from the menu. An archive file will be compiled and the **Organizer** opens (see Figure 16.6).

3. In the Organizer, make sure the **latest archive file** is selected and click the **Validate** button. If you have not set up the app correctly in iTunes Connect, you will get an error and will have to go back to the website to correct any problems. Otherwise, it asks you to log in with your developer ID, and validation will begin. This may take a while. If you get a message that there are no issues, you are ready to submit to the App Store.

4. Click the **Distribute** button. Click the **Submit to App Store** option button. Click **Next**.

5. Enter your **developer login information**. (It may already be there.) Select an **identity**. The identity is your **Distribution Profile** you created earlier. It may already be filled in. If so, check to make sure that it is your Distribution Profile. Click the **Next** button. You will get a message "Your application is being uploaded." This may take a while. When it is complete, you will get a success message. Your app is now waiting to be reviewed by Apple.

Figure 16.6 Xcode Archive Organizer.

The app review process is very thorough and may take several weeks to complete. After the app is accepted, it will be available for purchase. If it is rejected, Apple will inform you of the reason and give you a chance to correct the problems. Generally, your first app takes the longest to get reviewed. Future apps typically get a less-thorough review because you have demonstrated that you can conform to the App Store requirements. Congratulations! You are now in the iOS app business.

App Distribution for the Enterprise

App distribution within an organization differs between iOS and Android. Generally, distribution is easier because you are not required to conform to the specifications of the Play or App stores.

Android Enterprise Distribution

Distributing Android apps within an organization is very easy. You prepare an APK just like you did for the Play Store, and then you give it to your users. The easiest way to do this is by sending users an e-mail with the APK attached. If users open the e-mail on an Android device, the device automatically asks if they want to install it. However, for this to occur, users must have set their device to accept apps from unknown sources. To do this, go to the Settings app on the Android device and check the box next to Unknown Sources. Unfortunately, this item is not located in exactly the same spot in Settings on every Android device. Some common locations are under Applications or Security.

Another approach would be to set up an internal website to distribute the app. Again, the user must check the box next to Unknown Sources. Although these are the two most common approaches, because Android is open, you can choose whatever method works for your organization.

Many organizations also implement mobile device management (MDM) solutions to manage their mobile devices and app distribution. These systems can help organizations implement security controls on devices owned by employees as well as devices owned by the enterprise. In addition, they can also be used to distribute both in-house and purchased apps to users. A detailed discussion of MDM is well beyond the scope of this book.

iOS Enterprise Distribution

Distribution of apps within the organization is a bit more complicated in iOS than it is in Android. The first step is to get an iOS Enterprise Developer license. The cost of the license is $299 per year but allows unlimited distribution of apps within the organization. You cannot sell apps in the App Store with this license. Organizations that want to do both internal and public development need both an Enterprise Developer license and an iOS Developer license.

Distributing within the organization requires setting up both an enterprise distribution certificate and an enterprise distribution provisioning profile. These are then packaged with the app using Xcode. There is no need to use iTunes Connect with in-house apps. However, the provisioning profile expires after a year. Prior to that time, a new profile must be created, packaged with the app, and redistributed, or the app will stop working.

After an app is compiled with the appropriate certificate and profile, it can be distributed through third-party MDM, systems or the app file can be sent directly to the users for installation.

Testing and Fragmentation

Testing is a critical component of app development. This is especially true for Android because of the wide array of devices that the operating system is installed on. However, it is critical that apps developed on either platform be tested on real devices prior to release. Testing an app is very much like testing any other piece of software in that a comprehensive test plan must be established and followed. Testing should also be performed by individuals outside the development team.

A comprehensive test plan should include thorough black box unit testing, including equivalence partitioning, boundary value analysis, and cause-effect graphing. Fortunately, the innate organization of apps into individual screens makes it easy to test each screen as a unit. To use equivalence partitioning in a screen, identify all the possible outcomes of the user interaction with the screen and identify the input or other data that would lead to that outcome. For example, in the ContactActivity screen in the MyContactList app, there would be nine possible outcomes (refer back to Figure 2.7). Each navigation button opens the corresponding screen, the Toggle button enables and disables editing, the Save button saves the contact, the Picture button opens the camera and returns a photo, the Phone buttons open the phone app and dial the correct number, and the Change Birthdate button changes the birthday. Each of these outcomes should be tested in every iteration of the app.

In boundary value analysis, the limits for each input should be identified, and each side of the limit should be tested. Again, using the ContactActivity screen as an example, one limit might be that the app shouldn't store birthdays that are a future date. A test for this limit would enter a date equal to the date the app is being tested and the next day. The today's date test should be displayed; the next day's date should result in an error message. Other boundary values for this screen might include entering too many and too few digits for a telephone number.

Finally, in cause-effect graphing, each outcome identified in equivalence partitioning is examined to identify the possible paths that could lead to the expected outcome. For example, the Save button on the ContactActivity screen should either save the contact or alert the user to any errors that may have caused the save to fail. Should the contact be saved only if all the inputs on the screen have data, or is some subset acceptable? Will the app save only a name? If a street address is entered, are the city and state required? All possible combinations that lead to either a saved contact or an error message should be tested.

The testing just described may initially be performed on the Android Emulator or the iOS Simulator, but it should also be performed on an actual device. This is especially true for apps that access the hardware features of the device. Apps that use location or other sensors cannot be adequately tested in either the Android Emulator or the iOS Simulator.

After all the unit tests have been passed successfully, the app should be tested for usability. The ability to provide help and/or training in the use of your app is extremely limited. Users should be able to figure out how to use it with relative ease. This requires testing by someone unfamiliar with the app. Developers have a relatively difficult time testing this themselves because they are too familiar with the way the app should work. Both Google and Apple provide extensive guidelines for human-computer-interaction (HCI) design that you should study and follow to help ensure the app is easy to use.

The final set of tests requires access to a variety of devices. Because of the large number of manufacturers that provide Android devices, this is a much more difficult problem in Android than in iOS. For Android, you should have at least one device that runs the minimum SDK and one that runs the target SDK. You also should have one device for each screen size supported by your app. (You can limit screen size in the manifest like you did for minimum and target SDK.) This set of devices should be considered the minimum number required. If possible, you should also test devices from different manufacturers. There are differences, and these can cause interesting problems. There are companies that for a fee will help test your app on a range of different devices. However, you can also use market share data about what devices and OS versions are most prevalent in the market you are targeting. For example, if your app would not be relevant to users outside of your own country, you can focus your efforts on the devices that are actually in use in your country.

Why Did That Happen?

One of our Android apps uses a standard list similar to what you have seen in Chapter 6, "Lists in Android: Navigation and Information Display." The app worked fine. Then we started getting complaints from users who had a new phone from a specific manufacturer. The manufacturer had made some changes that required a specific attribute value in the ListItem to display properly. Although this change couldn't have been foreseen by us, it does illustrate the need to test on multiple devices.

The iOS world has a much more limited set of devices, and the platform is more standardized between devices. However, Apple has continued to increase the variability of hardware specs across its lineup, so it is increasingly important to test on as many devices as possible. For example, if your app supports 3D Touch, you need to make sure to test on devices that support this technology and devices that don't.

Keeping Up with the Platform

Both Apple and Google make changes to their respective operating systems on a regular basis. This can be challenging for developers with apps "in the wild." Updates to the operating system can and, although infrequently, do disrupt apps that previously ran fine. To avoid problems with users of your app or to prevent getting bad reviews in the app stores, it pays to keep on top of platform changes.

Keeping up with changes to the OS is not rocket science, but it does require diligence. At a minimum, as soon as the new OS is released, you should recompile your app to include the new version as a target. Correct any errors that occur when you do this, until you get a new version that can be tested on the emulator or simulator. Once it is running well there, run it on an actual device with the updated OS installed and run through your complete test plan to ensure that it works on that device. Finally, test the new version of your app on a device running an older version of the OS. When you are satisfied that your app works, release an upgrade to the app through the appropriate app store.

Beyond the bare minimum previously outlined, as a registered developer you also have access to prerelease software so you can test your app in advance of the general release to the public. For instance, Apple typically releases the first beta version of a new version of iOS and Xcode at its WWDC conference in June, several months before the public release in September. Because most iOS users update their devices very quickly after the public release, it is very important that you have tested your app thoroughly before the release.

Why Did That Happen? (Continued)

One of our Android apps uses GPS coordinates from the device to record information. After a new release to the OS, any app that was running on an updated device would "Force Close" almost immediately after the app opened. A "Force Close" is a cardinal sin in the Android world, and users will quickly come to hate your app if it happens even infrequently. This was a difficult problem because the app ran on the emulator and on many devices, but not those with the updated OS! The only way we could figure it out was to run debug with Eclipse (used in an earlier version of ths book), connected to a phone with the updated OS, and step through the code line by line. It turned out that the new OS was reporting the GPS coordinates in a slightly different manner than older versions did. We had to modify the code to handle both situations to get the app to run on both the new and older OS. This problem was not detectable by just recompiling the app to use the new SDK.

Summary

Publishing apps have both similarities and differences in Android and iOS. They both require the same type of information to be entered for the app that is to be sold. However, the exact procedure is different. Prior to publication of an app, thorough testing is required. An app that crashes frequently or does not do what it says it does will not pass the Apple review process. An Android app that has the same problems may be allowed to be published, but it will get bad reviews and may be eventually removed by Google. After you have published apps, it is imperative that you keep up with platform changes. New versions of the OS can create problems for apps that currently run perfectly.

Exercises

1. Compile the Android version of MyContactList for release. Send an e-mail to yourself or a friend with the APK attached. Install it on the Android device.

2. Write a test plan for the ContactList screen for both the Android and iOS platforms. How are they similar? Different?

3. Look up the app publication policies for Android and iOS. Describe any similarities and differences between them.

APPENDICES

Fixing Code Issues Using Android Studio

Android Studio is an Integrated Development Environment (IDE) that provides many tools to support the development of Android apps. The book has used many of these tools in the development of the MyContactList app. However, there are many tools in the IDE that help the developer produce robust code that both conforms to Android conventions and performs well. In this appendix, we will demonstrate how to use the Inspect Code tool to improve our finished app.

Improving the Code

While striving to produce "bulletproof" code is every developer's objective, often when we get down in the weeds of development, we take shortcuts, try things and forget them, ignore conventions, and skip other good coding practice just to get the app working. If we forget to go back and correct these issues, it can lead to an app that does not perform as expected once we get it in the hands of the user. The Inspect Code in Android Studio can help us correct these oversights.

Analyzing the Code

The first step is to run the inspection tool. This is relatively easy since it is just a menu selection. From the top line menu choose **Analyze > Inspect Code....** The **Specify Inspection Scope** dialog will be displayed (Figure A.1). Using this dialog, you can narrow the scope of the analysis. The scope can be narrowed by limiting what files are inspected in the project or by what types of things the inspector looks for. The inspection of the code takes some time so with larger apps you may want to limit the scope to reduce the amount of time you have to wait. Since the MyContactList app is not that big, choose **Whole project**. Since we do not use unit tests, deselect **Include test sources**. Click **OK**.

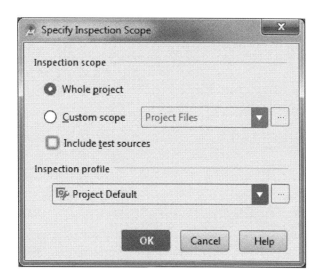

Figure A.1 Inspection scope dialog.

The **Inspecting Code...** progress dialog will be displayed (Figure A.2). This shows the tests being run and the files being processed as the inspection proceeds. If you would like to continue working on things in the app while you wait for the results you can click Background button.

Figure A.2   Inspecting code progress dialog.

When the inspection is complete, the results will be displayed in the Inspection panel at the bottom left of the IDE (Figure A.3). The top line identifies the total number of issues found and below that are a categorized list of these issues. The first set of categories is any **Lint** issues found. Lint is a tool included with Android studio that identifies potential structural issues with the code. These issues include problems with reliability, efficiency, and maintainability with your code. After the Lint issues are other issues that may impact the app's ability to perform as intended, including potential bugs and class structure issues.

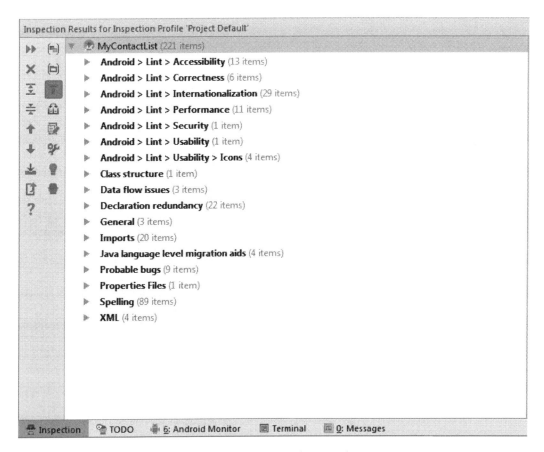

Figure A.3   Inspection results.

Fixing Issues

The code inspection can also support fixing the identified issues. The inspection panel can be used to address an issue ranging from just opening the file with the problem to actually correcting the error. Click the **disclosure** arrow to the left of **Android > Lint > Correctness**. Then click the **arrow** to disclose the items in **Missing commit()....** Finally, open the items under **ContactSettingsActivity.java** and select the select the first line that reads **Consider using 'apply()'...** (Figure A.4).

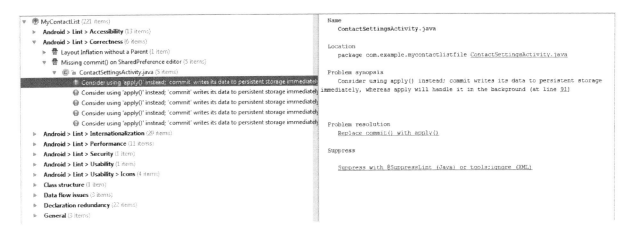

Figure A.4 Using the inspector to identify and fix issues.

A panel will open to the right of the inspection results panel that will explain the issue, identify where it occurs (both file and line), and suggest a problem resolution. Finally, the window will provide an option to suppress reporting of the issue. Use this option sparingly, if at all. You want to know of any potential problems!

To fix this issue, first click the **line number** in the **Problem synopsis** section. The file will open, and the cursor will be placed on the line with the error in it. Examine the line of code and then click **Replace commit() with apply()** in the **Problem resolution** section. Notice that the code is changed. If you understand, the problem and suggested resolution, you can skip opening the file and just click the suggested resolution. However, if you do not, you should examine the problem and suggested resolution closely. Some suggested resolutions will make your code operate different from intended. This likely means you need to examine the problem in more detail before you address a fix.

Next, open the **Imports** issue in the **Inspection panel**. Drill down to **Unused Imports > ContactActivity.java** and select the first **Unused import** line. Unused imports occur when you delete code that required an import. The import is not automatically removed when all code that requires the import is removed from the file. While unused imports do not have an impact at runtime, they can slow compilation and lead to code that is more difficult to maintain. In the **Resolution panel**, click **Delete unnecessary import**. Note that the issue is removed from the Inspection panel and the next issue is highlighted. You can go through all the unused imports in this manner to clean up your code.

While this appendix is not intended to show you how to fix all the issues in the app, we will address one more item. Drill down in **Android > Lint > Internationalization** through **Hardcoded text to app** and select the first **Hardcoded string** issue. As noted in the core of the book, Android prefers text to be stored in a resource file and then referred to in the code. This allows you to run a program to change the language of the app by changing the language in the resource file. You can do this by creating resource files for all the languages you want your app to be readable in. Click the **line number** in the **Problem synopsis** section in the **Resolution panel**.

The XML file that contains the hardcoded text will be opened, and the line with the text (android:text=) will be highlighted. Select the **text** between the quotation marks and press **Alt-Enter**. A dialog will open (Figure A.5) that gives options on how to address the issue.

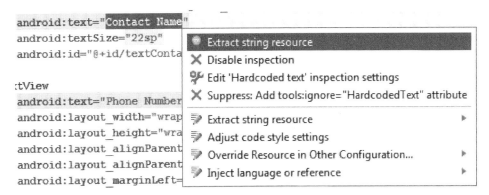

Figure A.5 Fixing hardcoded text.

Click **Extract string resource**. The **Extract Resource** dialog will be displayed. Note that the Resource value is the highlighted text, and the Resource name suggestion matches the text but is all lowercase and does not have spaces in it. You can change the name if you wish but do not change the value. Click **OK**. Note that `android:text="Con-tact Name"` is now `android:text="@string/contact_name"`. The actual value is now stored as a resource with the name `contact_name` in the strings.xml file in the values folder, and its value for the layout is pulled from there. Open **the strings.xml** file to see this resource value.

The Inspection results will often update as you correct the issues. However, many times these will not. Once you have fixed a number of issues, it may be necessary to run the inspection again to see what you have left to correct.

APPENDIX B

ConstraintLayouts in Android

Constrained Layouts are a new addition to Android. These layouts are similar to Relative Layouts, in that all widgets are positioned with respect to other UI elements. However, they are purported to be more flexible than Relative Layout, and Android Studio's layout editor is designed to support the creation of the layout without need to edit the XML directly. They allow a flatter design without the need for nested layouts. In the past, more complex UI designs required the developer to nest layouts within layouts to get the look required for the app. Nesting layouts can have an impact on processing efficiency, and thus ConstraintLayout provides a potential solution. Note that depending on the speed of your machine, this tutorial may be frustrating. Updating the layouts as you make changes often significantly lags your operations. Additionally, the ConstaintLayout is in beta. We found that at times the exact same sequence of steps leads to different results. If you are unsuccessful with placing a widget after several attempts, it may be easiest to delete the widget and start over.

Download and Install ConstraintLayout

The ConstraintLayout is not currently a part of the standard Android SDK and must be installed separately. The first step is to get the components with the SDK Manager. Choose **Tools > Android >SDK Manager**. When the SDK Manager opens, select the **SDK Tools** tab and open **Support Repository**. Select **ConstraintLayout for Android** and **Solver for ConstraintLayout**. Next, click **Show Package Details** and note the version (currently at 1.0.0-beta4). Click **OK** and then choose accept and click **Finish**. The next step is to add a dependency in your app so that you can use the layout. Open **build.gradle (Module:app)**. Add the following line in the dependencies section:

```
compile 'com.android.support.constraint:constraint-layout:1.0.0-beta4'
```

You will now need to sync the gradle files. Click **Sync Now** at the top right of the screen. Once the sync is complete, you can begin working with ConstraintLayout.

Creating a UI with ConstraintLayout

To demonstrate the use of ConstraintLayout, we will rebuild the layout for the Settings activity using this type of layout as the root rather than RelativeLayout. Right-click on the **layout folder** in the Project Explorer and select **New > Layout resource file**. In the **New Resource File** window, type the name as **activity_settings_constraint** and type the **Root** element as **android.support.constraint.ConstraintLayout**. Click **OK**. The layout editor will open. If you get a rendering problem, click **refresh** (look for it in the rendering error message). Once you get a full layout, you are ready to begin.

For your layout design to work correctly, each widget must have a minimum of one horizontal and one vertical constraint. Constraints are relative to other widgets or the parent layout. To start, drag a **TextView** to the layout. Your screen should look similar to Figure B.1. Working with ConstraintLayout requires working with the Blueprint view and the properties window to the right of it.

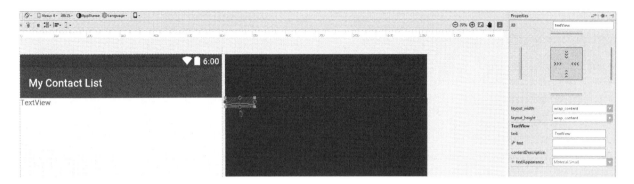

Figure B.1 ConstraintLayout with TextView.

Note the blue dots on each edge of the TextView in the Blueprint. These are the points where constraints are attached to the widget and are referred to as the constraint handles. Center your pointer in the **center of the top constraint handle**. Click and hold and **drag** toward the top of the blueprint. This is a little touchy. You want the constraint to point to the dashed line. When you get it there, the TextView should move down a little. Next, do the same with the **left constraint handle**. When done correctly, your blueprint should look like Figure B.2. Don't worry if it didn't work right the first time. It is fairly easy to redo the constraint. Just click and release in the constraint handle you want to change. The existing constraint will be removed, and you can try again. Note that sometimes it is easier to work in the design rather than the blueprint view. If you are having trouble placing constraints using blueprint, try the design view. It works the same way.

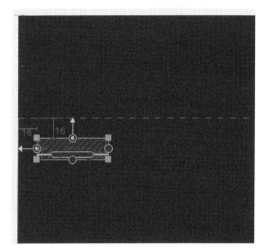

Figure B.2 TextView with initial constraints.

Notice that the distance from the top and left defaults to 16dp. In the MyContactList app, this distance was set to 15dp. This is easy to change. Click in the **TextView** and then click on one of the **16s** displayed at the top of the **Properties panel** on the right. Enter 15 for each constraint. Enter **textSortContact** as the id for the widget in the textbox above where you changed the distance for the constraint. Enter **Sort Contacts by:** in the Text textbox below the constraint display in the Properties panel.

Now drag a **RadioGroup** to the blueprint. Repeat the previous process, except make the top constraint point to the bottom of the **TextView**. Set the left constraint dimension to **35dp** and the top dimension to **10dp**, rather than the default 16. Also, at the top of the Properties panel, change the Id to **radioGroupSortBy**. Note that when you drag the RadioGroup to the blueprint, it will partially cover the TextView. It is probably easiest to position the top constraint first; otherwise the editor isn't sure if you are trying to attach the left constraint to the parent or the TextView. Once you have the RadioGroup positioned, grab the **lower right corner square** on the widget. The squares are **resize handles**. Resize the RadioGroup as shown in Figure B.3. The size is temporary, so don't worry about the exact size.

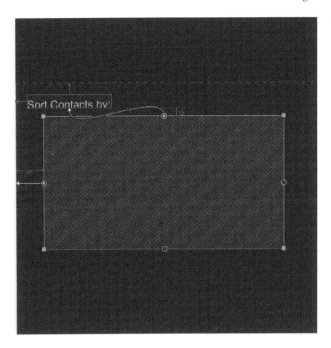

Figure B.3   Resized RadioGroup.

Next, grab a **RadioButton** and drag it onto the **RadioGroup** in the **Component Tree** (Figure B.4). Depending on the speed of your machine, the RadioButton may not look like it's positioned correctly. Ignore that for now and change the id to **radioName** and the text to **Name** in the Properties panel. A RadioGroup is a LinearLayout, so there are no constraints to be used on widgets placed inside it. The only way to ensure the correct order is to examine the Component Tree. Drag two more **buttons** to the **RadioGroup** in the **Component Tree**. Change their Ids to **radioCity** and **radioBirthday** and text to **City** and **Birthday**. Once you have completed adding all the radio button operations, click on the **RadioGroup** widget. In the Properties panel, change the **layout_width** and **layout_height** to **wrap_content**. Again, the display may not look correct, but as long as the radio buttons appear under the radio group in the component tree, it will display correctly.

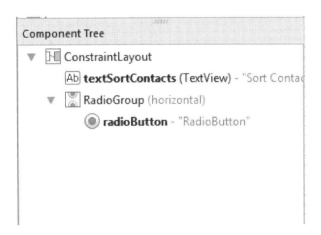

Figure B.4   RadioButton properly placed in the Component Tree.

Drag another **TextView** to the blueprint below the **RadioGroup**. Drag the **top constraint** to the RadioGroup and set the distance to **15dp**. Drag the **left constraint** to the edge screen and set the distance to **15dp**. Change its Id to **textSortOrder** and Text to **Sort Order:**. Add another **RadioGroup** and two **RadioButtons**, like you did for the first RadioGroup. Set the **top constraint** of the RadioGroup to **10dp** below the **Textview** and the **left constraint** to **35dp**. Give it an id of **radioGroupSortOrder**. Give the first RadioButton the id **radioAscending** and the second **radioDescending**. Give the two buttons the text **Ascending** and **Descending**, respectively. Finally, click on the **RadioGroup** and change the height and width to **wrap_content**.

The final step is to add the navigation bar. Drag a **ConstraintLayout** from the Layout section of the Palette to somewhere near the bottom of the blueprint. Click the **bottom constraint handle** of the layout and drag to the **bottom of the blueprint**. Change the distance from 16dp to **0dp**. Next, grab the **right constraint handle** and drag to the right side of the screen. Change the distance to **0dp**. Now grab the **left constraint handle** and drag to the **left side of the screen**. Change the distance to **0dp**. Click the **Show Constraints** button on the toolbar above the design view (which looks like an eye), and your display should now look similar to Figure B.5.

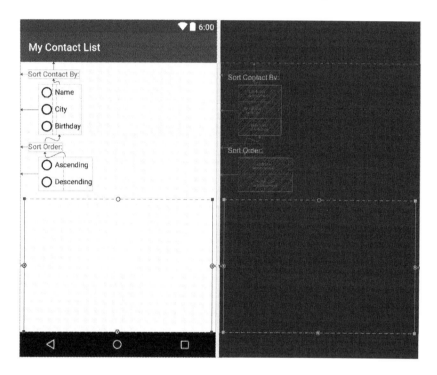

Figure B.5 Initial placement of navbar.

Change the width of the layout to **match_parent** and height to **100dp**. Note that sometimes changing this causes the other size to change. If the layout disappears, click on it in the component tree and change back to **match_parent** and **100dp** height. Now we are going to add the background color. Click **View all properties** at the bottom of the **Properties panel**. Locate the **background property** and click on it. Then click the **...** on the right to the left of the wrench symbol. The **Resources dialog** window will open. Click on the **Color** tab on the left side and then type **navbar** in the search box. Double-click **navbar_background**. Scroll to the bottom of the Properties panel and click **View fewer properties**. Verify that the left, right, and bottom constraint remain 0.

The next step is to add the ImageButtons to the navigation bar. Drag an **ImageButton** into the **navigation bar** (on design view, blueprint view, or component tree). The **Resource dialog** will display. Verify that the **Drawable** tab is selected, and type **mapicon** in the Search box. Double-click **mapicon**. Note that the icon may not display. Verify that the ImageButton is indented in the new layout in the Component Tree. If it is not, drag it there. Select the **ConstraintLayout** in the **Component Tree** and then change its width property to **wrap_content**. Grab the **right constraint handle** of the **ImageButton** and drag to the **right side of the screen**. It will likely move all the way to the right of the layout. Then grab the **left constraint handle** and drag to the **left side of the screen**. Your display should look similar to Figure B.6.

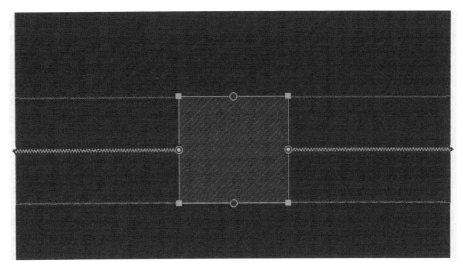

Figure B.6   Placement of ImageButton.

Select the **ConstraintLayout** and note that both constraint lines are squiggly and extend to each edge. The squiggly lines occur when you have two opposing constraints. The initial placement for a widget with opposing constraints is centered. This placement can be changed by changing the **Horizontal Bias** in the **Properties panel**. Make sure the **ImageButton** is selected, and look at the **Properties panel** below the constraint diagram and above layout_width. You should see a bar with a circle and the number 50 in the middle of it (Figure B.7). The 50 indicates that each constraint equal weight and the widget will be centered. If you drag the circle to the right or left, you can change this bias so that the widget is to one side or the other. While you're looking at the Properties panel, change the Id to **imageButtonMap**. Make sure you leave the Horizontal Bias at **50**.

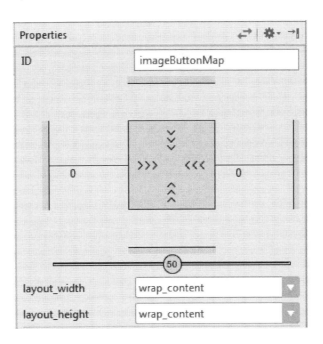

Figure B.7   Horizontal Bias specification.

Drag another **ImageButton** to the navigation bar **ConstraintLayout** to the left of the map **ImageButton**. It should show up on the blueprint to the left of the map button. Choose **contactlisticon** as the drawable for this button and give it the Id **imageButtonList**. Next grab the **right constraint handle** of the new ImageButton and drag it to the **left constraint handle on the map button.**

The new button should move toward the map button. Change its margin from 8 to **20**. If the new button is not aligned vertically with the map button, click on it and drag up or down until it is. Repeat this procedure for another **ImageButton**. However, place this one to the **right of the map button**. Choose **settingsicon** for its image and drag its **left constraint** to the **right constraint of the map button**. Change the left margin value to **20** and give it an Id of **imageButtonSettings**.

Your layout is ready to be used. Open the **ContactActivitySettings.java** file and change the setContent line in the onCreate method so that the activity uses the new layout:

```
setContentView(R.layout.activity_settings_constraint);
```

Run the program. You should see no difference.

Final Thoughts

ConstraintLayout is still in beta and does not appear to be completely stable. Additionally, if your development machine is not that fast, or if you develop on a virtual machine (like I do), you may find using these layouts are more trouble than they are worth. If the editor cannot change the display fast enough to keep up with your pace of work it is a productivity killer. That said, ConstraintLayout appears to be a great way to configure interfaces without the need to directly code XML. Hopefully future versions of Android Studio and the ConstraintLayout components will become more stable and efficient, and this layout can become an important part of Android app development.

APPENDIX C

Introduction to Swift

If you want to develop an app for iOS, you have two choices for languages: Objective-C and Swift. The former is the traditional language used in the Apple development ecosystem since the late 1980s. The syntax of Objective-C left beginning developers scratching their heads, while the reliance on C often made the language constrained. So when Apple introduced Swift at WWDC in June 2014, developers in the audience became very excited. The language was significantly simplified from Objective-C and thoroughly modern. It won StackOverflow's Most Loved designation in 2015, and was in second place in 2016. It is now considered the default option for any app developed for Apple's operating systems, including iOS, watchOS, macOS, and tvOS.

In this Appendix, you will see how the Swift language works and learn some of the patterns that are required to become a proficient Swift developer.

Getting Started: On the Playground

Along with Swift, Apple also introduced the Playground as a place to experiment and learn the Swift language. In this Appendix, you will use the Playground to explore the language and its features. Throughout the appendix, you are encouraged to experiment on your own by expanding the examples and adding details. As is always the case when learning a programming language, the more you practice and experiment the faster you will learn it. You can find more details about the language in the official guide to the language: https://developer.apple.com/library/content/documentation/Swift/Conceptual/Swift_Programming_Language.

Most questions can also be answered by simple Google searches, which will likely lead you to StackOverflow. As you look for information about the language, you should be aware that the language has changed dramatically since it was released. Swift 3 is the current version, so be aware that code examples you see online may be for Swift 1 and 2, and sometimes those are no longer relevant. Fortunately, Xcode will allow you to check a project for outdated syntax and offer to upgrade to the current version of Swift.

To get started with Swift, create a new Playground in Swift by selecting **File > New > Playground**. Name it **LearningSwift** and choose **iOS** for the Platform. Click **Next**. Select a location for the playground in the next screen and click **Create**. This will create a new editor window where you can enter code and have it execute immediately. Figure C.1 shows the initial Playground with one line added. Go ahead and type that line in.

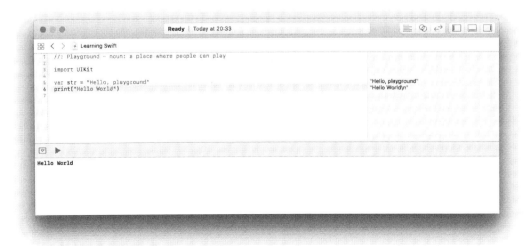

Figure C.1   Playground.

You have created the quintessential first program, Hello World. You'll notice that the `print` statement was not entered inside a method or class. It is in fact a complete program. The right side of the Playground functions like a running debugger and provides useful feedback on the program you're writing. The bottom area is called the Debug area and shows any output from the program. In this case, the Hello World string is output. Usually the Playground executes whenever you make changes to the program, but you can also manually execute it by clicking the blue arrow above the debug area. If the right side bar isn't showing up, make sure it is wide enough to show output by dragging the divider between white and gray to the left. You can also try clicking the blue triangle to execute the code or show/hide the debug area at the bottom.

Variables and Constants

In Swift, variables are declared by using the `var` keyword followed by the name of the variable. Listing C.1 shows a few examples of variables being declared.

Listing C.1   Declaring variables

```
1    var name = "Jane Austen"
2    var age = 42
3    var price = 19.95
4    var salePrice: Double = 25
5    var lastName: String
6    var title: String?
```

This illustrates several properties of variables in Swift

- Swift is strongly typed, but will infer the types of variables, so in line 1, the type of `name` can be inferred to be String because the initial value is set to a String.

- The `age` variable in line 2 is an Int, and price in line 3 is a Double.

- You can also explicitly indicate the type as shown in line 4 where `salePrice` is a Double. This is necessary when the initial value isn't enough to infer the type, or when no initial value can be provided as shown in line 5.

- If a value cannot be specified when the variable is declared, you can declare it as *optional*, as shown in line 6 by adding a question mark after the type. We will discuss optionals in more detail later in this appendix.

Constants are declared in the same way as variables, except by using the keyword `let` instead of `var`. Constants can be declared without an initial value, but once assigned, the value cannot be changed. Swift programmers tend to prefer constants over variables, as they have some performance benefits and leads to safer code. If you know a value isn't going to change, you might as well declare it as a constant.

One curiosity in Swift is that when you make assignments, the whitespace around the equal sign has to be balanced—that is, if you have a single space before the equal sign, you must also have a single space after the equal sign.

Arrays and Dictionaries

You can create arrays very easily by declaring a variable and adding the elements in square brackets as shown in Listing C.2.

Listing C.2   Working with Arrays

```
1    var colors = ["blue", "green", "red"] //Declare an array and assign three values to it
2    let green = colors[1]    //Retrieve the value from the second element and assign it to a constant
3    colors[2] = "white"      //Change the value of the 3rd element
4    colors.append("yellow")  //Add a new element. Have to append to expand the array
5    let numColors = colors.count   //Returns the number of elements in the array
6    let yellow = colors.last     //Retrieve the last element in the array
7    var empty:[Int] = []            //Declare an empty array set to hold only Int values
```

Dictionaries are key-value pairs, which are created in a similar way to arrays as shown in Listing C.3.

Listing C.3   Working with Dictionaries

```
1   var productColor = [String:String]() //Create a new empty dictionary
2   productColor = [                       //Assign values to the dictionary
3       "X12": "blue",
4       "C45": colors[1],
5       "B32": "purple"
6   ]
7   let blue = productColor["X12"]     //Retrieve value from one of the dictionary entries
8   productColor["C45"] = "black"      //Set value for dictionary entry
9   var emptyDict: [String:Float] = [:] //Create an empty dictionary. This notation only works where
                                        //type information can be inferred
```

Note that line 1 shows an alternative approach to creating an empty dictionary to that shown in line 9. The difference between the two is that in line 1, the type information is included at the time the object is created, whereas in line 9, the type information is provided when the variable is declared. When the array is created, the compiler will infer the data types from the declaration, so they don't need to be included. Of course, in this example, it doesn't make much difference whether the type information is on the right or the left of the equal sign, but in cases where the array isn't initialized immediately, or a new array is created later in the code, the notation in line 9 makes more sense.

Control Flow

Swift supports the usual array of control flow statements and loops. Listing C.4 shows an if-else statement. Notice the lack of parentheses around the Boolean expression.

Listing C.4   Example of an If-Else Statement

```
1   if salePrice < 20 {
2       print("What a find!")
3   } else {
4       print("That's expensive!")
5   }
```

Listing C.5 shows an example of a switch statement, which is similar to many other programming languages. It examines a variable (age, in this case), and compares it with a number of different values to find a match. A few things to note about switch statements in Swift:

- You can use ranges to describe the values to compare to, as shown in lines 3, 7, 9, 11, and 13.
- Ranges can be closed (lines 3, 7, 9) or half open (lines 11 and 13). Closed ranges include the values as listed (e.g., values 0, 1, 2, 3, and 4 are all included in line 3), whereas a half open range doesn't include the upper bound (e.g., 130 is not included in the range in line 11).
- Switch statements don't "fall through," so you don't need a break for each case.
- The default clause is optional if the rest of the cases are exhaustive.

The switch statement in Swift is generally more powerful than what is available in other languages, so you should spend some time studying what is available.

Listing C.5   Switch Statement

```
1     var description = ""
2     switch age {
3     case 0...4:
4         description = "toddler"
5     case 5, 6:
6         description = "ready for school"
7     case 7...12:
8         description = "tweenager"
9     case 13...19:
10        description = "teenager"
11    case 20...130:
12        description = "adult"
13    case Int.min..<0:
14        description = "Undefined age"
15    default:
16        description = "Undefined age"
17    }
```

Swift includes three separate loop constructs: while, repeat-while, and for-in. The for-in loop is well suited to iterating over collections, such as arrays and dictionaries. Lines 1–5 in listing C.6 show an example of a for-in loop that goes through an array of numbers and calculates the sum.

Lines 7–9 shows how you can use a range to loop a predetermined number of times. In this case, the loop goes through 10 times. If you enter this code in the Playground, you will see in the right margin how many times each loop is executed.

Listing C.6   Example of For-In Loop

```
1     let prices = [12.34, 34.56, 32.43]
2     var sum:Double = 0
3     for price in prices {
4         sum += price
5     }
6
7     for i in 1...10 {
8         print(i)
9     }
```

The while and repeat-while loops are very similar to what is available in a number of other languages, including Java and C#, so they will not be covered here.

Optional Variables

One of the unique concepts in Swift is that of optional variables. If a variable is declared to be optional, that means that it doesn't have to have a value. This is similar to nil in other languages, but even value types like Int and Booleans can be optional in Swift. Whereas nil in many languages is simply a pointer to nothing, in Swift it is the absence of a value. To declare an optional variable, you simply add a question mark after the data type, like this:

```
var length:Int?
```

You can initialize an optional variable right away, but you don't have to. Once you have declared a variable as optional, you will need to deal with it being optional when you want to access it. This means the compiler will complain if you don't explicitly guard against null-pointer reference errors. When you want to access the optional value, you have two options:

1. Force unwrap the variable.
2. Check whether the variable has an actual value before unwrapping it.

Unwrapping is simply the process of accessing the value of the variable. To force unwrap the value of the optional, you place an exclamation point after the variable name. So you might have code like this:

```
if length! > 9 {
    print ("long")
} else {
    print("short")
}
```

In this case, you tell the compiler not to worry—that there will be a value for length when this code executes. If there isn't a value, the program will crash with this error message:

```
fatal error: unexpectedly found nil while unwrapping an Optional value
```

To check for whether the variable has an actual value, you use a special version of the if statement that can help with ensuring that you always have a value for an optional variable. In the MyContactList app, when a Contact is being displayed on the screen, the contact may have a picture associated with that object. The code for associating the picture with the control looks like this:

```
if let imageData = currentContact?.image as? Data {
    imgContactPicture.image = UIImage(data: imageData)
}
```

This if statement combines a check for whether an optional value has a value with a constant declaration. In this case, currentContact is declared as an optional, but more importantly, the image property value needs to be cast to Data. If there is no value in image, the cast will fail. By using an if let, the cast will only happen if there is an actual value in the image property, and the second line will then be sure to have data to work with. When using the if let statement, the compiler will know that the optional variable can be used safely inside the curly braces of the if let, and will not insist on the exclamation point.

Declaring and Calling Functions

Compared to Objective-C, function declarations in Swift are much easier to read and write, but they are still very flexible and powerful. Figure C.2 shows an example of a function signature that illustrates most of the features of functions in Swift. If you are familiar with methods in Java or C#, this should be relatively well-known to you.

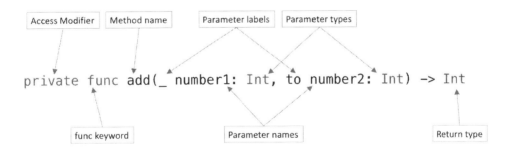

Figure C.2 Method signature.

- Access modifiers are placed in front of the function signature and designates whether functions are private or public to the class they are declared in.
- The func keyword specifies that a function is being declared.
- Parameter names are listed in front of the parameter type separated by a colon.
- Return types are specified at the end of the function signature. If no value is returned, simply omit everything after the parameter parenthesis.

Calling the function provided previously can be done like this:

```
var result = add(number1: 12, number2: 3)
```

This is fairly straightforward, but notice the use of the parameter names. This makes it easier to understand what each parameter means when you call the method.

You can also add labels to functions. Then you declare a function like this:

```
func subtract(number1:Int, from number2:Int) -> Int {
    return number2 - number1
}
```

where `from` is a label to make it easier to read the method when you call it, which would look like this:

```
result = subtract(number1: 10, from: 12)
```

This results in function calls that are easier to read—almost like sentences. In the subtract function it becomes very clear that the first number is subtracted from the second. If a label is specified in a method declaration, it must be used in a function call, and if no label is specified, the parameter name is used as the label. If you want to omit a label from a parameter, you replace it with an underscore:

```
func subtract(_ number1:Int, from number2:Int) -> Int {
    return number2 - number1
}

result = subtract(10, from: 12)
```

This can sometimes make the function call even easier to read, as in the example noted.

Function Types and Closures

One of the interesting aspects of Swift is that you can treat a function as a type. That means you can pass a function as a parameter to another function, and a function can return a function. For example, consider the code in Listing C.7.

Listing C.7   Examples of Function Types

```
1    func add(_ number1: Int, to number2: Int) -> Int
2    {
3        return number1 + number2
4    }
5
6    func subtract(_ number1:Int, from number2:Int) -> Int
7    {
8        return number2 - number1
9    }
10
11   var math: (Int, Int) -> Int
12   math = add
13   var n = math(2, 3)
14   math = subtract
15   n =  math(2, 3)
16
17   func calculate(symbol: Character) -> (Int, Int) -> Int {
18
19       func doNothing(n1: Int, n2: Int) -> Int { return 0 } //Nested function
20
21       switch symbol {
22       case "+":
```

(continued)

Listing C.7   Examples of Function Types (*continued*)

```
23              return add
24          case "-":
25              return subtract
26          default:
27              return doNothing
28          }
29      }
30
31      math = calculate(symbol: "+")
32      n = math(2, 4)
```

Here, lines 1–9 show the add and subtract methods created earlier. Then, line 11 defines a variable, math, to be any function that takes two integers and returns an integer. Line 12 assigns the add function to the math variable, and calls the math function in line 13 with two actual numbers. This will actually call the add method and return the result 5. Line 14 then reassigns the math function to the subtract method, and line 15 then gets the result −1.

It gets more interesting with the calculate function in line 17. This function defines a return type that matches the math function, and we can thus return any function that matches this pattern. The switch statement in lines 21–27 uses the symbol parameter to decide which function to return. The default case returns a function called doNothing that is declared in line 19. This is a *nested function* that is declared inside another function. Nested functions can be called inside the function, or they can be returned as results as seen here.

Try creating multiply and divide functions, and modify the switch statement to return these functions as appropriate.

Sometimes, function types can be left unnamed. In this case, they are called closures. This is often used with completion handlers, as you will see later in this appendix.

Classes and Structs

Swift is a powerful object-oriented language that uses the same object model as you are used to from Java and C#. However, there are a few interesting quirks. First, let's take a look at a Book class as shown in Listing C.8. Create a new Playground called BookPlayground for this example.

Listing C.8   Book Class

```
1       class Book: CustomStringConvertible {
2           var title: String
3           var author: String
4           var year: Int
5           var borrower: String? {
6               didSet { //Observer called when value is changed
7                   if borrower != nil && oldValue != nil { borrower = oldValue }
8               }
9           }
10          var isOut: Bool { //read-only property
11              get {
12                  if borrower != nil { return true }
13                  else { return false }
14              }
15          }
16          //Implementing the CustomStringConvertible protocol
17          var description: String { return "\(title) by \(author) (\(year))" }
18
19          init() { //Initializer (Constructor)
20              title = ""
21              author = ""
22              year = 0
23          }
```

(*continued*)

Listing C.8 Book Class (*continued***)**

```
24
25        //Initializer with parameters
26        init(_ title: String, by author: String, publishedIn year:Int) {
27            self.title = title
28            self.author = author
29            self.year = year
30        }
31
32        func lendOut(to borrower: String){
33            if !isOut {
34                self.borrower = borrower
35            }
36        }
37
38        func returnBook() {
39            borrower = nil
40        }
41    }
```

Much of this is very similar to what you would expect from Java or C#.

- Line 1 declares the class with the name Book and specifies that the class conforms to the protocol `Custom-StringConvertible`. Inheritance and protocol conformance is declared exactly like in C#. After a colon after the class name, you can specify first a class to inherit from and then a list of protocols to conform to. Swift only allows single inheritance, so any class to inherit from must be listed first. This means that when you look at the code for a class like `Book`, you can't tell whether it's a subclass of `CustomStringConvertible` or it's conforming to the protocol. You have to know that `CustomStringConvertible` is a protocol to know which it is.

- Lines 2–17 declare a number of properties of the class. The first four (`title`, `author`, `year`, and `borrower`) are simple properties that can be set directly on any instance of an object. The question mark after the type on the `borrower` property specifies that this one is optional (a `book` doesn't have to have a `borrower`).

- Line 6 declares a listener, `didSet`, on the `borrower` property. This is called whenever the property has been changed. There is a corresponding property, `willSet`, that is called before the property is changed. Here, it is used to make sure that the borrower isn't changed if there's a previous lender already. Note that in a realistic application, you would probably want to also notify the user that the borrower didn't change. The `didSet` property receives the previous value as `oldValue`, so we simply check if `oldValue` is nil and change `lender` back to the `oldValue` if it wasn't.

- The `isOut` property in line 10 is read-only and uses a notation similar to the properties in C# to implement a `get` section that checks if the `borrower` is set and then returns `true`, and returns `false` if no borrower is set. If a `set` section was implemented, it could contain functionality to execute when changing the property, but in this case, the `isOut` property is calculated based on the `borrower` property, so it should not have a `set` section.

- The `description` property in line 17 is specified in the `CustomStringConvertible` protocol. When an object is printed (or passed in places where `String` is expected), the `description` property is used. By conforming to the `CustomStringConvertible` protocol, you can override the default behavior of the `description` property, which is to simply return the name of the object's class. This is similar to the ToString method in C# and toString in Java.

- Constructors in Swift are named `init`, but otherwise behave like constructors in Java and C# in that they ensure that all nonoptional properties have been initialized. In the `Book` class, there are two initializers— one that takes no parameters (lines 19–23), and one that takes parameters (lines 26–30). Notice in line 26 that the initializers are declared just like methods, with parameter lists and argument labels. They just don't have a method name of their own and no return type. The underscore in the beginning of the parameter list specified that no label is given for the argument, so when it is called, there is no identifying label.

- Lines 27–29 use the keyword `self` to refer to the current object instance. This is the same as the `this` keyword in Java and C#.
- Lines 32–36 declare a method (which is a function declared in a class) called `lendOut`. This method is an alternative to using the `borrower` property to specify the current borrower of the book. This method uses the `isOut` property to check if the book should be lent out.
- Finally, the `returnBook` method in lines 38–40 simply sets the `borrower` to nil, indicating that there is no current lender of the book.

Figure C.3 shows how the Book class can be used and manipulated in the Playground.

Figure C.3 Interacting with objects of the Book class.

The actions in Figure C2 should be fairly self-explanatory, but a few notes are required.

- Line 44 uses the parameterized initializer to create a `Book` object assigned to `b1`. Notice how the labels make the method easy to read.

- The next few lines call `isOut` and `borrower` on the `b1` object. You can observe the results of these calls in the right sidebar (`false` and `nil` as expected). In real code, you would of course not make calls like these, as they have no effect on the program, but as you play around in the Playground, it's an easy way to do a quick check on the state of an object.

- After the call to `lendOut`, the full status of the object is observed. You bring this up by hovering over the description in the sidebar. You will see two small icons come up. One is for QuickLook and the other is called **Show Result**, which you click to bring up the object status as shown. In this example, the object state is examined after calling the `lendOut` method (line 47), and then attempting to set the `borrower` property to Jim in line 48. Notice that the `borrower` is still Joe. Then the book is returned in line 50 by calling the `returnBook` method. This causes the `borrower` to become `nil`.

- Lines 54–58 show how to initialize an object using the default initializer and setting values using the properties.

- Lines 62–68 create an array containing the two objects, and then print out the status of each one taking into account whether the book is lent out or not. Notice in line 64 that the reference to the Book object (`b`) is used on its own to get the String description of the object, since the `Book` class conforms to the `Custom-StringConvertible` protocol.

As an exercise, you can incorporate the information about the borrower into the Book's own description, so the `for` loop simply contains a single `print(b)` statement.

Inheritance and Protocols

One of the important concepts of object-oriented programming is inheritance, which allows for creating simpler and more efficient code by allowing one class to inherit all the properties of another class. This gives the benefit of polymorphism, where a variable can be declared to hold a particular type in the code, but at runtime, any object declared of that class or any of its subclasses can be assigned to the variable.

Inheritance in Swift works exactly like it does in Java and C#. And the syntax for inheritance is exactly the same as in C#. You simply specify the name of the super class after the name of the class, so if we wanted to declare a `PhotoBook` class that would inherit from `Book`, it would look like this:

```
class PhotoBook : Book {
    var imageTitle: String?
}
```

Swift allows only for single inheritance, and similarly to Java's Object and C#'s object classes, Swift has a class called `NSObject`, which is the top-most class in the inheritance hierarchy.

To allow for a class to have multiple identities, object-oriented programmers turn to interfaces in Java and C#. The same concept is called a *protocol* in Swift, and rather than implement an interface, Swift classes are said to *conform* to a protocol. But the concepts are the same: A protocol defines a set of methods and properties, and when a class conforms to the protocol, any variable declared to hold a type of the protocol will be able to hold an object of any class that conforms to the protocol. Specifying that a class conforms to a protocol is also done in the class declaration line, by simply adding the protocol after the super class like this:

```
class MyClass: SuperClass, MyProtocol, AnotherProtocol
```

As you can see, classes can conform to multiple protocols. A protocol can declare that some methods are optional, but otherwise, the class will need to implement all methods declared in all the protocols.

Completion Handlers

When you make a call to a web service—for example, to geocode an address—it takes a long time for that call to complete, so we often don't want to block the program from continuing while waiting for the result to come back. Instead, the method call to the web service can be handed off to a *completion handler*, which will then handle the result when it comes back. This is also called asynchronous programming.

In Chapter 13, "Maps and Location in iOS," you will see the bit of code shown in Listing C.9, which uses a geocoder to convert an address into a placemark that can be placed on a map.

Listing C.9   Calling a Method with a Completion Handler

```
1    @IBAction func addressToCoordinates(_ sender: Any) {
2        let address = "\(txtStreet.text!), \(txtCity.text!), \(txtState.text!))"
3        geoCoder.geocodeAddressString(address) {(placemarks, error) in
4            self.processAddressResponse(withPlacemarks: placemarks, error: error)
5        }
6    }
7
8    private func processAddressResponse(withPlacemarks placemarks: [CLPlacemark]?, error: Error?) {
9        //Method body omitted
10   }
```

The code here is fairly easy to explain. In line 3, it calls the `geocodeAddressString` method and hands the completion off to the method `processAddressResponse`, which is declared in line 8. Two of the method's parameters, `placemarks` and `error`, are populated by the call to the web service.

But the notation here doesn't tell us the whole story. For instance, what is the data type of those two parameters when they show up in line 3 and where are they declared? If you look up the documentation for `geocodeAddressString` (option-click CLGeocoder, and then scroll down to find the method), you will find that its declaration looks like this:

```
func geocodeAddressString(_ addressString: String, completionHandler: @escaping
                                              CLGeocodeCompletionHandler)
```

As you can see, this method takes two parameters, whereas it only took one parameter (`address`) in the call above. To understand this, we have to dig a little further and understand the `completionHandler` argument in the `geocodeAddressString` declaration. This is a block of code—also called a closure, or a nested function—that can be passed around as a parameter. Here's the declaration of that closure:

```
typealias CLGeocodeCompletionHandler = ([CLPlacemark]?, Error?) -> Void
```

This declares a method type that takes two parameters, an array of `CLPlacemark` objects and an `Error` object, and returns `Void`. So when you call the `geocodeAddressString` method in line 3 of Listing C.9, the compiler knows that you are calling the `CLGeocodeCompletionHandler`, and can infer the types of the parameters, which is why there is no type information in line 3. You could include the types in that call:

```
geoCoder.geocodeAddressString(address) {(placemarks: [CLPlacemark]?, error: Error?) in
```

Writing the call to the `geocodeAddressString` method in a different way might also help increase our understanding It can be written like this:

```
geoCoder.geocodeAddressString(address, completionHandler: {(placemarks: [CLPlacemark]?, error: Error?) in
```

This version is functionally equivalent to the previous calls to the method; it just includes that second parameter, `completionHandler`, explicitly. Swift just allows for a shorthand notation of dropping that parameter, and that is the notation that is most commonly used when using completion handlers.

You can also declare a completion handler as a variable if you need to use the same completion handler multiple times. Listing C.10 shows how that would look.

Listing C.10   Calling a Method with a Completion Handler

```
1   let myCompHandler: ([CLPlacemark]?, Error?) -> Void = {
2       (placemarks, error) in
3       //Implementation of code to handle the completion (show address on map)
4   }
5
6   geoCoder.geocodeAddressString(address, completionHandler: myCompHandler)
7
```

The completion handler is declared like a constant, but the type is that of a method that matches the required signature of a `CLGeocodeCompletionHandler`. Line 2 sets up the names of the parameters as they will be used inside the completion handler, the body of which was omitted here. Line 6 shows how this completion handler is called.

Index

81777813R00195

Made in the USA
Lexington, KY
21 February 2018